Welcome to a year of opportunities

I hope that by the end of 2018, this *Handbook* looks completely different. I hope it's dog-eared and creased from being pulled out of your car glovebox so many times. I hope it's stained with suntan lotion and ice-cream, and scattered with scribbled notes and folded-down corners – all reminders of special days in the country.

Because this isn't a book to hide in a drawer. It's your guide to the huge number of opportunities that await you as a National Trust member in 2018.

This year, we're celebrating Women and Power, marking 100 years of women gaining the right to vote. So do look out for themed events near you, and how to get involved. As an admirer of Virgina Woolf's work, I'm particularly looking forward to 'A Room of One's Own' launching at Monk's House, Woolf's former home. This is one of five of our places with fascinating female histories, where we are inviting artists and activists to spend time. 'A Room of One's Own' will creatively explore their inspiring legacies and reflect on how perceptions of, and attitudes towards, women have changed across time – I can't wait to see the outcome.

Wherever this *Handbook* leads you, it should help you to get the most from a huge range of amazing places, indoors and out. Your membership helps to protect those places for generations to come.

I want to thank you on behalf of everyone at the National Trust for your invaluable support. Here's to a year of exploration, inspiration and discovery – and of making sure this *Handbook* looks crumpled, creased and very well used by the end of it…

John Orna-Ornstein
Director of Curation and Experience

Using your *Handbook* for days out to treasure

All of the entries in your *Handbook* include a range of information to help you get the most from every visit. Here's what all of the symbols mean...

This table shows you when places are open

Example place		M	T	W	T	F	S	S
House								
11 Feb–4 Nov	11–5	M	T	W	T	F	S	S
5 Nov–28 Nov	12–5	M	T	W	T	F	S	S
1 Dec–9 Dec	10:30–4:30	M	T	W	T	F	S	

Last entry to house and tea-room 20 minutes before closing.

These are opening times.
A letter means the place or facility is **open** on this day.
A grey dot means it's **closed**.
Any special notes about opening times are shown down here.

These symbols tell you something about the place. You'll find them above its description

| 1939 | Acquisition date |
| Historic house |
| Castle/fort |
| Church/chapel |
| Watermill |
| Windmill |
| Other buildings |
| Public house |
| Archaeological site |
| Farm/farm animals |
| Garden |
| Countryside/park |
| Coast |
| Nature reserve |
| Places to stay |
| Campsite |
| Licensed for weddings |
| Available for functions |

These symbols tell you about accessibility. You'll find them towards the bottom of each listing

| Designated parking |
| Drop-off point |
| Transfer available |
| Accessible toilet |
| Catering accessible |
| Shop accessible |
| Induction loop |
| Photograph album |
| Virtual tour |
| Seats/seating available |
| Braille (guide or menu) |
| Large print (guide or menu) |
| Steps/uneven terrain |
| Ramped access or slopes |
| Level access/terrain, paths |
| Lifts |
| Stairclimber |
| Stairlift |
| Narrow corridors |
| Wheelchairs available |
| Accessible route and/or map available |
| Powered mobility vehicle |

Need help? Contact Supporter Services Centre, National Trust, PO Box 574, Manvers, Rotherham, S63 3FH

As you make plans, don't forget ...

#1
We're open more than you think
We're keeping doors (and gates) open longer, so you can enjoy the places you love more than ever, all year round. Worth remembering when you're thinking about things to do come rain or shine. Talking of which...

#2
You'll never need to have the same experience twice
Nature is constantly changing, of course, but so are the events run by many National Trust places. Indoors and outside, right through the year, and covering everything from Lord of the Rings trails to Elizabethan jewellery exhibitions, it's best to expect the unexpected.

#3
Last entry is 30 minutes before closing time
If you're planning a quick stroll after work or fancy a last-minute summer picnic, make sure you don't cut it too fine.

#4
It's easy to stay up-to-date
To find out what's planned near you (and to make sure we've not had to change opening times for any reason), download the National Trust app, head to **nationaltrust.org.uk**, seek us out on social media or simply chat to staff and volunteers on your next visit.

#5
Our *Getting Here* guide can help in remote places
The postcodes for some destinations in this *Handbook* won't get you all the way. For more detailed maps and directions, order your free *Getting Here* guide. To request a copy call 0344 800 1895 or visit **nationaltrust.org.uk/gettinghere**

#6
Our *Land Map* can give you a headstart on history
This interactive map tells the full story behind the land we look after and 300+ war memorials. Get an insider's view at **ntlandmap.org.uk**

Make the most of your membership with these digital tools

Website
Take a closer look by visiting **nationaltrust.org.uk**

app
500+ places in your pocket. Just search 'National Trust' in your app store

My National Trust
Easily manage your membership online at **nationaltrust.org.uk/mynationaltrust**

Social media
Ask questions, share your experiences or just say 'hi'

Planning your journey
By car: rac.co.uk/route-planner

By bike: sustrans.org.uk

By train: nationalrail.co.uk or 03457 484950

By taxi (from a station): traintaxi.co.uk

By public transport (England, Wales and Scotland): traveline.info or 0871 200 2233

By public transport (Northern Ireland): translink.co.uk or 028 9066 6630

By public transport (London): tfl.gov.uk or 0343 222 1234

Need help? Call us on 0344 800 1895 (9 to 5:30 weekdays, 9 to 4 weekends)

Ready to discover how much you can do?

As a National Trust member, there are so many ways to experience the places you love – whatever the season. So from exhibitions in pop-up pavilions to chalking the White Horse, how will you make the most of your membership this year?

Looking for carriages, ceramics or canvases?
Find the collections you care about on page 436

Find those 'whoa' moments indoors

However foggy and drizzly it might be, you're still guaranteed spectacular sights inside our historic houses. Let Elizabethan art, Jazz Age interiors or even a pink pineapple pavilion spark your imagination – or banish the January blues in the warmth of a tropical glasshouse.

Discover the secrets of spring

A fawn darting through the trees? A waft of wild garlic in the air? The year's first bluebells in bloom? Head for our walking trails and cycle routes as nature stirs into life this spring, and see what moments of magic you discover.

No bike? No problem.
Turn to page 433 to find out where to hire kids' and adults' cycles (or bring your own bike to dozens of special places with very special cycle routes)

Between January and April, why don't you …

- *Plant snowdrops with our gardeners*
- *See new art inspired by ancient places*
- *Sketch the year's brightest daffodils*
- *Share a spring picnic (bring a brolly, just in case)*
- *Take a guided wildflower tour*

Do more at the places you love

Whether it's a weekly visit to read under a favourite tree, a tick on your bucket list as you go surfing for the first (but definitely not last) time, or a family trip to give flour milling a try, the summer months are perfect for putting special places at the heart of your plans.

Indulge your passions.
Love industrial landmarks? Inspired by starlight sleepovers? Whatever warms your heart, find perfect places by theme on page 433

Make yourself at home in the sun

Why not take inspiration from our 50 things to do before you're 11¾, and fly a kite, explore a cave, try rock climbing or simply walk barefoot across the sand?

Look out for special events too – from evening theatre shows (remember your hamper) to bioblitzes, where you can record your local wildlife.

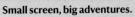

Small screen, big adventures.
Turn to page 439 for locations used in *Poldark* and other TV favourites

Between May and August, why don't you …

- *Watch a film on a beanbag under the stars*
- *Make a feast from our homegrown ingredients*
- *Book a break in a lighthouse keeper's cottage*
- *Load a scone with cream and jam*
- *Crest the coastal waves in a kayak*

7

Gather memories this harvest time

Ready to carve a show-stopping pumpkin? Or shake apples from a tree to make a lip-smacking pie? As autumn colours transform the landscape, crunch your way through fallen leaves and try fruit picking and ghostly Hallowe'en trails. Many places reveal their secrets at our Heritage Open Days, too.

Spooky spots and ghoulish goings-on.
To share spine-chilling thrills at some of the most haunted historic houses and castles, turn to page 433

Between September and December, why don't you ...

Send sycamore seeds spinning through the air

Capture golden landscapes on a photography course

Go camping in the late autumn sun

Relive servant life on a behind-the-scenes tour

Give your wellies a midwinter workout

Celebrate traditions old and new

Whether Christmas means mince pies with friends, a new bauble to take pride of place on your tree, or a tour round a Victorian Christmas home, we're ready to celebrate with you. And once the presents are all unwrapped, why not join us for a wintry stroll and steaming pot of tea with the people you love (or maybe for a little peace and quiet all by yourself).

Discover timeless fashions.
Want to see Victorian festive outfits close up – or even try on a Tudor jester's hat for size? Find special places with costume collections on page 436

Cornwall

Cotehele Quay on the Tamar
Competition entry from Sue Rowlands

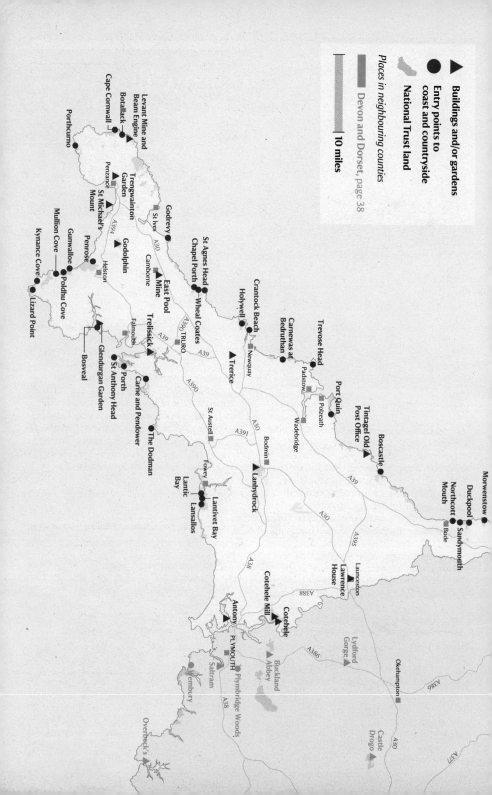

Buildings and/or gardens
Entry points to coast and countryside
National Trust land
Places in neighbouring counties

Devon and Dorset, page 38

10 miles

Porthcurno
Cape Cornwall
Botallack
Levant Mine and Beam Engine
Penzance
Trengwainton Garden
St Michael's Mount
Godrevy
St Ives
Chapel Porth
St Agnes Head
Wheal Coates
Godolphin
Camborne
East Pool Mine
Gunwalloe
Penrose
Helston
Poldhu Cove
Mullion Cove
Kynance Cove
Lizard Point
Bosveal
Glendurgan Garden
Falmouth
Trelissick
St Anthony Head
Carne and Pendower
The Dodman
Porth
St Austell
A30
A394
A30
A39
A390
A391
A30
A38
A388
A386
A30
A386
A377

Holywell
Crantock Beach
Newquay
Carnewas at Bedruthan
Trevose Head
Padstow
Port Quin
Polzeath
Wadebridge
Bodmin
Boscastle
Tintagel Old Post Office
Morwenstow
Duckpool
Northcott Mouth
Sandymouth
Bude
A395

Trerice
Lanhydrock
Fowey
Lantic Bay
Lansallos
Lantivet Bay
Cotehele Mill
Cotehele
Lawrence House
Launceston
Antony
PLYMOUTH
Buckland Abbey
Plymbridge Woods
Saltram
Trengwainton
Overbeck's

Lydford Gorge
Okehampton
Castle Drogo
TRURO

Antony

Torpoint, Cornwall PL11 2QA

⌂ ✿ 🎥 1961

Antony sits within a magnificent landscape garden

Still the family home of the Carew Poles after hundreds of years, this beautiful early 18th-century house has fine collections of paintings, furniture and textiles. The landscape garden offers sweeping views to the River Lynher and includes a formal garden with topiary, a knot garden and sculptures. **Note**: Woodland Garden (not National Trust), free admission for members when house open.

Eat, shop, stay: tea-room offering light lunches and afternoon tea. Picnics welcome in the grounds. Gift shop with souvenirs, plants and local produce. Small second-hand bookshop.

Things to see and do: Indoors Quizzes and trails. **Outdoors** Garden and family events. Modern sculpture throughout garden and Woodland Garden. Games and croquet on lawn. Den-building. Quizzes and trails. **Dogs**: assistance dogs only.

Access: 🅿 ♿ 🚻 🏠 🅿 💻 ♪ ∴
House ♿ ⬇ Grounds ♿ ➡ ⬇
Parking: 250 yards.

Antony		M	T	W	T	F	S	S
House, garden, shop and tea-room								
3 Apr–31 May	12–5	·	**T**	**W**	**T**	·	·	·
3 Jun–30 Aug	12–5	·	**T**	**W**	**T**	·	·	**S**
4 Sep–31 Oct	12–5	·	**T**	**W**	**T**	·	·	·
Woodland Garden								
1 Mar–31 Oct	11–5:30	·	**T**	**W**	**T**	·	**S**	**S**

House: open 12:30 to 4:30. Timed ticket entry to house allocated on arrival. Also open Good Friday and Easter Sunday, Sunday 6 May, Sunday 27 May and Bank Holiday Mondays.

Boscastle

near Tintagel, Cornwall

🏞 🏛 ♿ 1955

There has been a fishing and trading port here for centuries and you can still watch boats come and go between the high cliffs that guard the snaking harbour entrance. Much of Boscastle can be discovered on foot, with footpaths leading in all directions. You can walk in the footsteps of the young Thomas Hardy through the wildlife-rich ancient woodland in the Valency Valley, or explore the rare medieval field system known as 'the Forrabury Stitches' high above the village. Nearby is the striking lookout building on Willapark headland, and the historic churches of Minster and Forrabury. **Note**: toilet by main car park (not National Trust).

Boscastle: the snaking natural inlet leading to the harbour

Looking down on the harbour at Boscastle

Eat, shop, stay: harbourside café with courtyard seating. Large shop and visitor centre offering a wide range of gifts, seasonal plant sales plus a wealth of guides and information about the local area. Second-hand bookshop. Five holiday cottages. Free Wi-Fi throughout.

Things to see and do: children's quiz/trail. Coasteering available nearby. Visitor centre shows short film about the 2004 flood. Why not combine with a visit to Tintagel Old Post Office, four miles down the coast? **Dogs**: welcome on walks and in café courtyard.

Access: 🅿️ 🚻 ♿ **Grounds** ♿
Sat Nav: use PL35 0HD. **Parking**: 100 yards, pay and display, not National Trust (charge including members).

Find out more: 01840 250010 or boscastle@nationaltrust.org.uk

Boscastle	M	T	W	T	F	S	S
Shop, café and visitor centre							
Open all year	*	M	T	W	T	F	S	S

*Opening times vary throughout year, ranging from 10:30 to 4 in winter to 10 to 5:30 in high summer. Closed 25 and 26 December.

Bosveal

near Mawnan Smith, Falmouth, Cornwall

🏛️ ⛴️ 🚗 🛏️ 1980

Many walks take in woodland valleys, secluded coves and the soft, sheltered shores of the Helford River and Falmouth Bay. **Note**: toilets and refreshments at nearby Glendurgan Garden. Holiday cottages at Bosloe and Durgan. For Sat Nav use TR11 5JR.

Find out more: 01326 252020 or bosveal@nationaltrust.org.uk

Botallack

on the Tin Coast, near St Just, Cornwall

🏠 🍴 🏛️ ⛴️ 🚗 🛏️ 🍽️ 1995

On the wild Tin Coast, the famed Crowns engine houses (above) cling to the foot of the cliffs in a landscape transformed by its industrial past. Part of the Cornish Mining World Heritage Site, and the filming location for Wheal Leisure in BBC's *Poldark*, from here Cornish miners changed the world. **Note**: industrial landscape with numerous mine shafts and mining remains – please keep to paths and tracks.

Eat, shop, stay: light refreshments with views to the Isles of Scilly (opening days/times vary, check before visiting), pasties, cakes, ice-cream, hot and cold drinks. Picnic blankets to borrow. Two can stay at romantic Botallack Count House Cottage, with dramatic coastal views.

Things to see and do: film and displays in the Workshop celebrating the Tin Coast and *Poldark*. Explore mining history on the outdoors trail and enjoy an easy clifftop walk to Levant Mine. **Dogs**: welcome everywhere on short leads. Please take care near mine shafts and cliff edges.

Access:
Sat Nav: use TR19 7QQ. Beware, some Sat Navs misdirect. Keep to the B3306 until you reach Botallack village. **Parking**: just beyond Botallack Count House.

Find out more: 01736 786931 or botallack@nationaltrust.org.uk

Botallack
Botallack Workshop café open most days (telephone for details).

Cape Cornwall

on the Tin Coast, near St Just, Cornwall

🏛 ⚓ 🚗 ⛺ 1987

The distinctive headland of Cape Cornwall (below) juts out into the ocean where two great bodies of water meet. Once a heavily industrialised landscape, it is now part of the Cornish Mining World Heritage Site, and a wild and rugged home to many seabirds which nest on the Brisons rocks. **Note**: narrow lanes, unsuitable for caravans. Car park toilets open Easter to end October. Building works.

Eat, shop, stay: light refreshments (not National Trust) available from Easter to end of October, including drinks, pasties, sandwiches, cakes and, when available, crab and lobster landed at Cape Cornwall. Many facilities in St Just. Holiday cottage in nearby Cot Valley.

Things to see and do: perfect beach for rock-pooling and wild swimming. Working cove for crab and lobster fishermen. Short walk to the top of the Cape for views to the Isles of Scilly. **Dogs**: welcome, except on the beach and slipway from Easter to October.

Access: 🅿
Sat Nav: use TR19 7NN for Cape Cornwall car park. **Parking**: at Cape Cornwall, Porth Nanven (Cot Valley) and Ballowall.

Find out more: 01736 786931 or capecornwall@nationaltrust.org.uk

Carne and Pendower

near Veryan, Cornwall

🏛 ⚓ 🚗 ⛺ 1961

The beach at Pendower, with Carne Beach beyond

Two of the best beaches on the Roseland peninsula: fine stretches of sand and rock pools, popular with families. Walks along the coast and inland reveal the area's wildlife – great for butterflies in summer and birds in winter. Lots of history to discover nearby, from Bronze Age to Cold War. **Note**: seasonal toilets in both car parks.

Eat, shop, stay: Tea by the Sea van at Carne (concession) serves tea, cake and tempting treats. The tenant-run Hidden Hut is nearby at Porthcurnick Beach. You can stay close to Carne Beach at the five holiday cottages at Gwendra and Caragloose.

Things to see and do: the beaches are ideal for swimming and rock-pooling. A path leads inland to Carne Beacon, one of Britain's largest Bronze Age barrows. Downloadable walking trails cover the wider area. **Dogs**: seasonal dog restrictions on beaches (please keep under control near livestock).

Access:
Sat Nav: for Carne use TR2 5PF; Pendower TR2 5PF (turn right at sign for Pendower Beach). **Parking**: car parks at both Carne and Pendower.

Find out more: 01872 580553 or carne@nationaltrust.org.uk

Carnewas at Bedruthan

near Padstow, Cornwall

🏛️ 🛍️ 1930

Since Victorian times this has been one of the most popular destinations on the Cornish coast, known for its spectacular clifftop views of giant rock stacks striding across Bedruthan Beach (not National Trust). Those with a head for heights can climb down the cliff staircase to the beach (closed during the winter) but beware of being cut off by the tide. For a longer walk, follow the coast path to Park Head and the sheltered cove of Porth Mear beyond.

Carpets of spring and autumn squill bedeck these clifftops, and birds nesting from March include linnets, stonechats and skylarks. **Note**: unsafe to enter the sea here at any time.

Eat, shop, stay: shop offering a range of gifts, many locally sourced and produced, and popular tea-room (concession) with adjoining clifftop tea-garden. Picnic area. Bunkhouse and holiday cottages offering expansive sea views at Park Head.

Things to see and do: children's quiz and walks leaflet. Simple play area. Carnewas awarded 'dark sky status', so ideal for stargazing. Why not combine with a visit to Trerice (9 miles away)? **Dogs**: welcome under control.

Access: 🅿️ 🚻 🚾 🍴 Car park and cliff top ♿ ➡️
Sat Nav: use PL27 7UW. **Parking**: on site.

Find out more: 01637 860563 or carnewas@nationaltrust.org.uk

Carnewas at Bedruthan		M	T	W	T	F	S	S
Tea-room*								
10 Feb–23 Mar	11–4	M	T	W	T	F	S	S
24 Mar–28 Oct	10:30–5	M	T	W	T	F	S	S
27 Dec–31 Dec	11–4	M	·	·	T	F	S	S
Shop								
10 Feb–23 Mar	10:30–4	M	T	W	T	F	S	S
24 Mar–28 Oct	10–5	M	T	W	T	F	S	S
3 Nov–30 Dec	10:30–4	·	·	·	·	·	S	S

Cliff staircase closed from 29 October to mid-February.
*Telephone 01637 860701 to check opening times in winter.

Carnewas at Bedruthan: the view from the cliff staircase looking across the beach towards the giant rock stacks

Chapel Porth

near St Agnes, Cornwall

🖼️ 1957

Chapel Porth: popular with families and surfers

At the foot of a steep valley between high heathery cliffs, Chapel Porth Beach is a shingle strip at high tide and a huge expanse of sand at low tide – popular with families and surfers. The area is steeped in mining history, with many remains to be discovered on walks. **Note**: seasonal toilets. Take care not to get cut off by incoming tide. Seasonal lifeguards.

Eat, shop, stay: Chapel Porth Beach Café open daily in summer and most winter weekends (01872 552487). Picnics welcome. Pubs, cafés and shops nearby in St Agnes (none National Trust).

Things to see and do: great walking country – the coast path and inland paths link you with Porthtowan, St Agnes Head and the World Heritage Site mining remains at Charlotte United, Wheal Coates and Trevellas.
Dogs: seasonal dog ban on the beach (Easter Sunday to 30 September inclusive).

Access: 🅿️ 🐕 🅿️ 🔼 🚻 ♿
Sat Nav: use TR5 0NS. **Parking**: car park (very busy in summer). Additional parking at nearby Wheal Coates and St Agnes Head.

Find out more: 01872 552412 or chapelporth@nationaltrust.org.uk

Cotehele

St Dominick, near Saltash, Cornwall PL12 6TA

🏠 ✝️ 🖼️ 🌼 🛥️ 🛏️ 🍴 1947

The Edgcumbes built their rambling granite and slate-stone home high above the River Tamar, and it remained in their family for nearly 600 years. Time has stood still here. The Hall, with its ancient timber roof and displays of weaponry, and the warren of tapestry-clad rooms beyond have changed little since Tudor times. The 5-hectare (12-acre) garden features historic daffodils, terraces, ponds and orchards with 150 local apple varieties. The Valley Garden, with medieval stewpond and dovecote, leads to Cotehele Quay – thriving in Victorian times – where you'll find 1899 Tamar sailing barge *Shamrock*, lime kilns and the Discovery Centre. **Note**: the house has no electricity, so feel free to bring a torch.

Little changed since Tudor times, Cotehele looks down on the River Tamar from its high vantage point

Eat, shop, stay: restaurant near house serving hot lunches and cakes. Tea-room on quay offering light lunches, cakes and cream teas. Gift shop and plant centre. Art and craft gallery featuring West Country artists. Second-hand bookshop. Picnic area. Eight holiday cottages on estate.

Things to see and do: **Indoors** 'Words and Pictures' features the work of people who were inspired by and influenced Cotehele. First World War exhibition including local memories. **Outdoors** Play area. Year-round events and walks. **Dogs**: welcome throughout estate. Assistance dogs only in formal garden.

Access: [icons]
Building [icons] Grounds [icons] ➡
Sat Nav: ignore from Tavistock, follow brown signs. **Parking**: at house and on quay.

Find out more: 01579 351346. 01579 352711 (Barn Restaurant). 01579 352713 (shop) or cotehele@nationaltrust.org.uk

Cotehele		M	T	W	T	F	S	S
House								
10 Mar–28 Oct	11–4	M	T	W	T	F	S	S
29 Oct–31 Dec*	11–4	M	T	W	T	F	S	S
Garden and estate								
Open all year	Dawn–dusk	M	T	W	T	F	S	S
Restaurant, tea-room, gallery, shop, plant sales								
10 Feb–9 Mar**	10–4	M	T	W	T	F	S	S
10 Mar–28 Oct	10–5	M	T	W	T	F	S	S
29 Oct–31 Dec	10–4	M	T	W	T	F	S	S

*Hall only. Christmas garland from 17 November. Everything closed 25 and 26 December, except garden and estate.
**Tea-room on quay open daily from 1 January.

The medieval stewpond and dovecote at Cotehele

Cotehele Mill

St Dominick, near Saltash, Cornwall PL12 6TA

[icons] 1947

The working waterwheel at 19th-century Cotehele Mill

A peaceful walk alongside the Morden stream from Cotehele Quay takes you to the restored 19th-century Cotehele Mill. On Thursdays and Sundays you can watch corn being ground into flour. Traditional woodworker and potter on site, as well as re-created wheelwright's, saddler's and blacksmith's workshops. Look out for baking days. **Note**: nearest toilets and parking at Cotehele Quay.

Eat, shop, stay: Cotehele flour, gifts and ice-cream for sale. The Edgcumbe tea-room at nearby Cotehele Quay serves light lunches and cream teas. Snacks available from the kiosk on the quay. Picnics welcome in meadow. Two holiday cottages.

Things to see and do: **Indoors** Events, including milling and bakery demonstrations, as well as dress-up days. Opportunity to mill grain at the hand quern. Interpretation boards. **Outdoors** Family trails. **Dogs**: welcome, but assistance dogs only in bakery and mill.

Access: Building Grounds 🏛️
Parking: on Cotehele Quay (at the mill by arrangement only). Shuttlebus from Cotehele House.

Find out more: 01579 350606 (mill).
01579 351346 (Cotehele) or
cotehele@nationaltrust.org.uk

Cotehele Mill		M	T	W	T	F	S	S
10 Mar–30 Sep	11–4:30	M	T	W	T	F	S	S
1 Oct–28 Oct	11–4	M	T	W	T	F	S	S

Crantock Beach

near Newquay, Cornwall

 1956

Close to Newquay, this feels like a different Cornwall: Crantock Beach is an expanse of golden sand, great for sandcastles and surfing. Wonderful walking country – through the dunes on Rushy Green, alongside the gentle waters of the Gannel Estuary, or around the headland of West Pentire, carpeted with wild flowers. **Note:** danger, unpredictable currents.

Eat, shop, stay: refreshments available at Crantock village and West Pentire. Fern Pit café (not National Trust), across the Gannel Estuary from Crantock Beach, is accessible by ferryboat at high tide during the main season or by footbridge at low tide.

Things to see and do: surf school and board hire. Spot seals from the coast path. There are vibrant displays of summer wild flowers to discover in the fields above nearby Polly Joke Beach. **Dogs:** welcome under control everywhere, including the beach.

Access: ♿🐕
Sat Nav: use TR8 5RN for Crantock Beach and TR8 5QS for Treago Mill. **Parking:** on site (height restriction barrier when unmanned) and at Treago Mill for Polly Joke Beach (also known as Porth Joke).

Find out more: 01208 863046 or
crantockbeach@nationaltrust.org.uk

The Dodman

Penare, near Gorran Haven, Cornwall

🏛️🚶🌊🅿️ 1919

The highest headland on Cornwall's south coast, with massive Iron Age ramparts. Great walking, wildlife and beaches on either side. **Note:** park at Penare: footpaths to Hemmick Beach and Dodman Point. For Sat Nav use PL26 6NY and carry on down hill. Sorry no toilet.

Find out more: 01872 580553 or
thedodman@nationaltrust.org.uk

Duckpool

near Bude, Cornwall

🚶🌊 1960

Remote beach with rock pools at the mouth of the wooded Coombe Valley, overlooked by cliffs carpeted with wild flowers. **Note:** toilets open seasonally. For Sat Nav use EX23 9JN.

Find out more: 01208 863046 or
duckpool@nationaltrust.org.uk

Crantock Beach near Newquay: golden sand and dunes

East Pool Mine

Pool, near Redruth, Cornwall TR15 3NP

🏠 🏛 1967

East Pool celebrates the extraordinary lives of the people who worked at the very heart of the Cornish Mining World Heritage Site. With two giant beam engines, preserved in their towering engine houses, this is a great place for all the family to discover the dramatic story of Cornish mining.

One of the towering engine houses at East Pool Mine

Eat, shop, stay: small shop selling gifts, food and souvenirs, also a good selection of minerals and Cornish history books. You can enjoy a hot drink (or even an ice-cream) indoors or at our picnic bench in the sun.

Things to see and do: view the working beam engine and hands-on exhibits. Family activities, trails and free guided tours. Trevithick Cottage, home of the celebrated Cornish engineer Richard Trevithick, is nearby at Penponds. **Dogs**: welcome in outdoor areas.

Access: 🅿 🅿 ♿ ♿ ♿ ♿ ♿ Grounds ➡
Taylor's Engine House ♿ Michell's Engine House ♿ ♿
Sat Nav: for main site, use TR15 3NH; for Trevithick Cottage use TR14 0QG.
Parking: for main site, use Morrisons' car park (far end). Additional parking at Michell's Engine House nearby.

Find out more: 01209 315027 or eastpool@nationaltrust.org.uk
Trevithick Road, Pool, Cornwall TR15 3NP

East Pool Mine		M	T	W	T	F	S	S
Mine and Taylor's Engine House								
17 Mar–27 Oct*	10:30–5		T	W	T	F	S	
Michell's Engine House								
17 Mar–27 Oct*	12–4		T	W	T	F	S	
Trevithick Cottage								
4 Apr–24 Oct	2–5			W				

*Open Easter Monday and Bank Holiday weekends in May and August (times as above). Winter opening available for arranged visits.

Glendurgan Garden

Mawnan Smith, near Falmouth, Cornwall TR11 5JZ

🏠 ❄ ♿ 🚻 1962

Glendurgan Garden was described by its creators, the Quakers Alfred and Sarah Fox, as a 'small peace [sic] of heaven on earth'. Visitors can find out why it proved to be just this for the Foxes and their 12 children by exploring

Glendurgan's three valleys, running down to the sheltered beach at Durgan on the Helford River. There's a puzzling maze, created by Alfred and Sarah to entertain the family. You can enjoy camellias, magnolias and primroses in early spring, then rhododendrons and bluebells in May, followed by the exotic greens of summer and dramatic autumn colour in the trees. **Note**: steep paths, steps, uneven terrain.

Eat, shop, stay: tea-house (concession) serving homemade cakes, soups, sandwiches, light lunches and daily changing specials. Small shop and plant centre. Holiday lets – from waterside cottages for two, to large country houses for eight or more.

Things to see and do: Durgan Fish Cellar provides local history and wildlife information, beach chairs to borrow and children's activities. Durgan Beach with views of Helford River. Ten-minute introductory talks (call to check availability). **Dogs**: assistance dogs only in garden. Walks in surrounding countryside (details available at Glendurgan).

Access: 🅿️🐕♿🚻ℹ️ **Garden entrance** ♿ **Garden** 🚶
Parking: on site.

Glendurgan Garden, below, offers three valleys full of exotic treasures and cosy Durgan Fish Cellar, right

Find out more: 01326 252020 or glendurgan@nationaltrust.org.uk

Glendurgan Garden		M	T	W	T	F	S	S
10 Feb–31 Jul	10:30–5:30	·	T	W	T	F	S	S
1 Aug–31 Aug	10:30–5:30	M	T	W	T	F	S	S
1 Sep–28 Oct	10:30–5:30	·	T	W	T	F	S	S

Last entry one hour before closing. Closes dusk if earlier. Open Bank Holiday Mondays.

Godolphin

Godolphin Cross, Helston, Cornwall TR13 9RE

🏠🏛️🚻♿🥤🚶 2000

Hidden in shaded woodland, Godolphin escaped modernisation and contemporary fashions. The granite-faced terraces and sunken lawns of the Side Garden have seen little change since the 16th century, and Victorian farm buildings tell the story of Godolphin as a tenant farm. The estate, once busy with prosperous tin mines, is now part of the Cornish Mining World Heritage Site and is wonderful walking country, rich in archaeology, rare plants and wildlife. There are panoramic views from the top of Godolphin Hill. The historic house is a holiday home, where you can stay and experience the splendour that mining riches bought. **Note**: house is open to visitors on limited dates between holiday lets (please check before visiting).

Eat, shop, stay: small tea-room in the Piggery serving drinks, sandwiches, cakes, ice-cream. Local gifts and souvenirs. Picnic benches in the orchard or borrow a blanket to relax in the garden. You can soak up the out-of-hours atmosphere by staying in Godolphin House.

The 16th-century Side Garden, above, at Godolphin, and flowers in the gardener's potting shed, below

Things to see and do: gardener's potting shed has information on flora and fauna. Free guided tours and waymarked walks. Discover the active conservation programme of the farm buildings. Barefoot trail from Easter to October. **Dogs**: welcome outdoors on short leads. Water bowl and dog biscuits available.

Access: 🅿️ 🐕 ♿ 🚻 📷 ♿ House ♿ ♿ 👥
Cider House ♿ ↕ **Garden** ♿ ♿
Parking: 300 yards.

Find out more: 01736 763194 or godolphin@nationaltrust.org.uk

Godolphin		M	T	W	T	F	S	S
Garden and outbuildings								
1 Jan–28 Oct	10–5	M	T	W	T	F	S	S
29 Oct–31 Dec*	10–4	M	T	W	T	F	S	S
Estate								
Open all year	Dawn–dusk	M	T	W	T	F	S	S
House								
Limited opening**								

*Closed 24 and 25 December. **House open first Saturday to Thursday of every month, February to October (except August), plus weekends 1 to 16 December (please check house opening before visiting).

Godrevy

near Hayle, Cornwall

 1939

Long sandy beaches on St Ives Bay with wildlife-rich cliffs and walks. Godrevy café in dunes (concession) open most days. **Note:** unstable cliffs and incoming tides. Toilets open in top field. For Sat Nav use TR27 5ED. Car-parking fields on headland open in summer, subject to weather and ground conditions. Café open daily.

Find out more: 01872 552412 or godrevy@nationaltrust.org.uk

Gunwalloe

near Helston, Cornwall

 1974

Two family-friendly sandy beaches and reedbeds rich in wildlife. Between the two coves, a medieval church shelters behind Castle Mound. **Note**: lifeguards patrol Church Cove in summer holidays. Seasonal toilets. Dogs welcome all year at Dollar Cove, council-enforced ban at Church Cove (Easter to 1 October).

Find out more: 01326 222170 or gunwalloe@nationaltrust.org.uk

Holywell

near Newquay, Cornwall

1951

A classic North Cornish beach with a sweep of golden sand and a towering dune system. There's lots of history to explore, including the remains of an Iron Age castle on Kelsey Head, a Bronze Age barrow on Cubert Common and the holy well in a cave on the beach.

Eat, shop, stay: seasonal refreshments, traditional seaside shopping and pubs at Holywell and a convenience store and café year round at Cubert, 2 miles (none National Trust).

Holywell near Newquay: a paradise for beach lovers

Things to see and do: surf schools and board hire. Beach great for rock-pooling and building sandcastles. Seals can be seen from Kelsey Head. Wildlife-rich grasslands and coastline. **Dogs**: welcome everywhere, including the beach, but under close control, especially around livestock.

Access: Coast
Sat Nav: use TR8 5PF. **Parking**: on site.

Find out more: 01208 863046 or holywell@nationaltrust.org.uk

Kynance Cove

on the Lizard peninsula, Cornwall

1935

It's a ⅓-mile walk down to this famous beach, with its serpentine stacks, islands and caves, through rare Lizard heathland. **Note**: for Sat Nav use TR12 7PJ. Car park very busy in summer – arrive early to avoid disappointment. Seasonal dog ban on beach. Level access route to viewpoint only; path to beach steep and uneven. Café open Easter to November.

Find out more: 01326 222170 (Property Office). 01326 291174 (Rangers) or kynancecove@nationaltrust.org.uk

Lanhydrock

Bodmin, Cornwall PL30 5AD

1953

A tragic fire in 1881 meant that the Agar-Robartes family had to rebuild most of their 17th-century home. Out of the ashes came the country house you see today, presented as if time has stood still with the family having just popped out to tea. There are more than 50 rooms to discover – from the extensive kitchens, which reveal the servants' daily lives, to the elegant Victorian luxury of the family rooms. Outside is a garden, full of colour all year round and famed for its magnolias, and ancient woodlands with miles of footpaths to explore. The off-road cycle trails have different routes to suit all levels of experience, and you can even hire a bike when you get here.

Eat, shop, stay: the Park Café offers homemade dishes all year. At the house, there's the Stables tea-room, plus waitress service in the Victorian restaurant. Shop sells local food and gifts. Second-hand bookshop. A holiday cottage on the estate sleeps six.

Things to see and do: **Indoors** There's a remarkable early 17th-century ceiling in the gallery which survived the fire and is the oldest room in the house. As you explore you will experience everyday life in both the upstairs and downstairs worlds. Free children's trail daily. At Christmas, there's a traditional Victorian atmosphere. **Outdoors** Guided tours (telephone for availability) help you discover one of the great Cornish gardens, as well as the more remote corners of the parkland and riverside woods. There are waymarked routes for exploring alone, as well as family-friendly cycle trails and a popular adventure playground. **Dogs**: dog-friendly walks throughout the estate (assistance dogs only in house and garden).

The Long Gallery ceiling at Lanhydrock, above, survived the devastating fire. Visitors exploring the parkland, right and below

Access:
House **Grounds**
Sat Nav: use PL30 4AB (1 Double Lodges).
Parking: 600 yards.

Find out more: 01208 265950 or lanhydrock@nationaltrust.org.uk

Lanhydrock		M	T	W	T	F	S	S
House and garden								
1 Mar–31 Oct	11–5:30	M	T	W	T	F	S	S
1 Dec–31 Dec*	11–4	M	T	W	T	F	S	S
Estate and cycle trails								
Open all year	Dawn–dusk	M	T	W	T	F	S	S
Refreshments								
Open all year	10–5	M	T	W	T	F	S	S

March and October: house closes at 5. November to February: refreshments close at 4. House entry by timed tickets at busy periods (last ticket available 45 minutes before closing). *Selected rooms only. Everything closed 25 December. House closed 26 December.

Lansallos

between Polperro and Polruan, Cornwall

🏛️⚓🏕️🛏️🅰️ 1936

East of the Fowey Estuary is a long stretch of unspoilt coast loved by walkers, with abundant wild flowers and birds. From Lansallos church, a path ambles down the valley to a west-facing sandy beach. A picnic and a nose for adventure are all you need for the perfect day. **Note**: nearest toilets at Lantivet Bay car park.

Eat, shop, stay: Highertown Farm campsite offers relaxed and unspoilt camping, or you could stay at Old and West House holiday cottages, with their far-reaching views over open countryside and the bay below.

Things to see and do: downloadable walking trails. Play trails alongside the valley path at Lansallos. Great coast for kite-flying, paddling and bathing. Walking west along the coast path leads to Lantivet and Lantic Bays. **Dogs**: welcome, under close control around livestock.

Access: 🦽
Sat Nav: use PL13 2PX for Lansallos.
Parking: at Lansallos.

Find out more: 01726 870146 or lansallos@nationaltrust.org.uk

The way down to Lansallos Beach

Lantic Bay

near Polruan, Cornwall

⚓🏕️🛏️ 1959

Large shingly secluded beach on a beautiful bay, great spot for paddling and picnicking, well worth the climb back up. **Note**: sorry no toilet. Beach is down a very steep path with steps. Beware of rip tides. Nearest postcode for Sat Nav is PL23 1NP.

Find out more: 01726 870146 or lanticbay@nationaltrust.org.uk

Lantivet Bay

between Polruan and Lansallos, Cornwall

⚓🏕️🛏️🅰️ 1976

Great starting point for walks along this unspoilt sweep of coast, with its small rocky coves. Access to coast path. **Note**: toilets in car park. For Sat Nav use PL23 1NP. National Trust holiday cottages at nearby Triggabrowne Farm, between Lantivet and Lantic Bays.

Find out more: 01726 870146 or lantivetbay@nationaltrust.org.uk

Lawrence House

9 Castle Street, Launceston, Cornwall PL15 8BA

🏛️✳️ 1964

This Georgian town house, now a museum, hosts special exhibitions. Large display of costumes and a children's toy room. **Note**: leased to Launceston Town Council. Open 26 March to 26 October, Monday to Friday, 10:30 to 4:30. Also open the second Saturday of each month.

Find out more: 01566 773277 or lawrencehouse@nationaltrust.org.uk

Levant Mine and Beam Engine

on the Tin Coast, near Pendeen, St Just, Cornwall TR19 7SX

 1967

Access: [icons] Reception [icon]
Engine house [icons] Grounds [icons]
Parking: 328 yards. Narrow lanes, unsuitable for coaches, caravans and motor homes. Please park at Geevor.

Find out more: 01736 786156 or levant@nationaltrust.org.uk

Levant Beam Engine		M	T	W	T	F	S	S
10 Feb–18 Feb	10:30–4:30	M	T	W	T	F	S	S
17 Mar–28 Oct	10:30–5	M	T	W	T	F	S	S

Access to man-engine tunnel by guided tour only.
Winter opening available for arranged visits.

Dramatically sited Levant Mine and Beam Engine

High up on the exposed cliffs of the Tin Coast is Levant, part of the Cornish Mining World Heritage Site, and at its heart, the restored 1840s beam engine running on steam. Here you can discover how Cornish miners, engineers and inventors risked everything to help shape the modern world. **Note**: exposed clifftop, uneven ground/mine ruins, please take care. Engine steaming (timed tickets available on arrival).

Eat, shop, stay: light refreshments, including hot and cold drinks, pasties and ice-cream with outdoor picnic benches. Small shop selling books, minerals, souvenirs and postcards. You can stay in the heart of the Tin Coast at nearby Botallack Count House Cottage (sleeps two).

Things to see and do: Indoors Restored beam engine steams daily. **Outdoors** Waymarked walks to Botallack and Geevor. Free guided tours of mining landscape, archaeology and tunnel to the man-engine shaft. Rock-breaking and mineral-washing activity. **Dogs**: welcome on short leads. Take care at cliff edges and in mining remains.

Lizard Point

on the Lizard peninsula, near Helston, Cornwall

[icons] 1935

This is mainland Britain's most southerly point, infamous as a site of shipwrecks in the past and overlooking what is still one of the busiest shipping lanes in the world. The cliffs and farmland are incredibly rich in wildlife. From the Wildlife Watchpoint you can see seals and occasionally dolphins, as well as the iconic Cornish choughs, which breed close by. At Bass Point, a short walk along the coast path, you'll find the tiny Lizard Wireless Station. This is dedicated to Marconi's world-changing experiments, which took place in this simple hut on the cliffs.

Visitors exploring Polpeor Cove, beneath Lizard Point

Dark storm clouds sweep in above a wild sea beside the derelict lifeboat station at Polpeor Cove, Lizard Point

Eat, shop, stay: highly rated Polpeor Café at Lizard Point (concession) open all year – weather-dependent – with outside seating and great views. Gifts on sale at the information point (Easter to end October). Quirky holiday cottage adjoining the Lizard Wireless Station on Bass Point.

Things to see and do: take a walk along the coast path for superb coastal views, or try one of the inland routes to search for rare and unique plants. **Dogs**: welcome on leads (please note that livestock graze in some areas).

Access: [icons] Lizard Wireless Station [icon]
Sat Nav: use TR12 7NT.
Parking: at Lizard Point.

Find out more: 01326 222170 (Property Office). 01326 291174 (Rangers/Wireless Station) or lizard@nationaltrust.org.uk

Lizard Point		M	T	W	T	F	S	S
Wildlife Watchpoint*								
1 Apr–16 Sep	10–4	M	T	W	T	F	S	S

*Weather permitting. Telephone for opening times of the Lizard Wireless Station at Bass Point.

Morwenstow

near Bude, Cornwall

[icon] 1956

The realm of a great Victorian character – Parson Hawker. Hawker's Hut, driftwood-built, is on the cliff edge near his church. **Note**: sorry no toilets. For Sat Nav use EX23 9SR. Rectory Tea-rooms (tenant-run) open seasonally for cream teas and more.

Find out more: 01208 863046 or morwenstow@nationaltrust.org.uk

Mullion Cove

on the Lizard peninsula, near Helston, Cornwall

[icons] 1945

Originally built in the 1890s, the picturesque harbour at Mullion Cove shelters a small fishing fleet from powerful westerly storms. **Note**: toilets open seasonally. Dogs on leads welcome all year. Kayaking and boat trips available. Parking 200 yards approximately, not National Trust (charge including members).

Find out more: 01326 222170 or mullioncove@nationaltrust.org.uk

Northcott Mouth

near Bude, Cornwall

[icon] 1981

Quiet and ruggedly beautiful, this small rocky beach opens up to expansive sand and rock pools as the tide drops. **Note**: sorry no toilets. Dogs welcome, under control. Lifeguards in high season. For Sat Nav use EX23 9ED.

Find out more: 01208 863046 or northcottmouth@nationaltrust.org.uk

Penrose

near Helston, Cornwall

🏛️ 🏊 🚲 👪 🚤 1974

Home to Loe Pool, Cornwall's largest natural lake, Penrose is a mix of woods, farmland, parkland, cliffs and beaches: a great place to explore. There are 16 miles of bridleways and footpaths, including a trail around the pool and many coast path links. **Note**: to maintain the sense of peace at Penrose we don't allow watercraft on the pool.

Eat, shop, stay: Stables Café (concession) with parkland views – open daily, Easter to November, and at weekends all year. Picnics welcome in the neighbouring walled garden. There are several holiday cottages around Penrose, some hidden away and others with sea or lake views.

A popular easy-access route across Penrose's parkland

Things to see and do: you can hire a bike at Helston, try the easy-access route from Helston to the café, or pick a downloadable trail to follow. **Dogs**: welcome under control, please note livestock graze in the fields.

Access: Helston Drive ♿ ▶
Sat Nav: use TR13 0RA for Fairground car park. **Parking**: several small car parks around Loe Pool, plus the Fairground car park (not National Trust) in Helston.

Find out more: 01326 222170 or penroseestate@nationaltrust.org.uk

Penrose		M	T	W	T	F	S	S
Stables Café								
29 Mar–26 Oct	10–4	M	T	W	T	F	S	S
27 Oct–30 Dec	10–4						S	S

Poldhu Cove

on the Lizard peninsula, near Helston, Cornwall

🏕️ 🏊 🚲 👪 ⛺ 1984

Poldhu (above) is an unspoilt beach popular with locals and visitors. The beach, dunes and reedbeds are designated as a Site of Special Scientific Interest for their rich wildlife. South of the cove the Marconi Monument and visitor centre celebrate Poldhu's role as the site of the first transatlantic wireless signal. **Note**: car park and toilets not National Trust. Members pay for parking.

Eat, shop, stay: the café at Poldhu Beach is open all year (not National Trust). A Trust campsite is close by at Teneriffe Farm, near Mullion, and there are holiday cottages further away at Bass Point, Penrose and Cadgwith.

Things to see and do: popular surf school offers lessons for all the family with ex-professional Dan Joel. **Dogs**: welcome on coast path. Council-enforced beach ban from Easter to 1 October.

Access: 🅿️ Marconi Centre ♿ ♿ ▶
Sat Nav: use TR12 7BU. **Parking**: on site, not National Trust.

Find out more: 01326 222170. 01326 240293 (Teneriffe Farm Campsite) or poldhucove@nationaltrust.org.uk

Port Quin

near Wadebridge, Cornwall

 1936

Once a busy fishing port, Port Quin is now a peaceful sheltered inlet on an outstanding stretch of unspoilt coast. Nearby are the headlands of Pentire and the Rumps, with spectacular views and wild flowers; Lundy Bay at the foot of a wildlife-filled valley; and Pentireglaze Haven with great rock-pooling. **Note**: nearest toilets in Polzeath, 3 miles (not National Trust).

Doyden Castle on the cliffs by Port Quin

Eat, shop, stay: pubs, cafés and shops in Polzeath (not National Trust). Holiday cottages, including the quirky Doyden Castle and a number of coastal apartments and characterful cottages.

Things to see and do: seals, rare bats, corn buntings and puffins to spot. Well-preserved Iron Age ramparts on the Rumps. Sea kayaking and coasteering available nearby. **Dogs**: welcome under control. Seasonal dog ban on Polzeath Beach (including Pentireglaze Haven).

Access: Coast and beach
Sat Nav: use PL29 3SU for Port Quin; PL27 6QY Pentireglaze and Pentire Farm; PL27 6QZ Lundy Bay. **Parking**: at Port Quin, Lead Mines (Pentireglaze) and Lundy Bay. Also at Polzeath (not National Trust).

Find out more: 01208 863046 or portquin@nationaltrust.org.uk

Porth

on the Roseland peninsula, near Portscatho, Cornwall

 1958

Creekside and coastal footpaths make for great walking and wildlife spotting, or spend the day on the beach at Towan. **Note**: for Sat Nav use TR2 5EX. The Thirstea Company seasonal van (concession) serves drinks, cakes, sandwiches and ice-cream. Toilets. Holiday cottages here and nearby Bohortha.

Find out more: 01872 580553 or porth@nationaltrust.org.uk

Porthcurno

near Penzance, Cornwall

 1994

Soft, white shell beach with freshwater stream, surrounded by turquoise seas. Great for watching birds, basking sharks and dolphins. **Note**: for Sat Nav use TR19 6JU. Parking and toilets not National Trust (charge including members).

Find out more: 01736 761853 or porthcurno@nationaltrust.org.uk

St Agnes Head

near St Agnes, Cornwall

1967

A patchwork of gorse and heather carpets these clifftops high above the Atlantic Ocean, overlooked by lofty St Agnes Beacon. **Note**: for Sat Nav use TR5 0NU. Nearest café and toilets at Chapel Porth.

Find out more: 01872 552412 or stagneshead@nationaltrust.org.uk

St Anthony Head

on the Roseland peninsula,
near Portscatho, Cornwall

 1959

Guarding the eastern entrance to Falmouth harbour, this headland has been strategically important for centuries. It commands magnificent views up the Fal Estuary and across Falmouth Bay towards the Lizard, and you'll find plenty of historic fortifications from various eras to explore.

Eat, shop, stay: you can stay here in the old officers' quarters on the headland itself (two adapted for disabled visitors), or nearby at Bohortha and Porth holiday cottages. There are many wonderful spots for picnicking. At Porth there's a seasonal tea-van (concession).

Things to see and do: tours of St Anthony Battery on certain dates each summer. There's a bird hide for spotting peregrine falcons. You can walk the coast path or scramble down to Molunan Beach. **Dogs**: welcome.

Access: ⊞ ☍
Sat Nav: use TR2 5HA. **Parking**: on site.

Find out more: 01872 580553 or stanthonyhead@nationaltrust.org.uk

View from the Battery Observation Post, St Anthony Head

St Michael's Mount

Marazion, Cornwall TR17 0HS

⊞ ✝ ✿ ⚏ 1954

Unique and magical St Michael's Mount, Marazion

This iconic rocky island, crowned by a medieval church and castle, is home to the St Aubyn family and a 30-strong community of islanders. Visiting the Mount, you are immersed in history, islanders' tales and legends like the famous 'Jack the Giant Killer'. There's a subtropical terraced garden to explore, and spectacular views of Mount's Bay and the Lizard from the castle battlements. If the tide is high, you can take an evocative boat trip to the island harbour; at low tide you walk across the ancient cobbled causeway from Marazion on the mainland, as pilgrims have done for centuries. **Note**: steep climb to the castle over uneven, cobbled, historic pathway. St Aubyn Estates/National Trust partnership. Members have to pay for car parking and boat trips to the Mount at high tide.

Eat, shop, stay: Island Café for pasties, sandwiches, ice-cream. Sail Loft for Newlyn fish specials, homemade bread, cakes. Both serve local ales, cider, cream teas. Island and Courtyard shops sell emerging contemporary artists' ranges, local produce, jewellery, homewares. St Aubyn Estates run all.

Things to see and do: **Indoors** Children's castle quest. Find out more about the castle's history by asking our knowledgeable room guides. Sunday church services (Whitsun to September). **Outdoors** Storytelling and family activities during school holidays. **Dogs**: assistance dogs only in castle and garden.

Access: 🚻♿🧸📷🎦🅿️ Castle 🪜 Village ♿♿
Parking: numerous spaces in Marazion, opposite St Michael's Mount, not National Trust (charge including members).

St Michael's Mount: looking up at the iconic castle from its subtropical, steeply terraced garden

Find out more: 01736 710265 (information, tides and boats) or stmichaelsmount@nationaltrust.org.uk
stmichaelsmount.co.uk
Estate Office, King's Road, Marazion TR17 0EL

St Michael's Mount		M	T	W	T	F	S	S
Castle								
18 Mar–29 Jun	10:30–5	M	T	W	T	F	·	S
1 Jul–31 Aug	10–5:30	M	T	W	T	F	·	S
2 Sep–26 Oct	10:30–5	M	T	W	T	F	·	S
Garden								
16 Apr–29 Jun	10:30–5	M	T	W	T	F	·	·
5 Jul–31 Aug	10–5:30	·	·	·	T	F	·	·
6 Sep–28 Sep	10:30–5	·	·	·	T	F	·	·

Last admission one hour before castle closes (remember to allow enough time for travel from mainland). Telephone for details of opening arrangements in November and December.

Sandymouth

near Bude, Cornwall

 1978

A popular destination, yet Sandymouth remains unspoilt and breathtakingly beautiful. You'll find an extreme difference between the beach at low tide – when it is a huge sweep of sand and rocky outcrops – and at high tide, when it shrinks back to a pebbly cove, backed by twisted cliffs.

Eat, shop, stay: Sandymouth Café (concession, open seasonally) has outdoor and indoor seating and also sells beach goods. Pubs, shops and cafés in Kilkhampton and Bude (none National Trust).

Things to see and do: surf school. Fantastic rock-pooling and coastal walks. Look out for the waterfall and amazing geological formations backing the beach. You may also catch sight of skylarks, song thrushes and stonechats. **Dogs**: welcome everywhere, including the beach, but under close control (especially around livestock).

Access: 🅿️ 🚾 ♿ Coast and beach ♿
Sat Nav: use EX23 9HW. **Parking**: on site.

Find out more: 01208 863046 or sandymouth@nationaltrust.org.uk

Sandymouth							
Café at Sandymouth open seasonally, telephone 01288 354286.							

Tintagel Old Post Office

Fore Street, Tintagel, Cornwall PL34 0DB

🏠 ❄️ 1903

A medieval manor house in miniature, at more than 600 years old this is one of Cornwall's oldest domestic buildings. Used by a number of businesses throughout the Victorian period,

Tintagel Old Post Office: a manor house in miniature

its final function was as the village's letter-receiving office. The cottage garden hidden at the back offers a welcome retreat. **Note**: nearest toilet 54 yards in Trevena Square (not National Trust).

Eat, shop, stay: small souvenir shop in the Post Room selling craft items, gifts and books inspired by the Old Post Office's history and events. Picnics are welcome in the relaxing cottage garden at the back of the house.

Things to see and do: **Indoors** Events all year, including traditional craft workshops, baking demonstrations and activities to provide entertainment during school holidays.
Outdoors Family trail, games and dressing-up.
Dogs: assistance dogs only.

Access: 🅿️ 📷 ♿ 👓 📷 Building ♿ ♿ 🚻
Grounds ♿ ♿
Parking: pay and display village car parks, not National Trust (charges including members). Nearest Trust parking at Glebe Cliff in Tintagel, ½ mile.

Find out more: 01840 770024 or tintageloldpo@nationaltrust.org.uk

Tintagel Old Post Office		M	T	W	T	F	S	S
10 Feb–18 Feb	11–4	M	T	W	T	F	S	S
5 Mar–25 Mar	11–4	M	T	W	T	F	S	S
26 Mar–23 Sep	10:30–5:30	M	T	W	T	F	S	S
24 Sep–28 Oct	11–4	M	T	W	T	F	S	S

Trelissick

Feock, near Truro, Cornwall TR3 6QL

🏠 🏛 ✛ 🛏 ⛵ 🍽 | 1955 |

Trelissick is set on its own peninsula, with panoramic views over the Fal Estuary. The house provides the perfect setting to enjoy the ever-changing seascape and countryside steeped in Cornish history. Visitors can explore meandering paths through the woodland garden, leading to exotic plants and formal lawns with herbaceous borders bursting with colour. There are also longer walks to discover through the historic parkland, which sweeps down towards the estuary, and along Lamouth Creek to the Iron Age promontory fort and 18th-century quay at Roundwood.

Eat, shop, stay: Crofters Café open daily. Barn Restaurant and Courtyard Room both available for functions and private hire. Large shop with plant and garden centre. Second-hand bookshop. Cornish art and craft gallery. Six holiday cottages on the estate.

Things to see and do: Indoors Don't miss the life story of Ida Copeland. At Christmas, illuminated house and garden during evening openings. **Outdoors** Trelissick beach is perfect for skimming stones and paddling.

Trelissick: inside the Solarium, above, and heading towards the beach, below

Dogs: welcome on woodland walks. Assistance dogs only in garden.

Access: 🅿️ 🚻 ♿ ♿ ♿ 🚪 ♿ 🚻 Reception ♿ ♿
House ♿ ♿ ♿ Garden ♿ ♿ ♿ ➡ ♿ ♿
Parking: 80 yards.

Find out more: 01872 862090 or trelissick@nationaltrust.org.uk

Trelissick		M	T	W	T	F	S	S
Garden, café, shop, gallery and bookshop								
Open all year	10:30–5:30*	M	T	W	T	F	S	S
House								
20 Jan–18 Nov	11–5**		M	T	W	T	F	S	S
Parkland and walks								
Open all year		M	T	W	T	F	S	S

*1 January to 9 February and 29 October to 31 December: closes 4:30. Garden closes dusk if earlier. **20 January to 9 February and 29 October to 18 November: closes 4. Late-night openings and Christmas illuminations in December. Closed 25 and 26 December. Some areas, including house, occasionally close for private events.

Trengwainton Garden

Madron, near Penzance, Cornwall TR20 8RZ

🧩 🛏 1961

Here in this warm sheltered garden, you can follow in the footsteps of the great 1920s plant hunters to see colourful species that flowered in Britain for the first time. Award-winning magnolias and rhododendrons are still nurtured by those with a passion for plants, and subtropical varieties from around the world thrive in the shelter of the walled gardens, including a kitchen garden built to the dimensions of Noah's Ark. Winding wooded paths follow a half-mile incline to sea views across Mount's Bay, and the descent via the drive is bordered by a stream garden and open meadows.

Eat, shop, stay: award-winning tea-room (concession) with indoor and outdoor seating. Shop sells local gifts, food, souvenirs and Trengwainton-inspired plants. Second-hand bookshop and gallery in the former head gardener's cottage. Nearby, you can stay in an 18th-century former laundry house (sleeps nine).

Things to see and do: seasonal spotter sheets. Holiday activities, including Easter Egg hunts, pumpkin fun and Christmas lantern walk. Second World War 'Dig for Victory' plot. Why not visit Godolphin on the same day? **Dogs**: welcome on leads.

Access: 🅿️ 🚻 ♿ 🚪 ⬆️ 🎫 ⬆️ 🅿️ Reception ♿ Tea-room ♿ Garden ♿ ▶️ 🦮 ♿
Sat Nav: TR20 8RZ. **Parking**: 150 yards.

Find out more: 01736 363148 or trengwainton@nationaltrust.org.uk

Trengwainton Garden		M	T	W	T	F	S	S
11 Feb–28 Oct	10:30–5	M	T	W	T	.	.	S

Open Good Friday. Tea-room opens at 10.

Trengwainton Garden: the eccentric kitchen garden, above, and walking in the dog-friendly garden, below

Trerice

Kestle Mill, near Newquay, Cornwall TR8 4PG

🏠 ❄ 🧺 🔔 🍸 1953

Tucked away down winding lanes, just a stone's throw from Newquay, you'll find Trerice. Once the Cornish seat of the Arundell family, Trerice is an Elizabethan manor house with tales waiting to be discovered of prosperous origins, decline, partial ruin and 20th-century restoration. From the highest point of Trerice's lovely garden, views stretch out over a landscape rich in history, where ancient trees and boundaries speak eloquently of the past. Built from golden elvan stone, with ornate gables and a magnificent hall window, this grand house on a small scale inspired local writer Winston Graham's 'Trenwith' in the *Poldark* novels.

Eat, shop, stay: famous for lemon meringue pie, the barn restaurant serves light meals, snacks, freshly baked treats and cream teas. Shop selling local products, souvenirs and plants. The west wing of the house contains a holiday flat that sleeps two.

Enjoying a game of kayling on the lawn at Trerice, above, and the house in autumn, below

Things to see and do: **Indoors** Costume days, introductory talks and conservation events. Replica armour to try on. **Outdoors** Family activities and trails, Cornish 'kayles' and other traditional games. **Dogs**: welcome in car park only.

Access:  House 🏛🚻♿ Barn 🏛♿ Garden ♿🏛➡♿

Sat Nav: enter Kestle Mill A3058. **Parking**: 300 yards. Electric vehicle charging point available.

Find out more: 01637 875404 or trerice@nationaltrust.org.uk

Trerice		M	T	W	T	F	S	S
3 Mar–28 Oct	10:30–5*	M	T	W	T	F	S	S
3 Nov–23 Dec**	11–4	.	.	.	.	.	S	S

*House opens 11. **Selected rooms, garden, shop and restaurant open.

The distinctive outline of Trevose Head, seen from the west

Things to see and do: wonderful coastal walks with views and chances to watch wildlife. Access to Booby's Bay Beach. Carnewas at Bedruthan, just a few miles along the coast, is another spectacular coastal destination. **Dogs**: welcome under control. Please be aware of ground-nesting birds and keep to signed footpaths.

Find out more: 01208 863046 (North Cornwall office) or trevosehead@nationaltrust.org.uk

Trevose Head

near Padstow, Cornwall

 2016

Jutting into the Atlantic, Trevose Head commands views for miles along the coast. Exposed western cliffs contrast starkly with a gentler eastern coastline. Home of Trevose lighthouse (owned by Trinity House) and Padstow Lifeboat Station, it's also famed for nesting corn buntings and skylarks, and rare plants, such as wild asparagus. **Note**: sorry no toilets. Be careful of the sheer-sided round hole and quarry near Dinas Head.

Eat, shop, stay: convenience store and pub/café in St Merryn and Harlyn (1 to 2 miles). None National Trust. Picnics welcome.

Wheal Coates

near St Agnes, Cornwall

🏛♿🚻 1956

Dramatic mining ruins – an iconic Cornish sight – on the clifftops, carpeted with heather and gorse. **Note**: for Sat Nav use TR5 0NT. Follow the coast path for a lovely walk down to Chapel Porth Beach for nearest café and toilets.

Find out more: 01872 552412 or whealcoates@nationaltrust.org.uk

Additional coastal and countryside car parks in Cornwall

Strangles Beach	EX23 0LQ	St Agnes Beacon	TR5 0NU	Chyvarloe	TR12 7PY
Glebe Cliff, Tintagel	PL34 0DL	Reskajeage Downs	TR14 0JG	Predannack	TR12 7EZ
Lundy Bay	PL27 6QZ	Derrick Cove	TR14 0JG	Poltesco	TR12 7LR
Pentireglaze	PL27 6QY	Fishing Cove	TR27 5EE	Nare Head	TR2 5PQ
Trevose Head	PL28 8SL	Trencrom	TR27 6NP	Lamledra (Vault Beach)	PL26 6JS
Park Head	PL27 7UU	Carn Galver	TR20 8YX	Coombe Farm	PL23 1HW
Treago Mill (Polly Joke)	TR8 5QS	Cot Valley	TR19 7NS	Hendersick	PL13 2HZ

Devon and Dorset

Bridleway through heathland overlooking Studland Bay

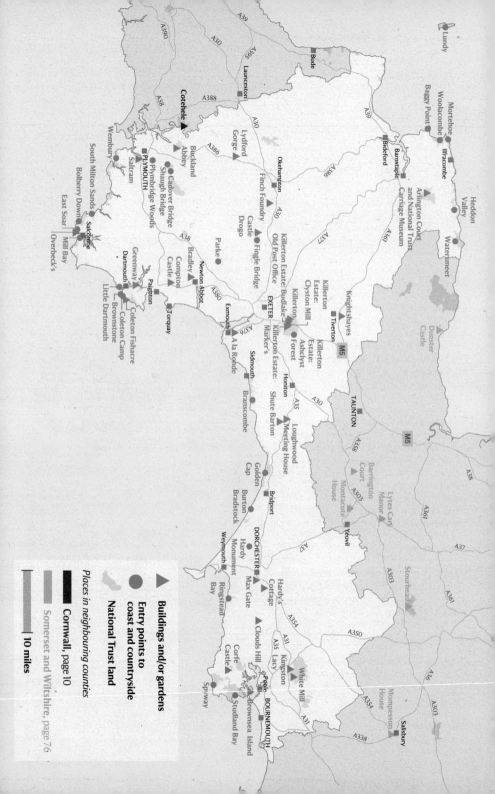

Lundy

Bude

Launceston

A39

A30

A395

A388

A30

A386

Cotehele ▲

A390

A38

Buckland Abbey ▲

Lydford Gorge ▲

Okehampton

Wembury

South Milton Sands

Bolberry Down

East Soar

Overbeck's

Mill Bay

Salcombe

Saltram ▲

PLYMOUTH ■

Shaugh Bridge

Plymbridge Woods ●

Cadover Bridge ●

Castle Drogo ▲

Finch Foundry ▲

Fingle Bridge ▼

Parke ●

Bradley ▲

Compton Castle ▲

Greenway ▲

Dartmouth ●

Little Dartmouth

Coleton Fishacre ▲

Coleton Camp

Brownstone

Paignton

Torquay

Newton Abbot

A380

A38

Exmouth

A la Ronde ▲

Killerton Estate: Budlake

Old Post Office ■

Killerton Estate: Clyston Mill ■

EXETER ■

Marker's ■

Killerton Estate: Ashclyst Forest ●

Killerton ▲

Killerton Estate: Shute Barton ▲

Sidmouth

Branscombe

Honiton

Knightshayes ▲

Tiverton ■

A396

A361

Bideford

Barnstaple

Arlington Court and National Trust Carriage Museum ▲

Baggy Point ●

Woolacombe

Mortehoe

Ilfracombe

Heddon Valley ●

Watersmeet ●

A39

A361

M5

Dunster Castle

A377

A35

A30

A38

A358

M5

TAUNTON ■

Loughwood Meeting House ▼

Golden Cap ●

Burton Bradstock

Bridport

A37

Montacute House

Barrington Court ▼

A303

Lytes Cary Manor ▼

Yeovil

Stourhead

A37

A361

A36

A303

Salisbury

Weymouth

DORCHESTER ■

Hardy Monument ●

Max Gate ▲

Ringstead Bay

Hardy's Cottage ▼

Clouds Hill ▼

Corfe Castle ▲

Kingston

White Mill ▼

Spyway

Studland Bay

Brownsea Island

Poole

BOURNEMOUTH ■

A31

A35

A351

A354

A350

A338

A36

Mompesson House

Places in neighbouring counties

■ Cornwall, page 10

Somerset and Wiltshire, page 76

Buildings and/or gardens ▼

● Entry points to coast and countryside

National Trust land

|‎ 10 miles

A la Ronde

Summer Lane, Exmouth, Devon EX8 5BD

 1991

Full of creativity and treasures from around the world, this amazing 16-sided house was the work of cousins Jane and Mary Parminter in the 1790s. Step inside and enter another world, one where their imaginations ran wild in design and ornamentation. They decorated walls with feathers, shells and pictures made of seaweed and sand, and every space contains mementoes from their travels. With the 360° touchscreen virtual tour, you can view the fragile shell gallery made with 25,000 shells. Outside, there's a sense of harmony around the orchard, hay meadow and colourful borders, and views over the Exe Estuary. **Note**: small and delicate rooms. Photography welcome without flash.

Eat, shop, stay: licensed tea-room serving morning coffee, light lunches and afternoon tea. Indoor and outdoor seating with views of the Exe Estuary. Borrow a blanket for a picnic. The shop features gifts, local food and keepsakes. Second-hand book sales.

Things to see and do: Indoors Eclectic collections. Trails, papercrafts and dressing-up. Tinkle the ivories. **Outdoors** Orchard, hay meadow and colourful borders. Estuary views. Garden games, croquet, seasonal activities and tours. **Dogs**: dogs on leads welcome everywhere (excluding house).

Access: ⬚⬚⬚⬚⬚⬚⬚⬚ House ⬚⬚⬚
Grounds ⬚ ➡
Sat Nav: postcode unreliable, enter Summer Lane. **Parking**: on site.

Find out more: 01395 265514 or alaronde@nationaltrust.org.uk

A la Ronde		M	T	W	T	F	S	S
3 Feb–9 Mar	*		M	T	W	T	F	S	S
10 Mar–28 Oct	11–5		M	T	W	T	F	S	S

*House: open by guided tour only Monday to Friday (first tour 11); at weekends and 12 to 16 February open 11 to 5 on a free-flow basis. Grounds, shop and café: open 10:30 to 5:30. Last orders in café at 5. Last entry to house at 4.

Tulips light up a border in the garden at A la Ronde in Devon, above, while inside, every corner is full of wonderfully eclectic collections, below

Arlington Court and the National Trust Carriage Museum

Arlington, near Barnstaple, Devon EX31 4LP

🏛 ✝ 🐾 ❀ ♿ ⬆ 1949

Hidden in the lichen-draped landscape of North Devon, Arlington is a surprise and a delight. The starkly classical exterior of the house gives no clue to what lies inside – recently redisplayed to share the passions of the Chichester family who lived here. The stable block houses a nationally important display of more than 40 carriages, from grand state coaches to humble governess cars. The garden is restored to its colourful Victorian glory, and the conservatory's exotic plantings reveal the Chichesters' world travels. New this year: find out more about how the Chichester ladies made their mark in a man's world.

Eat, shop, stay: seasonal produce grown in the walled garden is used in the tea-room. Reduced menu in winter. Two holiday cottages on edges of estate, sleeping two or three (dogs welcome).

Things to see and do: Indoors Bat-cam for watching rare bats. Rooms in the cellar tell the servants' stories. Children's activities.

Outdoors Two woodland play areas. Bring your walking boots for exploring the large estate. **Dogs**: welcome on leads in garden, Carriage Museum and wider estate.

Access: 🅿 ♿ 🚻 ℹ 🏷 📷 🖥 VT ♿ ⚫ 🖐
House 🔶🔶♿ Museum 🔶⬍♿ Grounds ➡🔶♿
Sat Nav: from South Molton, don't turn left into unmarked lane (deliveries only).
Parking: 150 yards.

Find out more: 01271 850296 or arlingtoncourt@nationaltrust.org.uk

Arlington Court		M	T	W	T	F	S	S
10 Feb–9 Mar	11–4*	M	T	W	T	F	S	S
10 Mar–27 Oct	11–5*	M	T	W	T	F	S	S
28 Oct–23 Dec	11–4	·	·	·	·	·	S	S

*Garden, shop and tea-room open 10:30. Grounds open all year, dawn to dusk.

Spring and autumn fun at Arlington Court and the National Trust Carriage Museum, Devon, above and below

Baggy Point

near Croyde, Devon

⚿ ♨ 🚲 🚗 | 1939

Exploring Baggy Point in Devon, above and below

Baggy Point is the impressive headland at Croyde, once owned by the Hyde family and overlooking one of the best surfing beaches in the South West. Huge coastal views out to Lundy Island, great walking and opportunities to climb, surf and coasteer make it a must-do destination for anyone visiting North Devon. Baggy Point also appeals to wildlife and nature lovers – keep a look out for seals and porpoises, as well as many bird species, including peregrine falcons, linnets and Dartford warblers. **Note**: toilets and outdoor shower in courtyard next to car park.

Eat, shop, stay: Sandleigh tea-room, garden and shop (tenant-run) serves drinks and food grown in the walled garden. Open-air covered

seating area overlooking garden. Tea-room is next to car park, close to beach slipway. Car-park kiosk serves cold drinks and snacks.

Things to see and do: free family activity pack to borrow (or download). Walks leaflets available from car-park kiosk. Easy-access route to the Point. Arlington Court and the National Trust Carriage Museum nearby. **Dogs**: welcome on leads (except for seasonal ban on Croyde Beach, May to September).

Access: 🅿♿ 🏛 ➡
Sat Nav: use EX33 1PA. **Parking**: car park in Moor Lane, Croyde.

Find out more: 01271 870555 or baggypoint@nationaltrust.org.uk

Bolberry Down

between Salcombe and Hope Cove, near Malborough, Devon

♨ 🚲 | 1938

The starting point for a spectacular stretch of coast between Salcombe and Hope Cove, including the headlands of Bolt Head and Bolt Tail and the sandy beach at Soar Mill Cove. The majestic ragged cliffs have claimed countless ships over the centuries. There's an easy-access clifftop route.

Eat, shop, stay: refreshments and meals available at Oceans Reach (not National Trust). Walkers' Hut café (tenant-run) at East Soar Outdoor Experience serves hot drinks and homemade cakes, and there are also catered camping options and a pretty holiday cottage.

Things to see and do: level circular trail (just under a mile), accessible for most wheelchair users and pushchairs. **Dogs**: welcome (on leads where animals grazing).

Access: 🅿♿ 🚹 🏛 ➡
Sat Nav: use TQ7 3DY. **Parking**: at Bolberry Down and Hope Cove (not National Trust).

Find out more: 01752 346585. 01548 561904 (East Soar Outdoor Experience) or bolberrydown@nationaltrust.org.uk

Bradley

Totnes Road, Newton Abbot, Devon TQ12 6BN

⚏ ✝ ❉ 1938

Surrounded by riverside meadows and woodland, this unspoilt medieval manor house is still a relaxed family home. There are original features to look out for, such as the medieval cat hole and drip stones, as well as the peaceful chapel that was licensed for services in 1428. **Note**: sorry no toilet. Parking from 10:30 on open days.

Eat, shop, stay: table-top shop selling honey, souvenirs, gifts and postcards. Picnics welcome in the meadows surrounding the house and garden.

Things to see and do: free children's trail. Open-air theatre performances in the garden. Walks in Bradley meadow and woodland. For a truly medieval experience, why not visit nearby Compton Castle? **Dogs**: welcome in meadows and woodland. Assistance dogs only in garden and house.

Access: ⓟ ⓓ ▱ ♿ ⓘ ⊘ Building ♿ ♿ ⚤
Grounds ♿ ♿ ➡
Sat Nav: TQ12 1LX directs to gate lodge (follow driveway for parking). **Parking**: in meadow (for designated parking call 07745 236836).

Find out more: 01803 661907 or bradley@nationaltrust.org.uk

Bradley		M	T	W	T	F	S	S
3 Apr–27 Sep	11–5	·	**T**	**W**	**T**	·	·	·

Also open Bank Holiday Monday, 7 May.

Branscombe

on the Jurassic Coast, near Seaton, Devon

⚏ ⛭ ⚒ ⛺ 1965

Nestling in a valley that reaches down to the sea on East Devon's dramatic Jurassic Coast, the village of Branscombe is surrounded by picturesque countryside with miles of tranquil walking through woodland, farmland and beach. Charming thatched houses, forge and restored watermill add to the timeless magic of the place. **Note**: nearest toilets at information point, village hall and beach car park.

Eat, shop, stay: Old Bakery tea-room (tenant-run) serving sandwiches, cakes and cream teas. Quality ironwork on sale from the Old Forge. Forge Cottage, just across the road, is a holiday cottage in an ideal location for exploring the village and coast.

Things to see and do: trail (graded as easy) winding up from the beach to the village, passing Manor Mill, Old Bakery and Old Forge. The beach is great for swimming and picnics. **Dogs**: welcome on leads in the Old Bakery garden, orchard, beach and wider countryside.

Access: ▣ Old Bakery tea-room ♿ ⚤
Mill ♿ ⚤ Grounds ♿
Sat Nav: use EX12 3DB. **Parking**: next to Old Forge, limited spaces. Also village hall and beach car parks (neither National Trust).

Find out more: 01752 346585 or branscombe@nationaltrust.org.uk

Branscombe		M	T	W	T	F	S	S
Manor Mill*								
1 Apr–28 Oct	2–5	·	·	·	·	·	·	**S**
Old Forge								
Open all year	10–5**	**M**	**T**	**W**	**T**	**F**	**S**	**S**

*Manor Mill also open Wednesdays 25 July to 29 August.
**Telephone 01297 680481 to check forge opening times. For details of the Old Bakery tea-room opening, telephone 01297 680764.

Still a family home, medieval Bradley in Devon sits surrounded by woodland and riverside meadows

Brownsea Island

Poole Harbour, Poole, Dorset

1962

The perfect day's adventure, this island wildlife sanctuary is easy to get to but feels like another world from the moment you step ashore. The island sits in the middle of Poole Harbour, with dramatic views to the Purbeck Hills. Thriving natural habitats, including woodland, heathland and a lagoon, have created havens for wildlife, such as the red squirrel and a huge variety of birds. The island is rich in history too. It is the birthplace of the Scouting and Guiding movements, and there are the remains of daffodil farming, pottery works and Maryland village to explore. **Note**: half-hourly boat service from 10 (not National Trust). Wheelchair boat service. No access to castle. Voluntary donation to enter the Dorset Wildlife Trust area (including members).

Eat, shop, stay: Villano Café; coffee bar; self-service hot drinks at the Outdoor Centre. Engine Gift Shop selling National Trust gifts, local products, Brownsea Island souvenirs and ice-cream. Scout and Guide Trading Post sells memorabilia. Two harbour-front holiday cottages.

Things to see and do: family activities, tree-climbing trail, Tracker Packs and natural play area. Events, walks and talks. Open-air theatre. Outdoor activity and visitor centres. Buggy tours for less-mobile visitors (booking advised). **Dogs**: assistance dogs only.

Access: [symbols] **Buildings** [symbols] **Grounds** [symbols]
Sat Nav: for Sandbanks Jetty use BH13 7QJ; for Poole Quay BH15 1HP. **Parking**: near Sandbanks and Poole Quay, not National Trust (charge including members).

Find out more: 01202 707744 or brownseaisland@nationaltrust.org.uk

Brownsea Island		M	T	W	T	F	S	S
Hourly boat service from Poole Quay and Sandbanks*								
10 Feb–11 Mar	10–4	.	.	.	.	.	S	S
Full boat service from Poole Quay and Sandbanks**								
17 Mar–28 Oct	10–5	M	T	W	T	F	S	S

*Winter weekend opening: boats from Poole and Sandbanks run hourly from 10. **Full boat service from Poole and Sandbanks runs every 30 minutes from 10. Shop and Villano Café: open until last boat. Winter Bird Boats (booking essential) from Poole offer Brownsea landings on 6 and 21 January and 4 February, or cruises on 13 January and 16 February.

Splendid isolation: Brownsea Island in Dorset, above and below, can only be reached by boat

Brownstone

Brownstone Road, Kingswear, Devon TQ6 0EH

 1981

Spectacular views on a coastal walk that leads to a rare Second World War gun battery at Froward Point. **Note**: naturally uneven coastal paths, steep in places – be aware of cliff edges and keep children and dogs supervised.

Find out more: 01803 752776 (Rangers) or brownstone@nationaltrust.org.uk

Buckland Abbey

Yelverton, Devon PL20 6EY

🏠✝🔧🎫🅿☕ 1948

Hundreds of years ago, Cistercian monks chose this tranquil valley as the perfect spot in which to worship, farm their estate and trade. The abbey, later converted into a house, today combines furnished rooms with museum galleries bringing to life the story of how seafaring adventurers Sir Richard Grenville

and Sir Francis Drake changed the shape of Buckland Abbey and the fate of England. Outdoors you'll find the walled kitchen garden, Cider House garden and wild garden; the impressive medieval Great Barn; community growing areas; orchards and woodland walks with far-reaching views and late spring bluebells. **Note**: abbey interior presented in association with Plymouth City Museum.

Eat, shop, stay: Ox Yard Restaurant serves freshly cooked local produce, often using ingredients grown in the kitchen garden. Picnics welcome in garden and grounds. Shop selling gifts and plants. Galleries and second-hand bookshop. Holiday cottage.

Buckland Abbey, Devon: the museum galleries, above, and the abbey bathed in the light of a setting sun, below

Things to see and do: **Indoors** Don't miss the famous Drake's Drum. **Outdoors** Higher Paddock natural play area and zip wire for younger visitors. Year-round events, estate walks and trails. **Dogs**: welcome on leads in farmland and on woodland walks. Assistance dogs only in garden.

Access: 🅿️🚊🧋🦽🚻🎨🖥️🍴🔈♿
Abbey 🦽♿ **Visitor Welcome** 🦽♿
Grounds 🦽🧋➡️📷♿
Sat Nav: do not use. **Parking**: 150 yards.

Find out more: 01822 853607 or
bucklandabbey@nationaltrust.org.uk

Buckland Abbey		M	T	W	T	F	S	S
6 Jan–4 Feb*	10–4	.	.	.	.	.	S	S
10 Feb–28 Oct	10–5**	M	T	W	T	F	S	S
29 Oct–31 Dec†	10–4	M	T	W	T	F	S	S

*Access to abbey by tour only (places limited);
**Abbey opens 11. †November: access to abbey, Monday to Friday, by tour only (places limited); Saturday and Sunday free-flow. December: free-flow access to ground floor only; 27 to 31 December access by tour only (places limited). Everything closed 24 to 26 December.

Burton Bradstock

on the Jurassic Coast, near Bridport, Dorset

🏖️🚢 1973

One of the main gateways to Dorset's Jurassic Coast, with easy access to spectacular sandstone cliffs and miles of unspoilt beaches. Hive Beach is a hugely popular family destination, part of Chesil Bank – the largest shingle ridge in the world. Nearby, Burton Cliff glows bright gold in the sunlight.

Eat, shop, stay: tenant-run Hive Beach Café on Chesil Bank serving local seafood.

Things to see and do: events through the year, some especially for families. Paddling, swimming and outdoor activities. Circular and clifftop walks. Chesil Bank popular for angling.
Dogs: welcome. Dog-free zone on Hive Beach, 1 June to 30 September.

Access: 🅿️🦽
Sat Nav: use DT6 4RF. **Parking**: on site.

Burton Bradstock: Burton Cliff on Dorset's Jurassic Coast

Find out more: 01297 489481 or
burtonbradstock@nationaltrust.org.uk

Cadover Bridge

on Dartmoor, near Shaugh Prior, Devon

🏛️🏖️ 1960

Tranquil moorland by the River Plym with pools. Starting point for walks across open moors and tors or ancient woodland.
Note: for Sat Nav use PL7 5EH.

Find out more: 01626 834748 or
cadoverbridge@nationaltrust.org.uk

Castle Drogo

Drewsteignton, near Exeter, Devon EX6 6PB

🏠🏚✝🎏🍴🍽 1974

High above the ancient woodlands of the Teign Gorge stands Castle Drogo. Inspired by the rugged Dartmoor tors that surround it, the castle was designed and built by renowned 20th-century architect Sir Edwin Lutyens. Nothing is normal at Drogo, as the castle is currently undergoing a major conservation project to save it, by making it watertight. The inside has been redisplayed taking inspiration from the stories of Drogo, bringing to life darkened spaces and displaying the collection in creative new ways. A scaffolding viewing tower enables you to see the craftsmanship of the modern-day stonemasons. **Note**: access may be restricted or changed due to building works. Restrictions apply to viewing tower.

Eat, shop, stay: popular licensed café in the visitor centre, with outside seating, serving light meals, homemade cakes and scones. Picnics welcome in orchard and grounds. Shop stocking gifts, local beers, jams and a good-sized plant centre. Holiday cottage nearby at Chagford.

Castle Drogo in Devon, below, sits high above the ancient woodlands of the Teign Gorge, right

Things to see and do: Indoors Programme of specialised guided tours, family trails and events. **Outdoors** Lutyens-designed terraced garden, games on the lawn. Walks into the Teign Gorge, views across Dartmoor, riverside paths. **Dogs**: welcome on leads in grounds and wider estate. Assistance dogs only in formal garden.

Access: 🅿♿🄳♿♿♿♿📷💻♿🅰🅿
Building ♿♿♿ **Grounds** ♿♿♿➡♿♿
Parking: 400 yards from visitor centre.

Find out more: 01647 433306 or castledrogo@nationaltrust.org.uk

Castle Drogo		M	T	W	T	F	S	S
Castle								
3 Mar–4 Nov	11–5	M	T	W	T	F	S	S
Garden, visitor centre, café and shop								
1 Jan–2 Mar*	11–4	M	T	W	T	F	S	S
3 Mar–4 Nov	10–5:30	M	T	W	T	F	S	S
5 Nov–31 Dec**	11–4	M	T	W	T	F	S	S
Estate								
Open all year	Dawn–dusk	M	T	W	T	F	S	S

*Closed 15 to 24 January. **Closed 24 to 26 December.

Clouds Hill

Bovington, Dorset BH20 7NQ

🏠 1937

In this tiny woodsman's cottage you can discover the essentials and the luxuries chosen by T. E. Lawrence after he had abandoned the 'Lawrence of Arabia' persona and remodelled himself as a private in the army at Bovington Camp. Much of the furniture and fittings was designed by Lawrence himself.

Clouds Hill, Dorset: T. E. Lawrence's simple home

Eat, shop, stay: self-service tea and coffee available. Small shop selling gifts, books and Lawrence memorabilia.

Things to see and do: you can visit the nearby homes of Thomas Hardy – Max Gate and Hardy's Cottage – along the very roads on which Lawrence himself rode. **Dogs**: welcome on leads in grounds only.

Access: ⦂⦂ **Building** ♿🄹 **Grounds** ♿
Parking: on site.

Find out more: 01929 405616 or cloudshill@nationaltrust.org.uk

Clouds Hill		M	T	W	T	F	S	S
1 Mar–31 Oct	11–5			W	T	F	S	S

Timed tickets may apply on busy days. No electric light, so last admission at dusk.

Coleton Camp

between Dart Estuary and Brixham, Devon

 1981

Great walks along the coast path to Scabbacombe and Man Sands beaches on this rugged stretch of coast. **Note**: naturally uneven coastal paths, steep in places – be aware of cliff edges and keep children and dogs supervised. For Sat Nav use TQ6 0EQ.

Find out more: 01803 753010 or coletoncamp@nationaltrust.org.uk

Coleton Fishacre

Brownstone Road, Kingswear, Devon TQ6 0EQ

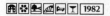 1982

This evocative 1920s Arts and Crafts-style house, with its elegant art deco interiors, perfectly encapsulates the spirit of the Jazz Age. The former country home of the D'Oyly Carte family, it has a light, joyful atmosphere and inspiring sea views. You can glimpse life 'upstairs and downstairs' and try on 1920s clothing in the popular handling room. In the RHS-accredited garden, paths weave through glades and past tranquil ponds and rare tender plants from New Zealand and South Africa; many exotic plants thrive beneath the tree canopy. You can walk down to a coastal viewpoint through the valley garden.

Eat, shop, stay: 1920s-inspired award-winning Café Coleton serving light bites, hearty lunches and cakes and bakes. Shop selling souvenir guides, china, gifts, food, music and plants. Why not stay in Chauffeur's Flat or Coleton Barton Cottages and enjoy after-hours access to the garden?

Things to see and do: family trails in the house and garden. Daily guided garden walks from Easter to October, led by a member of the garden team. Events, including open-air theatre. Wild play area. **Dogs**: welcome on short leads in garden and Café Coleton. Tethering rings by house.

Access: [symbols] Building [symbols] Grounds [symbols]
Parking: 20 yards from reception; overflow parking 150 yards.

Find out more: 01803 842382 or coletonfishacre@nationaltrust.org.uk

Coleton Fishacre		M	T	W		F	S	S
10 Feb–28 Oct	10:30–5	M	T	W	T	F	S	S
3 Nov–23 Dec	11–4	·	·	·	·	·	S	S
24 Dec–31 Dec	11–4	M	·	·	T	F	S	S

1920s Coleton Fishacre, Devon, perfectly encapsulates the joyful spirit of the Jazz Age

Compton Castle

Marldon, Paignton, Devon TQ3 1TA

🏠➕🔆🚻🚪 1951

Compton Castle, Devon: medieval fortified manor house

A rare survivor, this medieval fortified manor house set amid rolling hills has high curtain walls and two portcullises. It was once the home of Sir Humphrey Gilbert, and his descendants still live here today. Outside, you can discover roses climbing pergolas, knot and herb gardens and a picnic orchard. **Note**: hall, sub-solar, solar, study, kitchen, scullery, guard room and chapel open. Credit cards not accepted.

Eat, shop, stay: table-top shop selling souvenirs, guidebooks, gifts and postcards. Picnics welcome in the lower orchard. Why not stay a little longer and have a holiday in the bewitching Watchtower? Castle Barton restaurant (not National Trust) opposite.

Things to see and do: family activities, including history and squirrel trails for children, medieval dressing-up and garden games. You can join a 1½-mile circular walk opposite the castle. Events, such as Easter Egg hunts. **Dogs**: welcome in the lower orchard on leads. Assistance dogs only in castle and garden.

Access: 🅿️💻♿·· Building 🔍🏠 Grounds 🔍🏠
Parking: in Castle Barton's car park for cars and campervans, opposite entrance, 100 yards. Overflow parking on grass verges at castle entrance.

Find out more: 01803 661906 or comptoncastle@nationaltrust.org.uk

Compton Castle		M	T	W	T	F	S	S
3 Apr–31 Oct	10:30–4:30	·	**T**	**W**	**T**	·	·	·
Open Bank Holiday Mondays, including Easter Monday.								

Corfe Castle

Corfe, Wareham, Dorset BH20 5EZ

🏠🚻🚪 1982

This fairytale fortress is an evocative survivor of the English Civil War, partially demolished by the Parliamentarians in 1646. It's a favourite haunt for adults and children alike – all ages are captivated by these romantic ruins with their breathtaking views. There are 1,000 years of the castle's history as a royal palace and fortress to be discovered here. Fallen walls and secret places tell tales of treachery and treason around every corner. Corfe Castle's brooding presence is a backdrop to some of Britain's most beautiful coast and countryside. Corfe Common and Hartland Moor are close by – you can explore them by walking or cycling, discovering rare wild flowers and masses of wildlife along the way. **Note**: steep, uneven slopes; steps; sudden drops throughout castle. All/parts of castle close in high winds.

Corfe Castle in Dorset: fairytale fortress

Eat, shop, stay: 18th-century tea-room serving cream teas – summer garden with unrivalled castle views and log fire in winter. Shop in village square, with locally made gifts. Castle View visitor centre. Two holiday cottages in village, plus several more in wider Purbeck area.

Why not share your pictures with us? #nationaltrust

Corfe Castle: the formidable trebuchet, above, and a family explores the romantic ruins of this evocative survivor of the English Civil War, left

Things to see and do: action-packed programme of fun family history events runs from April until September, with something most weekends and school holidays. Highlights include Saxon and Viking and Civil War re-enactments, wildlife events, open-air theatre and winter lights. Throughout the year, discover the castle's trebuchet and children's activities. Beyond the castle walls, you can explore a wildlife-rich landscape of hills and heathland on walks through Purbeck. Downloadable walks include: the Purbeck Ridgeway – Corfe Castle to the coast (a walk along the roof of Purbeck taking in Old Harry Rocks); and the Corfe Common history walk, exploring the historic landscape around Corfe Castle. **Dogs**: welcome on short leads.

Access: [P] [D] [WC] [⬆] [🔊] [♿] [•] [◉] Grounds [♿]
Sat Nav: use BH20 5EZ. **Parking**: 800 yards uphill walk. Norden park and ride (½ mile) and West Street in village, neither National Trust (charge including members).

Find out more: 01929 481294 (ticket office). 01929 480921 (shop). 01929 481332 (tea-room) or corfecastle@nationaltrust.org.uk

Corfe Castle		M	T	W	T	F	S	S
1 Jan–28 Feb	.10–4	M	T	W	T	F	S	S
1 Mar–31 Mar	10–5	M	T	W	T	F	S	S
1 Apr–30 Sep	10–6*	M	T	W	T	F	S	S
1 Oct–31 Oct	10–5	M	T	W	T	F	S	S
1 Nov–31 Dec	10–4	M	T	W	T	F	S	S

Tea-room closed for refurbishment 8 to 12 January. Shop closed 9 January. Castle, shop and tea-room: closed 1 March and 25 to 26 December. *Shop and tea-room: close 5:30.

East Soar

between Salcombe and Hope Cove, near Malborough, Devon

 [⬆] [📷] 1950

This is a great starting point for exploring the isolated and rugged coast between Bolt Head and Bolt Tail. There's lots of history to discover, including the remains of Bronze Age settlements, shipwrecks and a top-secret Second World War installation. There is a waymarked one-mile route to Overbeck's, overlooking Salcombe. **Note**: sorry no toilet.

Eat, shop, stay: the quirky Walkers' Hut café (tenant-run) at East Soar Outdoor Experience serves hot drinks and homemade cakes. There are also catered camping options and a pretty holiday cottage. Nearby Overbeck's offers crab sandwiches and cream teas with sea views.

Things to see and do: this is a good stretch of coast for wildlife-spotting – look out for cirl buntings, silver-studded blue butterflies and large flocks of swallows and house martins gathering for their autumn migration.

Access: [P] [♿]
Sat Nav: use TQ7 3DR.
Parking: at East Soar car park.

Find out more: 01752 346585. 01548 561904 (Walkers' Hut) or eastsoar@nationaltrust.org.uk

The wild and rugged coastline at East Soar in Devon offers wonderful walking opportunities

Devon and Dorset

Finch Foundry

Sticklepath, Okehampton, Devon EX20 2NW

🏠 ✜ ♿ 1994

A blacksmith works the forge at Finch Foundry, Devon

The foundry was a family-run business producing a range of tools for West Country industries, including farming and mining, in the 19th century. The huge waterwheels and tilt hammer spring into action during regular demonstrations. Products of the business are displayed in the carpenters' workshops. Outside is a delightful cottage garden. **Note**: narrow entrance to car park, plus height restrictions.

Eat, shop, stay: cosy tea-room, with tables in the garden, offering snacks, cakes, ice-cream, hot and cold drinks. Gift shop, plant sales.

Things to see and do: **Indoors** Family activities, stories, demonstrations and tours of machinery. Blacksmithing event on St Clement's Day in November. **Outdoors** Starting point for moorland walks. Delightful cottage garden containing Tom Pearse's summerhouse. **Dogs**: welcome in all areas (excluding tea-room).

Access: 🅿️♿🔊🔉📷 Foundry ♿ 👫 Grounds ♿
Parking: on site (height/width restrictions).

Find out more: 01837 840046 or finchfoundry@nationaltrust.org.uk

Finch Foundry		M	T	W	T	F	S	S
3 Mar–28 Oct	11–5	M	T	W	T	F	S	S
3 Nov–23 Dec	11–3	·	·	·	·	·	S	S

Demonstrations of the working machinery throughout day. Open for St Clement's Day, 24 November (patron saint of blacksmiths).

Fingle Bridge

Teign Gorge, near Drewsteignton, Exeter, Devon

🚻 ♿ 1990

This popular spot lies at the bottom of the Teign Gorge on Dartmoor, where a 17th-century bridge crosses the river. There's much to explore – Fingle Woods, downstream, offers miles of footpaths; while upstream you can climb up towards Castle Drogo, which sits on a ridge high above the river. **Note**: uneven terrain. Fingle Woods are being restored and managed in partnership with the Woodland Trust.

Eat, shop, stay: you're welcome to picnic in the meadow by the river. Refreshments available at the Fingle Bridge Inn (not National Trust) and at Castle Drogo café, where there is also a National Trust shop, at the top of the gorge.

17th-century Fingle Bridge in the Teign Gorge, Devon

Things to see and do: abundant birdlife, including bats and butterflies, to spot. Iron Age hill forts, riverside walks, ancient woodlands and views down the Teign Gorge. 'Wild Tribe' events in the meadow (booking essential). **Dogs**: welcome under close control.

Access: 🚻♿
Sat Nav: for Fingle Bridge car park use EX6 6PW; Castle Drogo car park EX6 6PB; Steps Bridge car park EX6 7EQ. **Parking**: Fingle Bridge (access over narrow packhorse bridge) for Fingle Woods. Additional parking Castle Drogo main car park or Steps Bridge in Teign Valley.

Find out more: 01647 433356 or finglebridge@nationaltrust.org.uk

Golden Cap

on the Jurassic Coast, near Bridport, Dorset

 1961

Golden Cap, Dorset: the highest point on the south coast

Spectacular countryside estate on the Jurassic Coast – England's only natural World Heritage Site. The great rocky shoulder of Golden Cap is the south coast's highest point, with breathtaking views in all directions. Stonebarrow Hill is a good starting point for discovering the 25 miles of footpaths around the estate.

Eat, shop, stay: small volunteer-run shop and information centre (open Easter to October), with toilets and bunkhouse, in the old radar station at Stonebarrow car park, Charmouth. Six holiday cottages, mostly thatched, make ideal bases for getting to know the wider estate.

Things to see and do: play trail on Langdon Hill. Smugglers' trail on Stonebarrow Hill. Family activities and events all year. Charmouth Beach for fossils and traces of 185 million years of Earth's history. **Dogs**: welcome.

Access: 🦽
Sat Nav: for Stonebarrow use DT6 6RA; Langdon Hill DT6 6EP. **Parking**: at Stonebarrow Hill and Langdon Hill.

Find out more: 01297 489481 (Golden Cap) or goldencap@nationaltrust.org.uk

Golden Cap
Stonebarrow shop and information centre open seasonally, Easter to October.

Greenway

Greenway Road, Galmpton, near Brixham, Devon TQ5 0ES

🏠❄️🛏️🔔🚂 2000

Here you are given a glimpse into the lives of the famous author Agatha Christie and her family. Their atmospheric holiday home is set in the 1950s, when Greenway overflowed with friends and family, gathered together for holidays and Christmas. The family were great collectors and the house is brimming with their books, archaeology, Tunbridgeware, silver and porcelain. The informal woodland garden drifts down the hillside towards the sparkling Dart Estuary and the Boathouse, scene of the crime in *Dead Man's Folly*. Please consider 'green ways' to get here:. ferry (shuttle bus available from quay), steam train, cycling or walking. **Note**: booking essential for car parking (01803 842382). Train halt ½ mile (woodland walk; shuttle bus).

Greenway, Devon: the atmospheric holiday home of Agatha Christie and her family is set in the 1950s

A seat with a view at Greenway

Eat, shop, stay: Barn Café serving lunches and sweet treats. Tack-room open at peak times offering drinks, ice-cream and snacks. Shop selling souvenir guides, Agatha Christie books and plants. Second-hand bookshop. Four holiday cottages, with after-hours access to the garden.

Things to see and do: why not start your visit with an introductory film in the Stables? Guided garden tours daily until October. Events such as open-air theatre. Family activities, including croquet, tennis and trails. **Dogs**: welcome on garden paths on short leads (tethering rings available in courtyard).

Access: ⓅⒹⒹⒶⒶⒶⒶⒶⒶⒶⒶⒶⒶⒶ
Buildings ⒶⒶⒶ Garden ⒶⒶ
Parking: spaces must be booked – same-day booking possible by telephone. No parking on Greenway Road or Galmpton.

Find out more: 01803 842382 (Greenway car-park booking and infoline). 01803 882811 (Greenway Ferry Company). 01803 555872 (Dartmouth Steam Railway and River Boat Company) or greenway@nationaltrust.org.uk

Greenway		M	T	W	T	F	S	S
10 Feb–28 Oct	10:30–5	M	T	W	T	F	S	S
3 Nov–23 Dec	11–4	·	·	·	·	·	S	S
24 Dec–31 Dec	11–4	M	·	·	T	F	S	S

Hardy Monument

Black Down, near Portesham, Dorset

🏠🏊 1938

Memorial to Vice-Admiral Hardy, Flag-Captain of HMS *Victory* at Trafalgar, designed to look like a spyglass. Views over the Channel. **Note**: nearest postcode for Sat Nav is DT2 9HY. Open 28 March to 30 September, Wednesday to Sunday, 11 to 4 (subject to weather conditions).

Find out more: 01297 489481 or hardymonument@nationaltrust.org.uk

Hardy's Cottage

Higher Bockhampton, near Dorchester, Dorset DT2 8QJ

🏠❄ 1948

Hardy's Cottage, Dorset: Thomas Hardy's childhood home

You can find yourself 'far from the madding crowd', as you explore Hardy's rural childhood home and the birthplace of his literary land of 'Wessex'. Visitors are invited to make themselves at home, whether sitting next to the fire or wandering through the quintessential cottage garden. **Note**: nearest toilet at visitor centre.

Eat, shop, stay: postcards, gifts and Thomas Hardy's books are on sale at the cottage, and at Hardy's Birthplace Visitor Centre near the car park. Café (not National Trust) at the visitor centre.

Things to see and do: why not combine your visit with a trip to Max Gate, Hardy's later home in Dorchester, and Clouds Hill, the retreat of Hardy's friend T. E. Lawrence? **Dogs**: welcome on leads in the garden and woods only.

Access: [symbols] Building [symbol] Grounds [symbols]
Parking: 700 yards (not National Trust). Free to members displaying valid Trust car-parking sticker. Telephone for accessible parking arrangements.

Find out more: 01305 262366 or hardyscottage@nationaltrust.org.uk

Hardy's Cottage		M	T	W	T	F	S	S
4 Jan–25 Feb	10–4				**T**	**F**	**S**	**S**
1 Mar–31 Oct	11–5	**M**	**T**	**W**	**T**	**F**	**S**	**S**
1 Nov–30 Dec	11–4				**T**	**F**	**S**	**S**

Last admission 45 minutes before closing (dusk if earlier). Admission through visitor centre (open daily 10 to 4, café last orders 3:45), 590 yards from cottage. Timed tickets may apply on busy days (especially Mondays when school groups visit) – check before visiting.

Heddon Valley

on Exmoor, near Combe Martin, Devon

[symbols] 1963

The dramatic West Exmoor coast, favourite landscape of the Romantic poets, offers not only the beautiful Heddon Valley, but also Woody Bay and the Hangman Hills to explore. There are spectacular coastal, moorland and woodland walks. Nature highlights include one of the UK's last surviving colonies of high brown fritillary butterflies, which can be seen in July and August on the bracken-clad hillsides

Two views of Heddon Valley, Devon, above and below

of the Heddon Valley. Look out for the rich diversity of fungi in autumn. High above the valley sits a Roman fortlet, the remains of which are still visible today.

Eat, shop, stay: shop selling walking equipment and clothing, maps, postcards, local history books, Exmoor products, gifts and ice-cream. Heddon Orchard Bothy offers basic accommodation – equivalent to camping without a tent.

Things to see and do: all-terrain children's buggies and all-terrain mobility scooter available to borrow (call 01598 763556 to book mobility scooter). **Dogs**: welcome.

Access: [symbols] Countryside [symbols]
Sat Nav: use EX31 4PY. **Parking**: opposite Trust shop.

Find out more: 01598 763402 or heddonvalley@nationaltrust.org.uk

Heddon Valley		M	T	W	T	F	S	S
Shop								
24 Mar–28 Oct	10:30–5*	**M**	**T**	**W**	**T**	**F**	**S**	**S**

Open 11 to 4 on March weekends. *Also open 11 to 4 from 10 September.

Killerton

Broadclyst, Exeter, Devon EX5 3LE

[icons] 1944

Would you give away your family home for your political beliefs? Sir Richard Acland did just that with his Killerton Estate in the heart of Devon, when he gave it to the Trust in 1944. Today you'll find a welcoming Georgian house set in 2,600 hectares (6,400 acres) of working farmland, woods, parkland, cottages and orchards. There's plenty of calm space in the glorious garden, beautiful year-round with rhododendrons, magnolias, champion trees and formal lawns. You can explore winding paths, climb an extinct volcano, discover an Iron Age hill fort and take in distant views towards Dartmoor. More family home than grand mansion, the relaxed house holds the National Trust's largest fashion collection, with selected items exhibited annually.

Eat, shop, stay: table service in the highly rated Killerton Kitchen restaurant. Lighter bites in the Stables Café or Dairy Café on busier days. Picnics welcome. Plant centre, bookshop and shop selling gifts and award-winning estate produce. Five holiday cottages on the estate.

Things to see and do: Indoors Interactive, family-friendly house. You're welcome to play the piano, read library books and sit on chairs. Family trail to find hidden mice.
Outdoors You can walk, run and cycle throughout the estate, which is made up

Welcoming Killerton in Devon, this page and opposite: visitors are encouraged to play the piano in this relaxed house, have an outdoor adventure or enjoy the views

of parkland, woods, orchards and rolling Devon countryside. Winding garden paths to the Bear's Hut, ice house and chapel. There are giant redwoods, rhododendrons and far-reaching views to discover. Many seasonal events and trails, including Easter trails, cider and apple festival and Christmas at Killerton.
Dogs: welcome in the parkland and estate. Assistance dogs only in garden and chapel grounds.

Access: [icons]
House [icons] Grounds [icons]
Sat Nav: postcode leads to house, so follow brown signs to main car park. **Parking**: main car park 280 yards. Additional smaller car parks, including Ashclyst Forest Gate, Ellerhayes Bridge, Danes Wood.

Find out more: 01392 881345 or killerton@nationaltrust.org.uk

Killerton		M	T	W	T	F	S	S
House and Killerton Kitchen restaurant								
10 Feb–23 Mar	11–4	M	T	W	T	F	S	S
24 Mar–4 Nov	11–5	M	T	W	T	F	S	S
24 Nov–31 Dec*	11–4	M	T	W	T	F	S	S
Chapel, garden, Stables Café, shop and plant centre**								
1 Jan–9 Feb	11–4	M	T	W	T	F	S	S
10 Feb–31 Dec*	10–5:30	M	T	W	T	F	S	S
Park								
Open all year	8–7	M	T	W	T	F	S	S

House: entry by timed tickets at peak times. Fashion collection exhibition open with house, 10 February to 4 November. *Special Christmas opening until 6 January 2019: closes at 3 on 24 December, everything except park closed 25 December, house closed 26 December. **Open 9 on Saturdays. Garden and park: open daily to 7, or dusk if earlier. Dairy Café: open at peak times.

Killerton Estate: Ashclyst Forest

near Broadclyst, Exeter, Devon

🏕 | 1944

One of the largest woods in East Devon, with waymarked trails for exploring. A haven for butterflies, bluebells and birds. **Note**: for Sat Nav use EX5 3DT, follow signs to Ashclyst. Nearest toilets, café and shop at main Killerton car park.

Find out more: 01392 881345 or ashclystforest@nationaltrust.org.uk

Killerton Estate: Budlake Old Post Office

Broadclyst, Killerton, Exeter, Devon EX5 3LW

🏠 | ❀ | 1944

Visiting this old village post office with its cottage garden and intriguing outbuildings is like stepping back into the 1950s. **Note**: nearest parking and toilets at Killerton. Open 1 April to 31 October, Monday, Tuesday, Wednesday and weekends, 1 to 5.

Find out more: 01392 881345 or budlakepostoffice@nationaltrust.org.uk

Killerton Estate: Clyston Mill

Broadclyst, Exeter, Devon EX5 3EW

🏭 | 🏕 | 1944

A historic working water-powered corn mill in a picturesque setting by the River Clyst. **Note**: nearest parking and toilets in Broadclyst village. Open 1 April to 31 October, Monday, Tuesday, Wednesday and weekends, 1 to 5.

Find out more: 01392 462425 or clystonmill@nationaltrust.org.uk

Killerton Estate: Marker's

Townend, Broadclyst, Exeter, Devon EX5 3HS

🏠 | 1944

A medieval hall-house with a thatched roof, smoke-blackened timbers, a rare painted screen, garden and cob summerhouse. **Note**: nearest parking and toilets in Broadclyst village. Open 1 April to 31 October, Monday, Tuesday, Wednesday and weekends, 1 to 5.

Find out more: 01392 461546 or markers@nationaltrust.org.uk

Kingston Lacy

Wimborne Minster, Dorset BH21 4EA

🏠 | 🏛 | ❀ | ♿ | 🅿 | ⛺ | ☕ | 1982

Home to the Bankes family for over 300 years, Kingston Lacy is a monument to the family's exceptional taste and desire to surround themselves with beauty. After the family lost their Corfe Castle stronghold to the Parliamentarians in the Civil War, they moved here and gradually created an astonishing

Kingston Lacy, Dorset: a corner of the garden, opposite, the impressive façade, above, and opulent Spanish Room, below

Italian palace in the heart of rural Dorset. Today you can discover an internationally acclaimed art collection, including paintings by Rubens, Velázquez and Titian, exquisite carvings and lavish interiors. There's even more to explore outside, with sweeping lawns, a Japanese Garden, kitchen garden, woodland and parkland walks – look out for the award-winning herd of Red Ruby Devon cattle – and a huge 3,500-hectare (8,500-acre) countryside estate to enjoy. **Note**: timed tickets only. Some rooms may close at short notice. Low light levels.

Eat, shop, stay: hot meals at lunchtime, light bites, cream teas and cakes in the Stables Café. Drinks, cakes and ice-cream available in kitchen garden (March to October). The old kitchen shop stocks local food, plants, gifts and souvenirs. Second-hand bookshop. Holiday cottage.

Things to see and do: **Indoors** Lavish interiors, world-class art collection, sculptures and wood carvings (levels of light are kept low to protect these treasures). **Outdoors** The garden changes with the seasons from snowdrops, blossom and bluebells to summer flowers and autumn colour. There are deckchairs for relaxing on the lawn, or why not explore the kitchen garden or join a garden tour? Activities all year include guided walks, family trails and evening events. Longer walks across the estate include a riverside route past Eye Bridge or the Iron Age hill fort of Badbury Rings, home to 14 varieties of orchid. **Dogs**: welcome on leads in café courtyard and 'horseshoe' seats, park, woodlands and wider estate.

Snowdrops smother the ground in spring at Kingston Lacy

Eye Bridge, Pamphill Green and Badbury Rings, where there is a charge on point-to-point race days (including members).

Find out more: 01202 883402 or kingstonlacy@nationaltrust.org.uk

Kingston Lacy		M	T	W	T	F	S	S
House								
1 Mar–28 Oct	11–5	M	T	W	T	F	S	S
Part of house: for exhibition or seasonal experience only								
1 Jan–28 Feb	11–4	M	T	W	T	F	S	S
29 Oct–26 Nov	11–4	M	T	W	T	F	S	S
1 Dec–31 Dec	11–4*	M	T	W	T	F	S	S
Garden, park, shop and café								
Open all year	10–4**	M	T	W	T	F	S	S

House: last admission one hour before closing; open by timed entry tickets only, bookable online in advance (limited places available on day); some rooms and areas may close at short notice (please check before visiting). *Christmas experience: Friday, Saturday and Sunday, house open to 6 and garden (with light displays) to 7. Everything closed 17 January and 25 December. **1 March to 28 October: close 6.

Access: 🅿️♿🚻🖼️📷♿🚗📷🎧⠿◻️
Building ♿ **Grounds** ♿📷♿♿
Sat Nav: unreliable, follow B3082 to main entrance. Use BH21 4EL for Eye Bridge; BH21 4EE for Pamphill Green; DT11 9JL for Badbury Rings. **Parking**: on site or at

Knightshayes

Bolham, Tiverton, Devon EX16 7RQ

 1972

One of the finest in the South West and the only existing 'garden in a wood', Knightshayes' garden is a masterpiece of architectural planting. As well as one of the largest plant collections in the National Trust, there are hidden glades and pathways to discover and far-reaching views. The Gothic Revival house is a rare example of the genius of William Burges, whose opulent designs are guaranteed to inspire extremes of opinion. Alongside this, the restored walled garden merges full productivity with aesthetic appeal and it's one of the best examples of a Victorian kitchen garden in the country. **Note**: access to the house and garden may be restricted during spring and winter.

Eat, shop, stay: Stables Café serves hot meals, made using ingredients from the kitchen garden, also soups, sandwiches, cakes and drinks. Conservatory tea-room offers snacks, cakes, ice-cream and drinks. Picnics welcome. Well-stocked shop and plant centre, with plants from the Knightshayes collection.

Things to see and do: **Indoors** Family trails around the house. Traditional Victorian Christmas. **Outdoors** Play areas. Animal topiary. Kitchen garden restoration project. Events, including outdoor music in the summer, Christmas fairs and illuminations. **Dogs**: welcome on leads in parkland and woods; in formal garden, November to February only.

Access: 🅿️♿🏛️♿♿♿⛲📷📱♿👁️📷
House ♿♿♿ **Stables** ♿♿♿ **Gardens** ♿➡️♿
Sat Nav: do not use, follow brown signs on nearing Tiverton/Bolham. **Parking**: on site.

Find out more: 01884 254665 or knightshayes@nationaltrust.org.uk

Knightshayes		M	T	W	T	F	S	S
1 Jan–25 Feb	10–4	M	T	W	T	F	S	S
26 Feb–28 Oct	10–5	M	T	W	T	F	S	S
29 Oct–2 Dec	10–4	M	T	W	T	F	S	S
3 Dec–31 Dec	10–5	M	T	W	T	F	S	S

House: opens 11; selected rooms open January and February; downstairs only November and December. Parkland and woodland: open 7:30 to 5:30. Garden, café and shop: open to 5:30, July and August. Everything closed 24, 25 and 26 December. Mid-Devon Show, Saturday 28 July (expect delays).

Knightshayes in Devon: the Gothic Revival house is a rare example of the genius of William Burges

Little Dartmouth

near Dartmouth, Devon

🏛🏊🚶 1970

A gentle coastal landscape west of Dartmouth, with wonderful views, wild flowers and the remains of a Civil War encampment.
Note: toilets at Dartmouth Castle (not National Trust). For Sat Nav use TQ6 0JP.

Find out more: 01752 346585 or littledartmouth@nationaltrust.org.uk

Loughwood Meeting House

Dalwood, Axminster, Devon EX13 7DU

✝ 1969

Atmospheric 17th-century thatched Baptist meeting house dug into the hillside.
Note: sorry no toilet. Open daily, 10 to 5. Services held twice yearly (details at Meeting House).

Find out more: 01752 346585 or loughwood@nationaltrust.org.uk

Lundy

Bristol Channel, Devon

🍴✝🍷🏛🛏🏊🚶🐕 1969

Undisturbed by cars, this wildlife-rich island, designated the first Marine Conservation Area, encompasses a small village with an inn, Victorian church and the 13th-century Marisco Castle. **Note**: financed, administered and maintained by the Landmark Trust. Ferry from Bideford or Ilfracombe. MS *Oldenburg* fares (including members), discounts available.

Lundy in the Bristol Channel, Devon: visitors can stay on this wildlife-rich island

Eat, shop, stay: tavern serving hot and cold food and drinks. Convenience shop selling souvenirs, Lundy stamps, snacks and ice-cream. Holiday cottages (not National Trust).

Things to see and do: scuba diving, walking, letterboxing, bird and wildlife-watching.
Dogs: assistance dogs only.

Access: 🚗🚻♿ Building 🏛 Grounds 🌳
Sat Nav: use EX34 9EQ for Ilfracombe; EX39 2EY for Bideford. **Parking**: at Bideford and Ilfracombe, not National Trust (charge including members).

Find out more: 01271 863636 or lundy@nationaltrust.org.uk   The Lundy Shore Office, The Quay, Bideford, Devon EX39 2LY

Lundy

MS *Oldenburg* sails from Bideford or Ilfracombe up to four times a week from the end of March until the end of October carrying both day and staying passengers. A helicopter service operates from Hartland Point from November to mid-March, Mondays and Fridays only, for staying visitors.

Lydford Gorge

Lydford, near Tavistock, Devon EX20 4BH

[♿] [1947]

This magical legend-rich river gorge (the deepest in the South West) offers a variety of adventurous walks. The gorge provides a truly breathtaking experience: around every corner the River Lyd plunges, tumbles, swirls and gently meanders as it travels through the steep-sided, oak-wooded valley. There are amazing features carved out by the water over thousands of years, from the 30-metre Whitelady Waterfall to the turbulent pothole called the Devil's Cauldron. Throughout the seasons there is an abundance of wildlife and plants to see, from woodland birds to wild garlic in the spring and fungi in the autumn. **Note**: rugged terrain, vertical drops. Booking required for Tramper.

Lydford Gorge, Devon: a visitor enjoys the freedom that a Tramper offers, above. The breathtaking gorge, below

Eat, shop, stay: shop selling gifts, books, local food and drink, outdoor wear and plants. Two tea-rooms at either end of the gorge serving light lunches, soup, sandwiches, cream teas, cakes and ice-cream. Takeaway drinks and food available.

Things to see and do: waterfall suspension bridge, wildlife-themed and bushcraft activities, spotter sheets, Hallowe'en trail in October half-term, children's play area, bird walk and bird hide along the old railway line. **Dogs**: welcome on leads (excluding tea-rooms).

Access: [icons]
Buildings [icon] Gorge [icon]
Sat Nav: EX20 4BH (Devil's Cauldron entrance); EX20 4BL (waterfall entrance).
Parking: on site.

Find out more: 01822 820320 or lydfordgorge@nationaltrust.org.uk

Lydford Gorge		M	T	W	T	F	S	S
Gorge, shop and tea-rooms								
3 Mar–28 Oct	10–5	**M**	**T**	**W**	**T**	**F**	**S**	**S**
Gorge (part of), shop and tea-room								
3 Nov–23 Dec	11–3:30	·	·	·	**T**	**F**	**S**	**S**

Waterfall tea-room: opens 11, closing dependent on weather. October: last admission to gorge 3:30; shop and tea-room close at 4. Short walks to waterfall: open during daylight in January and February and Thursday to Sunday, 11 and 3:30 from 3 November to 23 December.

Max Gate

Alington Avenue, Dorchester, Dorset DT1 2FN

 1940

Max Gate, home to Dorset's most famous author and poet, Thomas Hardy, was designed by the writer himself in 1885. This atmospheric Victorian house is where Hardy wrote some of his most famous novels, including *Tess of the d'Urbervilles* and *Jude the Obscure*, as well as most of his poetry.

Eat, shop, stay: Thomas Hardy's books, souvenirs and small gifts on sale. Tea, coffee, cakes and ice-cream available.

Things to see and do: visit nearby Hardy's Cottage, the thatched cottage in which the writer was born and grew up, and Clouds Hill, the retreat of Hardy's friend T. E. Lawrence ('Lawrence of Arabia'). **Dogs**: welcome on leads in garden only.

Access: 🔎📷 Building 👆🚻 Garden 👆
Sat Nav: use DT1 2AJ. **Parking**: on roadside in front of the house (50 yards, limited spaces, not National Trust).

Max Gate in Dorset: view towards the house, above, and the Entrance Hall, below

Find out more: 01305 262538 or maxgate@nationaltrust.org.uk

Max Gate		M	T	W	T	F	S	S
4 Jan–25 Feb	10–4	·	·	·	**T**	**F**	**S**	**S**
1 Mar–31 Oct	11–5	**M**	**T**	**W**	**T**	**F**	**S**	**S**
1 Nov–30 Dec	11–4	·	·	·	**T**	**F**	**S**	**S**

Closes dusk if earlier.

Mill Bay

East Portlemouth, near Salcombe, Devon

 1991

There are sandy beaches at Mill Bay, Sunny Cove and Seacombe Sands, with rugged walking past coastguard lookouts towards Prawle. **Note**: for Sat Nav use TQ8 8PU. Toilets and Mill Bay Beach not National Trust.

Find out more: 01752 346585 or millbay@nationaltrust.org.uk

Mortehoe

near Ilfracombe, Devon

 1909

Gateway to a wild, remote coast with a rich history of wrecking and smuggling. Amazing walking, wildlife and sunbathing seals. **Note**: use EX34 7DT for village car park and toilets, not National Trust (charge including members). Town Farmhouse (tenant-run) offers cream teas in summer.

Find out more: 01271 870555 or mortehoe@nationaltrust.org.uk

The subtropical garden at Overbeck's in Devon, above and below, is filled with rare, exotic plants

Overbeck's

Sharpitor, Salcombe, Devon TQ8 8LW

🏛️ ❄️ ♿ 🎨 1937

Tucked away on the cliffs above Salcombe is this hidden paradise: a subtropical garden, bursting with colour, filled with exotic and rare plants and surprises round every corner, which surrounds the seaside home of scientist and inventor Otto Overbeck. The views from the garden over the estuary and coast are truly breathtaking. Inside, among Otto's eclectic collections – glimpses of a bygone age – are his 'Rejuvenator', once believed to cure all ills, and the melodious giant music box called a polyphon (you can choose a disc to play). Generations of children return to discover Fred the friendly ghost. **Note**: entrance path and grounds are very steep in places.

Eat, shop, stay: licensed tea-room serving cream teas and light lunches (crab sandwiches a speciality), terrace with sea views. Shop selling books, plants and unique gifts such as 'First Flight', a statuette inspired by the bronze girl in the garden.

Things to see and do: **Indoors** Activities, tours, trails and quizzes for children. **Outdoors** Garden trails, tours. Statue garden, secret paths, woodland areas and olive grove. The surrounding coast and beaches are great for exploring. **Dogs**: assistance dogs only.

Access: 🅿️ 🚪 🏠 🗺️ 📷 ♿ 🔌
Building 🏠 **Grounds** ♿
Sat Nav: follow brown signs through Malborough. **Parking**: small car park at top of drive and on approach lane. Additional parking at East Soar (1½ miles along coast path).

Find out more: 01548 842893 or overbecks@nationaltrust.org.uk

Overbeck's		M	T	W	T	F	S	S
10 Feb–28 Oct	11–5	**M**	**T**	**W**	**T**	**F**	**S**	**S**

Tea-room closes at 4:45.

Parke

near Bovey Tracey, Devon TQ13 9JQ

[icons] 1974

On the south-eastern edge of Dartmoor sits this tranquil historic parkland. Riverside paths follow the course of the River Bovey, as it meanders through woodlands and meadows rich in plants and wildlife. Look out for the medieval weir, walled garden and historic orchard.

Eat, shop, stay: Home Farm Café (not National Trust) – freshly cooked food from the seasonal menu board, coffee, teas and homemade cakes. Parke Lodge holiday cottage at the entrance to Parke.

The tranquil historic parkland at Parke in Devon

Things to see and do: orienteering trails to follow. Events, including Apple Day in autumn. Self-guided woodland trails leaflet available in courtyard. Dartmoor Pony Heritage Trust (not National Trust). **Dogs**: welcome throughout (on leads where stock grazing).

Access: [icons] Countryside [icons]
Sat Nav: use TQ13 9JQ.
Parking: on site (limited).

Find out more: 01626 834748 or parke@nationaltrust.org.uk

Parke	
Open every day all year	Dawn–dusk
Home Farm Café open 10 to 4 daily, plus Thursday, Friday and Saturday evenings (booking essential).	

Plymbridge Woods

near Plymouth, Devon

[icons] 1968

The wooded valley of the River Plym creates a link from the edge of Plymouth to the heights of Dartmoor. Footpaths lead through woodlands and alongside industrial ruins. There's also a family-friendly cycle path (NCN27) along an old railway line, a wooded mountain-bike trail and a variety of running routes.

Eat, shop, stay: mobile refreshment van in Plymbridge car park. Riverside picnic spots. A short cycle ride away is Saltram, with its popular Park Café and Chapel Tea-room in the garden.

Things to see and do: plenty of options for walkers, runners, cyclists and birdwatchers. Peregrine falcons can be watched from the viewpoint on Cann Viaduct in spring. Downloadable walking, cycling and orienteering trails. **Dogs**: welcome under close control.

Access: [icons]
Sat Nav: use PL7 4SR for Plymbridge.
Parking: at Plymbridge.

Find out more: 01752 341377 or plymbridgewoods@nationaltrust.org.uk

Plymbridge Woods, Devon: cycling on the old railway track

Ringstead Bay

on the Jurassic Coast, near Weymouth, Dorset

⊞ 🏛 1949

Ringstead Bay in Dorset, is a perfect shingle beach

This quiet, unspoilt stretch of the Jurassic Coast in West Dorset is like the seaside of childhood memories: a perfect sweep of shingle beach with rock pools inviting you to explore, backed by farmland and cliffs covered with flowers and butterflies. The seawater is incredibly clear and safe for bathing.

Eat, shop, stay: picnics welcome at the Trust car park at the top of the hill, with its views of the Jurassic Coast World Heritage Site. Shop and café at the beach car park (not National Trust).

Things to see and do: spectacular views of the bay and across to the Isle of Portland to enjoy. Why not walk out to the chalk headland of White Nothe? **Dogs**: welcome everywhere, especially on the South West Coast Path.

Access: 🔬
Sat Nav: use DT2 8NQ for Southdown.
Parking: on the clifftop farmland at Southdown Farm and at beach car park (not National Trust).

Find out more: 01297 489481 or ringsteadbay@nationaltrust.org.uk

Saltram

Plympton, Plymouth, Devon PL7 1UH

🏠 ❋ ⊞ 🏛 ▼ 1957

High above the River Plym, with magnificent views across the estuary, Saltram's rolling landscape parkland now provides wooded walks and open space for rest and play on Plymouth's outskirts. Saltram was home to the Parker family from 1743 and the house reflects their increasingly prominent lifestyle during the Georgian period. The magnificent decoration and original contents include Robert Adam's Neo-classical Saloon, original Chinese wallpapers, 18th-century oriental, European and English ceramics and a superb country-house library. Outside, the garden's planting offers something of interest all year, and there are also an 18th-century orangery and follies to explore. After wandering along scented pathways and the magnificent lime avenue, why not treat yourself to afternoon tea in the Chapel Tea-room?

Original Chinese wallpaper at Saltram, Devon

The magnificent Georgian façade and portico at Saltram, above, and the Library, right

Why not share your pictures with us? #nationaltrust

Eat, shop, stay: Park Café serving meals, drinks, snacks and ice-cream. The Chapel Tea-room in the garden offers light lunches and afternoon tea with waitress service. Shop selling seasonal gifts, local food, books and plants.

Things to see and do: **Indoors** The house is open 363 days a year. Dressing-up, guided tours, themed family trails, conservation in action. Visit at Christmas to see the house decorated. **Outdoors** Seasonal spectacles of winter snowdrops, spring daffodils, summer blooms and autumn colour in the garden. The park is ideal for anyone wanting a stroll with the dog, a run, cycle ride or simply to feed the ducks, whatever the weather. Garden illuminated at Christmas. Activities, '50 things', guided walks and tours throughout the year. Why not book the outdoor classroom for a Forest School session or a child's birthday? **Dogs**: very welcome in the park (identified on- and off-lead areas).

Access: [icons] House [icons]
Grounds [icons]
Sat Nav: enter Merafield Road, not postcode.
Parking: 50 yards.

Find out more: 01752 333500 or saltram@nationaltrust.org.uk

Saltram		M	T	W	T	F	S	S
House and Chapel Tea-room								
1 Jan–28 Feb†	11–3:30	M	T	W	T	F	S	S
1 Mar–31 Oct	11–4:30*	M	T	W	T	F	S	S
1 Nov–19 Nov†	11–3:30	M	T	W	T	F	S	S
Christmas at Saltram††								
20 Nov–30 Dec	11–8	M	T	W	T	F	S	S
Garden, Park Café and shop								
Open all year	10–5**	M	T	W	T	F	S	S
Park								
Open all year	Dawn–dusk	M	T	W	T	F	S	S

†Winter route. *11 to 12: house entry by guided tour only (places limited). Last house admission 45 minutes before closing. †† Christmas: house closes 4 on 24 December; everything (except park) closed 25 and 26 December. **Closes 4, November to February.

Shaugh Bridge

on Dartmoor, near Shaugh Prior, Devon

 1960

Ancient oakwoods and mossy boulders cloak the Plym Valley; riverside walks pass the atmospheric Dewerstone Rocks and industrial ruins. **Note**: for Sat Nav use PL7 5HD. Watch out for climbers on the Dewerstone Rocks.

Find out more: 01626 834748 (Dartmoor countryside office) or shaughbridge@nationaltrust.org.uk

Shute Barton

Shute, near Axminster, Devon EX13 7PT

 1959

Medieval manor house, with later Tudor gatehouse and battlemented turrets – now a holiday cottage. **Note**: open weekends, 19/20 May, 16/17 June, 20/21 October, 17/18 November (guided tour – no need to book).

Find out more: 01752 346585 or shute@nationaltrust.org.uk

South Milton Sands

Thurlestone, near Kingsbridge, Devon

 1980

This popular beach – a long sweep of golden sand and rock pools – edges a sheltered bay of crystal-clear water and looks out to the iconic Thurlestone Rock offshore. The nearby wetland is home to many bird species and is an ideal place to spot rare migratory visitors.

Eat, shop, stay: Beachhouse café (tenant-run) serving breakfast, lunch and dinner (locally caught fish).

Paddle-boarding at South Milton Sands in Devon

Things to see and do: great for swimming and watersports. Wetsuits, as well as windsurf and paddle boards, for hire (seasonal). The South West Coast Path offers great walks. **Dogs**: welcome on coast path and beach.

Access: 🅿️ ♿ Café and toilets ♿ Beach ♿ **Sat Nav**: use TQ7 3JY. **Parking**: behind beach.

Find out more: 01752 346585 or southmiltonsands@nationaltrust.org.uk

South Milton Sands
Beachhouse café seasonal opening, telephone 01548 561144.

Spyway

on the Purbeck coast, Langton Matravers, near Swanage, Dorset

🏠 🏛️ 🚻 ♿ ♿ 1982

Gateway to a dramatic coast of grassy clifftops teeming with wildlife, and Dancing Ledge. Fabulous walking – some steep slopes. **Note**: sorry no toilet. For Sat Nav use BH19 3HG.

Find out more: 01929 450002 or spyway@nationaltrust.org.uk

Studland Bay

Studland, near Swanage, Dorset

♿ ♿ ♿ ♿ 1982

This glorious slice of Purbeck coastline is famed for its 4-mile stretch of golden sand, gently shelving bathing waters and views of Old Harry Rocks and the Isle of Wight. With four beaches to choose from, Studland is loved by young families and watersports fans of all ages, and it includes the most popular naturist beach in Britain. The vast swathe of heathland behind the beach is a haven for native wildlife and features all six British reptiles. Footpaths and bridleways through sand dunes, woods and wild open landscape encourage you to explore. Wildlife to spot includes deer, insects and birds, as well as numerous wild flowers. Studland was the inspiration for Toytown in Enid Blyton's *Noddy*. **Note**: toilets at Shell Bay, Knoll Beach and Middle Beach; also South Beach (not National Trust).

Walkers at Old Harry Rocks, below, and the perfect sandy beach, right, at Studland Bay in Dorset

Eat, shop, stay: Knoll Beach Café on the beach with spectacular views of Old Harry Rocks; indoor and open-air seating. Log burner in winter. Wood-fired pizza oven in summer. Beach goods and seaside gifts for sale. Thirteen holiday cottages in the area.

Things to see and do: year-round events programme, family trails and multitude of watersports and beach sports – geocaching, slacklining, orienteering, beach volleyball, snorkelling, swimming, beach table tennis, paddle-boarding, sea kayaking and sailing. And don't forget sandcastles and rock-pooling. You can hire bikes or go horse-riding to explore inland. You can also hire a beach hut for the day or longer. Signposted trails, including one of the most popular coastal walks to Old Harry Rocks. Second World War remains tell of Studland's role in the build-up to D-Day. Five bird hides overlook Poole Harbour and Little Sea. Discovery Centre for private hire.
Dogs: welcome 1 May to 30 September on short leads. Under control in winter.

Access: 🅿️♿🚻♿📱 Grounds ♿🐕
Sat Nav: use BH19 3AQ for Knoll Beach.
Parking: at Shell Bay (7 to 9); South Beach (9 to 11); Knoll Beach and Middle Beach (9 to 8, or dusk if earlier).

Find out more: 01929 450500 or studlandbay@nationaltrust.org.uk

Studland Bay	
Shop and café	
Open every day all year	9:30–5*

*25 March to 27 October: open to 6 at weekends. July and August: open daily, 9 to 6. Reduced hours in winter, 10 to 4. Shop and café: closed 28 February, 1 March and 25 December.

Watersmeet, Devon: haven for wildlife and joy for walkers

Watersmeet

on Exmoor, near Lynmouth, Devon

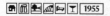 1955

This area, where the lush valleys of the East Lyn and Hoar Oak Water tumble together, is a haven for wildlife and offers excellent walking. At the heart sits Watersmeet House, a 19th-century fishing lodge, which is now a tea-garden, shop and information point. **Note**: deep gorge with steep walk down to house.

Eat, shop, stay: tea-garden serving hot and cold food and drinks in a magnificent wooded setting. Shop selling Exmoor produce and gifts, walking gear and maps. Nearby holiday cottages offer the chance of a longer stay to explore the area.

Things to see and do: Exmoor Spotter chart for families and 'Exmoor Coast of Devon' walks leaflet available. **Dogs**: allowed on leads in tea-garden.

Access: 🅿️🚻 Building 🦽 Grounds 🦽
Sat Nav: use EX35 6NT. **Parking**: pay and display (not National Trust) on Watersmeet Road; steep walk down to house. Trust car parks nearby at Combe Park and Countisbury. Please call to book accessible parking.

Find out more: 01598 752648 or watersmeet@nationaltrust.org.uk

Watersmeet	M	T	W	T	F	S	S
Tea-room and tea-garden*							
24 Mar–28 Oct 10:30–5*	M	T	W	T	F	S	S

*Open 11 to 4 from 10 September. March, November and December: open weekends, 11 to 4.

Wembury

near Wembury village, Plymouth, Devon

🏖️🚻🅿️ 1939

A great beach, and more: some of the best rock pools in the country, good surfing, masses of wildlife and views of a distinctive island – the Great Mewstone. Starting point for lovely coastal walks to Wembury Point and the Yealm Estuary. **Note**: toilet (not National Trust).

Eat, shop, stay: Old Mill Café serves coffees, homemade cakes, soups, pasties and ice-cream, as well as beach shop (tenant-run). Part of the old mill house adjoining the café, Mill Cottage is an idyllic holiday let right on the shore.

Things to see and do: Marine Centre full of information. Rock-pooling, surfing and snorkelling.

Dogs: welcome on coast path all year, and on beach 1 October to 30 April.

Access: [P] [icons] Café [icon]
Marine Centre [icon] Beach [icon]
Sat Nav: use PL9 0HP. **Parking**: just above beach.

Find out more: 01752 346585.
01752 862538 (Marine Centre) or
wembury@nationaltrust.org.uk

Wembury
For details of the Old Mill Café seasonal opening, telephone 01752 863280.

Discovering the excellent rock pools at Wembury, Devon

White Mill

Sturminster Marshall, near Wimborne Minster, Dorset BH21 4BX

 1982

An 18th-century corn mill with original wooden machinery, built on a Domesday Book site in a peaceful riverside setting. **Note**: open weekends, 31 March to 28 October, 12 to 5 (admission by guided tour, last tour 4). Open Bank Holiday Mondays.

Find out more: 01258 858051 or
whitemill@nationaltrust.org.uk

Woolacombe

near Ilfracombe, Devon

 1935

A golden beach and huge dunes, amazing surfing, perfect coves for rock-pooling and numerous headland walks with views of Lundy. **Note**: for Sat Nav use EX34 7BG (car park). Nearest toilets are by the beach (neither toilets nor car park are National Trust). Members have to pay for parking.

Find out more: 01271 870555 or
woolacombe@nationaltrust.org.uk

Additional coastal and countryside car parks in Devon and Dorset

Devon					
Countisbury	EX35 6NE	Ringmore	TQ7 4HR	Danes Wood	EX5 3LH
Combe Park	EX35 6LF	Snapes Point	TQ8 8NQ	Ellerhayes	EX5 4PY
Woody Bay	EX31 4QU	Prawle Point	TQ7 2BX		
Trentishoe Down	EX34 0PF	Scabbacombe	TQ6 0EF	**Dorset**	
Torrs Walk, Ilfracombe	EX34 8BA	Man Sands	TQ6 0EF	Cogden	DT6 4RJ
Hartland: Brownsham	EX39 6AN	Salcombe Hill	EX10 0NY	Lambert's Castle	DT6 5QJ
Exmansworthy	EX39 6AR	Dunsland	EX22 7AA	Acton	BH19 3JN
East Titchberry	EX39 6AU	Steps Bridge	EX6 7EQ	Dean Hill Viewpoint	BH19 3AA
Stoke	PL8 1JG	Hembury Woods	TQ11 0HW		
		Holne Woods	TQ13 7ST		

Lacock Abbey, Wiltshire

Somerset
and Wiltshire

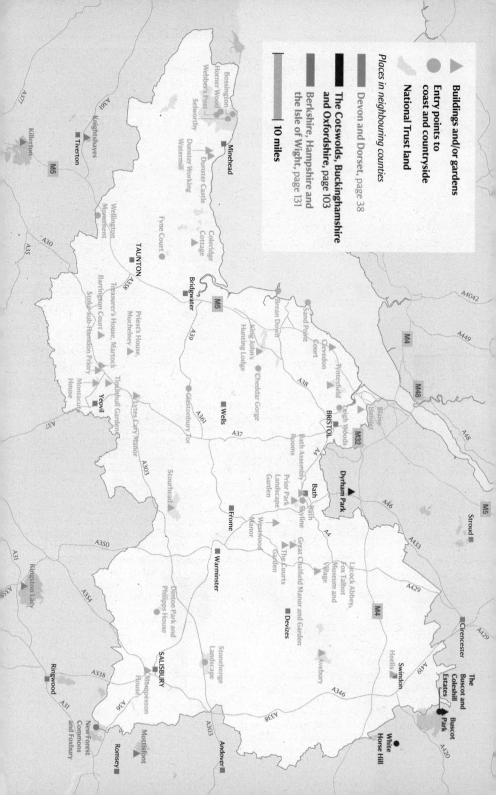

National Trust land

▶ Entry points to
coast and countryside

● Buildings and/or gardens

Places in neighbouring counties

Devon and Dorset, page 38

The Cotswolds, Buckinghamshire and Oxfordshire, page 103

Berkshire, Hampshire and the Isle of Wight, page 131

10 miles

Killerton

A377

Tiverton

Knightshayes

M5

A361

A30

A35

Wellington Monument

Bossington
Horner Wood
Webber's Post
Selworthy
Minehead

Dunster Working Watermill
Dunster Castle

Coleridge Cottage

Fyne Court

TAUNTON

A358

Treasurer's House, Martock
Barrington Court
Stoke-sub-Hamdon Priory
Montacute House

A37

Priest's House, Muchelney

Tintinhull Gardens
Yeovil

Lytes Cary Manor

A303

Bridgwater

M5

A39

King John's Hunting Lodge

Cheddar Gorge

Glastonbury Tor

A361

Wells

A37

Brean Down

Sand Point

Clevedon Court

Tyntesfield

Leigh Woods

BRISTOL

A4

M32

M48

Blaise Hamlet

A48

A4042

A449

M4

A38

Bath Assembly Rooms

Prior Park Landscape Garden
Bath Skyline

Bath

Dyrham Park

A46

M5

Stroud

A433

A429

Cirencester

A429

A419

The Buscot and Coleshill Estates
Buscot Park

A420

Westwood Manor

Great Chalfield Manor and Garden
The Courts Garden

Lacock Abbey, Fox Talbot Museum and Village

A4

A429

M4

Devizes

Avebury

Swindon

A419

Heelis

White Horse Hill

A346

Stourhead

A350

Frome

Warminster

A36

Stonehenge Landscape

Andover

A303

A338

Kingston Lacy

A31

A35

Dinton Park and Philipps House

SALISBURY

Mompesson House

Ringwood

A31

A338

A36

New Forest Commons and Foxbury

Mottisfont

Romsey

The early morning sun lights up part of the mysterious prehistoric stone circle at Avebury in Wiltshire

Avebury

near Marlborough, Wiltshire

🏠 ✝ 🍺 🏛 ❄ 👶 ♿ 1943

At Avebury, the world's largest prehistoric stone circle partially encompasses a pretty village. Millionaire archaeologist Alexander Keiller excavated here in the 1930s, and there is a museum bearing his name. Arranged in two parts, the Alexander Keiller Museum is divided into the Stables, displaying archaeological treasures from across the local area, and the Barn, a 17th-century threshing barn housing interactive displays and children's activities that reveal the story of this ancient landscape. Avebury forms part of the Stonehenge and Avebury World Heritage Site. Avebury Manor, on the edge of the village, was transformed in a partnership between the National Trust and the BBC, creating a hands-on experience that celebrates and reflects the lives of the people who once lived here. **Note**: English Heritage holds guardianship of Avebury Stone Circle (owned and managed by the National Trust). Toilets open during business hours.

Eat, shop, stay: Circles Café; Manor Tea-room (seasonal); Coach House Café (weekends and school holidays). Shop selling local gifts, including Avebury honey and books on the archaeology and mythology of the area. Holiday cottage (sleeping two) within the stone circle available all year.

Hands-on in the Kitchen at Avebury Manor

Things to see and do: **Indoors** Specialist talks and guided tours of the manor. Family activities in the museum and events during holidays. **Outdoors** Guided tours of the stone circle all year. Talks and guided tours of the landscape. Hunt for the golden hare at Easter or for witches' cats at Hallowe'en.
Dogs: assistance dogs only in Avebury Manor and garden and Circles Café. Elsewhere dogs on leads welcome.

Access: [icons] **Museum** [icons]
Manor [icons] **Grounds** [icons]
Sat Nav: use SN8 1RD. **Parking**: 300 yards. Please do not park on village streets.

Find out more: 01672 539250 or
avebury@nationaltrust.org.uk
National Trust Estate Office, High Street,
Avebury, Wiltshire SN8 1RF

Avebury		M	T	W	T	F	S	S
Stone circle								
Open all year	Dawn–dusk	M	T	W	T	F	S	S
Manor and garden								
10 Feb–24 Mar	11–4	M	T	W	T	F	S	S
25 Mar–27 Oct*	11–5	M	T	W	T	F	S	S
28 Oct–30 Dec	11–4	M	T		T	F	S	S
Museum								
1 Jan–24 Mar	10–4	M	T	W	T	F	S	S
25 Mar–27 Oct	10–6	M	T	W	T	F	S	S
28 Oct–31 Dec	10–4	M	T	W	T	F	S	S

Shop/café open daily. Last entry to manor one hour before closing; timed tickets during peak times. In winter, part of garden and museum may be closed. Everything except stone circle closed 24 to 26 December. *Manor closed 20 to 22 June.

Barrington Court

Barrington, near Ilminster, Somerset TA19 0NQ

[icons] 1907

Colonel Lyle, whose family firm became part of Tate & Lyle, rescued the partially derelict 16th-century Court House in the 1920s, surrounding it with a productive estate. A keen collector of architectural salvage, Colonel Lyle filled the house with his collection of panelling, fireplaces and staircases. Now without furniture, the light, empty spaces provide atmospheric opportunities to explore freely. The walled White Garden, Rose and Iris Garden and Lily Garden were influenced by Gertrude Jekyll, with playing fountains, vibrant colours and intoxicating scents. The original kitchen garden supplies the restaurant and continues the Lyle family's vision of self-sufficiency.
Note: independently run artisan workshops (opening times vary).

Barrington Court in Somerset offers atmospheric interiors and a gracious garden to explore

Eat, shop, stay: Strode dining and tea-rooms offering tea, homemade cakes and meals with ingredients often grown in the kitchen garden. Children's menu available. Shop selling gifts, plants and award-winning cider and apple juice. Second-hand bookshop. Artisan workshops. Holiday cottage in Strode House.

Things to see and do: **Indoors** House tours and children's trail, seasonal events. Activities in artisan workshops. **Outdoors** Trails and tours. Seasonal events, including Easter Egg hunts. **Dogs**: assistance dogs only in formal garden.

Access: [icons]
Building [icon] **Grounds** [icons]
Sat Nav: misdirects visitors to rear entrance – follow brown signs from Barrington village.
Parking: 200 yards.

Find out more: 01460 241938 or barringtoncourt@nationaltrust.org.uk

Barrington Court		M	T	W	T	F	S	S
5 Jan–4 Feb	10:30–3	·	·	·	·	**F**	**S**	**S**
9 Feb–4 Nov	10:30–5	**M**	**T**	**W**	**T**	**F**	**S**	**S**
9 Nov–30 Dec	10:30–3	**M**	·	·	·	**F**	**S**	**S**

Open 1 January, 10:30 to 3.

Bath Assembly Rooms

Bennett Street, Bath, Somerset BA1 2QH

[icons] 1931

The Assembly Rooms were at the heart of fashionable Georgian society. The Fashion Museum is on the lower ground floor. **Note**: limited access during functions. Bath Assembly Rooms is run by Bath and North East Somerset Council. Entry charge for the Fashion Museum (including members). Open daily 10:30 to 6 (closes at 5 in January, February, November and December). Closed 25 and 26 December. Last admission one hour before closing.

Find out more: 01225 477789 or bathassemblyrooms@nationaltrust.org.uk

Bath Skyline

Bath, Somerset

[icon] 1959

One of Bath's unique features, leading to its World Heritage Site designation, is its 'green setting' – encircling meadows and wooded hillsides where you can walk and relax with grandstand views over the historic cityscape. There's a 6-mile Bath Skyline waymarked walk, plus shorter routes to follow from the city centre. **Note**: sorry no toilet or parking.

Eat, shop, stay: there are many places to picnic around the Skyline. Food and snacks are available nearby at Prior Park Landscape Garden. Also from Widcombe cafés, the American Museum in Britain and the Holburne Museum (none National Trust, some entry fees).

Things to see and do: 'Walk to the view' is a 3-mile self-led circular route starting from the Abbey. Geocaching trail and other family activities. Bath parkrun every Saturday. Regular

Bath Skyline, Somerset, offers sweeping city views

guided walks. **Dogs**: welcome under control (on leads in some areas). Cattle grazing April to November.

Access: 🦽➡️
Parking: none on site, nearest city centre.

Find out more: 01225 833977 or bathskyline@nationaltrust.org.uk

Blaise Hamlet

Henbury, Bristol BS10 7QY

🏠 1943

Delightful hamlet of nine picturesque cottages, designed by John Nash in 1809 for Blaise Estate pensioners. **Note**: access to green only; cottages not open. Sorry no toilet.

Find out more: 01275 461900 or blaisehamlet@nationaltrust.org.uk

Bossington

on Exmoor, near Minehead, Somerset

🏠🚻♿🐕 1944

Part of the Holnicote Estate, Bossington is a peaceful coastal hamlet on the edge of the Bristol Channel with distinctive thatched cottages. From here you can wander down to the pebble beach, where there's plenty of coastal wildlife to spot and far-reaching views to Wales and along the Exmoor coastline. **Note**: nearest toilets in car park.

Eat, shop, stay: barbecues provided in the picnic field next to the car park. Kitnors tea-room is open seasonally for cream teas and light lunches (not National Trust). Why not stay here longer? The picturesque part-thatched Lower House holiday cottage sleeps ten.

Things to see and do: look out for old limekilns and Second World War sea defences. You can walk to the ruined coastguard lookout on Hurlstone Point – a top spot for porpoise sightings. **Dogs**: welcome on leads.

Access: ♿
Sat Nav: use TA24 8HF. **Parking**: on site.

Find out more: 01643 862452 or bossington@nationaltrust.org.uk

Kite-flying on Bossington Beach, Somerset

Brean Down

near Weston-super-Mare, North Somerset

 1954

One of Somerset's most striking coastal landmarks: a dramatic limestone peninsula jutting out into the Bristol Channel (above). You can relax on the beach at the foot of the down or take a walk along this spectacular 'natural pier' to the fort, which provides a unique insight into Brean's military past. **Note**: steep climbs and cliffs; please stay on main paths. Tide comes in quickly.

Eat, shop, stay: Cove Café – with winter woodburner or summer courtyard and picnic benches – serving cooked breakfasts, lunches or tea and cakes. Shop with popular ice-cream bar, buckets, spades, beach games and souvenirs. Holiday apartment (sleeps four).

Things to see and do: you can walk to the end of the down and discover the historic fort, spotting birds, feral goats and flowers on the way. Downloadable circular walk available. Events throughout year. **Dogs**: welcome on leads, please note stock may be grazing on the down.

Access: 🚻 Building 🐾 ♿
Sat Nav: use TA8 2RS.
Parking: at Cove Café and shop.

Find out more: 01278 751874 or breandown@nationaltrust.org.uk

Brean Down									
Café and shop									
1 Jan–28 Feb	10–4	M	T	W	T	F	S	S
1 Mar–31 Oct	9–5	M	T	W	T	F	S	S
1 Nov–31 Dec*	10–4	M	T	W	T	F	S	S

*Closed 25 December.

Cheddar Gorge

in the Mendips, near Wells, Somerset

 1910

At almost 400 feet deep and three miles long, Cheddar is England's largest gorge. It was formed during successive ice ages, when glacial meltwater carved into the limestone, creating steep cliffs. The gorge (below) is a haven for wildlife and contains many rare plants, including the Cheddar pink. **Note**: terrain is steep away from the road. Caves and car parks privately owned (charge including members).

Eat, shop, stay: seasonal shop and information centre providing leaflets, information on National Trust membership, local information and walks, gifts and souvenirs. Free Wi-Fi and computer tablets available for use to help plan days out in the area.

Things to see and do: four-mile circular gorge walk (details from shop and information centre) and Strawberry Line (NCN26) cycle route to Cheddar. **Dogs**: welcome on leads in shop and gorge.

Access: 🐾
Sat Nav: use BS27 3QE. **Parking**: car parks on both sides of gorge, not National Trust (charge including members).

Find out more: 01934 744689 or cheddargorge@nationaltrust.org.uk

Cheddar Gorge		M	T	W	T	F	S	S
Shop and information centre								
10 Feb–4 Nov	10–5	M	T	W	T	F	S	S
10 Nov–16 Dec	10–5						S	S

Clevedon Court

Tickenham Road, Clevedon,
North Somerset BS21 6QU

🏠🔆 1961

Featuring rare domestic architecture from the medieval period, the house is in remarkable condition and has played home to Clevedon's lords of the manor for centuries. The house was bought by Abraham Elton in 1709 and it is still the much-loved family home of his descendants today. **Note**: the Elton family opens Clevedon Court for the National Trust.

Eat, shop, stay: kiosk serving cream teas and soft drinks.

Things to see and do: extensive collection of Elton Ware pottery, Nailsea glass and prints of industrial archaeology. Family guide and children's quiz/trail. **Dogs**: assistance dogs only.

Access: 🅿️ 🔲 🔲 🔲 🔲 🔲 👓 🖼
Building 🔲 🔲 Grounds 🔲
Parking: 50 yards (unsuitable for trailer or motor caravans). Alternative parking 100 yards east of entrance in cul-de-sac.

Find out more: 01275 872257 or clevedoncourt@nationaltrust.org.uk

Clevedon Court		M	T	W	T	F	S	S
1 Apr–30 Sep	2–5			**W**	**T**			**S**

Tea kiosk and car park open 1:15. House entry by timed ticket, not bookable. Open Bank Holiday Mondays.

Coleridge Cottage

35 Lime Street, Nether Stowey, Bridgwater, Somerset TA5 1NQ

🏠🔆 1909

Home to Samuel Taylor Coleridge for three years, this simple house – the birthplace of literary Romanticism – was where he wrote his best-known poems. Now an award-winning experience offers the chance to immerse yourself in 18th-century sights and sounds. Coleridge's poetry is brought to life in the cottage (below) and wildflower garden.

Eat, shop, stay: tea-room serving light refreshments. Shop selling gifts reflecting Coleridge's life and work.

Things to see and do: Indoors Writing with a quill, dressing up in Georgian costumes or following a family trail. **Outdoors** You can listen to poetry in the garden, or draw water from the well.

Access: 🖼 🔲 🖼 Building 🔲 🔲 Garden 🔲 🔁
Parking: in pub car park (not National Trust).

Find out more: 01278 732662 (Infoline). 01643 821314 or coleridgecottage@nationaltrust.org.uk

Coleridge Cottage		M	T	W	T	F	S	S
3 Mar–28 Oct	11–5	**M**	**T**	**W**	**T**	**F**	**S**	**S**
1 Dec–16 Dec	11–4	·	·	·	·	·	**S**	**S**

Wednesdays: may open 12 (please telephone prior to visiting). Private tours/educational visits by arrangement.

The Courts Garden

Holt, near Bradford on Avon,
Wiltshire BA14 6RR

🔆 1943

This curious English country garden (right) is a hidden gem. Garden rooms of different styles, shaped by the vision of past owners and gardeners, reveal themselves at every turn. You'll find herbaceous borders, quirky topiary, a peaceful water garden, arboretum, kitchen garden, naturally planted spring bulbs and a redesigned sunken garden.

Eat, shop, stay: seasonal produce from the kitchen garden for sale, as well as a small selection of gifts and guidebooks. Sales from the second-hand bookshop support conservation work. Rose Garden tea-room serving lunch and afternoon tea. Picnics welcome in the arboretum.

Things to see and do: discover garden history and seasonal highlights in the Orchard Room. Trails and a hidden wildlife garden for young explorers. Keen gardeners can pick up tips from the friendly team. **Dogs**: assistance dogs only.

Access: ♿🚲🚼🎵👓🅿 Garden 🚶♿➡️♿
Parking: 80 yards in village hall car park (not National Trust). Follow signs for overflow parking. Please avoid parking on village streets.

Find out more: 01225 782875 or courtsgarden@nationaltrust.org.uk

The Courts Garden		M	T	W	T	F	S	S
3 Feb–25 Feb	11–5:30	·	·	·	·	·	S	S
26 Feb–28 Oct	11–5:30	M	T	·	T	F	S	S

Tea-room open as garden, last orders 45 minutes before closing.

Dinton Park and Philipps House

Dinton, Salisbury, Wiltshire SP3 5HH

🏠🚽♿ 1943

Tranquil rolling parkland, perfect for walks and picnics, surrounds a neo-Grecian house designed by Jeffry Wyatville in 1820. **Note**: the house is closed in 2018. The park is open daily all year. Sorry no toilet.

Find out more: 01672 538014 or sw.customerenquiries@nationaltrust.org.uk

Dunster Castle

Dunster, near Minehead, Somerset TA24 6SL

🏰✿♿🅿🍽 1976

Dramatically sited on top of a wooded hill, a castle has existed here since at least Norman times. Its impressive medieval gatehouse and ruined tower are a reminder of its turbulent history. The castle that you see today, owned by the Luttrell family for over 600 years, became an elegant country home during the 19th century. The terraced garden displays varieties of Mediterranean and subtropical plants, while the tranquil riverside wooded garden below, with its natural play area, leads to the historic working watermill. There are panoramic views over the Bristol Channel and surrounding countryside from the castle and grounds.

Eat, shop, stay: 17th-century stables shop selling local and regional gifts and guidebooks. Light refreshments available at the Camellia House. Riverside tea-room and shop selling stoneground flour at Dunster Working Watermill. Places to eat and drink in Dunster village (not National Trust).

Things to see and do: **Indoors** Interactive exhibitions and 'Chapters' bring stories to life. Tours of kitchens and behind the scenes. Explore the vaulted Victorian reservoir beneath the Keep Garden. **Outdoors** Events, including living history. **Dogs**: welcome in parkland and garden on short leads.

Sumptuous table settings at Dunster Castle, Somerset

Dunster Castle sits high on a steep wooded hill

Dunster Working Watermill

Mill Lane, Dunster, near Minehead, Somerset TA24 6SL

🏠 1976

Close to Dunster Castle on the peaceful River Avill is this fully operating 18th-century watermill, built on the site of a mill mentioned in the Domesday survey of 1086. With the recent installation of a new second waterwheel, this is now a very rare surviving example of a double-overshot mill (below). **Note**: admission to watermill inclusive with a Dunster Castle garden ticket.

Eat, shop, stay: the mill produces stoneground wholemeal flour from organic wheat, and the milling team packs porridge oats, jumbo oats and the mill's own muesli mix – all for sale in the shop. Riverside tea-room and garden serving light lunches and afternoon tea.

Things to see and do: milling often takes place on the first Wednesday of every month from April until September. A one-mile circular walk suitable for families takes in the mill and Dunster Castle. **Dogs**: welcome in the Watermill tea-room garden.

Access: 🅿️ Building 🔣🔣🔣
Parking: at Dunster Castle car park, 800 yards (enter from A39).

Find out more: 01643 821759 (mill). 01643 821314 (Dunster Castle) or dunstercastle@nationaltrust.org.uk

Dunster Working Watermill		
Open every day all year	10–5*	

*Closes at dusk if earlier. 7 and 8 December, open until 9 for 'Dunster by Candlelight'. Closed 24 and 25 December.

Access: 🅿️🔣🔣🔣🔣🔣🔣🔣🔣🔣
Castle 🔣🔣🔣🔣 Stables 🔣 Grounds 🔣🔣🔣
Parking: 300 yards (enter from A39).

Find out more: 01643 823004 (Infoline). 01643 821314 or dunstercastle@nationaltrust.org.uk

Dunster Castle		M	T	W	T	F	S	S
Castle								
1 Jan–2 Mar	Tour*	M	T	W	T	F	S	S
3 Mar–28 Oct	11–5	M	T	W	T	F	S	S
15 Dec–23 Dec	2–6	M	T	W	T	F	S	S
26 Dec–31 Dec	11–3	M	·	W	T	F	S	S
Garden, park, shop and tea-room								
Open all year	10–5**	M	T	W	T	F	S	S

*Entry by tour only at 11, 12, 1 and 2 (places limited). Behind-the-scenes tours available all year (telephone for details). 'Dunster by Candlelight': castle open 4 until 9, Friday 7 and Saturday 8 December. Everything closed 24 and 25 December. **Close dusk if earlier.

Fyne Court

near Bridgwater, Somerset

⬚⬚⬚⬚ 1967

This is a hidden gem in the Quantock Hills. While the house (former home of amateur scientist Andrew Crosse) no longer stands, the site remains simply beautiful within its woods and meadows. A great place for gentle walks, splashing in streams, building dens and discovering ruins (above). Information room in courtyard.

Eat, shop, stay: Courtyard tea-room serving light lunches, cream teas and cakes. Fyne Court Cottage (once a shooting lodge, then the family's retreat when the main house burnt down in a fire in 1894) is now a holiday cottage (sleeps six).

Things to see and do: three walking trails, including an accessible trail. Natural play and den-building areas for families. You can observe the skies at the Skyglade and enjoy a picnic in the walled garden. **Dogs**: welcome on leads.

Access: ⬚⬚⬚ Grounds ⬚➡
Sat Nav: use TA5 2EQ. **Parking**: on site.

Find out more: 01823 451587 or fynecourt@nationaltrust.org.uk

Fyne Court		M	T	W	T	F	S	S
Estate								
Open all year		M	T	W	T	F	S	S
Tea-room*								
10 Feb–18 Feb	10:30–3:30	M	T	W	T	F	S	S
12 Mar–4 Nov	10:30–4	M	T	W	T	F	S	S

*Also open weekends 24 February to 11 March and 10 November to 30 December. Opening can vary due to weather conditions.

Glastonbury Tor

near Glastonbury, Somerset

⬚⬚ 1933

Iconic tor, topped by a 15th-century tower offering spectacular views of the Somerset Levels, Dorset and Wiltshire. **Note:** 'sorry no toilet. For Sat Nav use BA6 8YA for nearest car park, not National Trust (charge including members).

Find out more: 01278 751874 or glastonburytor@nationaltrust.org.uk

Great Chalfield Manor and Garden

near Melksham, Wiltshire SN12 8NH

⬚⬚⬚⬚ 1943

A monkey, soldiers and griffins adorn the rooftops of this moated medieval manor, looking over the terraces of the romantic garden with topiary houses, rose garden and spring-fed fish-pond. All is lovingly looked after by the Floyd family. The manor has featured in several television dramas, including *Wolf Hall*. **Note**: home to the donor family tenants, who manage it for the National Trust. Charge for events outside normal opening times (including members).

Eat, shop, stay: guidebooks, postcards and plants for sale. Tea and coffee, homemade cakes and soup served in the Motor House (not National Trust).

Things to see and do: visits to house are by guided tour (limited). Garden and parish church may be enjoyed at any time (during opening hours). Map for cross-country walk to The Courts Garden available. **Dogs**: assistance dogs only.

Access: ⬚⬚⬚⬚⬚⬚⬚ Manor ⬚⬚
Garden ⬚➡

Great Chalfield Manor and Garden: medieval romance

Parking: 100 yards, on grass verge outside manor gates.

Find out more: 01225 782239 or greatchalfieldmanor@nationaltrust.org.uk

Great Chalfield		M	T	W	T	F	S	S
Manor								
1 Apr–28 Oct	Tour*		·	T	W	T	·	S
Garden								
1 Apr–28 Oct	1–5		·	·	·	·	·	S
3 Apr–25 Oct	11–5		·	T	W	T	·	·

*Manor admission by 45-minute guided tour (places limited, not bookable) Tuesday, Wednesday and Thursday at 11, 12, 2, 3 and 4; Sunday at 2, 3 and 4. Group visits welcome Friday and Monday (not Bank Holidays); please contact the tenant, Mrs Robert Floyd, on 01225 782239 (charge including members).

Heelis

Kemble Drive, Swindon, Wiltshire SN2 2NA

 2005

The Trust's award-winning central office is a remarkable example of an innovative and sustainable building. **Note**: shop and café open all year except 1 January, 2 April, 25 to 26 December. Admission to offices by booked guided tour only.

Find out more: 01793 817575 or heelis@nationaltrust.org.uk

Horner Wood

on Exmoor, near Minehead, Somerset

🏠🚻👦 1944

One of the largest and most beautiful ancient oak woods in Britain, Horner Wood is part of the Holnicote Estate. Home to an unusually rich variety of wildlife, the 324 hectares (800 acres) of woodland clothe the lower slopes of the surrounding moorland and follow river and stream valleys. **Note**: toilets in car park.

Eat, shop, stay: you can picnic by the river or enjoy a light lunch or cream tea at Horner Tea Garden or Horner Vale tea-room (neither National Trust). There are four holiday cottages on the Holnicote Estate for staying a bit longer.

Things to see and do: there's a 17th-century packhorse bridge and a Tudor iron-smelting site in the woods, plus some of Britain's rarest lichens, mosses and bats, and the General, a 500-year-old oak tree. **Dogs**: welcome under close control so as not to disturb wildlife and grazing animals.

Access: 🔁
Sat Nav: use TA24 8HY. **Parking**: on site.

Find out more: 01643 862452 or hornerwood@nationaltrust.org.uk

Horner Wood, Somerset: endless opportunities for fun

King John's Hunting Lodge

The Square, Axbridge, Somerset BS26 2AP

🏠 1968

This early Tudor timber-framed wool merchant's house (*circa* 1500) provides a fascinating insight into local history. **Note**: run as a local history museum by Axbridge and District Museum Trust. Open daily, 1 April to 31 October, 1 to 4.

Find out more: 01934 732012 or kingjohns@nationaltrust.org.uk

Lacock Abbey, Fox Talbot Museum and Village

Lacock, near Chippenham, Wiltshire SN15 2LG

🏠 ✝ 🍽 ✿ ♿ 🛏 1944

You can see why Ela of Salisbury chose this spot for her abbey in 1232: nestled alongside the River Avon in a rolling Wiltshire landscape, Lacock invites you to stay. The abbey bears testament to a legacy of almost 800 years of past owners with sophisticated taste, who sensitively turned it from a nunnery into a quirky family home, furnished with well-loved mementoes and furniture. Seasonal colour can be discovered in the wooded grounds, botanic garden, greenhouse and orchard. The museum celebrates William Henry Fox Talbot, who created the first photographic negative and established this as a birthplace of photography. Lacock has a homely feel, and the village, with its timber-framed cottages, is to this day a bustling community. **Note**: please check Abbey rooms winter openings. In autumn they may close due to heating repairs.

Eat, shop, stay: many places to eat and drink in Lacock village, including the Stables café and a recently opened tea-room in the Abbey. Two National Trust shops, independent village businesses and a beautiful holiday cottage make Lacock a great place to visit.

Lacock Abbey, Fox Talbot Museum and Village: once a nunnery, then a quirky family home, the Abbey sits in the midst of a rolling Wiltshire landscape

Things to see and do: **Indoors** The Abbey offers two distinct experiences: a peaceful ground-floor monastic cloister and first-floor furnished rooms. The museum provides an insight into the history of photography, which appeals to all ages and includes changing exhibitions. This year's focus is on women in Lacock's history. **Outdoors** The level grounds are great for picnics and walks. There are seasonally changing family trails in the Abbey grounds, open-air theatre events and a play area in the village. Lacock is a famous filming location, and its appearances include *Harry Potter*, *Wolf Hall* and *Pride and Prejudice*. **Dogs**: 1 November to 31 March welcome on short leads in Abbey grounds.

Access: 🅿️♿🚻🔍📷🎦🖥️🎵👓🚪♿
Abbey ♿♿ **Museum** ♿♿♿
Grounds ♿♿➡️♿♿

Sat Nav: may direct down closed road. Set to Hither Way, Lacock, for car park. **Parking**: 220 yards. No visitor parking on village streets.

Find out more: 01249 730459 or lacockabbey@nationaltrust.org.uk

Lacock Abbey		M	T	W	T	F	S	S
2 Jan–9 Feb*	11–4	M	T	W	T	F	S	S
10 Feb–28 Oct	10:30–5	M	T	W	T	F	S	S
29 Oct–31 Dec*	11–4	M	T	W	T	F	S	S

Abbey: first-floor rooms and Courtyard Tea-room open 30 minutes later. Last admission to abbey rooms and last orders at tea-room 45 minutes before closing. Closed 25, 26 December and 1 January 2019. Village businesses operate independently. *Abbey cloister only, plus Great Hall at weekends (until 3:30).

Lacock Abbey, left, sits within graceful grounds, while the bustling village, above, is a famous filming location

Leigh Woods

Bristol

🏛️ 🚻 ♿ ⚐ 1909

A tranquil wilderness on Bristol's doorstep, with woodland, wildlife, Iron Age fort and wonderful views of the Avon Gorge and suspension bridge. Excellent network of paths, including 1¾-mile easy-access trail, links to the National Cycle Network and popular 'Yer Tiz' off-road cycle trail. Unique whitebeam trees grow in these woods. **Note**: toilet open during office hours.

Eat, shop, stay: picnics welcome.

Things to see and do: welcome hub. Natural play features. Events programme. Permanent orienteering course (map available to download). Iron Age hill fort – Stokeleigh Camp. Great views. Listen out for the calls of peregrine falcons. **Dogs**: welcome (but be aware of cattle in summer).

Access: 🅿️➡️
Sat Nav: use BS8 3QB for Leigh Woods car park (not National Trust). **Parking**: limited, on site (not National Trust).

Find out more: 0117 973 1645 or leighwoods@nationaltrust.org.uk

Bristol's famous suspension bridge seen from Leigh Woods

Lytes Cary Manor

near Somerton, Somerset TA11 7HU

🏛️ ✝️ 🚻 ❋ ♿ ⚐ 1949

Lytes Cary Manor in Somerset: lovingly restored

This intimate medieval manor house, with its beautiful Arts and Crafts-inspired garden, was originally the family home of the Elizabethan herbalist Henry Lyte. After years of neglect Lytes Cary was lovingly restored in the 20th century by Sir Walter Jenner and is arranged as it was in his time. A stroll around the garden rooms, divided by high yew hedges, reveals collections of topiary (including the Twelve Apostles), sensuous herbaceous borders and manicured lawns. A visit to this harmonious manor is wonderfully relaxing and uplifting. **Note**: parts of the garden may close occasionally.

Eat, shop, stay: small tea-room offering cakes and drinks. Picnic tables in the courtyard. Shop selling gifts, garden accessories and plants. Second-hand books. The west wing of the house is available as a holiday let, as is a Victorian cottage on the estate.

Things to see and do: tranquil walks on the wider estate and children's outdoor natural play area. Allotments are bursting with creative and colourful designs. **Dogs**: welcome on leads on estate walks only.

Access: 🅿️♿🚶🏠🔧🛗🎵♿🅿️ Building 🔧🍴♿
Tea-room 🔧🛗♿ Grounds 🔧♿
Parking: 40 yards.

Find out more: 01458 224471 or
lytescarymanor@nationaltrust.org.uk

Lytes Cary Manor		M	T	W	T	F	S	S
3 Mar–4 Nov	10:30–5*	**M**	**T**	**W**	**T**	**F**	**S**	**S**

*House: open 11 to 4:30. Tea-room: closes at 4:45. Timed
tickets at peak times. Estate walks open dawn to dusk.

Relaxing in the the garden at Lytes Cary Manor

Mompesson House

The Close, Salisbury, Wiltshire SP1 2EL

🏠 ✿ 1952

Visiting Salisbury's Cathedral Close, you
step back into a past world. As you enter
Mompesson House, featured in the film
Sense and Sensibility, the feeling of leaving the
modern world behind deepens. The tranquil
atmosphere is enhanced by the magnificent
plasterwork, graceful oak staircase and fine
period furniture, which are the main features of
this perfectly proportioned Queen Anne town
house. Mompesson House has one of the finest
displays of English 18th-century drinking
glasses and a collection of stumpwork, a
fascinating example of raised embroidery. The
garden, with traditional herbaceous borders
and pergola, is an oasis of calm in Salisbury.

Eat, shop, stay: the garden tea-room has
indoor and outdoor seating and serves tea,
coffee, light bites and cakes. The shop in
the courtyard offers a range of gifts for you
and your home.

Things to see and do: exhibition,
family trails and croquet on the lawn.
Dogs: assistance dogs only.

Access: 🅿️ 🚻 ♿ 🖼 📷 🚶 ∴ ⊘
Building 🔈 🏔 Grounds 🔈 🏔
Parking: 260 yards in city centre, not
National Trust (charge including members).

Find out more: 01722 335659 or
mompessonhouse@nationaltrust.org.uk

Mompesson House		M	T	W	T	F	S	S
10 Mar–4 Nov	11–5	**M**	**T**	**W**	**T**	**F**	**S**	**S**
24 Nov–23 Dec*	11–3:30	·	·	·	**T**	**F**	**S**	**S**

*Ground-floor rooms decorated for Christmas.

Tranquil Mompesson House in Salisbury, Wiltshire

Montacute House in Somerset:
a beacon of Elizabethan pomp and style

Montacute House

Montacute, Somerset TA15 6XP

🏠 ✿ ♨ 🛏 [1931]

Built from golden Ham stone, Montacute House is set in a picturesque village sharing its name. It's a beacon of Elizabethan pomp and style, exemplified by walls of sparkling glass. Inside are tapestries, samplers and Britain's longest remaining Long Gallery, hosting portraits from the National Portrait Gallery. Outside, clipped lawns, wibbly-wobbly hedges, hidden paths and parkland entice exploration. Edward Phelips, a wealthy, ambitious lawyer and MP (who later prosecuted Guy Fawkes after the Gunpowder Plot), built this grand mansion to advertise his lofty position and success. More than 400 years later, does it still have its original power to impress?

Eat, shop, stay: café serving homemade seasonal lunches and tempting cakes to be enjoyed inside or out (dogs welcome in outside courtyard). Gift shop and plant sales. Monthly farmers' markets held March to December (excluding August). Two historic holiday cottages on the estate.

Things to see and do: Indoors National Portrait Gallery exhibition 'Elizabeth of Bohemia: the Winter Queen'. **Outdoors** Regular 'Elizabethan Welcome' tours and seasonal events. Family trails and swings. Tintinhull Garden and Barrington Court nearby. **Dogs**: welcome in garden and café courtyard (on short leads). Elsewhere, assistance dogs only.

Access: 🅿 ⛽ 📶 🏠 🖼 📷 🅰 Building 🏠 🖼 ♿
Grounds 🖼 ➡ ♿
Parking: on site.

Find out more: 01935 823289 or
montacute@nationaltrust.org.uk

Montacute House		M	T	W	T	F	S	S
House								
6 Jan–4 Mar	12–3						S	S
5 Mar–28 Oct	11–4	M	T	W	T	F	S	S
29 Oct–31 Dec	11–3*	M	T	W	T	F	S	S
Garden, parkland, café and shop								
3 Jan–4 Mar	11–4			W	T	F	S	S
5 Mar–28 Oct	10–5	M	T	W	T	F	S	S
29 Oct–31 Dec	10:30–4*	M	T	W	T	F	S	S

House: timed tickets may apply on busy days; some rooms may not be open due to essential conservation work. *22 to 31 December: house open 3 to 6:30; everything else 11 to 7. Everything closed 24 and 25 December.

Priest's House, Muchelney

Muchelney, Langport, Somerset TA10 0DQ

 1911

Medieval hall-house, built in 1308.
Note: private home. Sorry no toilet.
Open April to September, please call
for details of opening arrangements.

Find out more: 01935 823289 or
priestshouse@nationaltrust.org.uk

Prior Park Landscape Garden

Ralph Allen Drive, Bath, Somerset BA2 5AH

1993

Perched on a hillside overlooking Bath, this
elevated spot was chosen by Ralph Allen to
show off his estate to the city. The magical
landscape garden he created captures a
moment in time: 1764, the year of Allen's death.
There is a lot to discover, including winding
paths leading to hidden retreats, dramatic
views over Bath and a rare Palladian Bridge.
From summer onwards we're embarking on
a major conservation project to repair the
18th-century dams. Access to the lakes may be
restricted, but you'll have a once in a lifetime
opportunity to see the work in progress.
Note: no parking on site. Steep slopes,
steps, uneven paths. House not accessible
(not National Trust).

Eat, shop, stay: Tea Shed by the lakes
serves light snacks, cakes and refreshments
(please be aware that there is outdoor
seating only, in tea-garden). Small shop
next to visitor reception with a selection
of National Trust products.

Things to see and do: events and activities all
year. Free guided tours and seasonal trails. Tree
swings and natural play area. The Bath Skyline
6-mile circular walk is just minutes from the
garden. **Dogs**: welcome on short leads.

Access: ♿ Grounds
Parking: on site for disabled visitors only.
Car parks in city centre, 1 mile (steep, uphill
walk). Frequent bus services from bus station
or City Sightseeing bus (Skyline route)
from city centre.

Find out more: 01225 833977 or
priorpark@nationaltrust.org.uk

Prior Park Landscape Garden		M	T	W	T	F	S	S
6 Jan–28 Jan*	10–4						S	S
1 Feb–2 Nov	10–5:30	M	T	W	T	F	S	S
3 Nov–30 Dec*	10–4						S	S

Last admission one hour before closing. Closes dusk if earlier
than 5:30. Tea Shed opening times vary. *Also open 1 January
and 26 December.

Prior Park Landscape Garden in Bath, Somerset

Selworthy

on Exmoor, near Minehead, Somerset

✝ 🏛 ♿ 🛏 1944

Selworthy is a good place to start discovering the wonderfully varied Exmoor landscapes within the 4,856-hectare (12,000-acre) Holnicote Estate. This is a timeless rural landscape of thatched cottages, a fine medieval church, walks through wooded combes and sweeping views across the vale to Dunkery Beacon, Exmoor's highest point.
Note: sorry no toilets.

Eat, shop, stay: Periwinkle tea-room and Clematis Cottage shop (not National Trust) are top spots for treats and trinkets. Or stay a little longer in the romantic, thatched Ivy's Cottage (sleeps two).

Things to see and do: a walk through the woods leads to Bury Castle, an Iron Age hill fort. The whitewashed church of All Saints looks out over the vale.
Dogs: welcome on leads.

Access: 🦽
Sat Nav: use TA24 8TP. **Parking**: on site.

Find out more: 01643 862452 or selworthy@nationaltrust.org.uk

Sprucing up the thatch at Selworthy in Somerset

Sand Point

near Kewstoke, Weston-super-Mare, North Somerset

🏛 ♿ ⛰ 1964

A natural pier into the Bristol Channel, north of Weston-super-Mare and Brean Down. Perfect for picnics; views across Sand Bay. **Note**: steep climbs and cliffs – please stay on main paths. Tide comes in quickly. Sorry, no toilets. For Sat Nav use BS22 9UD.

Find out more: 01278 751874 or sandpoint@nationaltrust.org.uk

Stoke-sub-Hamdon Priory

North Street, Stoke-sub-Hamdon,
Somerset TA14 6QP

 1946

Fascinating small complex of buildings,
formerly the home of priests serving the
Chapel of St Nicholas (now destroyed).
Note: sorry no toilet or parking. Please respect
the privacy of tenants in the main house.
Open April to September. Please telephone
for opening arrangements.

Find out more: 01935 823289 or
stokehamdonpriory@nationaltrust.org.uk

Stonehenge Landscape

near Amesbury, Wiltshire

 1927

You can wander freely through thousands of
acres of downland within the Stonehenge
and Avebury World Heritage Site (below).
The landscape around the famous stones is
studded with ancient monuments, such as the
Avenue and Cursus, and abounds with wildlife.
The visitor centre shuttle stops at Fargo
woodland on request. **Note**: English Heritage
manages stone circle, visitor centre/car park.
Bookings via english-heritage.org.uk. Pay and
display car park free to Trust members
(booking essential). Trust members enter free
(excluding International National Trust or
affiliate membership organisation members).

Eat, shop, stay: café and shop at visitor centre
(not National Trust).

Things to see and do: guided walks
and family activities throughout the year.
Dogs: assistance dogs only.

Access: [symbols]
Sat Nav: use SP3 4DX. **Parking**: at visitor
centre (English Heritage), free to Trust
members displaying Trust sticker. Booking is
recommended to guarantee a space. Limited
parking at Woodhenge.

Find out more: 0870 333 1181 (English
Heritage). 01980 664780 (National Trust) or
stonehenge@nationaltrust.org.uk

Stourhead

near Mere, Wiltshire BA12 6QF

🏠✝🍴🏛❄🛴🛌🔺🔔🍷 1946

'A living work of art' is how Stourhead was described when it first opened over 250 years ago. The world-famous landscape garden surrounds a glistening lake (above). There are towering trees, exotic rhododendrons, classical temples and a magical grotto to explore. Stourhead House was one of the first in the country to showcase Palladian architecture. With a unique Regency library, Chippendale furniture and inspirational paintings, this was a grand family home, shaped by generations of the Hoare family. Outside, views stretch across the Wiltshire countryside, and the lawns are perfect for picnics. Great for walking and wildlife spotting, with 1,072 hectares (2,650 acres) of chalk downs, ancient woods, Iron Age hill forts and farmland to explore.

Eat, shop, stay: spacious restaurant serving local, seasonal dishes. Shop with extensive garden and plant selection. Spread Eagle Inn. Ice-cream parlour serving snacks and refreshments. Red Lion pub, farm shop and art gallery (not National Trust). Picnics welcome. Holiday cottage by garden entrance.

Things to see and do: **Indoors** The house is the perfect start to your 'Genius of the Place' experience. Launching in March, 'Genius' uncovers the spirit and significance of this special place. Discover the characters and inspirations behind the creation of the landscape garden, Palladian mansion and surrounding estate. Explore behind the scenes on a guided tour (January and February).

Outdoors Your 'Genius of the Place' journey continues in the world-famous landscape revealing the origins of the design, temples and trees. The garden changes in harmony with the seasons: from spring blooms and fresh greens of summer, to spectacular autumn colours and exposed winter views. **Dogs**: garden – on leads after 4 (March to October); 3 (November); daytime (December to February).

Access: 🅿🕭♿🚻🗺📷💬📷 House 🦯♿♿
Landscape garden ➡♿♿
Parking: 400 yards. King Alfred's Tower, 100 yards.

Find out more: 01747 841152 or stourhead@nationaltrust.org.uk

Stourhead		M	T	W	T	F	S	S
Garden								
Open all year	9–5*	M	T	W	T	F	S	S
House								
10 Mar–11 Nov	11–4:30**	M	T	W	T	F	S	S
24 Nov–23 Dec†	11–3:30	M	T	W	T	F	S	S
King Alfred's Tower								
3 Mar–28 Oct	12–4	·	·	·	·	·	S	S

*30 March to 28 October: closes 6. **28 October onwards: closes 3:30. †Selected rooms only, decorated for Christmas. Everything closed 25 December. King Alfred's Tower: open more often at popular times, including Bank Holidays (please check before setting out).

Enjoying the garden at Stourhead, above, and the striking Regency Library, below

Tintinhull Garden

Farm Street, Tintinhull, Yeovil, Somerset BA22 8PZ

❀🧺🔔 1953

Order and abundance at Tintinhull Garden, Somerset

The vision of Phyllis Reiss, amateur gardener, lives on in this small yet perfectly formed garden. You can stroll among clipped lawns, glinting pools and welcome shaded areas that punctuate 'living rooms' of colour and scent. It's just the place to sit, relax and get away from it all.

Eat, shop, stay: quaint tea-room serving cakes and cream teas. Small shop and plant sales. You can soak up the atmosphere for longer by staying in the holiday cottage which forms part of Tintinhull House.

Things to see and do: village history exhibition (Tintinhull Archaeological Society). Why not combine with a visit to Montacute House or Lytes Cary Manor? Garden licensed for weddings. **Dogs**: welcome in courtyard only (reception has details of local walks).

Access: 🅿🕭♿🚻🗺💬📷 Building ♿♿
Gardens ♿➡♿
Parking: 150 yards.

Find out more: 01458 224471 or tintinhull@nationaltrust.org.uk

Tintinhull Garden		M	T	W	T	F	S	S
24 Mar–4 Nov	11–5	M	T	W	T	F	S	S

Tea-room closes at 4:45.

Treasurer's House, Martock

Martock, Somerset TA12 6JL

🏠 1971

Completed in 1293, this medieval house includes a Great Hall, 15th-century kitchen and an unusual wall-painting. **Note**: private home. Sorry no toilets or parking. Open April to September, please call for details of opening arrangements.

Find out more: 01935 823289 or treasurersmartock@nationaltrust.org.uk

Tyntesfield

Wraxall, Bristol, North Somerset BS48 1NX

🏠 ✝ ❁ ♣ ⊨ ⊤ 2002

At its heart Tyntesfield is a Victorian country house and estate, which serves as a backdrop to the remarkable story of the Gibbs family. Their tale charts the accumulation of wealth from the guano trade, transformation of a Georgian house to a Victorian Gothic masterpiece and the collection of more than 60,000 objects. Their achievements are celebrated through ornate Gothic carvings, flower-filled terraces, an abundant kitchen garden and an expansive estate nestled in the Somerset countryside. With each visit you'll experience a new side of Tyntesfield, as we close one door and open another. **Note**: house tickets may sell out quickly (booking advised). Major fire alarm system replacement project under way.

Eat, shop, stay: Cow Barn restaurant at Home Farm visitor centre offers seasonal homemade dishes using estate-grown ingredients. Shop with plant sales. Second-hand bookshop. For light bites while exploring, try the Pavilion Café. Holiday cottages on the estate provide opportunities for longer stays.

Things to see and do: **Indoors:** All year you'll have the chance to get a real insight into vital conservation work as different rooms and store rooms open and close. Exhibitions, murder mystery evenings and family storytelling. **Outdoors:** Free garden tours all year (check times on arrival). For young explorers there are three play areas, including a woodland adventure trail. Year-round events including open-air theatre, morning runs around the estate, guided walks, family activities and living history. **Dogs:** welcome all year, but some areas restricted (map available from ticket office).

Tyntesfield, North Somerset: height of Victorian Gothic

For information about getting to National Trust places, please see page 3

Access: 〔icons〕
House 〔icons〕 **Grounds** 〔icons〕
Parking: 550 yards.

Find out more: 0344 800 4966 (Infoline).
01275 461900 or
tyntesfield@nationaltrust.org.uk

Tyntesfield		M	T	W	T	F	S	S
House								
1 Jan–25 Feb	11–3	M	T	W	T	F	S	S
26 Feb–28 Oct	11–5	M	T	W	T	F	S	S
29 Oct–31 Dec	11–3	M	T	W	T	F	S	S
Estate and garden								
1 Jan–25 Feb	10–5	M	T	W	T	F	S	S
26 Feb–28 Oct	10–6	M	T	W	T	F	S	S
29 Oct–31 Dec	10–5	M	T	W	T	F	S	S

Last entry to house one hour before closing. Timed tickets to house (limited numbers): booking via website advised. Shop and restaurant close 30 minutes before estate and garden. 24 and 31 December house closes at 2, estate closes at 3. Everything closed 25 December.

Tyntesfield: the Hall Staircase with a bust of former owner William Gibbs, left.
Below, a young visitor explores the garden

Webber's Post

on Exmoor, near Minehead, Somerset

〔icons〕 1944

Walking at Dunkery Beacon, near Webber's Post, Somerset

This fine lookout on the Holnicote Estate commands views over Horner Wood and the wild expanse of moorland stretching up to Dunkery Beacon, the highest point on Exmoor. With many trails, this is a beautiful setting for many different pastimes – walking, cycling, horse-riding, picnicking or simply enjoying the view. **Note:** sorry, no toilets.

Eat, shop, stay: a great spot for a picnic, offering classic Exmoor views across Horner Wood and moorland. Four holiday cottages on the nearby Holnicote Estate make the perfect base for getting to know this beautiful area.

Things to see and do: an easy-access trail leads to Jubilee Hut, celebrating Queen Victoria's 1897 Diamond Jubilee. There are 4,000-year-old burial cairns to be discovered, and keep an eye out for Exmoor ponies.
Dogs: welcome under close control so as not to disturb wildlife and grazing animals.

Access: 〔icon〕
Sat Nav: use TA24 8TB and follow signs to Webber's Post. **Parking:** on site.

Find out more: 01643 862452 or
webberspost@nationaltrust.org.uk

Somerset and Wiltshire

Wellington Monument

near Wellington, Somerset

 1934

A striking memorial to the Duke of Wellington in an informal rural setting on the edge of the Blackdown Hills. **Note**: for Sat Nav use TA21 9PB. Sorry no toilet.

Find out more: 01823 451587 or wellingtonmonument@nationaltrust.org.uk

Westwood Manor

Westwood, near Bradford on Avon, Wiltshire BA15 2AF

 1960

Over the centuries, the residents of this small late medieval, Tudor and Jacobean house have modified the building to their own tastes, each leaving a permanent mark. The interiors are rich with decorative plasterwork, fine furniture and beautiful tapestries. Particular highlights are two rare keyboard instruments: a spinet and a virginal. **Note**: Westwood Manor is a family home, administered by the tenants.

Eat, shop, stay: guidebook telling the fascinating history of Westwood, postcards and CD of Elizabethan music recorded on the virginal and spinet. Tea and cake available at church hall next door (not National Trust).

A bird's-eye view of Westwood Manor, Wiltshire

Things to see and do: children's quizzes (house suitable for over fives). Close to Lacock Abbey, The Courts Garden at Holt and Great Chalfield Manor and Garden.

Access: ♿ ⦂⦂ ◎ Manor ♿ 🖼 Garden ♿
Parking: 90 yards.

Find out more: 01225 863374 or westwoodmanor@nationaltrust.org.uk

Westwood Manor		M	T	W	T	F	S	S
1 Apr–30 Sep	2–5		**T**	**W**				**S**

Groups (eight people plus): please contact the tenant on 01225 863374 to arrange a private tour outside normal opening hours.

Additional coastal and countryside car parks in Somerset and Wiltshire

Somerset		King's Wood,		Wiltshire	
Sand Point	BS22 9UD	Mendip Hills	BS25 1DH	Whitesheet Hill	BA12 6RP
Staple Plain,		Ivy Thorn,		Win Green Hill	SP5 5AW
Quantock Hills	TA4 4DQ	Polden Hills	BA16 0TZ	Overton Hill	SN8 1QG
Holford	TA5 1SE	Walton Hill,		Pepperbox Hill	SP5 3QL
Quarts Moor	EX15 3UZ	Polden Hills	BA16 9RD	Cley Hill	BA12 7QU

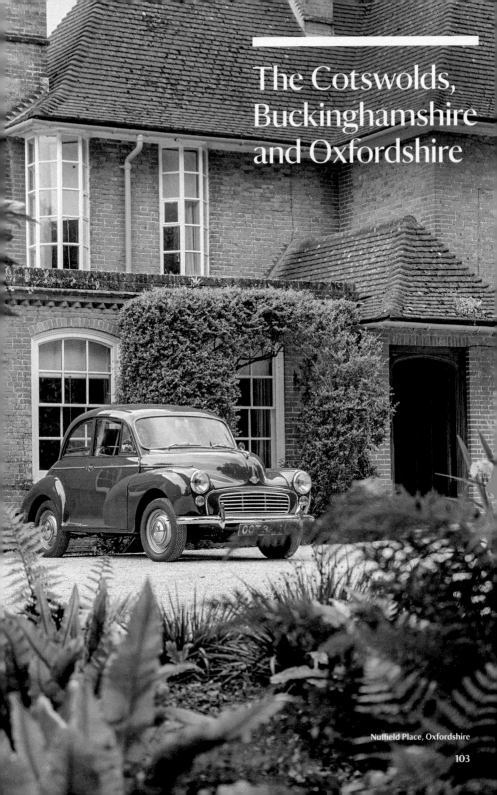

The Cotswolds, Buckinghamshire and Oxfordshire

Nuffield Place, Oxfordshire

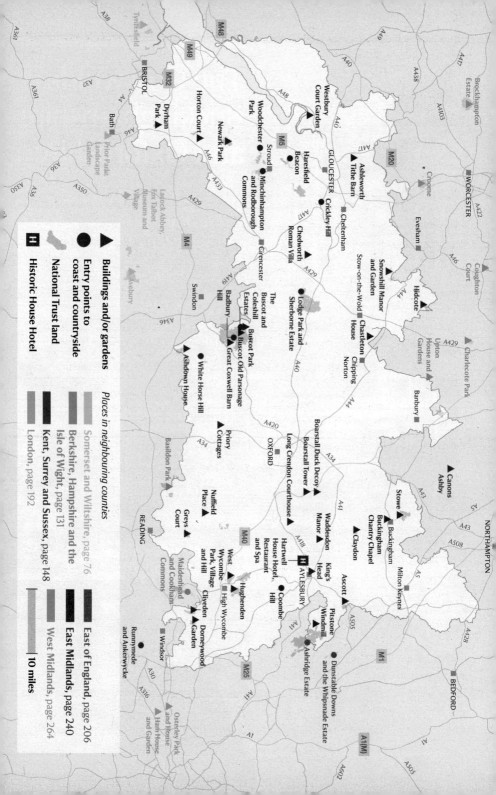

Buildings and/or gardens

▶ Entry points to coast and countryside

● National Trust land

H Historic House Hotel

Places in neighbouring counties

Somerset and Wiltshire, page 76

Berkshire, Hampshire and the Isle of Wight, page 131

Kent, Surrey and Sussex, page 148

London, page 192

East of England, page 206

East Midlands, page 240

West Midlands, page 264

10 miles

Brockhampton Estate

WORCESTER

Coughton Court

Evesham

Upton House and Gardens

Charlecote Park

Banbury

Canons Ashby

NORTHAMPTON

Stowe
Buckingham
Chantry Chapel

Claydon

Milton Keynes

BEDFORD

Ascott

King's Head

AYLESBURY H

Pitstone Windmill

Dunstable Downs and the Whipsnade Estate

Waddesdon Manor

Hartwell House Hotel, Restaurant and Spa

Ashridge Estate

Coombe Hill

Hughenden

Dorneywood Garden

West Wycombe Park, Village and Hill

High Wycombe

Cliveden

Maidenhead and Cookham Commons

Windsor

Runnymede and Ankerwycke

Ham House and Garden

Osterley Park and House

READING

Basildon Park

Greys Court

Nuffield Place

Priory Cottages

White Horse Hill

Ashdown House

Badbury Hill

Great Coxwell Barn

Buscot Park

Buscot Old Parsonage

The Buscot and Coleshill Estates

Lodge Park and Sherborne Estate

Long Crendon Courthouse

Boarstall Tower
Boarstall Duck Decoy

OXFORD

Swindon

Avebury

Lacock Abbey, Fox Talbot Museum and Village

Prior Park Landscape Garden

Bath

BRISTOL

Dyrham Park

Horton Court

Newark Park

Woodchester Park

Minchinhampton and Rodborough Commons

Stroud

Haresfield Beacon

Westbury Court Garden

GLOUCESTER

Crickley Hill

Chedworth Roman Villa

Cirencester

Ashleworth Tithe Barn

Cheltenham

Snowshill Manor and Garden

Hidcote

Stow-on-the-Wold

Chastleton House

Chipping Norton

Chantry Chapel

Ascott

Wing, near Leighton Buzzard,
Buckinghamshire LU7 0PR

[icons] 1949

Spring at Ascott in Buckinghamshire

Ascott House, an 'Old English' half-timbered manor, dates back to the 16th century. It was transformed by the Rothschilds towards the end of the 19th century and houses several exceptional collections. The extensive gardens are an attractive mix of formal and natural, with specimen trees, shrubs and beautiful herbaceous borders. **Note**: Ascott is a family home, administered by the de Rothschild family.

Eat, shop, stay: tea-room offering light lunches, afternoon tea, ice-cream and hot and cold drinks. Ticket kiosk selling guidebooks, calendars, postcards, plants, flowers and kitchen garden produce in season.

Things to see and do: Dutch Masters and paintings by Stubbs, Gainsborough and Reynolds. Fine furniture and amazing collection of oriental porcelain. Discover the Rothschilds' passion for innovative gardening. Relaxing cricket matches most summer weekends. **Dogs**: assistance dogs only.

Access: [icons] Building [icons]
Grounds [icons]
Sat Nav: nearest LU7 0PP. **Parking**: on site (218 yards).

Find out more: 01296 688242 or
ascott@nationaltrust.org.uk

Ascott		M	T	W	T	F	S	S
20 Mar–16 Sep*	1–6**		T	W	T	F	S	S

*Open Bank Holiday Mondays. Gardens open in aid of National Gardens Scheme, 1 May and 28 August (£5 entry, including members); house closed on NGS days.
**House open 2 to 5.

Ashdown House

Lambourn, Newbury, Oxfordshire RG17 8RE

[icons] 1956

Unique 17th-century chalk-block hunting lodge, with doll's-house appearance, built for the Queen of Bohemia by the Earl of Craven. The guided tour, which reveals an intriguing family history, leads up the staircase hung with fine 17th-century paintings. Outstanding rooftop views across three counties. **Note**: access to roof via 100-step staircase.

Things to see and do: guided staircase tour. White Horse Hill nearby. **Dogs**: on leads in woodland only.

Access: [icons] Building [icons] Grounds [icons]
Sat Nav: follow local brown signs from B4000.
Parking: in main estate car park, 437 yards.

Find out more: 01494 755569 (Infoline).
01793 762209 or
ashdownhouse@nationaltrust.org.uk

Ashdown House		M	T	W	T	F	S	S
House								
4 Apr–27 Oct	Tour*			W			S	
Woodland								
Open all year	Dawn–dusk	M	T	W	T		S	S

*House: admission by guided tour only, 2:15, 3:15 and 4:15 (advance booking not necessary).

Looking out from Ashdown House in Oxfordshire

Ashleworth Tithe Barn

Ashleworth, Gloucestershire GL19 4JA

 1956

Barn, with immense stone-tiled roof, picturesquely situated close to the River Severn. **Note:** sorry no toilet.

Find out more: 01452 814213 or ashleworth@nationaltrust.org.uk

Badbury Hill

Coleshill, near Swindon

 2011

This former plantation woodland is criss-crossed with easy circular walks, offering stunning views over the Upper Thames Valley. A spread of snowdrops heralds spring, followed by a carpet of bluebells. A copse of military-straight beech trees defines the Iron Age hill fort, currently under archaeological investigation.

Bluebells carpet woodland at Badbury Hill, near Swindon

Eat, shop, stay: three holiday cottages on the Buscot and Coleshill Estates.

Things to see and do: perfect woodland for family adventures and den-building. Natural play area with a large fallen tree to climb on. Great Coxwell Barn nearby. **Dogs:** under close control.

Access:
Sat Nav: use SN7 7NJ.
Parking: at countryside car park.

Find out more: 01793 762209 or badburyhill@nationaltrust.org.uk

Boarstall Duck Decoy

Boarstall, near Bicester, Buckinghamshire HP18 9UX

 1980

One of the very few remaining decoys in the country, providing fascinating insights into a rare aspect of rural life. **Note:** open Mondays and weekends, 10 March to 4 November, 11 to 5. Also open Good Friday.

Find out more: 01280 817156 or boarstalldecoy@nationaltrust.org.uk

Boarstall Tower

Boarstall, near Bicester, Buckinghamshire HP18 9UX

1943

Charming 14th-century moated gatehouse set in beautiful gardens, retaining original fortified appearance. Grade I listed. **Note:** access to upper levels is via a spiral staircase. Restricted opening due to building and restoration works, call for details before visiting.

Find out more: 01280 817156 or boarstalltower@nationaltrust.org.uk

Buckingham Chantry Chapel

Market Hill, Buckingham,
Buckinghamshire MK18 1JX

[✚][⊤][1912]

Atmospheric 15th-century chapel, restored by
Sir Gilbert Scott in 1875. Today it is a thriving
coffee shop and second-hand bookshop.
Note: open Tuesday, Wednesday, Friday and
Saturday, 2 January to 29 December, 10 to 3.
Volunteer-run, so opening subject to
availability (please contact property before
visiting). Open until 4 on Saturday.

Find out more: 01280 817156 or
buckinghamchantry@nationaltrust.org.uk

The Buscot and Coleshill Estates

Coleshill, near Swindon

[✚][🏛][⊤][❀][♿][🛏][1956]

These countryside estates on the western
border of Oxfordshire include the attractive,
unspoilt villages of Buscot and Coleshill, each
with a thriving tea-room. There are circular
walks of differing lengths and a series of
footpaths criss-crossing the estates, with
breathtaking countryside and wildlife at Buscot
Lock and Badbury Hill. **Note**: toilets in Coleshill
Estate office yard and next to village shop and
tea-room in Buscot.

Eat, shop, stay: Buscot tea-room offering
lunches and afternoon tea. Locally sourced
produce served at Coleshill shop and tea-room
and The Radnor Arms (none National Trust).
Three holiday cottages.

Things to see and do: guided walks
throughout the year, including tours of the
Second World War bunker. See the restored
watermill in action and visit the replica

Operations Base on special open afternoons.
Dogs: on leads near livestock and under close
control at all times.

Access: [♿]
Sat Nav: use SN6 7PT. **Parking**: at Buscot
village and by Coleshill Estate office.

The Buscot and Coleshill Estates, near Swindon

Find out more: 01793 762209 or
buscotandcoleshill@nationaltrust.org.uk

The Buscot and Coleshill Estates
Coleshill Watermill open second Sunday of the month: April to October, 2 to 5.

Buscot Old Parsonage

Buscot, Faringdon, Oxfordshire SN7 8DQ

[🏠][❀][1949]

Beautiful early 18th-century house with small
walled garden, on the banks of the Thames.
Note: sorry no toilets. Open Wednesdays,
4 April to 31 October, 2 to 6. Admission only by
written appointment with tenant (please mark
envelope 'National Trust booking').

Find out more: 01793 762209 or
buscot@nationaltrust.org.uk

Buscot Park

Faringdon, Oxfordshire SN7 8BU

⚏ ✷ ⬓ 1949

Lord Faringdon's family live in the house, maintain its interior, curate its contents on behalf of the Trustees of The Faringdon Collection and manage and develop the grounds and gardens. This unusual arrangement for a National Trust property gives it an idiosyncratic air and a different take on taste and presentation. As a result the whole entity becomes more fluid and more surprising. New works of art mingle with the old within the house, and new alleys and vistas stride out within the grounds. Paintings, statuary and objects by contemporary artists reinvigorate the whole – refreshing the spirit.

The Water Garden at Buscot Park in Oxfordshire

Eat, shop, stay: tea-room (not National Trust), serving cream teas, cakes, ice-cream and a selection of hot and cold drinks. Local honey and cider, peppermints, plants and kitchen garden produce (when available). Ice-cream also available in ticket office. Picnic area.

Things to see and do: occasional events in grounds and theatre (available for hire). **Dogs**: in Paddock (overflow car park) only.

Access: ⓟ ⓓ ⓔ ⓑ ⓕ ⓙ ⚌ House ⓗ ⓘ Grounds ⓗ ⓙ ⓚ ➡ ⓜ ⓑ **Parking**: on site.

Find out more: 01367 240932 (Infoline). 01367 240786 or buscotpark@nationaltrust.org.uk buscotpark.com

Buscot Park		M	T	W	T	F	S	S
House, grounds and tea-room								
30 Mar–28 Sep	2–6			W	T	F		
Grounds only								
3 Apr–25 Sep	2–6	M	T					

Weekend openings: 31 March; 1, 7/8, 21/22 April; 5/6, 12/13, 26/27 May; 9/10, 23/24 June; 14/15, 28/29 July; 11/12, 25/26 August; 8/9, 22/23 September, 2 to 6 (tea-room open 2 to 5:30). Last admission to house one hour before closing. Open Bank Holiday Mondays.

Chastleton House

Chastleton, near Moreton-in-Marsh, Oxfordshire GL56 0SU

⚏ ✷ 1991

Within the warm, weathered Cotswold stone walls of this ancient country house, lie faded elegant interiors full of myths and memories – a compelling time capsule of 400 years of family life. Discover the secrets they hide, then explore the garden, a sleeping beauty preserved in graceful decline.

Eat, shop, stay: plants, local ice-cream, home-grown produce and honey from Chastleton's hives for sale. Second-hand books in the stables. Light refreshments available most days in the local church (not National Trust). Picnics welcome in the Brewhouse garden.

Chastleton House, Oxfordshire: myths and memories

Things to see and do: Indoors You can experience the romantic decline of a country manor, watch our introductory film and enjoy our family explorer packs. **Outdoors** Croquet on the lawn. **Dogs**: on leads in car park and Dovecote Field. Assistance dogs only in garden.

Access: ⬚⬚⬚⬚⬚⬚⬚⬚
Building ⬚ **Garden** ⬚
Sat Nav: misleading, follow brown signs.
Parking: footpath to house, steep in places, 273 yards.

Find out more: 01494 755560 (Infoline).
01608 674355 or
chastleton@nationaltrust.org.uk

Chastleton House		M	T	W	T	F	S	S
7 Mar–4 Nov	1–5*			W	T	F	S	S

*Last entry one hour before closing.

Chedworth Roman Villa

Yanworth, near Cheltenham,
Gloucestershire GL54 3LJ

🏛 1924

Cradled in a beautiful wooded valley and fed by a natural spring, this high-status Roman villa saw imperial fashions and local spirits living side by side. Nature took over and hid the magnificent mosaics, intricate hypocaust systems, bathhouses and ancient water-shrine for more than 1,500 years until Victorian gamekeepers rediscovered the site. The National Trust has, in turn, looked after Chedworth's Roman treasures and Victorian legacy for nearly a century, providing its modern villa guests with new facilities, as well as astonishing archaeology to enjoy. It remains a hidden place of natural beauty and continual discovery.

Eat, shop, stay: café serving sandwiches, soup, jacket potatoes, cakes, snacks, hot and cold drinks and ice-cream. You can find Roman-themed souvenirs, books and games, seasonal plants and National Trust gifts in the shop.

Things to see and do: Indoors Guidebooks, audio guides, free guided tours. Activities, including Roman dressing-up for children.

The west range at Chedworth Roman Villa, Gloucestershire, bottom, and contemporary dress, below

Costumed interpreters and living history events. **Outdoors** Family activities and trails (Bank Holiday weekends and school holidays). **Dogs**: assistance dogs only.

Access: ♿🅿️♿♿♿♿📷🖥️♿ Reception ♿♿
West Range ♿♿♿ Grounds ♿♿➡️♿
Parking: on lane at entrance, plus woodland overflow (March to October).

Find out more: 01242 890256 or chedworth@nationaltrust.org.uk

Chedworth Roman Villa		M	T	W	T	F	S	S
10 Feb–24 Mar	10–4	M	T	W	T	F	S	S
25 Mar–28 Oct	10–5	M	T	W	T	F	S	S
29 Oct–25 Nov	10–4	M	T	W	T	F	S	S

Children and adults alike are welcome to get hands-on at Chedworth Roman Villa

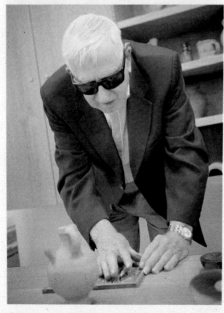

Claydon

Middle Claydon, near Buckingham, Buckinghamshire MK18 2EY

🏛️✝️🍃♿🔔♿⛓ 1956

Elegant Georgian Claydon in Buckinghamshire

Nestled in peaceful parkland, the Georgian exterior hides a lavish interior filled with oddities. The collection encompasses the unique and wonderful, as well as stunning carvings and portraits of interesting characters from 300 years of Verney family history. An inspirational place, where Florence Nightingale, Lady Verney's sister, spent her summers. **Note**: garden entry charges apply (including members).

Eat, shop, stay: second-hand bookshop, courtyard shops, galleries and tea-room (not National Trust). Picnics welcome.

Things to see and do: **Indoors** Historical costume exhibition. Children's activities, trails and dressing-up. **Outdoors** The classic English garden opened by the Verney family. **Dogs**: welcome on leads in the park.

Access: 🅿️♿♿♿♿♿📷📺♿∷
House ♿♿♿ Grounds ♿♿➡️♿
Parking: on site.

Find out more: 01296 730349 or claydon@nationaltrust.org.uk

Claydon		M	T	W	T	F	S	S
10 Mar–4 Nov	11–5	M	T	W	·	·	S	S
Open Good Friday.								

Cliveden

Cliveden Road, Taplow, Maidenhead,
Buckinghamshire SL1 8NS

🏛️ ❖ ♿ 🐾 | 1942 |

High above the River Thames with panoramic views over the Berkshire countryside, these gardens capture the grandeur of a bygone age. Over the course of 350 years, each family added their own extravagant touch, creating a series of distinct gardens. From carpets of spring bulbs and vibrant floral displays on the elaborate Parterre, to the intimate Rose Garden and rich autumn colour in the oriental Water Garden, each area is designed purely for enjoyment, and all echo Cliveden's rich history of politics, passion and pleasure. Miles of walks meander through majestic woodlands and along riverbank paths, while a giant yew-tree maze, storybook-themed play area and acres of space to run around in, make this a great place to play. **Note**: mooring charge on Cliveden Reach, £10 per 24 hours (including members), does not include entry.

Eat, shop, stay: Orangery Café (refurbishment this spring/summer) serving lunch (12 to 2:30) and snacks. Outdoor kiosk (dog-friendly) serving light refreshments. Doll's House 'grab-and-go' beside play area, designed for families. Shop, including plant sales. Picnic areas.

The gardens at Cliveden, Buckinghamshire, capture the grandeur of a bygone age

Things to see and do: Indoors Short guided
tour of part of the house (now a hotel) on
certain days. Greys Court and Hughenden
nearby. **Outdoors** More than 30,000 plants
create striking displays on the Parterre in
spring and summer, with thousands more
flowers filling the Long Garden each season.
The Rose Garden blooms from late June.
Walking and fitness trails. Highlights for
families include a play area, maze, free seasonal
trails, woodland play trail and den-building
area. Events include open-air theatre, family
fun days, guided garden walks and workshops.
Boat trips on the Thames, April to October
(additional charge including members).
Dogs: welcome under close control in
woodlands only.

Access: 🅿️🚌♿🚻🔤🏞️🎧🗺️📷
House (hotel) 🔤♿♿🚼♿ **Garden** 🔤♿♿➡️♿
Sat Nav: for gardens use Cliveden Road and
SL1 8NS. For woodlands use SL6 0HJ.
Parking: on site.

Sweeping lawns at Cliveden, below, and
autumn fun in the majestic woodlands, above

Find out more: 01628 605069 or
cliveden@nationaltrust.org.uk

Cliveden	M	T	W	T	F	S	S
Garden, shop, café and woodland							
Open every day all year	10–5*						

House and chapel: limited opening April to October
(call for details). House: admission by timed ticket only
from Information Centre. *1 January to 4 February and
29 October to 31 December: estate closes 4. Everything
closed 24 and 25 December.

Coombe Hill

Butler's Cross, near Wendover,
Buckinghamshire

🏛️🎠♿👥 1918

Nationally important chalk grassland site
and the highest viewpoint in the Chilterns.
Stunning views over the Aylesbury Vale.
Note: picnic area and play trail. Sorry no toilet.
For Sat Nav use HP17 0UR.

Find out more: 01494 755573
(Hughenden Estate Office) or
coombehill@nationaltrust.org.uk

Crickley Hill

Birdlip, Gloucestershire

♿ 1935

Sitting high on the Cotswold escarpment with
views towards the Welsh hills, Crickley Hill
overlooks Gloucester and Cheltenham.
Note: car park and visitor centre not National
Trust. For Sat Nav use GL4 8JY. Parking charges
(including members).

Find out more: 01452 814213 or
crickleyhill@nationaltrust.org.uk

Dorneywood Garden

Dorneywood, Dorney Wood Road, Burnham,
Buckinghamshire SL1 8PY

❄️ 1942

Ministerial residence since 1954 with country
garden. Afternoon teas. Open selected
afternoons (dates may change at short notice).
Note: no photography. Visitor details recorded
for security reasons. House and garden open
daily, 7 to 18 July, 2 to 4:30. Garden open
Wednesday and Thursday, 2 May to 26 July and

15 August to 20 September, 2 to 4:30. Booking
essential. May close at short notice, please
check before travelling.

Find out more:
dorneywood@nationaltrust.org.uk

Dyrham Park

Dyrham, near Bath,
South Gloucestershire SN14 8HY

🏛️✝️❄️♿ 1961

Dyrham Park, South Gloucestershire: intriguing treasures

Dyrham is a place of exploration. Parkland
adventurers can savour far-reaching views
towards the Welsh hills or encounter the
resident herd of majestic fallow deer, while
in the garden we are creating a haven of
tranquillity and inspiration. Sumptuous
planting in the pool garden contrasts with the
Dutch formality of the avenue and parterre,
as well as with the wilder wooded terraces.
The house is an intimate encounter with the
17th century. There are treasures gathered
from across the world, reflecting an age of

exploration and empire and revealing the personal passions of William Blathwayt – Secretary at War to William III. The house interior will be evolving throughout the year, as we develop new ways of revealing Dyrham's stories.

Eat, shop, stay: tea-room serving lunch, cakes and refreshments. Courtyard and garden kiosks (with outdoor seating) offering drinks, ice-cream and snacks on busy days. Shop selling plants, books, local products and gifts. Second-hand bookshop. Indoor and outdoor picnic tables at Old Lodge.

Things to see and do: **Indoors** Events and activities all year, including a range of house tours. **Outdoors** Guided tours of the park and garden. Family trail through the park, with natural play zones and fun things to discover along the way. Play area at Old Lodge. Borrow a Tracker Pack to help explore nature. The Cotswold Way passes next to Dyrham Park, linking into longer walks. Nearby Prior Park Landscape Garden offers great views and access to the Bath Skyline, where you can enjoy a 6-mile circular walk through beautiful woodlands, meadows and historic features.
Dogs: assistance dogs only. Dogs permitted on leads in small area next to car park.

Access:
House **Grounds**
Sat Nav: use SN14 8HY and enter via A46.
Parking: 20 yards from visitor centre.

Find out more: 0117 937 2501 or dyrhampark@nationaltrust.org.uk

The sweeping parkland at Dyrham Park, right and below, offers miles of walks and family trails to delight all ages

Discovering the Pool Garden at Dyrham Park

Dyrham Park		M	T	W	T	F	S	S
House								
1 Jan–9 Feb	Tour	M	T	W	T	F	S	S
10 Feb–28 Oct	11–5	M	T	W	T	F	S	S
29 Oct–31 Dec*	Tour	M	T	W	T	F	S	S
Park, garden, shop, tea-room and basement								
1 Jan–9 Feb	10–4	M	T	W	T	F	S	S
10 Feb–28 Oct	10–5	M	T	W	T	F	S	S
29 Oct–31 Dec*	10–4	M	T	W	T	F	S	S

Last admission one hour before closing. 5, 12 and
19 September; 7, 14, 21 and 28 November; 5 and 12 December:
everything closed until 1. Behind-the-scenes tours of the
house in winter. *Everything closed 24 and 25 December.

Great Coxwell Barn

Great Coxwell, Faringdon, Oxfordshire SN7 7LZ

 1956

Former 13th-century monastic barn, a favourite
of William Morris, who would regularly bring
his guests to wonder at its structure.
Note: sorry no toilet; narrow access lanes
leading to property. Open daily, dawn to dusk.

Find out more: 01793 762209 or
greatcoxwellbarn@nationaltrust.org.uk

Greys Court

Rotherfield Greys, Henley-on-Thames,
Oxfordshire RG9 4PG

🏠 ❀ ♿ 1969

Set in the rolling hills of the Chilterns, Greys
Court is a picturesque Tudor manor house
surrounded by layers of history, intimate walled
gardens and glorious wooded parkland. The
house is warm and welcoming, unfurling the
memories of the Brunner family through the
rooms of their comfortable home. Across the
perfect lawn, a medieval tower and patchwork
of mellow brick buildings conceal an English

Greys Court, Oxfordshire: the intimate
walled garden, below, and homely kitchen, bottom

country garden. Through an ancient arch,
seasonal blooms are revealed, from bright
bulbs through clematis and wisteria to glorious
peonies and roses in the summer. Winter walks
in the woodland are a must.

Eat, shop, stay: tea-room serving morning
coffee, afternoon tea, lunches and snacks.
Shop selling books, gifts, souvenirs and plants.
Seasonal organic produce and plants from
the gardens (when available).

Things to see and do: **Indoors** Enjoy the
elegant, comfortable rooms of the Brunner
family home. **Outdoors** Discover many
'rooms' in the walled gardens and rambling
woodland walks. Visit Nuffield Place nearby.
Dogs: welcome on leads (excluding walled
gardens and play area).

Access: 🅿️🚶♿🏛️📷🏠📖 House ♿
Tea-room ♿ Grounds ♿🚶
Parking: 220 yards.

Find out more: 01491 628529 or
greyscourt@nationaltrust.org.uk

Greys Court		M	T	W	T	F	S	S
Garden, tea-room and shop								
Open all year	10–5*	M	T	W	T	F	S	S
House guided tours								
1 Jan–28 Feb	11–3†	M	T	W	T	F	·	·
1 Mar–31 Oct	11–12	M	T	W	T	F	S	S
1 Nov–30 Nov	11–3†	M	T	W	T	F	·	·
1 Dec–31 Dec	11–12	M	T	W	T	F	S	S
House								
1 Mar–31 Oct	1–5	M	T	W	T	F	S	S
1 Dec–31 Dec*	1–4	M	T	W	T	F	S	S

*1 January to 4 February and 29 October to 31 December:
closes 4. **House tickets available from visitor reception
(places limited). †Weekend tours in January, February and
November at 11 and 12; free-flow from 1. Everything opens
at 12 on 2 September for annual village fête. Closed 24 and
25 December.

Haresfield Beacon

near Stroud, Gloucestershire

🏠 ♿ 1931

Prominently positioned on three spurs of the
Cotswold escarpment. Views across the Severn
Estuary towards the Forest of Dean and Brecon

Why not share your pictures with us? #nationaltrust

Beacons. The wildlife is some of the best in the Cotswolds and there's a wealth of archaeological features, including long and round barrows, a hill fort and cross dyke. **Note**: Cotswold Way National Trail runs through estate.

Eat, shop, stay: pubs in Randwick and Haresfield (not National Trust). Ice-cream vendor (not Trust) in Shortwood car park on sunny days. Picnics welcome.

Things to see and do: bluebells and butterflies to spot and woods to explore – there are superb veteran beech trees on Shortwood's slopes. Great place to fly a kite and watch buzzards and kestrels. **Dogs**: welcome on leads near livestock. Dog bins available in Shortwood car park.

Access: 👤
Sat Nav: use GL6 6PP for Shortwood car park.
Parking: at Shortwood.

Find out more: 01452 814213 or haresfieldbeacon@nationaltrust.org.uk

Hartwell House Hotel, Restaurant and Spa

Oxford Road, near Aylesbury,
Buckinghamshire HP17 8NR

🏛️ ♣ ⚓ 🛏️ 🔔 ⊤ 2008

Elegant Grade I listed stately home, having both Jacobean and Georgian façades, contains magnificent main hall with exceptional ceiling and elegant drawing-rooms serving morning coffee or afternoon tea. Set in beautifully landscaped grounds, including ruined Gothick church, lake, bridge and 36 hectares (90 acres) of parkland. Only one hour from central London. **Note**: access is for paying guests of the hotel, including for luncheon, afternoon tea and dinner. Children over the age of six welcome. Held on a long lease from the Ernest Cook Trust.

Find out more: 01296 747444. 01296 747450 (fax) or info@hartwell-house.com hartwell-house.com

Hidcote

Hidcote Bartrim, near Chipping Campden, Gloucestershire GL55 6LR

♣ 🔔 ⊤ 1948

One of the outdoor 'rooms' at Hidcote in Gloucestershire

This world-famous Arts and Crafts garden nestles in a North Cotswolds hamlet. Created by the talented and wealthy American horticulturist Major Lawrence Johnston, Hidcote's colourful and intricately designed outdoor 'rooms' are full of surprises, which change in harmony with the seasons. Many of the unusual plants found growing in the garden were collected from Johnston's plant-hunting trips around the world. Wandering along the narrow paved pathways, you come across secret gardens, unexpected views and plants that burst with colour.

Eat, shop, stay: Barn Café, plus Winthrop's Café. The National Trust's largest plant centre. Shop selling exclusive Hidcote souvenirs. Picnics welcome in the picnic area, close to the car park.

A peaceful spot for contemplation at Hidcote

Things to see and do: themed activities and workshops throughout the season. You can play croquet on the Great Lawn, or tennis using period wooden racquets (activities are weather dependent). **Dogs**: assistance dogs only.

Access: [icons]
Visitor reception [icon] Grounds [icons]
Sat Nav: follow signs to Mickleton.
Parking: 100 yards.

Find out more: 01386 438333 or hidcote@nationaltrust.org.uk

Hidcote		M	T	W	T	F	S	S
Garden, shop and Winthrop's Café								
3 Feb–4 Mar	11–4						S	S
5 Mar–1 Apr	10–5	M	T	W	T	F	S	S
2 Apr–23 Sep	10–6	M	T	W	T	F	S	S
24 Sep–28 Oct	10–5	M	T	W	T	F	S	S
3 Nov–16 Dec	11–4						S	S

Garden: last admission one hour before closing. Barn Café and plant centre: open 5 March to 28 October.

Horton Court

Horton, near Chipping Sodbury,
South Gloucestershire BS37 6QR

[icons] 1949

Atmospheric Norman hall and Tudor loggia, in the beautiful secluded setting of Horton Court's historic grounds. **Note**: main manor house is tenanted and not open to the public. Sorry no toilets. Advance booking may be required. Limited opening from April. Please telephone for opening details and booking arrangements.

Find out more: 01453 842644 (Newark Park) or hortoncourt@nationaltrust.org.uk

Hughenden

High Wycombe, Buckinghamshire HP14 4LA

[icons] 1947

It's hardly surprising that the unconventional Victorian Prime Minister Benjamin Disraeli so loved Hughenden. His handsome home, set in an unspoilt Chiltern valley with its views of ancient woods and rolling hills, is full of the fascinating personal memorabilia of this charismatic and colourful statesman. Disraeli's hillside retreat later became the headquarters for a top-secret, Second World War operation that put Hughenden high on Hitler's target list. The basement exhibition, 1940s living-room and ice-house bunker bring wartime Britain to life. The estate also offers a variety of walks, rewarding visitors with perfect views of the Chiltern Hills.

Eat, shop, stay: Stableyard café serving hot meals, sandwiches, cakes and drinks. Dizzy's tea-room and Grab & Go coffee shop open weekends and holidays only. Shop stocks local produce, as well as Disraeli and 'Hillside' memorabilia. Second-hand bookshop, plants and estate produce available.

Things to see and do: **Indoors** Historical introductory talks throughout the day. **Outdoors** Woodland walks. Children's trails in Walled Garden and woodland play at the top of the picnic orchard. **Dogs**: welcome on short leads in orchard and gardens. Assistance dogs only in manor.

Hughenden, Buckinghamshire, sits in an unspoilt valley

A corner of the garden at Hughenden

Access: 🅿️ 🚗 ♿ 🚻 📷 🎧 📱 💺 ♿ 📷
Manor ♿ 🏠 🚹 ♿ Grounds ♿ 🏠 ➡️ ♿
Parking: on site.

Find out more: 01494 755565 (Infoline).
01494 755573 or
hughenden@nationaltrust.org.uk

Hughenden								
House*								
1 Jan–5 Jan	11–3	M	T	W	T	F	·	·
22 Jan–9 Feb	11–4**	M	T	W	T	F	S	S
10 Feb–28 Oct	11–5	M	T	W	T	F	S	S
29 Oct–31 Dec	11–3	M	T	W	T	F	S	S
Gardens, café and shop								
Open all year	10–5†	M	T	W	T	F	S	S

*House: admission by timed ticket at certain times;
**Open 12 to 3 on weekdays. †1 January to 4 February and
29 October to 31 December: closes 4. Shop opens at 11 all
year. Whole property closed 24 and 25 December.

King's Head

King's Head Passage, Market Square, Aylesbury,
Buckinghamshire HP20 2RW

🏠 🍽️ 1925

Historic public house dating back to 1455, with
a pleasant family atmosphere. This is one of
England's best-preserved coaching inns.
Note: Farmers' Bar leased by Chiltern Brewery.
Open Monday to Saturday all year (apart from
25 December), 11 to 11, and Sundays, 7 January
to 30 December, Bank Holiday Mondays and
other public holidays, 12 to 10:30.

Find out more: 01296 718812 (Farmers' Bar).
01280 817156 (National Trust) or
kingshead@nationaltrust.org.uk

Lodge Park and Sherborne Estate

Aldsworth, near Cheltenham,
Gloucestershire GL54 3PP

🏠 🚻 🛏️ 🔔 ♿ 🍽️ 1983

Within the tranquil Sherborne Estate sits
England's only surviving 17th-century deer-
coursing grandstand. Lodge Park was built in
1634 to satisfy John 'Crump' Dutton's love of
gambling and entertaining. Don't miss the
dramatic views from the roof. The Sherborne
Estate has a variety of peaceful walks through
the Cotswold countryside. **Note:** toilets at
Lodge Park only.

Lodge Park on the Sherborne Estate, Gloucestershire

Eat, shop, stay: tea, cake, ice-cream and plants
for sale at Lodge Park, when open. Tea-room and
shop in Sherborne village (not National Trust).

Nearby holiday cottages: Deer Park Lodge at Lodge Park, West Lodge in Sherborne and 9 Arlington Row in Bibury.

Things to see and do: living history, family events, children's quizzes, lawn games, historic shepherd's hut, woodland play trail and beautiful walks in Bridgeman landscape at Lodge Park. Country walks across the wider estate. **Dogs**: on leads in Lodge Park grounds and near livestock. Under control at all times.

Access: 🅿️🅿️🎫🎫📷📷 Lodge 🔥🔥🔥
Sat Nav: for Lodge Park use GL54 3PP; for Sherborne Estate use GL54 3DT (Ewe Pen Barn) or GL54 3DL (Water Meadows).
Parking: on site for Lodge Park. For Sherborne Estate use either Ewe Pen Barn or Water Meadows car parks.

Find out more: 01451 844130 or lodgepark@nationaltrust.org.uk

Lodge Park and Sherborne Estate		M	T	W	T	F	S	S
Lodge Park								
10 Feb–18 Feb	11–4	·	·	·	·	·	S	S
2 Mar–28 Oct	11–4	·	·	·	·	F	S	S
Sherborne Estate								
Open all year	Dawn–dusk	M	T	W	T	F	S	S

Lodge Park: open Bank Holiday Mondays; occasionally closes for private functions (telephone to confirm openings).

Long Crendon Courthouse

Long Crendon, Aylesbury, Buckinghamshire HP18 9AN

 1900

Superb example of a 14th-century courthouse with a wealth of local history – the second building acquired by the National Trust. **Note**: extremely steep stairs. Sorry no toilet. Parking limited. Open Wednesdays and weekends, 10 March to 4 November, 11 to 5. Volunteer-run, so opening subject to availability (please call before visiting). Open all public and Bank Holidays.

Find out more: 01280 817156 or longcrendon@nationaltrust.org.uk

Minchinhampton and Rodborough Commons

near Stroud, Gloucestershire

🏛️🔀 1913

These historic Cotswold commons (above), traditionally grazed, are famed for rare flowers and butterflies, prehistoric remains and far-reaching views. Minchinhampton Common contains a nationally important complex of Neolithic and Bronze Age burial mounds, while Rodborough Common's limestone grasslands have abundant wild flowers, including rare pasqueflowers and many varieties of orchid.

Eat, shop, stay: many great picnic spots (no tables). The historic Winstones ice-cream factory is on Rodborough Common; ice-cream vans usually found in Reservoir car park in summer. Several pubs around the edge of both commons (none National Trust). Two holiday cottages nearby.

Things to see and do: the commons are great places to walk, picnic, spot butterflies or fly a kite, and there are events throughout the year.

Downloadable Rodborough Common butterfly walk available. **Dogs**: welcome everywhere (under close control near livestock). Dog bins in car parks.

Access:
Sat Nav: use GL5 5BJ for Minchinhampton; GL5 5BP Rodborough. **Parking**: at Reservoir car park on Minchinhampton Common; Rodborough Fort car park on Rodborough Common.

Find out more: 01452 814213 or minchinhampton@nationaltrust.org.uk

Newark Park

Ozleworth, Wotton-under-Edge, Gloucestershire GL12 7PZ

🏠 🏛 ✳ 🐾 📷 1949

With splendid views from the Cotswold escarpment, Newark Park is a secluded estate with a historic country home at its heart. From Tudor beginnings to dramatic rescue by a 20th-century Texan, the house has many stories to tell. The informal garden and estate provide space to play, explore and contemplate. **Note**: toilets in car park (additional toilets in Newark House).

Eat, shop, stay: gift shop on the first floor of Newark House and plant sales next to visitor reception. Tea pavilion in the garden serving light lunches, cakes, drinks and ice-cream. Outdoor seating, with indoor seating available in house. Holiday cottage.

Things to see and do: **Indoors** Exhibitions in house. **Outdoors** Waymarked walks and geocaching on estate. Open-air theatre, croquet on the lawn with peacocks for company. Seasonal garden specials include snowdrops, cyclamen and wild garlic.
Dogs: welcome on leads in garden and estate (please mind peacocks and grazing livestock).

Access: 🅿 🚻 📷 🏠 💺 👜 ♿
Building 🅰 🅱 🅲 Grounds 🅰
Sat Nav: only works when approaching from north; if approaching from south follow brown signs from Wotton-under-Edge and A46.
Parking: 100 yards from house.

Find out more: 01453 842644 or newarkpark@nationaltrust.org.uk

Newark Park		M	T	W	T	F	S	S
3 Feb–28 Feb	11–4	M	·	W	T	F	S	S
1 Mar–4 Nov	11–5	M	·	W	T	F	S	S
10 Nov–16 Dec	11–4	·	·	·	·	·	S	S

Estate walks open daily dawn to dusk (weather permitting). Reduced car park opening in winter.

Newark Park, Gloucestershire, below, sits high up in the Cotswolds. Far-reaching views from the Garden Hall, left

Nuffield Place

Huntercombe, near Henley-on-Thames,
Oxfordshire RG9 5RY

🏠 ✣ 2011

Nuffield Place, Oxfordshire: a corner of the sitting room

Nuffield Place was the home of William Morris, who rose from modest circumstances as a backyard bicycle repairer to become one of the richest men in the world. As founder of Morris Motors, Lord Nuffield was an innovator in mass production. He was also a great philanthropist, donating millions to charitable causes. Despite their great wealth, Lord and Lady Nuffield lived modestly in their Oxfordshire country home. The Arts and Crafts-style house is full of personal curiosities, such as the tool cupboard in Lord Nuffield's wardrobe, and gives an intriguing glimpse into the home life of this private couple.

Eat, shop, stay: tea-room serving light lunches and afternoon tea. Shop selling unique Nuffield Place mementoes, gifts, books and postcards.

Things to see and do: **Indoors** Immerse yourself in the wonderful storytelling of our passionate volunteers. **Outdoors** Charming Arts and Crafts-style garden with colourful herbaceous borders, kitchen garden and croquet lawn. Greys Court nearby.

Dogs: welcome on leads in the gardens and woodlands.

Access: 📄 House 🔽 Shop 🔽 Grounds 🔽
Parking: on site.

Find out more: 01491 641224 or nuffieldplace@nationaltrust.org.uk

Nuffield Place		M	T	W	T	F	S	S
26 Feb–4 Nov*	10–5**	M	T	W	T	F	S	S

*Closed 8 April, 24 June, 10 July. **House: access from 11; timed tickets may be used on busy days (available from visitor reception, places limited).

Pitstone Windmill

Ivinghoe, Buckinghamshire LU7 9EJ

✖ ✣ 1937

Believed to be the oldest postmill in England. Stunning views of the Chilterns. **Note**: access to windmill 262 yards via a grassy field track. Sorry no facilities. Limited parking. Open Sundays, 27 May to 26 August, 2:30 to 5:30 (also open Mondays, 28 May and 27 August).

Find out more: 01442 851227 or pitstonemill@nationaltrust.org.uk

Priory Cottages

1 Mill Street, Steventon, Abingdon, Oxfordshire OX13 6SP

🏠 1939

Now converted into two houses, these former monastic buildings were gifted to the National Trust by the famous Ferguson's Gang. **Note**: Priory Cottage South Great Hall only open. Administered by a tenant. Sorry no toilet. Open Tuesdays, 3 April to 25 September, 2 to 6. Admission by written appointment with tenant.

Find out more: 01793 762209 or priorycottages@nationaltrust.org.uk

Snowshill Manor and Garden

Snowshill, near Broadway,
Gloucestershire WR12 7JU

🏠 ❄ ⛟ | 1951 |

Charles Wade was a talented man who took delight in creating a home for his unlikely treasures. He was an artist and architect who collected beautiful and interesting objects, which for him were a celebration of good colour, craftsmanship and design. With a sense of fun and theatre, he took great pleasure in turning his home into a stage for the varied and curious finds. Next to the manor house is the humble cottage where Charles Wade lived, and both are surrounded by an intimate terraced garden, where he created 'different courts for different moods'. **Note**: entry by timed ticket (including members), places limited.

Eat, shop, stay: tea-room serving coffee, hot lunches and cream teas, using home-grown produce where possible. Shop selling gifts, plants and local produce. Second-hand bookshop. Picnic tables. Why not stay a while longer at one of four picturesque holiday cottages in the village?

Things to see and do: **Indoors** Family trail, handling collection and discovery talks. **Outdoors** Family trail, natural play area and introductory talks. **Dogs**: assistance dogs only.

Access: 🅿🚻🚽♿📷📱📹.♿
Manor ♿🚻 Garden ♿♿
Sat Nav: follow signs from centre of village.
Parking: 500 yards.

Find out more: 01386 852410 or
snowshillmanor@nationaltrust.org.uk

Snowshill Manor and Garden		M	T	W	T	F	S	S
Manor								
10 Mar–28 Oct	12–5	M	T	W	T	F	S	S
3 Nov–25 Nov	11–2:30	·	·	·	·	·	S	S
Garden, shop and tea-room								
10 Mar–28 Oct	11–5:30	M	T	W	T	F	S	S
3 Nov–25 Nov	10:30–3:30	·	·	·	·	·	S	S

Manor admission by non-bookable timed tickets (may run out on busy days). Last admission one hour before closing. Priest's House opens at 11.

Snowshill Manor, Gloucestershire, is bursting with interesting objects and unlikely treasures

Stowe

Buckingham, Buckinghamshire MK18 5EQ

🏠 ❀ ♨ 🔔 ⵂ 1990

Stowe, Buckinghamshire: one of the lakeside walks

The beauty of Stowe has attracted visitors since 1717. Picture-perfect views, lakeside walks and temples create a monumental landscape that changes with the seasons. Full of hidden meanings and classical references, the garden remains an earthly paradise. You will follow in the footsteps of 18th-century tourists by beginning your visit at the New Inn, now a visitor centre. From here it is a short walk or buggy-ride to the garden, where another world awaits. Our ongoing programme of works continues, as we return Stowe to its 18th-century glory. The sheer size and scale is perfect for either a steady stroll or vigorous ramble, and will leave you overwhelmed by its awe-inspiring splendour.

Eat, shop, stay: café inside New Inn serving fresh homemade food, such as light lunches, cakes, soups and scones. Shop selling local products inspired by Stowe, as well as gifts and plants. A second-hand bookshop is a must for bookworms. Picnics welcome.

Things to see and do: **Indoors** 18th-century parlour rooms in the New Inn. New Inn visitor centre provides details about visiting Stowe House State Rooms (not National Trust). House visitor centre open, includes exhibition and family-friendly activities. St Mary's Church open for visits. **Outdoors** Crisp winter walks, blooming spring displays, lazy summer days and vivid autumn colour – Stowe is forever changing. Fun family activities and outdoor events programme. We are restoring paths, statues and opening new garden areas all year, so there will be more to explore on every new visit. **Dogs**: welcome on leads (downloadable dog trail available). Tie-up points and water provided.

Access: 🄿♿🄺🄷🄻🄳🄹🄿 Visitor centre ♿🛗
Grounds ♿➡🦽
Parking: 545 yards.

Find out more: 01280 817156 or stowe@nationaltrust.org.uk

Stowe	
Open every day all year*	10–5**

*Gardens: closed 26 May (New Inn, parkland, café and shop open); recommended last entry 90 minutes before closing. **1 January to 4 February and 5 November to 31 December: closes 4. Closed 24 and 25 December.

Stowe: the Temple of British Worthies, below, and the elegant Palladian Bridge, left

Waddesdon Manor

Waddesdon, near Aylesbury,
Buckinghamshire HP18 0JH

🏛️🍴♿♿🔊🍷 1957

Baron Ferdinand de Rothschild started building the manor – managed by the Rothschild Foundation – in 1874 to display his outstanding collection of art treasures and entertain fashionable society. His choice of a French-style château, typical of the Loire Valley, surprises many visitors. The highest quality 18th-century French decorative arts are displayed alongside magnificent English portraits and Dutch Old Master paintings in 40 elegant interiors. Outside is one of the finest Victorian gardens in Britain, famous for its parterre and ornate working aviary, and enhanced with classical and contemporary sculpture. Today, the manor continues its tradition of entertainment and hospitality, with events celebrating food and wine. Visitors can explore Waddesdon's history, collections and gardens through changing exhibitions, talks and tours. **Note**: advance booking for house tickets essential for weekends and holidays for all visitors (including members). June Feast weekend and festive decorated interiors, November to December (charge including members).

Eat, shop, stay: two licensed restaurants for breakfasts, lunches and afternoon teas. Snacks and drinks at the Treaterie, Summer House and Coffee Bar. Gift and wine shop; regular wine tastings. Five Arrows Hotel in Waddesdon village. None National Trust.

Things to see and do: Indoors House timed ticket entry March to October, with furnished interiors displaying the collections (advance booking advised for weekends and holidays). Annual exhibitions. Talks and tours on aspects of the house, collection, archive and exhibitions with experts. November to December festive decorations in east wing only (advance booking essential). Rolling programme of films about Waddesdon's history, collections, aviary, gardens and cellars. **Outdoors** Daily free guided

garden walks and tours of the aviary and wine cellars, maps downloadable from waddesdon. org.uk. Woodland playground and den-building for children. Weekend and school holiday family events. Open-air film and theatre. Food festivals, Winter Light and Christmas fair. **Dogs**: welcome on leads in grounds and Stables Courtyard only.

Access: 🅿️♿🚻🏛️♿🔊📷🅿️♿
House ♿⬆️♿ **Coach House Gallery** ♿
Grounds ♿➡️♿
Parking: ¾ mile (frequent free shuttle service). Electric vehicle charging points in main car park.

Find out more: 01296 820414 or waddesdonmanor@nationaltrust.org.uk

Waddesdon Manor		M	T	W	T	F	S	S
Gardens, aviary, playground, wine cellars, shop, restaurants								
1 Jan–2 Jan	11–6	M	T	·	·	·	·	·
6 Jan–18 Mar	11–4	·	·	·	·	·	S	S
10 Feb–18 Feb	11–4	M	T	W	T	F	S	S
21 Mar–4 Nov	10–5	·	·	W	T	F	S	S
26 May–3 Jun	10–5	M	T	W	T	F	S	S
20 Oct–28 Oct	10–5	M	T	W	T	F	S	S
10 Nov–30 Dec**	11–6	·	·	W	T	F	S	S
31 Dec	11–6	M	·	·	·	·	·	·
House*								
21 Mar–28 Oct	12–4	·	·	W	T	F	S	S
26 May–3 Jun	12–4	M	T	W	T	F	S	S
Christmas House (partial opening)**								
10 Nov–30 Dec	11:30–6	·	·	W	T	F	S	S
31 Dec	11:30–6	M	·	·	·	·	·	·
Coach House Gallery								
25 May–28 Oct	11–5	·	·	W	T	F	S	S
26 May–3 Jun	11–5	M	T	W	T	F	S	S
20 Oct–28 Oct	11–5	M	T	W	T	F	S	S

House: open 11 to 4, weekends and Bank Holiday Mondays. *House: admission by timed ticket, available at waddesdon. org.uk or by calling 01296 820414 (booking fee). Advance booking of house tickets essential, especially on weekends, public and school holidays. Recommended last entry 2:30; last house entry 3:10. **Closed 24, 25 and 26 December.

Waddesdon Manor in Buckinghamshire: the north front of the French-style château, above, and opulent dining-room, left

West Wycombe Park, Village and Hill

West Wycombe, Buckinghamshire HP14 3AJ

🏠✝🍴⚓ 1943

Alongside this historic village lies an exquisite Palladian mansion (above). This lavish home and serene landscape garden reflect the wealth and personality of its creator, the infamous Sir Francis Dashwood, founder of the Hellfire Club. Still home to the Dashwood family and their fine collection, it remains a busy, private estate. **Note**: opened in partnership with the Dashwood family. The Hellfire Caves and café are privately owned and National Trust members receive a discount on the admission charge.

Eat, shop, stay: refreshments available at the Hellfire Caves and café (not National Trust), where members receive a discount. Variety of shops and pubs in the National Trust village, offering refreshments and local produce (none National Trust).

Things to see and do: **Indoors** Mansion guided tours, Monday to Thursday (free-flow access Sundays). **Outdoors** Centuries-old village with historic cottages and coaching inns. West Wycombe Hill, iconic Dashwood mausoleum and church with golden ball. **Dogs**: welcome on West Wycombe Hill. Assistance dogs only in park.

Access: 🅿️♿🏧📷🚻👓 Building 🔦🔦♿
Parking: 250 yards.

Find out more: 01494 755571 (Infoline). 01494 513569 or westwycombe@nationaltrust.org.uk

West Wycombe		M	T	W	T	F	S	S
Grounds								
1 Apr–30 Aug	2–6	M	T	W	T			S
House*								
3 Jun–30 Aug	2–6	M	T	W	T			S

*House: entry Monday to Thursday by guided tour (timed tickets); free-flow on Sundays and Bank Holidays. Last admission 45 minutes before closing.

Westbury Court Garden

Westbury-on-Severn, Gloucestershire GL14 1PD

❄ 1967

Originally laid out between 1696 and 1705, this is the only restored Dutch water garden in the country. There are canals, clipped hedges, working 17th-century vegetable plots and many old varieties of fruit trees. **Note**: credit cards not accepted.

Eat, shop, stay: light refreshments available in the local church (not National Trust) on Sunday afternoons.

Westbury Court Garden in Gloucestershire

Things to see and do: evening garden tours, Easter Egg trails and Apple Day. **Dogs**: welcome on short leads at all times.

Access: [icons] Pavilion [icon]
Summerhouse [icon] Garden [icons]
Parking: car park 300 yards from main road.

Find out more: 01452 760461 or westburycourt@nationaltrust.org.uk

Westbury Court Garden		M	T	W	T	F	S	S
7 Mar–31 May	10–5		·	W	T	F	S	S
1 Jun–30 Sep	10–5	M	T	W	T	F	S	S
3 Oct–28 Oct	10–5		·	W	T	F	S	S

Open Bank Holiday Mondays. Open other times by appointment.

White Horse Hill

Uffington, Oxfordshire

[icons] 1979

The White Horse at Uffington is part of an ancient landscape, steeped in history and mythology. It's the oldest chalk figure in the country, dated to the late Bronze Age about 3,000 years ago. Its linear form dominates the landscape, yet no one knows how it was made. The walls of an Iron Age hill fort are visible on the hilltop, the highest point in Oxfordshire. You can also look down on a valley known as The Manger and a natural outcrop known as Dragon Hill, where St George was said to have fought and slain the dragon.
Note: archaeological monuments under English Heritage guardianship. Sorry no toilet.

Scouring the chalk figure, above, at White Horse Hill in Oxfordshire, below

Things to see and do: guided walks and events to re-chalk the White Horse. Stunning views can be enjoyed from the top of the hill. Ashdown House woodland walks nearby.
Dogs: under close control at all times (stock grazing).

Access: 🅿️♿
Sat Nav: use SN7 7QJ. **Parking**: on site.

Find out more: 01793 762209 or whitehorsehill@nationaltrust.org.uk

Woodchester Park: view down the Woodchester Valley

Woodchester Park

Nympsfield, near Stroud, Gloucestershire

🏕️ 1994

This tranquil wooded valley contains a 'lost landscape': remains of an 18th- and 19th-century landscape park with a chain of five lakes. The restoration of this landscape is an ongoing project. Waymarked trails (steep in places) lead through picturesque scenery, passing an unfinished Victorian mansion.
Note: toilet not always available. Mansion managed by Woodchester Mansion Trust (not National Trust). Admission charges apply (including members).

Eat, shop, stay: seasonal café, shop and toilet facilities available at Woodchester Mansion (not National Trust).

The play trail at Woodchester Park, Gloucestershire

Things to see and do: waymarked trails through valley and popular woodland play trail for children built along shortest route, which includes rope swings, see-saw, balance beams and zip wire. Events throughout the year.
Dogs: under close control, on leads where requested.

Access: Grounds ♿
Sat Nav: nearest GL10 3TS, then follow signs.
Parking: accessible from Nympsfield road, 300 yards from junction with B4066.

Find out more: 01452 814213 or woodchesterpark@nationaltrust.org.uk

Additional countryside car parks in Gloucestershire and Buckinghamshire

Gloucestershire	
Mayhill	GL18 1JS
Dover's Hill	GL55 6PN
Buckinghamshire	
Ivinghoe Beacon	HP4 1NF
Pulpit Wood,	
Whiteleaf Fields	HP27 0NB

Berkshire, Hampshire and the Isle of Wight

The Needles Batteries and Headland, Isle of Wight

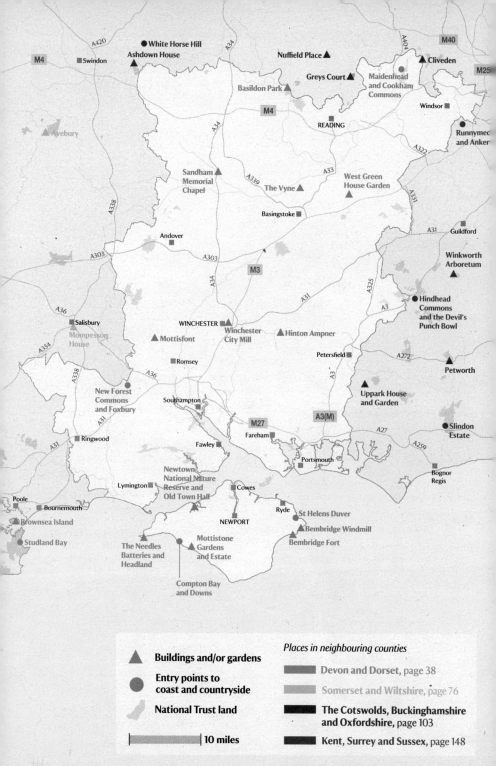

White Horse Hill ●
Ashdown House ▲
Swindon ■
A420
A34
M4
A34
M4

Nuffield Place ▲
Greys Court ▲
Basildon Park ▲
M40
Cliveden ▲
Maidenhead and Cookham Commons ▲●
Windsor ■
A404
M25

READING

A322

Runnymede and Anker ●

A338
A34

Sandham Memorial Chapel ▲
A339
The Vyne ▲
A33
West Green House Garden ▲
A331

Basingstoke ■

Avebury

A303
Andover ■
A303
M3
A34

A31
Guildford ■

Winkworth Arboretum ▲

A36
Salisbury ■
Mompesson House
A354
WINCHESTER ▲
Winchester City Mill ▲
Mottisfont ▲
Hinton Ampner ▲
A325
A3
Hindhead Commons and the Devil's Punch Bowl ●

Romsey ■
Petersfield ■
A272
Petworth ▲

A338
A36
A3
Uppark House and Garden ▲

New Forest Commons and Foxbury ●
Southampton ■
A31
M27
A3(M)
Fareham ■
Ringwood ■
Fawley ■
A27
A259
Slindon Estate ●

Portsmouth ■
Bognor Regis ■

Newtown National Nature Reserve and Old Town Hall ▲
Lymington ■
Cowes ■
Poole
Bournemouth ■
Ryde ■
St Helens Duver ●
NEWPORT ■
Brownsea Island ▲
Studland Bay ●
The Needles Batteries and Headland ●
Mottistone Gardens and Estate ▲
Bembridge Windmill ▲
Bembridge Fort ▲
Compton Bay and Downs

Legend

▲ Buildings and/or gardens

● Entry points to coast and countryside

National Trust land

▬ 10 miles

Places in neighbouring counties

Devon and Dorset, page 38

Somerset and Wiltshire, page 76

The Cotswolds, Buckinghamshire and Oxfordshire, page 103

Kent, Surrey and Sussex, page 148

Sitting within a secluded wooded parkland, Basildon Park in Berkshire contains fine furnishings and Old Masters

Basildon Park

Lower Basildon, Reading, Berkshire RG8 9NR

🏠 ✤ ♿ 1978

Sitting elegantly in 162 hectares (400 acres) of historic parkland and gardens, this 18th-century mansion was saved from destruction by Lord and Lady Iliffe in the 1950s, when it was derequisitioned after the Second World War. In a true labour of love, the Iliffes spent nearly 50 years renovating and returning the house to its former glory, acquiring a collection of fine furnishings and carefully selected Old Masters. The wooded parkland showcases glorious seasonal colour all year round, while the landscape has been restored to offer wonderful views, peaceful trails and picnic places. **Note**: entrance to main show rooms of mansion on first floor – 21 steps from ground level.

Eat, shop, stay: mansion tea-room serving coffee, lunch, afternoon tea and snacks. Shop selling books, plants, local food, ice-cream and much more.

Things to see and do: **Indoors** Exhibition 'At Home with Art, Treasures of the Ford Collection'. Guided house tours. **Outdoors** Woodland and parkland walks. Wild Play and family activities. **Dogs**: welcome on leads in grounds. Assistance dogs only in house.

Access: P♿ 🚻 ♿ ♿ 🅿️ 🔄 💻 📺 🎵 ⠿ 🅿️
Mansion ♿ ♿ Grounds ➡️ ♿
Sat Nav: not reliable, please follow brown tourist signs. **Parking**: 400 yards.

Find out more: 01491 672382 or basildonpark@nationaltrust.org.uk

Basildon Park	
Open every day all year	10–5*

*House: free-flow from 12, access by guided tour only 11 and 11:30 (tickets available from visitor reception, places limited). 1 January to 4 February and 29 October to 31 December: closes 4. Closed 24 and 25 December.

Bembridge Fort

Bembridge Down, near Bembridge,
Isle of Wight PO36 8QY

 1967

In a commanding position on top of Bembridge Down, this unrestored Victorian fort is open for volunteer-run guided tours. **Note**: sorry no toilets. Not suitable for children under ten. Open Tuesdays, 3 April to 30 October, 2 to 3:30 (access by guided tour only, booking essential).

Find out more: 01983 741020 or bembridgefort@nationaltrust.org.uk c/o Longstone Farmhouse, Strawberry Lane, Mottistone, Isle of Wight PO30 4EA

Bembridge Windmill

High Street/Mill Lane, Bembridge,
Isle of Wight PO35 5SQ

 1961

This little gem, the only surviving windmill on the Isle of Wight, is one of the island's most iconic images. Built *circa* 1700 and last operated in 1913, it still has most of its original machinery intact. Climb to the top and follow the milling process down its four floors. **Note**: steep steps inside the windmill.

Eat, shop, stay: the reception kiosk offers hot and cold drinks, including tea and a selection of coffees. Ice-cream, postcards, sweets, gifts and souvenirs also available. Picnic tables in grounds. Four holiday cottages nearby – Chert, Little Chert, Wydcombe and Knowles Farm cottages.

Things to see and do: Nature ID trails and children's activities during school holidays. Number of walks, including the start of Culver Trail. Bembridge Fort nearby. **Dogs**: welcome in grounds on leads. Assistance dogs only in windmill.

Access: 🅿️🗺️🖥️🧗📶 **Building** 🔥👫🏛️ **Sat Nav**: do not use, look for brown signs. **Parking**: free (not National Trust), 100 yards in lay-by.

Find out more: 01983 873945 or bembridgemill@nationaltrust.org.uk

Bembridge Windmill		M	T	W	T	F	S	S
10 Mar–28 Oct	10:30–5	**M**	**T**	**W**	**T**	**F**	**S**	**S**

Closes dusk if earlier. Conducted school groups and special visits March to end October (telephone or email to book).

Bembridge Windmill on the Isle of Wight is one of the island's most iconic images

Compton Bay and Downs

Compton, Isle of Wight

🛏️🔀 1961

The beach at Compton Bay and Downs, Isle of Wight

Compton offers a great day out with its sandy beaches and colourful cliffs. It's also a prime site for fossil-hunting – look out for dinosaur foot casts. The clifftops and downs are rich in wild flowers and butterflies and offer wonderful walks with breathtaking views.

Eat, shop, stay: licensed van selling hot and cold snacks, drinks and ice-cream. Two holiday cottages, Compton Farm Cottages, within walking distance – both ideally placed for exploring the coast and Downs.

Things to see and do: one of the best spots on the Isle of Wight for swimming, surfing and fossil-hunting. Scenic views from three walking trails available to download from the website. **Dogs**: welcome on beach between Hanover Point and Brook Chine all year.

Access: Compton Bay 🏖️
Sat Nav: use PO30 4HB. **Parking**: on site.

Find out more: 01983 741020 or comptonbay@nationaltrust.org.uk

Hinton Ampner

Hinton Ampner, near Alresford, Hampshire SO24 0LA

🏠➕🔀🔀🍽️ 1986

Hinton Ampner is the fulfilment of one man's vision. After a catastrophic fire in 1960, Ralph Dutton rebuilt his home in the light and airy Georgian style he loved. A passionate collector, he filled the sunny rooms with ceramics and art. Outside, Dutton designed a series of tranquil garden rooms, each with their own distinctive planting still apparent today. Geometric topiary, exotic-coloured dahlias and borders of repeat-flowering roses lead onto terraces with panoramic views across the South Downs. Extensive lawns, a park with ancient oaks and beech woodland provide plenty of space to stroll, play, relax and picnic.

Hinton Ampner, Hampshire: plenty of space for fun

The light and airy interior of Hinton Ampner

Eat, shop, stay: café serving seasonal dishes made using produce grown in our walled garden, homemade cakes and cream teas. Shop selling a range of locally sourced products and estate-grown plants. Second-hand bookshop. Picnics welcome.

Things to see and do: **Indoors** Conservation demonstrations throughout the year. **Outdoors** Estate walking trails and free seasonal garden walks. Events, including open-air theatre and music in the summer. Children's trails all year. **Dogs**: welcome on short leads in the grounds (assistance dogs only in the walled garden).

Access: 🅿️🅳🚽♿🎒🖼️🔌💻🎵📷🅰️
Building ♿🔵♿ Grounds ♿▶️♿
Sat Nav: use SO24 0NH – takes you to Hinton Arms pub, 21 yards west of main entrance.
Parking: on site.

Find out more: 01962 771305 or hintonampner@nationaltrust.org.uk

Hinton Ampner		M	T	W	T	F	S	S
Gardens, estate, shop and café*								
Open all year	10–5**	M	T	W	T	F	S	S
House								
10 Feb–24 Dec†	11–3:30	M	T	W	T	F	S	S

*Gardens: limited access in winter. **1 January to 4 February and 29 October to 31 December: close 4. †House: closed 24 to 30 November for Christmas set up. Everything closed 25 and 26 December.

Maidenhead and Cookham Commons

near Maidenhead, Berkshire

🏛️♿ 1934

This chain of ancient commons offers footpaths through broadleaf woodlands, chalk downland, marshes dotted with orchids and hay meadows buzzing with insects in summer. These rich habitats are great for spotting wildlife throughout the year – you might see emperor dragonflies, marbled white butterflies, redwings, skylarks and fieldfares.

Eat, shop, stay: numerous shops, restaurants, pubs and cafés in nearby Cookham, Cookham Dean, Golden Ball, Pinkneys Green and Maidenhead (none National Trust). Picnic on wildflower meadows.

Maidenhead and Cookham Commons in Berkshire

Things to see and do: enjoy walking and horse-riding along bridleways and tree-lined avenues. Let your imagination run wild on family-friendly routes, with great places to try den-building and bug-hunting. **Dogs**: welcome (please be mindful of ground-nesting birds and cattle grazing).

Access: ♿
Sat Nav: use SL6 6QD for Pinkneys Green.
Parking: numerous on site.

Find out more: 01628 605069 or maidenheadandcookham@nationaltrust.org.uk

Mottisfont

near Romsey, Hampshire SO51 0LP

🏛️ ✿ ♿ 1957

Ancient trees, babbling brooks and rolling lawns frame this 18th-century house with a medieval priory at its heart. Maud Russell made Mottisfont her home in the 1930s, bringing artists here to relax and create works inspired by Mottisfont's past, including an extraordinary drawing-room painted by Rex Whistler. We continue those artistic traditions today, with a permanent 20th-century art collection and major exhibitions in our top-floor gallery. Outside, carpets of spring bulbs, a walled rose garden, rich autumn leaves and a colourful winter garden create a feast for the senses all year round. Our world-famous collection of old-fashioned roses flowers once a year in June. There's space to run, jump and play, and always something for families to do.

Eat, shop, stay: Old Kitchen in house serving hot meals on china. Coach House Café in Stables offering lighter lunches on eco-friendly disposable tableware. Ice-cream parlour, additional kiosk in good weather. Shop and plant centre at Welcome Centre, second-hand bookshop in Stables.

The walled rose garden at Mottisfont in Hampshire, below, is at its peak in June, while winter, bottom, brings different delights

Berkshire, Hampshire and the Isle of Wight

Mottisfont stands proudly on rolling lawns. Primarily an 18th-century exterior, the house has a medieval priory at its heart

Things to see and do: Indoors Five major exhibitions in the art gallery every year – this year includes Heath Robinson and the bi-annual Open Exhibition. Changing layers of interpretation around the house, telling stories of the Russell family. **Outdoors** Free daily guided walks and talks. Family activities, including seasonal activity trails in school holidays and wild play areas. Open-air theatre events in summer. Other seasonal events throughout the year. Seasonal variety in the gardens. Wider estate to explore on foot or by bike. **Dogs:** welcome on short leads at all times in most of grounds, with some restrictions.

Access: ⬛⬛⬛⬛⬛⬛⬛⬛⬛ **House** ⬛⬛
Gallery ⬛ **Grounds** ⬛➡⬛⬛
Sat Nav: use SO51 0LN. **Parking**: on site.

Find out more: 01794 340757 or mottisfont@nationaltrust.org.uk

Mottisfont	
Open every day all year	10–5*

*1 January to 4 February and 5 November to 31 December: closes 4. House and gallery: open at 11. House: closed for short period in November. Timed tickets may apply at certain times. Gallery: closed for short periods in between exhibitions. Gardens: late openings, Thursday to Saturday, 8 to 24 June (rose season). Everything closed 24 and 25 December.

Mottistone Gardens and Estate

Mottistone, near Brighstone,
Isle of Wight PO30 4ED

❄ ⚓ 🏛 🚻 1965

Set in a sheltered south-facing valley, these gardens are full of surprises, with shrub-filled banks, hidden pathways and colourful herbaceous borders. Surrounding an attractive manor house (tenanted, not open), these 20th-century gardens have a Mediterranean-style planting scheme to take advantage of its southerly location, including drought-tolerant plants from subtropical regions. Other features include a monocot border, a small organic kitchen garden and a traditional tea-garden alongside The Shack, a unique cabin retreat designed as their summer drawing office by architects John Seely (2nd Lord Mottistone) and Paul Paget. There are also delightful walks across the adjoining Mottistone Estate.
Note: manor house open two days a year.

Eat, shop, stay: shop selling gifts, books, cards, postcards and ice-cream. Plant sales. Second-hand books. Tea-garden serving hot and cold drinks, soup, sandwiches, cake, cream teas and light refreshments. Three holiday cottages nearby – Mottistone Manor Farmhouse, Longstone Cottage and Rose Cottage.

Things to see and do: family events and garden tours. Flowerpot trail and estate walks. Newtown Old Town Hall and National Nature Reserve and The Needles Batteries and Headland nearby. **Dogs**: welcome on leads in the gardens, under close control around livestock on the estate.

Access: 🅿 🔾 ♿ 🔆 🔾 🎦 🖥 🚽 🅿
The Shack 🦽🍴 Garden 🦽🔆➡🚻
Parking: 50 yards.

Find out more: 01983 741302 or mottistonegardens@nationaltrust.org.uk

Mottistone Gardens		M	T	W	T	F	S	S
Gardens and shop								
11 Mar–25 Oct	10:30–5	M	T	W	T	.	.	S
Shop								
1 Nov–22 Dec	11–3	.	.	.	T	F	S	

Estate: open every day all year. Gardens: close dusk if earlier. House: open two days only, 27 May by guided tour, 9:30 to 12 (timed ticket, available on day); free-flow 1 to 5, and 28 May, 10:30 to 5 by free-flow (additional charges apply).

Exploring the colourful herbaceous borders and terraces at Mottistone Gardens and Estate on the Isle of Wight

The Needles Batteries and Headland

West High Down, Alum Bay,
Isle of Wight PO39 0JH

🏠🐕♿🚗 1975

You can walk from Freshwater Bay to The Needles Headland along Tennyson Down for stunning views of the coast. Then, perched high above The Needles, amid acres of this unspoilt countryside, is The Needles Old Battery, a Victorian fortification built in 1862 and used throughout both world wars. The Parade Ground has two original guns, and the battery's fascinating military history is brought to life with displays and models, plus a series of vivid cartoons by acclaimed comic book artist Geoff Campion. An underground tunnel leads to a searchlight emplacement with dramatic views over The Needles rocks. The New Battery, further up the headland, has an exhibition on the secret British rocket tests carried out there during the Cold War.
Note: steep paths and uneven surfaces. Spiral staircase to tunnel. Toilet at Old Battery only.

Eat, shop, stay: clifftop 1940s-style tea-room serving soup, sandwiches, cakes, cream teas and light refreshments. Picnic tables. Gift shop selling ice-cream, confectionery and gifts. Drinks, snacks and ice-cream available at New Battery. You can stay at the Coastguard clifftop holiday cottages.

Things to see and do: **Indoors** Family activity packs. Soldier and photo trails. **Outdoors** Clifftop walks to Tennyson Monument and beyond. **Dogs**: welcome on leads, assistance dogs only in upstairs tea-room, all dogs welcome downstairs.

Access: [icons]
Old Battery [icons] **New Battery** [icon]
Parking: no parking on site (limited disabled parking by arrangement). Nearest at Alum Bay, ¾ mile, not National Trust (minimum charge £5.50). Freshwater Bay, 3½ miles (not National Trust), or Highdown (196:SZ325856) 2 miles.

Find out more: 01983 754772 or needles@nationaltrust.org.uk

The Needles Batteries and Headland on the Isle of Wight, this page and opposite, provide ample opportunities for walks and wildlife-spotting

The Needles		M	T	W	T	F	S	S
Old Battery and tea-room								
10 Mar–28 Oct	10:30–5	M	T	W	T	F	S	S
Old Battery tea-room								
6 Jan–4 Feb	11–3	·	·	·	·	·	S	S
10 Feb–25 Feb	11–3	M	T	W	T	F	S	S
3 Nov–16 Dec	11–3	·	·	·	·	·	S	S
New Battery								
10 Mar–28 Oct	11–4	M	T	W	T	F	S	S
Needles Headland								
Open all year		M	T	W	T	F	S	S

Needles Batteries: close dusk if earlier and in high winds.
13 May: no disabled vehicular access due to Walk the Wight.
7 July: Old Battery early opening for Round the Island yacht race.

New Forest Commons and Foxbury

near East Wellow, Hampshire

🏕 1928

Woodland, grassland, heathland, bogs and mires make up the unique landscape of the New Forest Commons, a wilderness that's teeming with wildlife. The National Trust looks after commons at the following places: Bramshaw, Foxbury, Hale Purlieu, Hightown, as well as Rockford and Ibsley. Foxbury, a gateway to the New Forest, is a 150-hectare (370-acre) area of heathland restoration. Wide open spaces, gentle hillsides and hidden ponds are there to be discovered in this recovering landscape. This is a fragile conservation site for wildlife and we only allow access for special seasonal events. **Note**: all chargeable entrance and event fees in Foxbury apply to members.

Things to see and do: programme of events throughout the year at Foxbury focusing on the site's rich wildlife, including seasonal bird walks, volunteer tree-planting and Forest School for young children. **Dogs**: on leads or under close control March to July (due to nesting birds).

Access: 🦽
Sat Nav: for Foxbury use SO51 6AQ and look out for the Omega signs; Bramshaw Commons SO51 6AQ; Hale Purlieu SP6 2QZ; Hightown Common BH24 3HH; Rockford and Ibsley Commons BH24 3NA. **Parking**: for Foxbury at Half Moon car park on Blackhill Road.

Find out more: 01425 650035 or newforest@nationaltrust.org.uk

New Forest Commons and Foxbury
For your safety we would not advise access to the New Forest between dusk and dawn. Foxbury is accessible for special seasonal events only.

Ponies enjoy the freedom of the unfenced open spaces in New Forest Commons, Hampshire, above

Newtown National Nature Reserve and Old Town Hall

Newtown, near Shalfleet,
Isle of Wight PO30 4PA

Wander past flower-filled hay meadows and through ancient woodlands filled with rare butterflies and red squirrels down to the picturesque harbour. Newtown is the only National Nature Reserve on the island, owned and managed by the National Trust since 1963. Tucked away in a tiny hamlet adjoining the National Nature Reserve is a small and quirky 17th-century building, the only remaining evidence of Newtown's former importance. Bought for and donated to the National Trust by Ferguson's Gang, a group of young people in the 1930s battling against the sprawling development of England. **Note**: nearest toilet in car park by the visitor point.

Newtown National Nature Reserve, below, and Old Town Hall, above, on the Isle of Wight

Eat, shop, stay: postcards, guidebooks, maps and souvenirs available at the Town Hall. Hot and cold drinks and walks leaflets available at the visitor point. New this year: holiday cottage (sleeps four) on the National Nature Reserve.

Things to see and do: **Indoors** Children's quiz sheet. Exhibitions by local artists. **Outdoors** National Nature Reserve walks. Bird hides. Family activities. Seasonal events. **Dogs**: under close control on National Nature Reserve (please observe local signs).

Access: ⬛♿⬛♿⬛⬛ Building ♿♿⬛
Parking: 15 yards.

Find out more: 01983 531785 (Old Town Hall). 01983 531622 (visitor point) or newtown@nationaltrust.org.uk

Newtown		M	T	W	T	F	S	S
Nature Reserve								
Open all year		M	T	W	T	F	S	S
Old Town Hall								
11 Mar–18 Oct	10:30–5	·	T	W	T	·	S	S
Bird hide								
11 Mar–18 Oct	10–4	M	T	W	T	F	S	S

Old Town Hall, last admission 15 minutes before closing. Closes dusk if earlier.

A boardwalk at Newtown National Nature Reserve

St Helens Duver

near St Helens, Isle of Wight

🏛️🚗 1928

As well as inland walks and wildlife, St Helens Duver, Isle of Wight, offers beaches and glorious sea views

Sandy beaches, rock pools, sand dunes and coastal woods. The Duver itself was a Victorian golf course with royal patronage – evident from its short turf and undulating ground. Today, it's a fascinating place to look for wildlife, from burrowing digger wasps to wasp spiders and waterbirds over the harbour. **Note**: no toilets.

Eat, shop, stay: why not stay for longer at one of two charming holiday cottages close to the Duver? Old Church Lodge, a single-storey Victorian stone cottage sleeps four, while the Old Club House, an attractive wooden chalet overlooking the Duver, sleeps five.

Things to see and do: great spot for relaxing on the beach, exploring rock pools, admiring spring flowers or birdwatching across the harbour. You can take a coastal walk, or walk to Bembridge Windmill. **Dogs**: welcome under close control.

Access: 🔾
Sat Nav: use PO33 1XY. **Parking**: on site.

Find out more: 01983 741020 or sthelensduver@nationaltrust.org.uk

Sandham Memorial Chapel

Harts Lane, Burghclere, near Newbury, Hampshire RG20 9JT

✚ ❀ 1947

Lose yourself in Stanley Spencer's extraordinarily powerful paintings, recollecting his First World War service as a medical orderly and soldier, housed within this tranquil space. An exhibition area gives historical context before you enter the Chapel, while the garden is somewhere to pause and reflect afterwards or perhaps to picnic.

Tranquil Sandham Memorial Chapel, Hampshire

Inside the chapel, Stanley Spencer's powerful paintings recall his experiences during the First World War

Eat, shop, stay: small shop selling books, postcards, plants and local products. Picnics welcome.

Things to see and do: exhibition about the Chapel, paintings and the people who were instrumental in its creation. Orchard, beautiful wildflower meadow and new garden of reflection to explore. Events throughout the year. **Dogs**: in grounds on leads only.

Access: 🅿♿👁🔾📷📹🎫👓🅿 Chapel ♿
Visitor reception/exhibition ♿ Grounds ♿♿➡
Parking: opposite entrance to chapel.

Find out more: 01635 278394 or sandham@nationaltrust.org.uk

Sandham Memorial Chapel		M	T	W	T	F	S	S
1 Mar–28 Oct*	11–4			W	T	F	S	S
2 Nov–16 Dec	11–3					F	S	S

*2 June to 26 August open to 5, weekends only. Open Bank Holiday Mondays, 11 to 4. Car park opposite chapel available during normal opening hours, locked 15 minutes after closing. Chapel may be closed on certain days due to rehearsals for special events (please check before visiting).

The Vyne

Vyne Road, Sherborne St John, Basingstoke, Hampshire RG24 9HL

🏠➕♿✳♿🐕☂ 1956

In the early part of this year the major conservation project to repair the roof will be completed. Later we will be putting all the furniture back and opening the first floor again, so this is an ideal time to come and see how the property has been re-presented. Outside, acres of wildlife-rich gardens, meadows and woods create a wonderful space for relaxation

and exploration, while the play space gives children freedom to let their imagination take them on fantasy adventures. Sweeping lawns offer lakeside picnicking, and a short stroll reveals a cosy bird hide overlooking the water meadows.

Eat, shop, stay: tea-room serving light lunches, soup, sandwiches, cakes and scones. Gift shop and plant sales. Second-hand bookshops in house and garden. Picnics welcome.

Things to see and do: **Indoors** Events and activities all year. Free guided tours. **Outdoors** Open-air theatre. Garden tours, trails and woodland walks. **Dogs**: welcome on short leads in woodlands and most of gardens.

Access: 🅿♿♿♿♿♿🎦🎦📷📷:♿📷
House ♿🎦♿ **Grounds** ♿♿♿➡♿
Sat Nav: not reliable, follow brown tourist signs. **Parking**: on site, limited in winter (October to April) due to ground conditions.

Find out more: 01256 883858 or thevyne@nationaltrust.org.uk

The Vyne	
Open every day all year	10–5*

*1 January to 4 February and 5 November to 31 December: closes 4. House: opens 11 for visit by tour or timed ticket (telephone for details). Shop: opens 11. Last entry one hour before closing. Closed 24 and 25 December.

The Vyne in Hampshire sits beside a stately lake, above, and offers a boardwalk and bird hide, left, overlooking wildlife-rich water meadows

West Green House Garden

West Green, Hartley Wintney,
Hampshire RG27 8JB

[⌘] [1957]

Four seasons of beauty, contrast and
inspiration. Created by acclaimed garden
designer and writer Marylyn Abbott.
Note: maintained on behalf of the National
Trust by Marylyn Abbott. Facilities not
National Trust. Open Wednesday to Sunday,
7 March to 28 October, 11 to 4:30, 14 to
30 November, 11 to 4, and 1 to 23 December,
11 to 7. Also open Bank Holiday Mondays.

Find out more: 01252 844611 or
westgreenhouse@nationaltrust.org.uk

Winchester City Mill

Bridge Street, Winchester,
Hampshire SO23 9BH

[⌘] [⌘] [T] [1929]

This restored working watermill has stood at the
heart of the city of Winchester for a millennium
and is probably the oldest working watermill in
the UK. As the official Gateway to the South
Downs National Park, City Mill provides
information for visitors wishing to explore
local walks and attractions. **Note**: nearest
toilet 220 yards (not National Trust).

Eat, shop, stay: shop selling local produce,
gifts and books, as well as our freshly milled
wholemeal flour.

Things to see and do: tours, workshops and
exhibitions. School holiday quizzes and trails
and seasonal events for the whole family,
including Easter Egg hunts. Flour-milling
demonstrations every weekend and regular
baking demonstrations. **Dogs**: assistance
dogs only.

Access: [icons] Building [icon]
Sat Nav: do not use. **Parking**: at Chesil car
park or park and ride, neither National Trust
(charge including members).

Find out more: 01962 870057 or
winchestercitymill@nationaltrust.org.uk

Winchester City Mill		M	T	W	T	F	S	S
1 Jan–24 Dec	10–5*	**M**	**T**	**W**	**T**	**F**	**S**	**S**

*1 January to 4 February and 29 October to 24 December:
closes 4.

Winchester City Mill, Hampshire, spans the River Itchen

Kent, Surrey and Sussex

Birling Gap and the Seven Sisters, East Sussex

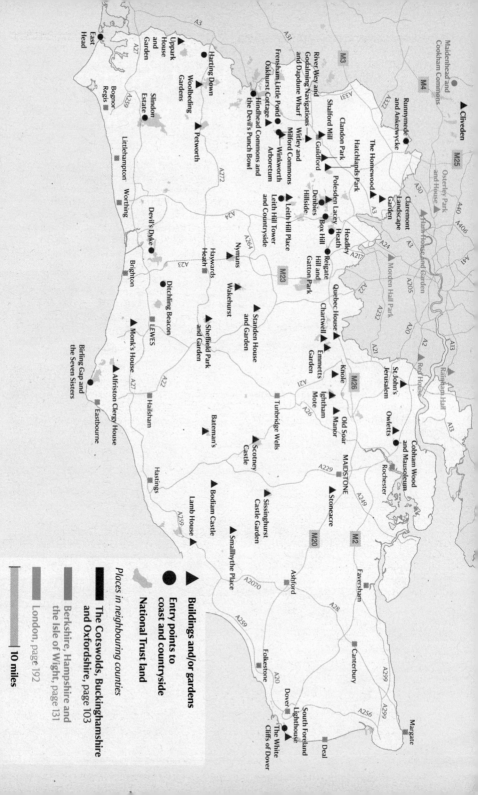

East Head

▲ Cliveden

Maidenhead and Cookham Commons

M4

M25

Osterley Park and House

A40

A41

Ham House and Garden

A406

A3

A31

M3

A322

A331

Runnymede and Ankerwycke

A30

A3

Morden Hall Park

A205

A232

A21

Red House

Rainham Hall

A13

A2

Uppark House and Garden

Woolbeding Gardens

Harting Down

Slindon Estate

River Wey and Godalming Navigations and Dapdune Wharf

Frensham Little Pond

Oakhurst Cottage

Hindhead Commons and the Devil's Punch Bowl

Shalford Mill

Witley and Milford Commons

Winkworth Arboretum

Clandon Park

Hatchlands Park

Guildford

Polesden Lacey

Denbies Hillside

Leith Hill Place

Box Hill

Leith Hill Tower and Countryside

The Homewood

Claremont Landscape Garden

Headley Heath

Reigate Hill and Gatton Park

Quebec House

Chartwell

Emmetts Garden

Ightham Mote

Knole

St John's Jerusalem

Owletts

Cobham Wood and Mausoleum

Rochester

Old Soar Manor

M26

Petworth

Littlehampton

Bognor Regis

Worthing

Devil's Dyke

Brighton

Hayward's Heath

Nymans

Wakehurst

Ditchling Beacon

LEWES

Standen House and Garden

Sheffield Park and Garden

Monk's House

Alfriston Clergy House

Birling Gap and the Seven Sisters

Eastbourne

Hailsham

Hastings

Batemans

Scotney Castle

Tunbridge Wells

Lamb House

Bodiam Castle

Sissinghurst Castle Garden

Smallhythe Place

Stoneacre

MAIDSTONE

M20

M2

Ashford

Faversham

Canterbury

Folkestone

Dover

Deal

Margate

South Foreland Lighthouse

The White Cliffs of Dover

A2070

A28

A299

A20

A256

A259

A229

A26

A21

A24

A217

A23

A272

A264

A24

A27

A259

A283

A22

Places in neighbouring counties

▲ Buildings and/or gardens

● Entry points to coast and countryside

National Trust land

The Cotswolds, Buckinghamshire and Oxfordshire, page 103

Berkshire, Hampshire and the Isle of Wight, page 131

London, page 192

10 miles

Alfriston Clergy House

The Tye, Alfriston, Polegate,
East Sussex BN26 5TL

 1896

Alfriston Clergy House in East Sussex

This rare 14th-century Wealden 'hall-house' was the first building to be acquired by the National Trust, in 1896. The thatched, timber-framed house is in an idyllic setting, with views across the River Cuckmere, and is surrounded by a tranquil cottage garden full of wildlife. **Note**: nearest toilet in village car park.

Eat, shop, stay: shop selling souvenirs, plants and gifts.

Things to see and do: **Indoors** Children's quizzes and trails. Varied events all year. **Outdoors** Short circular walks and longer hikes over the South Downs. **Dogs**: assistance dogs only.

Access: ⬚⬚⬚⬚⬚ Building ⬚⬚
Grounds ⬚⬚
Parking: 500 yards in village car parks (not National Trust).

Find out more: 01323 871961 or
alfriston@nationaltrust.org.uk

Alfriston Clergy House		M	T	W	T	F	S	S
3 Mar–4 Jul	10:30–5	M	T	W	·	·	S	S
6 Jul–29 Jul	10:30–5	M	T	W	·	F	S	S
30 Jul–31 Oct	10:30–5	M	T	W	·	·	S	S
3 Nov–16 Dec	11–4	·	·	·	·	·	S	S
Open Good Friday.								

Bateman's

Bateman's Lane, Burwash,
East Sussex TN19 7DS

⬚⬚⬚⬚⬚ 1940

Bateman's remains today as Kipling described it in 1902: 'A grey stone lichened house – AD 1634 over the door – beamed, panelled, with oak staircase all untouched and unfaked… It is a good and peaceable place, standing in terraced lawns nigh to a walled garden of old red brick and two fat-headed old oast houses with red brick stomachs and an aged silver-grey dovecot [*sic*] on top.' Much of Kipling's belongings remain as he left them. Paths wind through manicured lawns, a wildflower meadow and past Kipling's 1928 Rolls-Royce. A 17th-century working watermill stands beside the River Dudwell.

Rudyard Kipling's Bateman's in East Sussex

Bateman's remains much as Kipling left it

Eat, shop, stay: shop selling Kipling souvenirs and plants from the garden. Scullery bookshop specialising in pre-loved classic story books. Tea-room offering seasonal lunches, made using fresh produce from our kitchen garden, homemade cakes and light bites. Open-air seating in walled garden.

Things to see and do: **Indoors** Explore the house as Kipling left it. See where he set many of his best-known works. Seasonal talks and tours.

Outdoors Walks, trails and storytelling all year round. **Dogs**: welcome in the gardens on a short lead.

Access:
Building **Grounds**
Parking: 30 yards.

Find out more: 01435 882302 or batemans@nationaltrust.org.uk

Bateman's		M	T	W	T	F	S	S
House								
1 Jan–2 Mar*	11–4	M	T	W	T	F	S	S
3 Mar–28 Oct	11–5	M	T	W	T	F	S	S
29 Oct–31 Dec*	11–4	M	T	W	T	F	S	S
Garden, shop and tea-room								
Open all year	10–5**	M	T	W	T	F	S	S

*3 January to 2 March and 29 October to 30 November: entry to house on weekdays by guided tour only. **1 January to 4 February and 29 October to 31 December: closes 4. Closed 24 and 25 December.

Birling Gap and the Seven Sisters

near Eastbourne, East Sussex

1931

For drama, nothing beats the point where the sheer chalk cliffs of the South Downs meet the sea. One of the south coast's longest undeveloped stretches, the Seven Sisters are truly iconic. If you venture down the steps onto the beach, you can discover fascinating rock pools and the intricate wave-cut platform. The visitor centre, with its café and shop, is a delightful place to start or end your peaceful downland walk. Before you explore the rare chalk heath and grassland, why not pick up a Tracker Pack or get some friendly advice from a volunteer in the visitor centre?

Eat, shop, stay: licensed clifftop café serving hot and cold drinks, bottled beer and wine, light lunches, cream teas and cakes. Drinks and

sandwiches available to take away.
Seaside shop selling gifts and seasonal
items. Picnic area outside shop.

Things to see and do: **Indoors** Visitor centre.
Outdoors Rock-pooling, countryside walks and
stargazing. Crowlink downland, on top of the
Seven Sisters, Alfriston Clergy House and
Monk's House nearby. Events and activities for
all ages. **Dogs**: welcome, on leads in café, shop,
visitor centre and beach or near livestock.

Access: P🅿🅿🅿🅿🅿🅿 **Café** 🅿
Shop 🅿 **Beach** 🅿
Sat Nav: use BN20 0AB.
Parking: at Birling Gap.

Find out more: 01323 423197 or
birlinggap@nationaltrust.org.uk

Birling Gap and the Seven Sisters	
Café and shop	
Open every day all year†	10–5*

*1 January to 10 February and 29 October to 31 December:
closed 4. †Closed 24 and 25 December.

**The Seven Sisters provide a dramatic backdrop
to the beach at Birling Gap, East Sussex**

Bodiam Castle

Bodiam, near Robertsbridge,
East Sussex TN32 5UA

🅿🅿🅿🅿 1926

Bodiam Castle in East Sussex: brooding symbol of power

A brooding symbol of power for over 700
years, the strong stone walls of Bodiam Castle
rise up proudly from the peaceful river valley
setting. A wide moat encircles the seemingly
untouched medieval exterior. Once inside,
spiral stairways, tower rooms and battlements
with dizzying viewpoints are ripe for
exploration. **Note**: popular with schools.
Toilets in car park only.

Eat, shop, stay: shop selling gifts, castle-
themed products and local produce.
Tea-room serving homemade lunches,
teas, snacks and ice-cream.

The strong stone medieval walls of Bodiam Castle

Things to see and do: Indoors Story of Bodiam film and exhibition. Conservation programme revealing Bodiam's hidden collection. **Outdoors** Trails and guided walks. Events, including Easter Egg hunt and various family activities throughout the year. **Dogs**: welcome on leads in grounds only.

Access: ⯊🅿️♿🖼️♿♿♿📷💻🚻📷🔋🅰️ Castle ♿♿♿♿ Grounds ➡️♿
Parking: 400 yards.

Find out more: 01580 830196 or bodiamcastle@nationaltrust.org.uk

Bodiam Castle								
Castle								
1 Jan–2 Mar*	11–4	M	T	W	T	F	S	S
3 Mar–28 Oct	11–5	M	T	W	T	F	S	S
29 Oct–30 Nov*	11–4	M	T	W	T	F	S	S
1 Dec–31 Dec	11–4	M	T	W	T	F	S	S
Shop, tea-room and grounds								
Open all year**	10–5	M	T	W	T	F	S	S

*3 January to 2 March and 29 October to 30 November: entry to castle on weekdays by guided tour only. **1 January to 4 February and 29 October to 31 December: close 4. Closed 24 and 25 December.

Box Hill

Tadworth, Surrey

♿ 1914

A great place for family adventures: exploring the woods, braving the natural play trail, finding the tower or paddling in the River Mole at the stepping stones. On a clear day you can see for miles from the top of Box Hill, so if you're hiking up, the view is well worth it. You can pick up free walks guides from the shepherd's hut and outside the café, or find your own way along our many footpaths.

Eat, shop, stay: the Box Hill café has indoor and outdoor seating and serves light lunches, snacks, sandwiches and cakes. The servery offers takeaway hot drinks, sandwiches and cakes as well as the famous 'revival' flapjack!

Things to see and do: school holiday activities and walks guides available. You can borrow a children's Tracker Pack from the shepherd's hut to explore the wild and make the most of the outdoors. **Dogs**: under close control where livestock is grazing. Assistance dogs only in café.

Access: Café Grounds
Sat Nav: use KT20 7LB. **Parking**: off the Box Hill Zig Zag road (short walk to café and viewpoint).

Find out more: 01306 888793. 01306 878554 (learning and events) or boxhill@nationaltrust.org.uk

Box Hill	
Café	
Open every day all year	10–5*

*1 January to 4 February and 29 October to 31 December: closes 4. Closed 25 December.

Stepping Stones cross the River Mole at Box Hill, Surrey

Chartwell

Mapleton Road, Westerham, Kent TN16 1PS

1946

Chartwell, Kent: Clementine and Winston Churchill

Chartwell was a home and a place that truly inspired Sir Winston Churchill. The house is still much as it was when the family lived here, with pictures, books, gifts from around the world and personal mementoes. The studio contains the largest collection of Churchill's paintings and offers an insight into Churchill the painter, while the garden reflects Churchill's love of the landscape and nature, including the lakes he created. The woodland estate offers family walks, trails, den-building, swings and see-saws, a Canadian camp and opportunities to stretch your legs. You may come across our resident cat, Jock, making his daily inspection of the grounds. **Note**: house entrance by timed ticket (available on website). Chartwell can be challenging for less able.

Eat, shop, stay: café serving food inspired by Churchill's family cook – salads, light bites, cream teas, cakes and delicious desserts. Shop stocking Churchill memorabilia, books, ranges for the home and garden, plants and a special range of Jock the Cat items.

As well as being his home, Chartwell, above and right, inspired Winston Churchill and offered him an escape from heavy affairs of state

Things to see and do: Indoors Daily talks in the studio about Sir Winston's love of painting. New exhibition in winter displaying never-seen-before items. **Outdoors** New this year is the treehouse in the woods, similar to the treehouse Churchill built for his children. Guided tours of Churchill's family garden on selected days (March to October). The woodland trail offers great views of the house and connects with the hilly five-mile circular Weardale Walk to Emmetts Garden. Why not pick up some takeaway food from the Landemare Café and enjoy a picnic on the lower lawns by the lakes? **Dogs**: welcome on short leads in the garden and estate.

Access: 🅿️ 👕 🦽 🚐 🔊 📷 💻 🍽️ 🎧 👶 📱
Building 👟 🦽 🍽️ 👶 👥 Grounds 👟 🦽 👶
Parking: on site.

Find out more: 01732 868381 or chartwell@nationaltrust.org.uk

Chartwell		M	T	W	T	F	S	S
House								
24 Feb–28 Oct	11:30–5*	M	T	W	T	F	S	S
1 Dec–16 Dec	11–3	·	·	·	·	·	S	S
Garden, exhibition, studio, shop and café								
Open all year	10–5**	M	T	W	T	F	S	S

*House: entry by timed ticket (places limited) available from visitor welcome centre or 24 hours in advance via website or by calling 0344 249 1895. Last entry 50 minutes before closing. **1 January to 4 February and 29 October to 31 December: closes 4. Studio open times vary. Exhibition closes for short periods to change display. Whole site closed 24 and 25 December.

Clandon Park

West Clandon, Guildford, Surrey GU4 7RQ

🏛️🌼 1956

Clandon Park is the Trust's biggest restoration project in a generation, breathing new life into this Palladian marvel. **Note**: major restoration project under way. Access to the house and garden will continue to be possible for much of the year. Please check the website for the latest information on opening arrangements.

Find out more: 01483 222482 or clandonpark@nationaltrust.org.uk

Claremont Landscape Garden

Portsmouth Road, Esher, Surrey KT10 9JG

🌼 1949

Hidden in the heart of Surrey, this green oasis has always been a place to escape everyday life and enjoy simple pleasures. Formerly a sanctuary for some of the wealthiest and most influential people in the country, now everyone can enjoy this 'Capability' Brown landscape garden. The impressive turf amphitheatre offers wonderful views over the lake, and walks

Claremont Landscape Garden in Surrey: green oasis

The lake at Claremont Landscape Garden

take in key features such as the grotto and camellia terrace. Queen Victoria loved relaxing here from a young age, and the tradition of play continues today with nine-pin bowling, play areas and a cottage full of toys and games.

Eat, shop, stay: café (licensed) serving lunches and freshly baked cakes, biscuits and scones. Outside terraced seating area overlooking lake. Café is outside the pay barrier and close to the car park at the main entrance. Shop area within café. Free Wi-Fi.

Things to see and do: events throughout the year, including children's trails and crafts during school holidays. Guided walks. Belvedere Tower open on selected dates (April to October). Boat hire, subject to availability. **Dogs**: welcome on short leads between 1 October and 30 April only.

Access: 🅿️♿️🐕📷⬇️⬛🖊️ Grounds 🅿️➡️♿️ **Sat Nav**: unreliable; instead follow brown signs from Cobham and Esher. **Parking**: main car park at entrance. Space limited at busy times – please use car park in West End Lane opposite.

Find out more: 01372 467806 or claremont@nationaltrust.org.uk

Claremont Landscape Garden		M	T	W	T	F	S	S
1 Jan–31 Jan	10–4	M	T	W	T	F	S	S
1 Feb–25 Mar	10–5	M	T	W	T	F	S	S
26 Mar–28 Oct	10–6	M	T	W	T	F	S	S
29 Oct–31 Dec	10–4*	M	T	W	T	F	S	S

Café and shop close 30 minutes earlier than garden.
*Closed 24 and 25 December.

Cobham Wood and Mausoleum

near Cobham, Kent

🏠♿️ 2014

Sitting proud in historic woodland pasture, the 18th-century Darnley Mausoleum commands stunning views across the North Kent downs. **Note**: for Sat Nav use DA12 3BS. Mausoleum and South Lodge Barn normally open first Sunday of month, April to September, and selected other dates. Mausoleum open 12:30 to 4:30; South Lodge Barn 12 to 5.

Find out more: 01732 810378 or cobham@nationaltrust.org.uk

Denbies Hillside

near Dorking, Surrey

♿️ 1963

Denbies Hillside is a dramatic chalk escarpment with panoramic views of the Surrey countryside. It's a great place to walk, picnic and watch wildlife – you may even spot chalk downland species such as the Adonis blue and chalkhill blue butterflies.

Eat, shop, stay: picnic area with benches in Steers Field.

Denbies Hillside, Surrey: a dramatic chalk escarpment

Things to see and do: self-guided trail and spectacular views. Walk west along the North Downs Way to discover several Second World War pillboxes. Why not also visit nearby Hackhurst Downs? **Dogs**: welcome – please keep on leads when livestock are grazing.

Access:
Sat Nav: use RH5 6SR. **Parking**: at Ranmore West car park and Denbies Hillside.

Find out more: 01306 887485 or denbieshillside@nationaltrust.org.uk

Devil's Dyke

near Brighton, West Sussex

🛡️🏛️💺 1995

At nearly a mile long, the Dyke Valley is the longest, deepest and widest 'dry valley' in the UK. Legend has it that the Devil dug this chasm to drown the parishioners of the Weald. On the other hand, scientists believe it was formed naturally just over 10,000 years ago in the last ice age. The walls of the Iron Age hill fort can be seen when you walk around the hill, and there is a carpet of flowers and a myriad of colourful insects to discover in the valley.

Eat, shop, stay: Devil's Dyke pub (not National Trust) beside car park.

Things to see and do: self-guided walks leaflet, orienteering course map and family Discovery Packs available from information trailer (open April to September, weekends and some weekdays). Numerous bridleways offer great cycling.

Access: 🅿️🅿️♿🚻🚻♿➡️
Sat Nav: use BN1 8YJ. **Parking**: on site.

Find out more: 01273 857712 or devilsdyke@nationaltrust.org.uk

Devil's Dyke in West Sussex was formed during the last ice age

Ditchling Beacon near Brighton: the highest point in East Sussex

Ditchling Beacon

near Ditchling, Westmeston, East Sussex

 1953

Just 7 miles north of Brighton, at 248 metres above sea level, Ditchling Beacon is the highest point in East Sussex and offers panoramic views all around the summit. To the south visitors can see the sea, while to the north you look across the Weald or east–west across the Downs. The site also has the remains of an Iron Age hill fort. Situated on the South Downs Way, it makes an excellent place to start a walk heading west towards Devil's Dyke or east towards Black Cap and Lewes.

Eat, shop, stay: refreshments available from ice-cream van. Picnics welcome.

Things to see and do: great for bracing walks with amazing views on the South Downs. Traces of the rampart and ditch of the hill fort to discover. Why not visit nearby Ditchling Down? **Dogs**: welcome but must be kept on leads at all times.

Access: [Pd] [⚐]
Sat Nav: use BN6 8XG.
Parking: off Ditchling Road.

Find out more: 01323 423197 or ditchlingbeacon@nationaltrust.org.uk

East Head

near Chichester, West Sussex

 1966

One of the last surviving areas of natural coastline in West Sussex, with unspoilt sand dunes and fabulous views. **Note**: for Sat Nav use PO20 8AJ. Park at West Wittering Estate car park (not National Trust), charge including members.

Find out more: 01243 814730 or easthead@nationaltrust.org.uk

Emmetts Garden

Ide Hill, Sevenoaks, Kent TN14 6BA

1965

Emmetts is a garden to enjoy with friends and family. If you delve a little deeper, there are exotic plants collected from around the world and a host of stories to be discovered. Emmetts is known for its beautiful bluebells and spring colour, summer brings the romantic rose garden, followed by vibrant autumn foliage. It is a place where you can play games, picnic in our meadow or simply sit back and relax. Far-reaching views across the Weald of Kent can be enjoyed from the countryside walks. **Note**: restoration work under way in some areas of the garden this year.

Eat, shop, stay: the Old Stables serving cakes, bakes and light refreshments. Shop selling a variety of products for the home, garden and outdoors, books, souvenirs and children's toys. Venture outside to the plant area for an array of plants and garden products.

Things to see and do: **Indoors** Children's activities in the Discovery Cabin. **Outdoors** Children's trails (school holidays and December). Wild play area, including swings and a tepee. Garden tours. Walks available for surrounding countryside. **Dogs**: welcome on short leads in gardens and in the wider countryside.

Access: 🅿️🚐♿🚾👶🔊🚶♿ Grounds ♿➡️♿
Parking: 100 yards.

Find out more: 01732 751507 or emmetts@nationaltrust.org.uk

Emmetts Garden		M	T	W	T	F	S	S
10 Feb–31 Dec	10–5*	M	T	W	T	F	S	S

*Last entry 45 minutes before closing. 29 October to 31 December: closes 4. Closed 24 and 25 December.

Beautiful all year, Emmetts Garden in Kent is filled with exotic treasures

Frensham Little Pond

Priory Lane, Frensham, Surrey GU10 3BT

 1974

Frensham Little Pond, Surrey: a sanctuary for wildlife

Originally created in the 11th century to supply the Bishop of Winchester with fish, the pond and surrounding area is now a sanctuary for wildlife. The heathland is a colourful mosaic of purple heathers, fragrant bright-yellow gorse and rich green bracken with many footpaths to explore. **Note**: toilet available only when café open.

Eat, shop, stay: Tern Café serving snacks, homemade sandwiches and cakes (outside seating only). Picnics welcome (no barbecues please).

Things to see and do: bird hide and telescope next to café. **Dogs**: on leads from March to September and around café; no swimming in pond please.

Access: 🗘
Parking: at Priory Lane corner, Frensham and Grange Road.

Find out more: 01428 681050 (Rangers) or frenshamlittlepond@nationaltrust.org.uk

Frensham Little Pond		M	T	W	T	F	S	S
Café								
5 Jan–25 Mar	10–3*					F	S	S
26 Mar–28 Oct	10–5	M	T	W	T	F	S	S
2 Nov–30 Dec	10–3**					F	S	S

*12 to 18 February: open daily, 10 to 3. **Closed 24 and 25 December.

Harting Down

Harting Down, near South Harting, West Sussex GU31 5PN

📷 1994

A tapestry of downland with scattered scrub and woodland, rich in wildlife and steeped in history. **Note**: nearest toilets at South Harting or Uppark. Sat Nav unreliable.

Find out more: 01730 816638 or hartingdown@nationaltrust.org.uk

Hatchlands Park

East Clandon, Guildford, Surrey GU4 7RT

🏛️ ✻ 📷 1945

With open fields, ancient woodland and wildflower meadows, the parkland is perfect for relaxation and exploration. Our natural adventure area, with its tree house, balance beams, willow tunnels and bug hotel, is a great place for families to get even closer to nature. Nestled in the parkland is a Georgian country house, built for naval hero Admiral Boscawen and his spirited wife Fanny. The interior at

Why not share your pictures with us? #nationaltrust

Hatchlands Park is the earliest documented work in an English country house by celebrated Neo-classical architect Robert Adam. **Note**: only six ground-floor rooms open.

Eat, shop, stay: café in the original kitchen. Gift shop. Picnic areas.

Things to see and do: **Indoors** Guided mansion tours most Thursdays. Cellar tours (selected days). **Outdoors** Children's adventure area, courtyard garden and open-air theatre. **Dogs**: welcome under close control in designated areas. Dog-friendly Coach House Café.

Access: ⓟ♿🏠♿👶♿📷🚗🅿💷♿
Building 🔥♿🔥 **Grounds** 🔥➡♿
Sat Nav: misleading, instead follow brown signs to main entrance on A246 (grid reference TQ06349 51580). **Parking**: 300 yards.

Find out more: 01483 222482 or hatchlands@nationaltrust.org.uk

Hatchlands Park		M	T	W	T	F	S	S
House and garden								
1 Apr–28 Oct*	2–5†		T	W	T			S
Shop, café and park walks								
Open all year	10–5††	M	T	W	T	F	S	S

*Also open Bank Holiday Mondays and Fridays in August.
†Garden: open 10 to 5 on house open days. ††1 January to 4 February and 5 November to 31 December: closes 4. Closed 24 and 25 December.

The parkland at Hatchlands Park in Surrey is perfect for relaxation and exploration

Headley Heath

Headley Common Road, Headley Heath, Surrey KT18 6NN

 1946

With a wide network of tracks to explore and stunning views, Headley Heath is a perfect piece of countryside. **Note**: cattle grazing (please look out for notices and keep dogs on leads when nearby).

Find out more: 01306 885502 (Rangers) or headleyheath@nationaltrust.org.uk

Hindhead Commons and the Devil's Punch Bowl

near Hindhead, Surrey

 1906

Spectacular views from Hindhead Commons and uninterrupted walks to the Devil's Punch Bowl make this an unforgettable place to relax and take in some of the best countryside in the South East. Since the opening of the A3 tunnel, paths and bridleways have been reconnected and natural contours restored. Peace and calm now reign and the glorious landscape, with its carpets of purple heather in the summer and grazing Highland cattle, is there to enjoy. **Note**: renovation works to our café and car park are expected during the year.

Eat, shop, stay: café with indoor and outdoor seating, serving drinks, hot food, sandwiches and cakes.

Things to see and do: walks leaflets available from the café and shepherd's hut. Borrow a children's Tracker Pack at weekends to explore the wild and make the most of your visit. **Dogs**: under close control during bird-nesting season (March to October). Assistance dogs only in café.

Hindhead Commons and the Devil's Punchbowl, Surrey

Access: 🅿️ 🐕 ♿ 🚻 ⛰️
Café and shop 🔗 **Grounds** ➡️
Sat Nav: use GU26 6AB. **Parking:** off the London Road.

Find out more: 01428 681050 (Rangers). 01428 608771 (café) or hindhead@nationaltrust.org.uk

Hindhead Commons	
Café	
Open every day all year*	9–5**

*Closed 25 December. **1 January to 4 February and 29 October to 31 December: closes 4.

The Homewood

Portsmouth Road, Esher, Surrey KT10 9JL

🏠 ❋ 1999

Patrick Gwynne's extraordinary early 20th-century family home is a masterpiece of Modernist design in the midst of a picturesque garden. **Note:** administered on behalf of the National Trust by tenant. **Access by booked tour only, via minibus from Claremont Landscape Garden.** Toilets and café at Claremont. Additional charge for minibus and guided tour (including members). Usually open first and third Friday and the second and fourth Saturday of every month, 1 April to 31 October. 45-minute guided tours at 10:30, 11:30, 12:30, 2 and 3. Entry by booked tours only (call to book).

Find out more: 01372 476424 or thehomewood@nationaltrust.org.uk
c/o Claremont Landscape Garden, Portsmouth Road, Esher, Surrey KT10 9JG

Ightham Mote

Mote Road, Ivy Hatch, Sevenoaks, Kent TN15 0NT

🏠 ❋ 🐕 🛏️ 🍽️ 1985

Hidden away in a secluded Kent valley is this perfectly preserved medieval moated manor house. Created in the natural landscape almost 700 years ago, Ightham Mote is built from Kentish ragstone and great Wealden oaks. While its architecture and decoration trace the development of the English country house, its owners provide the stories of a once-cherished family home, evoking a deep sense of history. In the tranquil gardens there are streams and lakes fed by natural springs, an orchard, flower borders and a cutting garden. The wider estate offers walks with secret glades and countryside views. **Note:** very steep slope from visitor reception – passenger buggy or lower drop-off available.

Eat, shop, stay: Mote café (licensed) serving hot lunches, sandwiches, cream teas, cakes and

hot and cold drinks. Seating indoors and outside. Picnic facilities available. Shop selling gifts, local produce and plants.

Things to see and do: **Indoors** Year-round events, including introductory talks and tower tours, housekeeping events and family craft days. **Outdoors** Countryside walks and family fun days. Children's natural play area and den. **Dogs**: welcome on café patio and unticketed areas; assistance dogs only in ticketed areas.

Access: 🅿♿♿♿♿♿🅿🖥🎦🅿⚠🅿
Building 🅿🅿🅿🅿🅿 Grounds 🅿➡
Parking: 200 yards.

Find out more: 01732 810378 or ighthammote@nationaltrust.org.uk

Ightham Mote		M	T	W	T	F	S	S
House								
3 Mar–28 Oct	11–5	M	T	W	T	F	S	S
1 Dec–31 Dec*	11–3	M	T	W	T	F	S	S
Garden, café, exhibition and shop								
Open all year	10–5**	M	T	W	T	F	S	S

Estate open all year. *Partial access to house and grounds in winter. **1 January to 4 February and 29 October to 31 December: close 4. Closed 24 and 25 December.

Ightham Mote, Kent, rises from its mirror-like moat

Knole

Sevenoaks, Kent TN15 0RP

🏠🌸🅿 1946

Sitting proudly within Kent's last medieval deer-park, Knole offers something for everyone. Immerse yourself in the vast estate and follow in the footsteps of tourists who have visited Knole's show rooms for 400 years, where a world-class collection of paintings and furniture awaits. Spend the day and take in panoramic views from the top of the Gatehouse Tower, where you can also explore the life and loves of a former resident. If you only have an hour, take in the scale and magnificence of this 600-year-old estate by exploring the grand courtyards and tranquil Orangery. Find out how our conservators care for Knole's treasures in the conservation studio or wander the parkland, still populated by wild deer. **Note**: due to conservation work in show rooms, some rooms are closed.

A conservator hard at work at Knole in Kent

Eat, shop, stay: Brewhouse Café serving delicious hot and cold food, with outdoor seating available on the beautiful roof terrace. Enclosed picnic area in park. Gift shop, plant sales, and bookshop with children's area.

Things to see and do: **Indoors** Explore the vast property, including the atmospheric courtyards, Orangery, historic show rooms and tower. Discover Knole's stories in the Estate Office or dress in Tudor costume in the Visitor Centre. Join a highlights tour in the show rooms from Tuesday to Sunday (subject to availability). We also have an exciting programme of events all year. **Outdoors** Join a park walk or bat-spotting event to explore our ancient parkland, still home to a herd of wild deer. Geocache trail in the park. Special entry to Lord Sackville's private garden (Tuesdays, 3 April to 25 September). **Dogs**: welcome in parkland/courtyards on leads. Assistance dogs only in garden, tower, show rooms.

Access:
Show rooms 🦽🚹 Gatehouse Tower 🦽🚹
Park/garden 🦽♿➡🚻♿

Sat Nav: use TN13 1HU and follow brown signs to Sevenoaks High Street (concealed entrance opposite St Nicholas Church). **Parking:** 60 yards. Additional parking in town centre.

Find out more: 01732 462100 or knole@nationaltrust.org.uk

Knole		M	T	W	T	F	S	S
Show rooms								
27 Mar–4 Nov*	12-4		T	W	T	F	S	S
Tower, café, courtyards, shop, parkland								
Open all year	10-5**	M	T	W	T	F	S	S
Conservation studio								
3 Jan–29 Dec	10-5**			W	T	F	S	

*Entry by guided tours, 11 to 12; free-flow from 12. Open Bank Holidays, March to November. **November to January (inclusive): closes 4. Private garden: open Tuesdays, 3 April to 25 September, 11 to 4. Everything closed 24 to 25 December.

Clockwise from top left, mighty Knole glows in the setting sun; the Reynolds Room; a wild deer in the parkland

Lamb House

West Street, Rye, East Sussex TN31 7ES

 1950

Georgian home of writers Henry James and E. F. Benson, who depicted the property in the *Mapp and Lucia* stories. **Note:** open Mondays, Fridays and weekends, 3 June to 29 October, 11 to 5.

Find out more: 01580 762334 or lambhouse@nationaltrust.org.uk

Leith Hill Place

Leith Hill Lane, near Coldharbour, Dorking, Surrey RH5 6LY

 1945

Childhood home of English composer Ralph Vaughan Williams, once owned by the Wedgwood family and visited by Charles Darwin. Opened to the public in 2013 for the first time in 40 years, the house is being used as a trial base for new innovations. Glorious views over the South Downs. **Note:** parking access across sloping field (often muddy).

Leith Hill Place in Surrey

Eat, shop, stay: small kitchen run by volunteer bakers serving hot drinks and fresh bakes. Original AGA, stone-flagged dining-room and outside seating on terrace or courtyard garden. Camping at nearby Etherley Farm (not National Trust) or group stay at Henman Bunkhouse.

Things to see and do: free soundscape tour (timed tickets). You can play the piano and listen to music (often live). Children's trails and activities. Summer concerts. Small museum area with Vaughan Williams's piano displayed. **Dogs**: welcome on leads in grounds and some areas of house.

Access: P♿ D♿ ⬆♿ ♿ House ♿
Courtyard garden/south terrace ♿ ♿
Sat Nav: use RH5 6LU.
Parking: Rhododendron Wood car park, 437 yards, in Tanhurst Lane.

Find out more: 01306 711685 or leithhillplace@nationaltrust.org.uk

Leith Hill Place		M	T	W	T	F	S	S
23 Mar–28 Jul*	11–5					**F**	**S**	**S**

Open Bank Holiday Mondays. *Closed Sunday 29 July, due to RideLondon cycle race. For August to December opening times, please check website.

Things to see and do: **Indoors** Small exhibition room outlining the history of the tower. **Outdoors** Two free telescopes at top of the tower and walks leaflets covering the Leith Hill estate. **Dogs**: on leads on heathland (April to July).

Access: ♿
Sat Nav: for Rhododendron Wood and Starveall Corner use RH5 6LU; for Windy Gap RH5 6LX; for Landslip RH5 6HG. **Parking**: for tower use car parks at foot of hill.

Find out more: 01306 712711 or leithhill@nationaltrust.org.uk

Leith Hill		
Tower		
Open every day all year*	10–3	

*25 March to 28 October: open to 5. Closed 25 December.

Leith Hill Tower and Countryside, Surrey: unbeatable views

Leith Hill Tower and Countryside

near Coldharbour village, Dorking, Surrey

🏠 ♿ 1923

Built in 1765 by Richard Hull of Leith Hill Place, the top of Leith Hill Tower is the highest point in south-east England. From here there are unbeatable views north to the high-rise buildings of London, and to the south it's possible to see the sea sparkling through Shoreham Gap. This is glorious walking country, with iconic views of the local heathland and pastoral farmland landscapes. Every season is a riot of colour – starting with the spring bluebells at Frank's Wood, the early summer colour at the Rhododendron Wood, then the stunning autumnal displays of golds and reds. **Note**: steep spiral stairs to the top of the tower; no toilet or parking at tower.

Eat, shop, stay: hot and cold food and drinks available at Leith Hill Tower (not National Trust), tea and cake available at Leith Hill Place, when open. Picnics welcome, but no barbecues please. Self-catering accommodation at Henman Bunkhouse for up to 16 people.

Monk's House

Rodmell, Lewes, East Sussex BN7 3HF

🏠 ❄ ♿ 1980

Virginia Woolf's Monk's House in East Sussex

This small 17th-century weatherboarded cottage in the village of Rodmell was the country retreat of novelist Virginia Woolf and her husband Leonard and a meeting place for the Bloomsbury Group. The garden features the room where she created her best-known works and includes cottage garden borders, orchard, allotments and ponds. **Note**: no access to Rodmell from A26.

Eat, shop, stay: gift shop selling Woolf and Bloomsbury-related products.

Things to see and do: why not try your hand at a game of bowls? One of the favoured pastimes of the Woolfs. **Dogs**: allowed in garden on leads.

Access: 🅿 📷 🦽 Building 🔦 👥 Grounds 🔦
Sat Nav: do not use – wrongly indicates access across railway crossing. **Parking**: 100 yards (height restriction barrier).

Find out more: 01273 474760 or monkshouse@nationaltrust.org.uk

Monk's House		M	T	W	T	F	S	S
28 Mar–28 Oct	1–5		·	·	**W**	**T**	**F**	**S**	**S**

House: last admission 15 minutes before closing.
Open Bank Holiday Mondays. Garden: open 12:30 to 5:30.

Nymans

Handcross, near Haywards Heath, West Sussex RH17 6EB

🏠 ❄ 🍴 ♿ 🔔 ☂ 1954

One of the National Trust's premier gardens, Nymans was a creative retreat for the artistic Messel family. The garden showcases year-round colour and interest with rare and unusual plant collections of national significance. Discover hidden corners through stone archways, walk along tree-lined avenues, all the while surrounded by the lush countryside of the Sussex Weald. The comfortable yet elegant house, a partial ruin, reflects the personalities and stories of the talented Messel family. The adjoining woodland, with lake and bird hides, has plenty of opportunities to spot wildlife. A small gallery shows changing exhibitions throughout the year.

The house at Nymans, West Sussex: a partial ruin

Eat, shop, stay: large shop, plant and garden centre selling a collection of plants grown at Nymans. Café serving a choice of seasonal food. Kiosk open during busy periods. Woodland craft sales. Second-hand bookshop. Holiday cottage in woods.

Things to see and do: **Indoors** Gallery with year-round exhibitions. **Outdoors** Daily guided walks. Mobility buggy tours. Daily family activities, including trails and natural play.

Oakhurst Cottage

Hambledon, near Godalming, Surrey GU8 4HF

[icons] 1952

Timber-framed cottage offering a rare insight into domestic life in the mid-19th century, with a traditional garden to explore. **Note**: nearest toilets and visitor facilities at Winkworth Arboretum (4 miles approximately). Open Wednesdays, Thursdays and weekends, 1 April to 30 September, 2 to 5, and 3 to 31 October, 2 to 4. Admission by booked guided tour only at 2, 3 and 4 (last tour at 3 in October). Please call 01483 208936 to book. Also open Bank Holiday Mondays.

Find out more: 01483 208936 (Winkworth Arboretum) or oakhurstcottage@nationaltrust.org.uk

The heather garden, top, and woodland, above, at Nymans

Gardening and creative workshops. **Dogs**: in woodland only, on leads during bird-nesting season (1 March to 31 July).

Access: [icons]
House [icons] **Gallery** [icon] **Garden** [icons]
Parking: on site.

Find out more: 01444 405250 or nymans@nationaltrust.org.uk

Nymans	
Open every day all year*	10–5**

*Gallery closed for short periods to change exhibitions. 1 November to 28 February: house closed for winter conservation. **1 January to 4 February and 5 November to 31 December: closes 4. Closed 24 and 25 December.

Old Soar Manor

Plaxtol, Borough Green, Kent TN15 0QX

[icon] 1947

Dating from 1290, the remaining rooms of this knight's house offer a glimpse back to the time of Edward I. **Note**: sorry no toilet or tea-room. Narrow lanes, limited off-road parking. Open daily (excluding Fridays), 1 April to 30 September, 10 to 6.

Find out more: 01732 810378 or oldsoarmanor@nationaltrust.org.uk

Owletts

The Street, Cobham, Gravesend, Kent DA12 3AP

[icons] 1938

An architect's 17th-century family home with a varied history and architectural features, set within a relaxing, traditional garden. **Note**: parking available. Open Sundays, 1 April to 30 September, 11 to 5.

Find out more: 01732 810378 or owletts@nationaltrust.org.uk

Petworth

Petworth, West Sussex GU28 0AE

 1947

Home to an extraordinary collection of art, this magnificent 17th-century mansion stands as a monument to the evolving taste of one family over 900 years. Rooted in the powerful northern Percy dynasty, their journeys through the Tudor Reformation, the Gunpowder Plot, the Napoleonic Wars up to the present day, are reflected in the astonishing array of treasures that survives at Petworth. The palatial state rooms offer an infinity of paintings and sculptures, including major works by Van Dyck, Turner, Flaxman and Blake. From spring we celebrate the remarkable women of Petworth whose taste and influence quietly helped to shape the development of Petworth's famous collection and its wider cultural reputation. **Note**: additional charges may apply for some events, including Winter Art Exhibition.

Eat, shop, stay: Servants' Hall coffee shop serving barista-style coffee and tempting treats. Light lunches, afternoon teas and homemade cakes available in the Audit Room Café. Gift shops selling books, products inspired by the collection and locally sourced souvenirs.

Things to see and do: **Indoors** Free specialist talks and guided tours. Visit the servants' quarters, which evoke the hustle and bustle of domestic life. Exhibitions all year, with a festive display for the Christmas season.

Magnificent Petworth in West Sussex contains an extraordinary art collection, including works by Van Dyck and Turner

The Grand Staircase at Petworth, with its astonishing ceiling painting by Louis Laguerre

Outdoors The 283-hectare (700-acre) 'Capability' Brown deer-park, a landscape masterpiece, is a space for quiet reflection, offering views of the South Downs National Park. Download your own walk and get exclusive interactive information direct to your smartphone or tablet on the free Park Explorer. **Dogs**: under close control in Petworth Park. Assistance dogs only in Pleasure Ground.

Access: [icons] **Building** [icons] **Sat Nav**: use GU28 9LR. **Parking**: on A283, 700 yards. Separate car park for Petworth Park.

Find out more: 01798 342207 or petworth@nationaltrust.org.uk

Petworth		M	T	W	T	F	S	S
Mansion								
2 Jan–25 Mar	Tour	M	T	W	T	F	S	S
26 Mar–4 Nov	11–5	M	T	W	T	F	S	S
5 Nov–31 Dec	Tour	M	T	W	T	F	S	S
Pleasure Ground, shop and café								
Open all year	10–5*	M	T	W	T	F	S	S

13 January to 25 March: winter exhibition. 1 December to 31 December: selected rooms decorated for Christmas.
*1 January to 4 February and 5 November to 31 December: close 4. Closed 24 and 25 December.

Polesden Lacey

Great Bookham, near Dorking, Surrey RH5 6BD

🏛️❄️♿🚻🍽️ 1942

The lavish country retreat of Mrs Greville, a vivacious socialite who rubbed shoulders with the best in Edwardian high society, Polesden Lacey was a party house. Set within a quintessential English garden, it speaks of the many aspects of Edwardian social life, from the art of royal hospitality, to life in service. Indoors there are opulent collections of Fabergé, maiolica and fine art, including a world-renowned collection of Dutch Old Master paintings. Outside, the rose garden, herbaceous borders and the Long Walk offer opportunities for gentle exploration, while Graham Stuart Thomas's aromatic winter garden offers sunny colours during colder months. **Note**: additional charge may apply to certain events (including members).

Eat, shop, stay: Granary Café and Cowshed Coffee Shop offer seasonal dishes, snacks, coffee and ice-cream. Pop-up outlets open in

The gardens at Polesden Lacey, Surrey, are just as delightful in autumn, below, as in spring, above

warmer weather. Home and giftware, souvenirs and plants available to buy – all outside the pay perimeter. Second-hand bookshop in the grounds.

Things to see and do: **Indoors** Weekday house tours. Fabulous collections to enjoy. Seasonal programmes focus on a variety of stories to allow for vital conservation work. **Outdoors** The Grade II* listed gardens offer something for every season, blending Edwardian splendour with the majestic beauty of the ancient

woodlands on the wider 566-hectare (1,400-acre) estate. Rare birds, wild orchids, deer and other species to spot on four waymarked walks across this Site of Special Scientific Interest. Visitors can enjoy exploring the rose garden, herbaceous borders and Long Walk, while Graham Stuart Thomas's aromatic winter garden offers up sunny colours during colder months. **Dogs**: welcome on leads throughout the grounds (excluding formal gardens), countryside and farmland.

Polesden Lacey: carved panelling in the lavish Saloon

Access: [icons] **House** [icons] **Grounds** [icons]
Sat Nav: use KT23 4PZ. **Parking**: 200 yards.

Find out more: 01372 452048 or polesdenlacey@nationaltrust.org.uk

Polesden Lacey	
Open every day all year	10–5*

*House: opens 11; weekday access by guided tour only, 11 to 12:30; free-flow from 12:30. Admission by timed ticket at certain times. Last entry one hour before closing. 1 January to 4 February and 29 October to 31 December: closes 4. Closed 24 and 25 December.

Support the places you visit: please scan your member card for free parking ticket

Quebec House

Quebec Square, Westerham, Kent TN16 1TD

 1918

The Coach House at Quebec House in Kent: original charm

The childhood home of General James Wolfe, Quebec House retains much of its original charm and family feel. Interactive collections and objects belonging to Wolfe are used to explore Georgian family life and Wolfe's most celebrated victory at the Battle of Quebec in 1759.

Eat, shop, stay: second-hand books, souvenirs and guidebooks for sale in the Coach House, as well as hot and cold drinks and a selection of cakes.

Things to see and do: house guided tours at 12 and 12:30. Relive the dramatic battle to win Quebec in the exhibition. Why not explore the historic town of Westerham after visiting Quebec House? **Dogs**: welcome on short leads in the gardens.

Access: 🏛️🦽🏠📷♿📹♿
Building 🦽 **Grounds** 🦽🦽
Parking: 80 yards in main town car park on A25 (not National Trust).

Find out more: 01732 868381 or quebechouse@nationaltrust.org.uk

Quebec House		M	T	W	T	F	S	S
28 Feb–28 Oct	11–5*			W	T	F	S	S
3 Nov–16 Dec	1–4						S	S

*House: open for tours at 12 and 12:30; free-flow from 1.
Open Bank Holiday Mondays.

Reigate Hill and Gatton Park

near Reigate, Surrey

🏠🪜 1912

Reigate Hill commands sweeping views across the Weald to the South Downs. It's a great spot for walking, family picnics and watching wildlife. A short walk away is the 19th-century Reigate Fort. The complex is open every day and the fort buildings open for special events. To the east of Reigate Hill is Gatton Park, designed by Lancelot 'Capability' Brown. **Note**: areas of Gatton Park opened monthly by the Gatton Trust.

Eat, shop, stay: picnics welcome. Tea kiosk (not National Trust) at Wray Lane.

Reigate Hill and Gatton Park, Surrey: sweeping views

Reigate Hill and Gatton Park: numerous walks to enjoy

Things to see and do: walks detailed on noticeboards and downloadable from website. Chalk downland species, such as the Adonis blue butterfly, to spot, as well as mysterious military structures on Reigate Hill. **Dogs**: welcome, on leads when livestock grazing.

Access: ♿ ♿
Sat Nav: use RH2 0HX. **Parking**: at Wray Lane or Margery Wood car parks.

Find out more: 01342 843036 or reigate@nationaltrust.org.uk

Reigate Hill and Gatton Park
Reigate Fort buildings open by special arrangement.

River Wey and Godalming Navigations and Dapdune Wharf

Navigations Office and Dapdune Wharf, Wharf Road, Guildford, Surrey GU1 4RR

🏠 ♿ 🍽 1964

A hidden haven where you can take a boat trip, explore a restored barge, or enjoy scenic walks. Dapdune Wharf in Guildford brings to life stories of this historic waterway, along 20 miles of waterside towpath. A great place for children to have fun – and raid our dressing-up box. **Note**: boat trip charges, mooring and fishing fees apply to members.

Eat, shop, stay: small tea-room serving sandwiches, cakes, ice-cream and drinks. Small shop with plant sales. Picnic areas at Dapdune Wharf.

Things to see and do: **Indoors** Dressing-up clothes for children. **Outdoors** Year-round events, including activities for children at Dapdune and guided walks along towpath and beyond. River Festival in September. Overnight moorings available. **Dogs**: on leads at Dapdune Wharf and lock areas; elsewhere under control.

River Wey and Godalming Navigations in Surrey

Access: ♿♿♿♿♿♿ Grounds ♿
Parking: at Dapdune Wharf.

Find out more: 01483 561389 or riverwey@nationaltrust.org.uk

River Wey and Dapdune Wharf		M	T	W	T	F	S	S
Dapdune Wharf								
17 Mar–4 Nov	11–5	**M**	·	·	**T**	**F**	**S**	**S**

Open daily during local school half-term and summer holidays. 22 October to 4 November: closes one hour earlier. River trips from Dapdune Wharf, 11 to 4 (conditions permitting). Access to towpath during daylight all year.

Runnymede and Ankerwycke

Egham, near Old Windsor, Surrey

 1931

Seen by many as the birthplace of modern democracy, this picturesque open landscape beside the Thames was witness to King John's historic sealing of the Magna Carta more than 800 years ago. Today Runnymede and Ankerwycke offer the ideal space to enjoy ancient woodlands, countryside walks and picnics by the river, all within easy reach of the M25. Along with Lutyens' impressive Fairhaven Lodges, the peaceful landscape is also home to memorials for the Magna Carta, John F. Kennedy and Commonwealth Air Forces, making it the perfect place to remember and reflect upon important moments in world history.
Note: mooring and fishing (during fishing season) available for additional fee (including members).

Eat, shop, stay: tea-room serving freshly baked produce, morning coffee, light lunches and afternoon teas. Free Wi-Fi. Shop in tea-room offering Magna Carta-themed books, souvenirs and toys.

Things to see and do: family events, walks and talks throughout the year. River boat trips available with French Brothers Boat Hire (01784 439626). **Dogs**: welcome, but must be on leads near livestock.

Access: 🅿️ 🚻 🔬 📷 **Tea-room** 🦽 **Grounds** 🦽🦽
Sat Nav: use TW20 0AE and follow brown 'Runnymede Memorials' signs.
Parking: either side of A308 (seasonal opening).

Find out more: 01784 432891 or runnymede@nationaltrust.org.uk

Runnymede and Ankerwycke	
Tea-room	
Open every day all year	10–5*

*1 to 31 January and 29 October to 31 December: closes 3:30; 1 May to 31 August (weekends and Bank Holidays): closes 6. Car parks locked at dusk. Last entry one hour before closing. Closed 24 and 25 December.

The Magna Carta Memorial at Runnymede in Surrey

St John's Jerusalem

Sutton-at-Hone, Dartford, Kent DA4 9HQ

✠ ❀ 1943

Set within a secluded moated garden is this rare example of a 13th-century chapel built by the Knights Hospitaller. **Note**: private residence, maintained and managed by a tenant on behalf of the National Trust. Sorry no toilet or tea-room. Open Wednesdays, 4 April to 26 September, 2 to 6 and 3 to 31 October, 2 to 4.

Find out more: 01732 810378 or stjohnsjerusalem@nationaltrust.org.uk

Scotney Castle

Lamberhurst, Tunbridge Wells, Kent TN3 8JN

🏛 🏚 🎫 ❀ 🍴 1970

The medieval moated Old Scotney Castle lies in a peaceful wooded valley. In the 19th century its owner Edward Hussey III set about building a new house, partially demolishing the Old Castle to create a romantic folly, the centrepiece of his picturesque landscape. From the terraces of the new house, sweeps of

rhododendrons and azaleas cascade down the slope in summer, followed by highlights of autumn leaf colour, mirrored in the moat. In the house three generations have made their mark, adding possessions and character to the homely Victorian mansion which enjoys far-reaching views out across the estate.

Eat, shop, stay: the coach house tea-room offers a selection of hot meals and sandwiches, as well as homemade cakes and scones. Take home your own part of Scotney with local honey, Scotney Ale and plant sales available in the shop.

Scotney Castle, Kent: the romantic ruins of the moated old castle, left and above

Things to see and do: **Indoors** Children's trail around the house. Seasonal changing exhibitions and conservation demonstrations throughout the year. **Outdoors** Regular guided and self-led estate walks. Natural play and children's play areas. **Dogs**: welcome on leads in the garden and on the estate.

Access: 🅿 🅳 ♿ 🔆 📷 🎥 🎧
House 🔆 ♿ 🔆 **Grounds** 🔆 ➡ 🔆
Parking: 130 yards (limited), overflow parking 440 yards.

Find out more: 01892 893820 (Infoline). 01892 893868 or scotneycastle@nationaltrust.org.uk

Scotney Castle	
Open every day all year	10–5*

*House: opens 11; admission by timed ticket only, including members (places limited, early sell-outs possible). 1 January to 4 February and 5 November to 31 December: house open 11 to 3, everything closes at 4. Closed 24 and 25 December.

Shalford Mill

Shalford, near Guildford, Surrey GU4 8BS

 1932

You can sense the evocative stories of the past in the very structure of the mill, although the machinery no longer works. The wonderful story of the Ferguson's Gang is waiting for you – eccentric young women from the 1930s, determined to save the fabric of England for the future. **Note**: sorry no toilet or refreshments. Visits by guided tour only.

Things to see and do: **Indoors** Regular guided tours, evening talks and children's events. **Outdoors** Geocaching kits available on certain Sundays. **Dogs**: assistance dogs only.

Shalford Mill, Surrey: linked with the Ferguson's Gang

Access: [VT] [::] Building [♿] [♿]
Parking: none on site, off-street parking available near church.

Find out more: 01483 561389 or shalfordmill@nationaltrust.org.uk

Shalford Mill		M	T	W	T	F	S	S
25 Mar–31 Oct	Tour			W				S

Open Bank Holiday Mondays.

Sheffield Park and Garden

Sheffield Park, Uckfield, East Sussex TN22 3QX

[❄] [♿] [T] 1954

Water lilies at Sheffield Park and Garden, East Sussex

Colour, perfume and sound excite your senses as you enjoy winding paths, majestic trees, ponds and dappled glades. Falls, cascades and bridges are integral to the garden design. Planting is reflected in ponds so clear that the eye is tricked into thinking up is down. Bold and grand planting has a sculptural form in winter. Spring and summer bring vibrant blooms, fragrant arbours and splashes of colour. Autumn is a blazing kaleidoscope of greens, flame-reds, burnt oranges and bright yellows, planted for their combined display. The encircling park and woodland provide opportunities for further adventure. Dragonflies skit across the meadows, buzzards circle in the sky and kingfishers flash across the ponds.

Eat, shop, stay: tea-room serving homemade cakes, sandwiches, hot lunches and cream teas. Takeaway kiosk open seasonally. Shops in reception building and Coach House selling gifts, local products, gardening items and plants. Second-hand bookshop beside Coach House.

Things to see and do: events and trails in the school holidays and '50 things' self-led activities for families all year. Natural playtrail in Ringwood Toll – you can try den-building, balance beams, rope swing and much more. More than 120 hectares (300 acres) of parkland, with circular walks (just over 1 mile) of the River Ouse. Cricket matches most summer weekends. Carpets of bluebells in spring and outstanding autumn colour display. Walk Woods is open seasonally. Pulham Falls waterfall (12 to 1, Tuesdays and Fridays). Bluebell Railway – Sheffield Park station just a short walk across the parkland (weekend bus link spring/summer). **Dogs**: garden on short leads after 1:30; anytime on parkland. Off-lead in East Park.

Access: 🅿️♿🚻👶🔄📷🚽♿📹♿

Reception ♿🚻 **Tea-room** ♿♿

Garden ♿♿➡️♿🚻

Sat Nav: please look out for brown signs when approaching property. **Parking**: on site (overflow car park 600 yards in use when dry). Car park can become full during May and October.

Find out more: 01825 790231 or sheffieldpark@nationaltrust.org.uk

Sheffield Park and Garden	
Open every day all year	10–5*

Garden: last admission one hour before closing. *1 January to 4 February and 5 November to 31 December: closes 4 (last entry to garden 3). Garden, shop and tea-room: closed 24 and 25 December.

Numerous walks, below, are part of the many attractions at Sheffield Park and Garden. While the Cascade Bridge and Lower Woman's Way Pond, right, are typical of the garden's bold design

Sissinghurst Castle Garden

Biddenden Road, near Cranbrook, Kent TN17 2AB

🏠 🅿 ❀ ♿ 🚻 ⛴ 🍽 | 1967 |

Golden hues at Sissinghurst Castle Garden in Kent

Sissinghurst Castle Garden sits within the ruin of a great Elizabethan house surrounded by the rich Kentish landscape of woods, streams and farmland. The famous garden, with its fairytale tower, is the result of the creative tension between the formal design of Harold Nicolson and the lavish planting of Vita Sackville-West. The colour schemes, intimacy of the different garden 'rooms' and rich herbaceous borders are the epitome of an English garden. The wider estate, which includes a vegetable garden, lakes and rich variety of wildlife, is waiting to be explored, while our regular exhibitions tell Sissinghurst's stories and show how history and landscape have combined to shape this special place. **Note**: limited access for buggies and wheelchairs.

Eat, shop, stay: restaurant serving lunch and afternoon tea made with produce from our vegetable garden and farm (hot food available until 3). The Old Dairy, offering sandwiches, cakes and drinks. Second-hand bookshop and garden shop selling plants grown in the Sissinghurst nursery.

The distinctive turreted gatehouse, left, rises above Sissinghurst Castle Garden, while the South Cottage, above, is a far more modest building

Things to see and do: **Indoors** Exhibitions and daily talks. The Library contains the National Trust's most significant collection of 20th-century literature, and visitors can learn how we conserve it. **Outdoors** Welcome talks and '50 things' activities. Packs available from visitor reception to help you explore. Acres of ancient woodland and lakes. Panoramic views across the Wealden countryside. You can see animals on our working farm. Smallhythe Place, Lamb House and Stoneacre nearby.
Dogs: welcome on leads on estate. Assistance dogs only in garden and vegetable garden.

Access: 🅿️🅳🦽♿🚻🧷🛗🖼️📷🎵💡📷
Building 🔺🔺🔺 Grounds 🔺🔺➡️
Parking: 315 yards.

Find out more: 01580 710700 or sissinghurst@nationaltrust.org.uk

Sissinghurst Castle Garden		M	T	W	T	F	S	S
Garden								
17 Mar–31 Oct	11–5:30*	M	T	W	T	F	S	S
The South Cottage, tower and exhibitions								
1 Jan–16 Mar	11–4¹	M	T	W	T	F	S	S
17 Mar–31 Oct	11–5:30²	M	T	W	T	F	S	S
1 Nov–31 Dec	11–4¹	M	T	W	T	F	S	S
Shop and restaurant								
Open all year	10–5:30†	M	T	W	T	F	S	S
Estate								
Open all year	Dawn–dusk	M	T	W	T	F	S	S

*Garden: restricted access November to March; last entry 45 minutes before closing; for conservation reasons, no food, drink or buggies in garden (carriers provided). †Shop and restaurant: close 4:30, November to March. ¹South Cottage: last admission 3:30. Tower: closed for conservation work, January to April. ²South Cottage: closed June; limited timed tickets when open.

Slindon Estate

near Arundel, West Sussex

🏠🏛️📷🚣🚲👤📷 1950

The ancient Slindon Estate is an expansive patchwork of woodland, downland, farmland and parkland, with an unspoilt Sussex village at its centre. Countless historic features cover the landscape, such as Stane Street, the Roman road from Chichester to London soldiers once marched along. Slindon has a rich and wonderfully varied wildlife, and its sun-dappled woods are filled with wild flowers, with badgers and bats hunting there at dusk. The meadows are great places to spot butterflies and downland flowers, while expansive views take in the Weald and South Downs, continuing across the coastal plain to the sea.

Slindon Estate, West Sussex, an ancient patchwork of woodland, downland, farmland and parkland

The Slindon Estate hosts wonderfully varied wildlife

Eat, shop, stay: The Forge in Slindon village (tenant-run) stocks everything from locally baked bread, deli items, fruit and vegetables, to sandwiches, biscuits and cakes. Fresh coffee and tea, beer, light breakfasts, lunches and afternoon tea are also available.

Things to see and do: there are more than 25 miles of rights of way to explore on the estate, as well as the village to discover. **Dogs**: welcome under close control.

Access: 👤➡
Sat Nav: use BN18 0QY for Park Lane; BN18 0SP Duke's Road; BN18 1PH Bignor Hill.
Parking: at Park Lane, Duke's Road and Bignor Hill.

Find out more: 01243 814730 or slindonestate@nationaltrust.org.uk

Smallhythe Place

Smallhythe, Tenterden, Kent TN30 7NG

🏠 🌼 🔔 🍸 1939

Nestled among the rolling Kent countryside, the corridors of this early 16th-century cottage resonate with the vibrant spirit of its theatrical former owner, Victorian actress Ellen Terry. Bursting with memorabilia from her life-long career on stage, visitors can see unique theatrical artefacts and visit the Barn Theatre.

Eat, shop, stay: charming vintage tea-room attached to the Barn Theatre selling soup, sandwiches, cakes, as well as soft and alcoholic drinks.

Things to see and do: **Indoors** Diverse variety of plays and music performed in the Barn Theatre. **Outdoors** Open-air theatre in the garden throughout the summer. Sissinghurst Castle Garden, Lamb House and Stoneacre nearby. **Dogs**: allowed on leads in grounds.

Access: 👤🖼🎧📷♿ Building 👤🏠 Grounds 👤➡
Parking: 50 yards (not National Trust).

Find out more: 01580 762334 or smallhytheplace@nationaltrust.org.uk

Smallhythe Place		M	T	W	T	F	S	S
7 Mar–28 Oct	11–5		·	**W**	**T**	**F**	**S**	**S**

Tea-room: closes 30 minutes prior to closing.
Open Bank Holiday Mondays, 11 to 5.

Ellen Terry's portrait at Smallhythe Place in Kent

South Foreland Lighthouse

The Front, St Margaret's Bay, Dover, Kent CT15 6HP

🏠🚻♿🛏️🍽️ 1989

This historic landmark, dramatically situated on The White Cliffs, guided ships past the infamous Goodwin Sands and has a fascinating tale to tell. It was the first lighthouse powered by electricity and the site of the first international radio transmission. **Note: access to lighthouse by road is not permitted**. Nearest parking at White Cliffs Visitor Centre.

Kite-flying at South Foreland Lighthouse, Kent

Eat, shop, stay: loose-leaf tea and homemade cakes served in Mrs Knott's tea-room. Shop selling ice-cream, cold drinks and gifts.

Things to see and do: Indoors Tours run by knowledgeable guides. Interactive and hands-on displays. **Outdoors** Family fun with kite-flying and games. **Dogs**: in grounds only.

Access: 🚶♿🅿️📷🚻♿♿ Lighthouse ♿👨‍🦽
Tea-room ♿👨‍🦽 **Grounds** ♿
Parking: no onsite parking, nearest at White Cliffs (2 miles), or St Margaret's village car park (1 mile).

: 01304 853281 or southforeland@nationaltrust.org.uk

South Foreland Lighthouse		M	T	W	T	F	S	S
Lighthouse*								
26 Mar–28 Oct	11–5:30**	M	·	·	·	F	S	S
Tea-room								
3 Feb–25 Mar	11–3	·	·	·	·	·	S	S
26 Mar–28 Oct	11–5	M	T	W	·	F	S	S

*Significant conservation work at times. Please check website for most up-to-date opening times. Open daily during local school holidays. 28 October: closes at 3. **Last tour at 5.

Standen House and Garden

West Hoathly Road, East Grinstead, West Sussex RH19 4NE

🏠❄️♿🛏️🍽️ 1973

Nestled in the Sussex countryside with views across the High Weald, James and Margaret Beale chose an idyllic location to build their rural retreat. Designed by Philip Webb, the house is one of the finest examples of Arts and Crafts workmanship with Morris & Co. interiors and decorative art of the period. The 5-hectare (12-acre) hillside garden established by Mrs Beale is restored to its 1920s glory. Each garden room offers something for every season, from colourful spring bulbs to autumn shades. On the wider estate, footpaths lead

Standen House and Garden, West Sussex: 1920s glory

Vivid tulips at Standen House and Garden

into the woodlands and the High Weald Area of Outstanding Natural Beauty. **Note**: seasonal tours to top of water tower, £2 (suggested donation).

Eat, shop, stay: Barn Café serving homemade cakes, hot lunches and cream teas (Wi-Fi). Takeaway drinks, sandwiches and ice-cream. Arts and Crafts-inspired gifts in shop. Plant centre. Second-hand bookshop. Woodland craft. Kitchen garden produce. Picnics welcome. Holiday apartment within house.

Things to see and do: Indoors Daily talks. Changing exhibitions. Family Christmas. New this year: previously unseen rooms open. **Outdoors** Restored garden. 10,000 spring tulips. Woodland walks. Natural play area and trails (school holidays). **Dogs**: welcome on short leads in formal garden and woodland estate (seasonal grazing cattle).

Access: [icons] House [icons] Garden [icons]
Parking: 200 yards (steep hill).

Find out more: 01342 323029 or standen@nationaltrust.org.uk

Standen House and Garden		M	T	W	T	F	S	S
House, garden, café and shop*								
Open all year	10–5**	M	T	W	T	F	S	S
'Through Servants' Eyes' tours[1]								
2 Jan–31 Jan	11–2:30†	M	T	W	T	F	·	·
House tours[1]								
1 Nov–23 Nov	11–3†	M	T	W	T	F	·	·

*House: January, November, December, open 11 to 3:30; February to October, open 11 to 4:30, except weekdays; 1 to 9 and 19 to 28 February, tours only 11 to 12:55, free-flow from 1:30. [1]Admission by tour only. †Last tour departs.
**1 January to 4 February and 5 November to 31 December: close 4. Closed 24 and 25 December.

Stoneacre

Otham, Maidstone, Kent ME15 8RS

[icons] 1928

Medieval farmhouse surrounded by garden, orchard, rolling meadows and woodland. Home to famous designer and critic Aymer Vallance. **Note**: maintained on National Trust's behalf by tenant. Limited parking. Open Saturdays, 17 March to 22 September, 11 to 5:30. Last admission one hour before closing.

Find out more: 01622 861584 or stoneacre@nationaltrust.org.uk

Uppark House and Garden

South Harting, Petersfield, West Sussex GU31 5QR

[icons] 1954

High on its vantage point on the South Downs ridge, Uppark has views as far south as the Solent. Outside, the intimate garden is being gradually restored to its original 18th-century design, with plenty of space in the adjacent meadow to play and relax. Uppark's Georgian interiors illustrate the comfort of life 'upstairs', in contrast to the 'downstairs' world of its servants. Highlights include one of the best examples of an 18th-century British doll's-house in the country.

Uppark House and Garden, West Sussex, looks south

Visitors explore Uppark House and Garden

Eat, shop, stay: café (licensed) serving breakfast, lunches and afternoon tea. Shop selling books, plants, local food and much more.

Things to see and do: **Indoors** Rare 18th-century British doll's-house. **Outdoors** Garden tours (April to October). Open-air theatre and music in the summer. Harting Down, Hinton Ampner and Petworth House nearby. **Dogs**: welcome on short leads.

Access:
House **Garden**
Parking: 300 yards.

Find out more: 01730 825415 or uppark@nationaltrust.org.uk

Uppark House and Garden		M	T	W	T	F	S	S
Servants' quarters								
1 Jan–4 Feb	11-3	M	T	W	T	F	S	S
5 Feb–28 Oct	11-4	M	T	W	T	F	S	S
29 Oct–31 Dec	11-3	M	T	W	T	F	S	S
House (ground floor only)								
3 Mar–28 Oct	12:30-4*	M	T	W	T	F	S	S
Garden, shop and café								
Open all year	10-5**	M	T	W	T	F	S	S

*Ground floor: open 11 to 4 on Bank Holidays.
**Garden: limited access in winter. 1 January to 4 February and 29 October to 31 December: close 4. Everything closed 25 and 26 December.

Wakehurst

Ardingly, Haywards Heath, West Sussex RH17 6TN

1964

Wakehurst, the country estate of the Royal Botanic Gardens, Kew, is internationally significant for collections, scientific research and plant conservation. The gardens, wetland and woodland are delightful – there is also a nature reserve. You can also visit Kew's unique Millennium Seed Bank, where science and horticulture work side by side.
Note: funded and managed by the Royal Botanic Gardens, Kew. **Parking charges apply (including members)**.

Eat, shop, stay: Seed Café serving tea, coffee, cakes, bacon sandwiches, teacakes and soup. Redwoods Coffee Shop serving hot drinks and fresh patisserie. Stables Restaurant offering hot and cold food, plus cakes served all day. Gift shop. Plant centre (not National Trust).

Spring blossom at Wakehurst in West Sussex

Things to see and do: free daily guided tours. Seasonal festival programme, open-air theatre, lantern festival. Courses. Events all year. Willow sculpture trail. Adventurous Journeys and natural play areas for families. Kingfisher/badger-watching (charges apply). **Dogs**: assistance dogs only.

Access:
Buildings **Grounds**
Parking: 50 yards.

Find out more: 01444 894066 or wakehurst@kew.org. kew.org

Wakehurst		M	T	W	T	F	S	S
Garden*								
1 Jan–28 Feb	10-4:30	M	T	W	T	F	S	S
1 Mar–31 Oct	10-6	M	T	W	T	F	S	S
1 Nov–30 Dec**	10-4:30	M	T	W	T	F	S	S

*Mansion and Millennium Seed Bank: close one hour earlier. Shop: closes at 4, 2 January to 28 February; at 5:30, March to October; at 5, November to 1 January 2019. Catering facilities: close at 4, 2 January to 28 February; 5:15, 1 March to 31 October; 4:15, 1 November to 31 December. Shop closed Easter Sunday. UK National Trust members free (reciprocal agreements made between the Trust and other parties do not apply). **Closed 24 and 25 December.

The White Cliffs of Dover

Langdon Cliffs, Dover, Kent

🏠 ♿ ⛰ 🍽 1968

There can be no doubt that The White Cliffs of Dover are one of this country's most spectacular natural features. They are an official icon of Britain and have been a symbol of hope for generations. You can appreciate their beauty through the seasons by taking one of the country's most dramatic clifftop walks, which offer unrivalled views of the busy English Channel while savouring the rare flora and fauna found only on this chalk grassland. You can also learn more about the fascinating military history of The White Cliffs by taking a torchlit tour of Fan Bay Deep Shelter, a labyrinth of forgotten Second World War tunnels. **Note**: nearest toilets at White Cliffs. Age restrictions apply at Fan Bay.

Eat, shop, stay: shop selling gifts and outdoor goods. Coffee shop serving lunches, homemade cakes and afternoon teas. Both with unrivalled views of the Port of Dover. Homemade cakes and loose-leaf tea available in lighthouse tea-room.

Things to see and do: **Indoors** Lighthouse guided tours. Feeling adventurous? Why not take a walk to Fan Bay Deep Shelter and pick up a ticket for a torchlit tour of the Shelter and the newly uncovered sound mirrors? Descend deep into the cliffs and peer into the darkness of the hidden world beneath.

The labyrinthine Fan Bay Deep Shelter, left, lies deep under the iconic cliffs at The White Cliffs of Dover in Kent, above. Right, a couple enjoy a clifftop walk

Outdoors Natural play area. Spectacular viewpoints and photo opportunities. Events, talks and guided walks all year. Waymarked trail to South Foreland Lighthouse (only 2 miles away). **Dogs**: under close control at all times (animals grazing).

Access: 🅿♿🚾💺♿ 💺 Visitor centre 🚻 Fan Bay Deep Shelter 🔦 Countryside 🚶➡♿
Sat Nav: use CT15 5NA. **Parking**: on site, limited (please check before visiting Sundays and Bank Holidays, April to October).

Find out more: 01304 202756 or whitecliffs@nationaltrust.org.uk

The White Cliffs of Dover		M	T	W	T	F	S	S
Visitor Centre and shop								
1 Jan–4 Feb	10–4	M	T	W	T	F	S	S
5 Feb–28 Oct	10–5*	M	T	W	T	F	S	S
29 Oct–31 Dec**	10–4	M	T	W	T	F	S	S
Fan Bay Deep Shelter								
26 Mar–28 Oct	11–3	M				F	S	S

*2 July to 2 September: open to 5:30.
**Closed 24 and 25 December.

Winkworth Arboretum in Surrey, above and below, is the National Trust's only arboretum

Winkworth Arboretum

Hascombe Road, Godalming, Surrey GU8 4AD

❈ ⚘ 1952

The National Trust's only arboretum was born from one man's vision and passion. Dr Wilfrid Fox used the wooded valley and its lakes as a canvas for 'painting a picture' with trees. The fruits of his labour are an award-winning collection of more than 1,000 varieties of trees and shrubs set in the picturesque Surrey Hills, offering stunning combinations of colour with every changing season. Famous for vibrant autumnal foliage and endless carpets of bluebells in spring, the azaleas, magnolias, witch hazel and snowdrops make Winkworth worth visiting all year for beautiful scenery, a picnic or fun family events. **Note**: some steep slopes; banks of lake and wetlands only partially fenced.

Eat, shop, stay: small tea-room offering freshly baked scones, cakes and light lunches.

Things to see and do: events and guided walks throughout the year. **Dogs**: welcome on short leads.

Access: ♿🅿️🚻🐕🔄 Grounds ♿➡️
Parking: 100 yards.

Find out more: 01483 208477 or winkwortharboretum@nationaltrust.org.uk

Winkworth Arboretum		M	T	W	T	F	S	S
1 Jan–31 Jan	10–4	M	T	W	T	F	S	S
1 Feb–25 Mar	10–5	M	T	W	T	F	S	S
26 Mar–28 Oct	10–6	M	T	W	T	F	S	S
29 Oct–31 Dec	10–4*	M	T	W	T	F	S	S

Tea-room closes 30 minutes earlier than arboretum. Car-park gates locked at closing time. *Closed 24 and 25 December.

Witley and Milford Commons

Haslemere Road, Witley, Surrey GU8 5QA

 1921

Wonderful area of great contrasts, with extensive heathland views and secluded woodland glades. Trails available from car parks. **Note**: no toilets. For Sat Nav use GU8 5QA.

Find out more: 01428 681050 or witleymilfordcommons@nationaltrust.org.uk

Woolbeding Gardens

Midhurst, West Sussex GU29 9RR

 1957

A horticultural haven, Woolbeding Gardens is a masterpiece of colour and elegant design with a personal touch. This constantly evolving hidden gem boasts immaculate formal garden rooms with meticulously composed colour-themed borders, complemented by dramatic architectural follies and a waterfall that merges into the far-reaching landscape of the River Rother. **Note**: access by park-and-ride minibus from Midhurst only (booking essential).

Eat, shop, stay: Orchard Café serving barista-style coffee, speciality teas, and a selection of tempting treats. Shop selling gardening books, gifts and plants.

Things to see and do: join introductory talks and specialist Gardeners' Workshops. Enjoy the borders bursting with colour, find hidden follies waiting to be discovered and take in grand views of the countryside beyond.
Dogs: assistance dogs only.

Access: 🅿🚻♿ Reception ♿🔉 Garden ♿➡♿
Parking: none available. Access by complimentary park-and-ride minibus from Midhurst only.

Find out more: 0344 249 1895 or woolbedinggardens@nationaltrust.org.uk

Woolbeding Gardens		M	T	W	T	F	S	S
5 Apr–28 Sep	10:30–4:30	·	·	·	**T**	**F**	·	·

Advance booking essential. Access by park and ride only from Midhurst.

Woolbeding Gardens in West Sussex: masterpiece of colour and elegant design

London

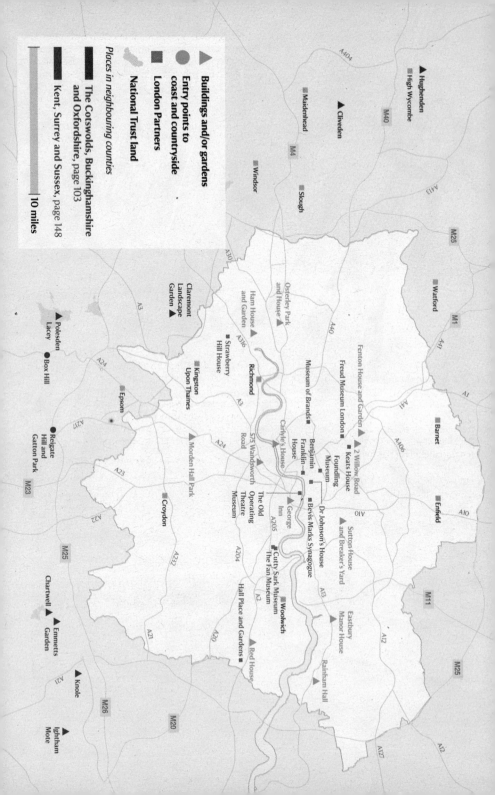

Buildings and/or gardens

Entry points to coast and countryside

London Partners

National Trust land

Places in neighbouring counties

The Cotswolds, Buckinghamshire and Oxfordshire, page 103

Kent, Surrey and Sussex, page 148

10 miles

Hughenden

High Wycombe

Cliveden

Maidenhead

Windsor

Slough

Watford

M40

M4

M1

M25

A404

A413

A41

M40

M4

A40

Claremont Landscape Garden

Ham House and Garden

Osterley Park and House

Fenton House and Garden

Freud Museum London

2 Willow Road

Keats House

Foundling Museum

Barnet

Enfield

Polesden Lacey

Box Hill

Strawberry Hill House

Richmond

Kingston Upon Thames

Epsom

Museum of Brands

Benjamin Franklin House

Carlyle's House

575 Wandsworth Road

Morden Hall Park

Croydon

Reigate Hill and Gatton Park

Dr Johnson's House

Bevis Marks Synagogue

Sutton House and Breaker's Yard

Eastbury Manor House

The Old Operating Theatre Museum

George Inn

Cutty Sark Museum

The Fan Museum

Woolwich

Hall Place and Gardens

Rainham Hall

Red House

Chartwell

Emmetts Garden

Knole

Ightham Mote

A30

A3

A24

A316

A3

A24

A205

A204

A2

A3

A13

A10

A10

A406

M23

A217

M25

A23

A22

A232

A20

A21

M25

M26

M20

M11

A1

A10

A12

A127

A12

A21

Carlyle's House

24 Cheyne Row, Chelsea, London SW3 5HL

🏠 ❀ 1936

Carlyle's House: 'A Chelsea Interior' by Robert Tait

'Let no woman who values peace of soul ever dream of marrying an author!' wrote Jane Carlyle in 1837. Her amusing letters about her husband, the sage of Chelsea, their friends (including Charles Dickens), impossible servants, noisy neighbours, builders, burglars and bedbugs bring this Victorian home to hilarious life.

Access: 🖼️📷 **Building** 🔲🍴 **Grounds** 🔲
Parking: limited on street, metered (charge including members).

Find out more: 020 7352 7087 or carlyleshouse@nationaltrust.org.uk

Carlyle's House		M	T	W	T	F	S	S
3 Mar–4 Nov	11–5			W	T	F	S	S
Open Bank Holiday Mondays.								

Eastbury Manor House

Eastbury Square, Barking IG11 9SN

🏠 ❀ 🔔 Ⴒ 1918

Elizabethan gentry house *circa* 1573. Little-altered, featuring early 17th-century wall-paintings and garden with bee-boles.

Tours, re-enactments, family days and crafts. **Note**: managed by London Borough of Barking and Dagenham. Some rooms are occasionally closed for functions. Independent tea-room and shop selling Tudor pottery, books and souvenirs. Special events and activities are charged at an additional cost. Open Thursdays and Fridays, 15 February to 14 December, 10 to 4 and Sundays, 1 April to 16 December, 11 to 4.

Find out more: 020 8227 2942 or eastburymanor@nationaltrust.org.uk

Fenton House and Garden

Hampstead Grove, Hampstead, London NW3 6SP

🏠 ❀ Ⴒ 1952

This 1686 town house, with views across London from the top of Hampstead's Holly Hill, is filled with world-class collections of ceramics, paintings, textiles and musical instruments. The ever-changing horticultural gem that is the garden, includes an orchard, kitchen garden, rose garden, terraces and lawns, and never fails to delight.

Delightful Fenton House and Garden in Hampstead

Eat, shop, stay: small shop area selling local and National Trust items, garden plants and produce.

Things to see and do: **Indoors** Collections talks, exhibitions and music events. **Outdoors** Garden events, including Apple Weekend. Keats House, the Freud Museum (both Trust London Partners) and 2 Willow Road are nearby. **Dogs**: assistance dogs only.

Access: 🏠🖥️🔲🖼️ Building 🔛🔛🔛 Grounds 🔛 **Parking**: none on site.

Find out more: 020 7435 3471 or fentonhouse@nationaltrust.org.uk

Fenton House and Garden			M	T	W	T	F	S	S
3 Mar–4 Nov	11–5						**W**	**T**	**F**	**S**	**S**

Open Bank Holiday Mondays and selected dates in December.

Delightful Ham House and Garden in Richmond

George Inn

The George Inn Yard, 77 Borough High Street, Southwark, London SE1 1NH

 1937

This public house, dating from the 17th century, is London's last remaining galleried inn. **Note**: leased to a private company. No table bookings (telephone for details). Open daily (apart from 25 and 26 December), 11 to 11.

Find out more: 020 7407 2056 or georgeinn@nationaltrust.org.uk

Ham House and Garden

Ham Street, Ham, Richmond TW10 7RS

 1948

On the banks of the River Thames, Ham is one of London's treasure houses and gardens. With a substantial collection of 17th-century paintings, furniture and textiles, Ham reveals what life looked like during the reigns of Charles I and II. You can learn how later generations protected their heritage by caring for their ancestors' treasured heirlooms. The ongoing re-creation of the 17th-century garden now features a large walled kitchen garden containing a collection of trained fruit, a formal lavender garden, woodland wilderness and two river meadows. **Note**: to protect fragile textiles, some rooms have low light levels.

Eat, shop, stay: the café serves lunches, teas and delicious cakes made on site using kitchen garden produce. Picnics are welcome and some tables are provided. The gift shop sells gifts for all occasions and plants, many Ham-grown.

Things to see and do: **Indoors** Art activities and trails during school holidays and weekends for families. **Outdoors** Discover more on a garden history or architecture tour. Enjoy our wildflower meadow by the Thames. **Dogs**: assistance dogs only.

Access: 🅿️🚻🚻🚻🚻🚻🚻🚻 House 🔛🔛🔛🔛 🔛 Café 🔛🔛🔛🔛 Gardens 🔛🔛🔛➡️🔛🔛 **Sat Nav**: takes you to stables on Ham Street nearby. **Parking**: none on site, nearest 380 yards (not National Trust) and on street.

Find out more: 020 8940 1950 or hamhouse@nationaltrust.org.uk

Ham House and Garden		M	T	W	T	F	S	S
House								
Open all year*	12–4	**M**	**T**	**W**	**T**	**F**	**S**	**S**
Garden, café and shop								
Open all year	10–5**	**M**	**T**	**W**	**T**	**F**	**S**	**S**

*Selected rooms only, January to March, November and December. **1 January to 4 February and 29 October to 31 December: close 4. Closed 24 and 25 December.

Morden Hall Park

Morden Hall Road, Morden, London SM4 5JD

🏛️🖼️📶🌀🐾🐕🍴 1941

Step into this 50-hectare (125-acre) oasis and you'll soon forget you're in bustling South London. Once a private country estate, the grounds were gifted to the National Trust to become a park for all people, and have been a local treasure ever since. Peaceful tree-lined riverside paths lead to wide open meadows and a collection of historic buildings which hint at an industrial past. The 1920s rose garden is a delight for the senses in summer and a perfect picnic spot, while a stroll on the immersive wetland boardwalk gives a rare glimpse into the secretive world of waterbirds.

Note: parking for visitors to Morden Hall Park only, five-hour maximum stay (including members). Admission charges apply to some events (including members).

Mordan Hall Park: a haven in bustling South London

Eat, shop, stay: garden centre offers expert advice and sells peat-free plants grown in National Trust nurseries. The Potting Shed Café in the former kitchen garden serves hearty fare, while the Stableyard Café offers light refreshments at weekends. Second-hand bookshop with period features.

Things to see and do: **Indoors** Regular exhibitions in the Stableyard Gallery. Hallowe'en and Christmas family events. **Outdoors** Open-air theatre and cinema during the summer. Family events at Easter, Hallowe'en and Christmas. **Dogs**: welcome on leads around buildings and mown grass, including rose garden. Within sight elsewhere.

Morden Hall Park: gifted as a park for all people

Access: 🅿️🚪🏷️♿🐕📷🏛️🚻👓🅰️
Snuff Mill ♿🏷️🍴♿ **Parkland** 🏷️♿➡️♿
Café and garden centre 🏷️♿
Sat Nav: use SM4 5JD and follow signs to Morden Hall Park Garden Centre.
Parking: 25 yards, next to garden centre.

Find out more: 020 8545 6850 or mordenhallpark@nationaltrust.org.uk

Morden Hall Park
Open every day all year

Potting Shed Café: open 9 to 6. Garden centre: open Monday to Saturday, 9 to 6; Sunday, 10:30 to 4:30. Rose garden and Stable Yard: open 8 to 6. 1 November to 1 March: all buildings and gardens close one hour earlier.

Osterley Park and House

Jersey Road, Isleworth, London TW7 4RB

🏠 ✳ 🎫 🍽 1949

A suburban palace caught between town and country, Osterley Park and House is one of the last surviving country estates in London. Past fields and grazing cattle, just around the lake the magnificent house awaits, presented as it would have been when it was redesigned by Robert Adam in the late 18th century for the Child family. A place for entertaining friends and clients, fashioned for show and entertaining, the lavish state apartments tell the story of a party palace. Recently returned family portraits and furniture now add a personal touch to grand rooms. 'Below stairs' see the contrast of the domestic quarters. Elegant pleasure gardens and hundreds of acres of parkland are perfect for whiling away a peaceful afternoon.

Eat, shop, stay: Stables Café, serving fresh seasonal dishes and homemade cakes (indoor and outdoor seating), and Brewhouse Coffee Shop (open seasonally). Gift shop, second-hand bookshop and plant sales in the Stables courtyard. Free Wi-Fi. Picnics welcome in the park and gardens.

Things to see and do: Indoors Year-round events and family activities. **Outdoors** You can stroll through colourful formal gardens, with herbaceous borders, ornamental vegetable beds and an established winter garden. With

meadows, woodland and a natural play trail with rope swings and stepping stones, you can let your imagination (and the children's) run wild. Why not enjoy a game of table tennis on the front lawn or a walk around the estate, with impressive views across Middle Lake towards the 18th-century house? Family-friendly multipurpose pathways are perfect for cycling, with trail maps and suggested routes available. **Dogs**: welcome on leads in parkland, with designated off-lead area.

Access: 🅿️ 🅳 📷 📷 📷 📷 📷 📷 📷 📷 📷
House 📷 📷 **Shop and bookshop** 📷 📷
Garden 📷 ➡️ 📷 📷
Sat Nav: enter Jersey Road and TW7 4RD.
Parking: 400 yards.

Find out more: 020 8232 5050 or osterley@nationaltrust.org.uk

Osterley Park and House	
Open every day all year	10–5*

*House: opens 11; last entry one hour before closing; selected rooms open in winter. Shop: open weekends only in January, February and November. 1 January to 4 February and 5 November to 31 December: closes 4. Closed 25 December.

One of the last surviving country estates in London, Osterley Park and House in Isleworth, this page and opposite, is an unlikely suburban palace

Rainham Hall

The Broadway, Rainham, London RM13 9YN

🏠 ❄️ 1949

Built in 1729 for an enterprising merchant, Rainham Hall has been home to nearly 50 different inhabitants, including a scientist-vicar, a *Vogue* photographer and local children, who attended a wartime nursery. One by one, we will be bringing their stories to life, through a changing exhibition programme.

Eat, shop, stay: the Stables Café serves seasonally inspired light lunches, freshly baked scones, cakes, barista coffee, teas and soft drinks. Gifts, guidebooks and postcards available.

Past residents' stories are brought to life at Rainham Hall

Things to see and do: **Indoors** Regular events, including family activities and seasonal festivities. **Outdoors** Almost 1½-hectare (3-acre) community garden.
Dogs: assistance dogs only.

Access: [icons] **House** [icons] [icons]
Café [icons] [icons] **Garden** [icons] [icons] ▶
Parking: 300 yards (not National Trust).

Find out more: 01708 525579 or rainhamhall@nationaltrust.org.uk

Rainham Hall		M	T	W	T	F	S	S
Stables Café and gardens								
3 Jan–30 Dec	10–5*	·	·	W	T	F	S	S
Hall								
10 Feb–30 Dec**	11–4	·	·	W	T	F	S	S

*Gardens: close earlier in winter. **Hall: open Bank Holiday Mondays. Whole site closed 24, 25, 26 and 31 December and 1 January 2019.

Red House

Red House Lane, Bexleyheath DA6 8JF

[icons] [icons] 2003

The only house commissioned, created and lived in by William Morris, founder of the Arts and Crafts Movement, Red House is a building of extraordinary architectural and social significance. An ongoing conservation project is gradually revealing Red House's secrets, including original Pre-Raphaelite wall-paintings and Morris's first decorative schemes.

Eat, shop, stay: William Morris shop housed in our Grade II* listed Coach House.
Café in original kitchen serving light lunches and a selection of cakes. Picnics welcome in the orchard.

Things to see and do: **Indoors** Award-winning film installation 'A poem of a house'. Exhibition of Philip Webb's personal effects. Wombat trails in school holidays. Guided tours.
Outdoors Garden tours. Lawn games.
Dogs: assistance dogs only.

Access: [icons] **Building** [icons] **Grounds** [icons] ▶
Sat Nav: use DA6 8HL – Danson Park car park.
Parking: at Danson Park, just over ½ mile.
Charge at weekends and Bank Holidays (including members).

Find out more: 020 8304 9878 or redhouse@nationaltrust.org.uk

Red House		M	T	W	T	F	S	S
3 Mar–28 Oct	11–5	·	·	W	T	F	S	S
2 Nov–16 Dec	11–4:30					F	S	S

Admission by guided tour only at 11, 11:30, 12, 12:30 and 1 (booking essential); free-flow 1:30 to 5 (4:30 in winter). Last admission 45 minutes before closing. Tea-room: last serving 4:30 (4 in winter). Open Bank Holiday Mondays.

Elegant simplicity at Red House, Bexleyheath

Sutton House and Breaker's Yard

2 and 4 Homerton High Street, Hackney,
London E9 6JQ

 1938

Transport yourself from buzzing Hackney into a
500-year-old country house full of twists and
surprises. Fine oak-panelled chambers, a great
hall, cellars, Tudor, Georgian, Victorian and
squatter rooms are all arranged around a
tranquil courtyard. Our garden playfully
celebrates its industrial past as a
car-breaker's yard.

Eat, shop, stay: treat yourself to tea and cake,
served on vintage crockery in the courtyard,
bookshop or among upcycled vehicles of the
Breaker's Yard garden.

Things to see and do: **Indoors** Toy treasure
chests playfully reveal secret, adventurous and
refined stories. Panels open to show hidden
features, such as 500-year-old graffiti.
Outdoors Breaker's Yard playground.
Seasonal events. **Dogs**: assistance dogs only.

Access: [icons] **Building** [icons]
Sat Nav: use E9 6JQ. **Parking**: none on site
and very limited nearby (not National Trust,
charge including members).

Playtime at Sutton House and Breaker's Yard, Hackney

Find out more: 020 8986 2264 or
suttonhouse@nationaltrust.org.uk

Sutton House		M	T	W	T	F	S	S
3 Feb–16 Dec	12–5						S	S
30 Mar–2 Apr	12–5	M				F		
7 Feb–14 Dec	12–5			W	T	F		

Open daily summer school holidays. Open Bank Holiday
Mondays and Good Friday (excluding December and January).
Many local community groups, schools and events in house all
year. If you would like to visit during quieter times please call.
Many late openings for events, contact property for details.

575 Wandsworth Road

575 Wandsworth Road, Lambeth,
London SW8 3JD

[icon] 2010

575 Wandsworth Road, Lambeth: detailed fretwork

Khadambi Asalache (1935–2006) turned this
modest Grade II listed Georgian terraced house
into a work of art. Featuring hand-carved
fretwork throughout, the house and
collections continue to inspire all who visit.
Note: sorry no toilets or café. Access by
booked guided tour only.

Access: House [icons]
Parking: none on site.

Find out more: 0344 249 1895 (bookings).
020 7622 4109 (enquiries) or
575wandsworthroad@nationaltrust.org.uk

575 Wandsworth Road		M	T	W	T	F	S	S
2 Mar–4 Nov*	Tour**					F	S	S

*Closed last Sunday of month. **Access by guided tour only
(approximately one hour) for up to six people (booking
essential, places limited, tickets released in February,
May and August).

2 Willow Road

Hampstead, London NW3 1TH

🏠 🆃 1994

Examining a model at 2 Willow Road, Hampstead

This late 1930s house, an architect's vision of the future, paints a vivid picture of the creative and social circles in which Ernö and Ursula Goldfinger moved. Today you can explore the intimate and evocative interiors, innovative designs, intriguing personal possessions and impressive 20th-century art collection. **Note**: sorry no toilet.

Eat, shop, stay: a small table in the entrance hall has property-related items available for sale.

Things to see and do: events, including late openings and tours. Fenton House nearby, as well as Keats House and the Freud Museum (both London Partners). **Dogs**: assistance dogs only.

Access: 🅿️ 🚪 📷 🖥️ 🎧 ⠿ ◎ **Building** ♿ 🚹
Parking: very limited, metered on-street parking nearby (not National Trust).

Find out more: 020 7435 6166 or 2willowroad@nationaltrust.org.uk

2 Willow Road		M	T	W	T	F	S	S
3 Mar–4 Nov	11–5*		·	W	T	F	S	S

*Entry by one-hour guided tour only at 11, 12, 1 and 2 (places limited, tickets available on day at door only). Wednesday to Friday, tours at 11 occasionally booked by groups. 3 to 5, self-guided viewing (timed entry when busy). Open Bank Holiday Mondays.

National Trust
Partner

London partners

'National Trust Partner' is an exciting venture between the National Trust and a selection of small, independent heritage attractions and museums within London. The Partnership aims to bring enhanced benefits to National Trust members living in London or for those visiting the capital for a day out, helping to provide increased opportunities to explore our rich and diverse heritage.

Entry charges: 50 per cent discount for members on presentation of a valid membership card. For full visiting information (and access), please see individual National Trust Partner websites.

Benjamin Franklin House

The world's only remaining home of Benjamin Franklin, featuring a unique 'Historical Experience'.

Underground: Charing Cross or Embankment.
Train: Charing Cross.

Find out more: 020 7925 1405 or benjaminfranklinhouse.org

Cutty Sark

Nineteenth-century tea clipper, once the fastest ship of her day, meticulously preserved to tell the stories of life on board.

Train: Cutty Sark (DLR) or Greenwich.

Find out more: 020 8312 6565 or rmgenquiries@rmg.co.uk   rmg.co.uk/cutty-sark

Bevis Marks Synagogue

Dated 1701, Britain's oldest surviving synagogue contains Cromwellian and Queen Anne furniture.

Underground: Liverpool Street or Aldgate.
Train: Liverpool Street.

Find out more: 020 7621 1188 or bevismarks.org.uk

Dr Johnson's House

Late 17th-century town house, once home to lexicographer and wit Samuel Johnson.

Underground: Chancery Lane or Blackfriars.
Train: Blackfriars.

Find out more: 020 7353 3745 or drjohnsonshouse.org

The Fan Museum

Unique collection of more than 4,000 fans, housed in elegant Georgian buildings.

Train: Cutty Sark (DLR) or Greenwich.

Find out more: 020 8305 1441 or thefanmuseum.org.uk

Freud Museum London

The final home of pioneering psychoanalysts Sigmund Freud and his daughter Anna.

Underground: Finchley Road.
Overground: Finchley Road & Frognal.

Find out more: 020 7435 2002 or freud.org.uk

Foundling Museum

Nationally important collection of 18th-century art, interiors, social history and music.

Underground: Russell Square, King's Cross, St Pancras or Euston. **Train**: King's Cross, St Pancras or Euston.

Find out more: 020 7841 3600 or foundlingmuseum.org.uk

Hall Place and Gardens

Stunning Tudor house with magnificent gardens.

Train: Bexley.

Find out more: 01322 526574 or hallplace.org.uk

Keats House

Elegant Regency villa where the Romantic poet John Keats wrote his best-loved poems.

Underground: Hampstead or Belsize Park.
Overground: Hampstead Heath.

Find out more: 020 7332 3868 or keatshouse@cityoflondon.gov.uk

The Old Operating Theatre Museum

Unique, atmospheric museum, hidden in the timbered Herb Garret of St Thomas's Church.

Underground: London Bridge.
Train: London Bridge.

Find out more: 020 7188 2679 or thegarret.org.uk

Museum of Brands

Intense experience of consumer culture: journey from Victorian times to your childhood.

Underground: Ladbroke Grove.

Find out more: 020 7243 9611 or museumofbrands.com

Strawberry Hill House

Horace Walpole's beautifully restored Gothic Revival castle by the Thames in Twickenham.

Train: Strawberry Hill.

Find out more: 020 8744 1241 or strawberryhillhouse.org.uk

nationaltrust.org.uk/londonntpartners

Wicken Fen National Nature Reserve, Cambridgeshire

East of England

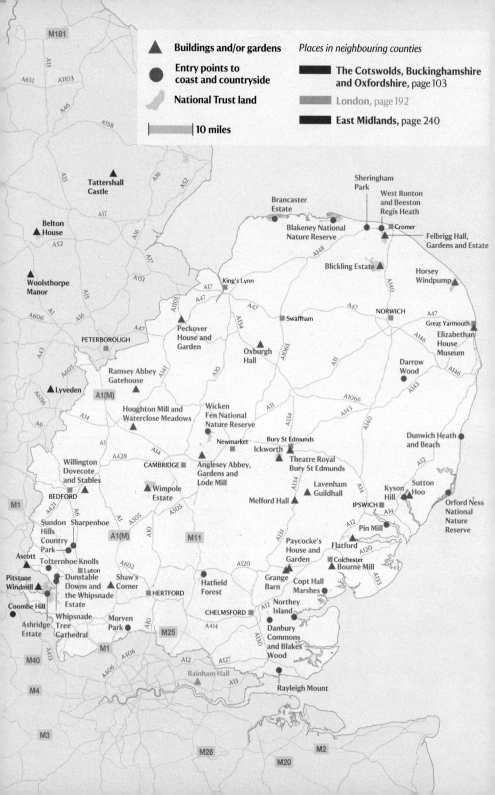

Buildings and/or gardens

Entry points to coast and countryside

National Trust land

10 miles

Places in neighbouring counties

The Cotswolds, Buckinghamshire and Oxfordshire, page 103

London, page 192

East Midlands, page 240

M181
A15
A631
A1103
A46
A158

Tattershall Castle
A16
A52
A17

Belton House
A16
A52

Woolsthorpe Manor
A15
A1
A16
A606
A1

Lyveden
A6116
A43
A605
A14
A6

Ramsey Abbey Gatehouse
A1(M)
A141

PETERBOROUGH
A47

Peckover House and Garden

King's Lynn
A17
A47
A134
A10

Brancaster Estate

Blakeney National Nature Reserve
A148

Sheringham Park

West Runton and Beeston Regis Heath
Cromer

Felbrigg Hall, Gardens and Estate

Blickling Estate
A140

Horsey Windpump

NORWICH
A47
A146

Great Yarmouth
Elizabethan House Museum

Swaffham
A1065

Oxburgh Hall

Darrow Wood
A143

A11
A1066
A143
A140
A146

Houghton Mill and Waterclose Meadows
A14
A1

Wicken Fen National Nature Reserve
A11

Newmarket

Bury St Edmunds
Ickworth

Theatre Royal Bury St Edmunds

Dunwich Heath and Beach
A12

Willington Dovecote and Stables
A428
A14

CAMBRIDGE

Anglesey Abbey, Gardens and Lode Mill

Lavenham Guildhall
A134

Kyson Hill
Sutton Hoo

BEDFORD
A421
A6
A1
A505

Wimpole Estate

Melford Hall

IPSWICH
A14

Orford Ness National Nature Reserve

Sundon Hills Country Park
Sharpenhoe
A1(M)
A10

Pin Mill

M1

Ascott
Totternhoe Knolls
A602

Luton
Dunstable Downs and the Whipsnade Estate
Shaw's Corner

M11

Paycocke's House and Garden

Flatford
A12
A120

Copt Hall Marshes

Colchester
Bourne Hill
A133

Pitstone Windmill

Coombe Hill
Ashridge Estate
M40
A413

Whipsnade Tree Cathedral

Morven Park

HERTFORD

Hatfield Forest
A120

CHELMSFORD
A12

Grange Barn

Northey Island
A130

M1
A406

A10
M25
A414

Danbury Commons and Blakes Wood

M4

Rainham Hall
A13

Rayleigh Mount

M3

M26

M20

M2

Anglesey Abbey, Gardens and Lode Mill

Quy Road, Lode, Cambridge, Cambridgeshire CB25 9EJ

🏠 🖼 ✿ 1966

When you step into this elegant home, you journey back to a golden age of country-house living. You can discover Lord Fairhaven's extensive collection and how we care for it, then explore the domestic wing to see how the staff serving Lord Fairhaven ran his household like clockwork. The celebrated garden, with its sweeping avenues, classical statuary and flower borders, offers captivating views, vibrant colours and delicious scents whatever the season. Children can play, explore and discover nature in the Wildlife Discovery Area. A visit to the historic working watermill on beautiful Quy Water will complete your day.

Eat, shop, stay: Redwoods restaurant serving sandwiches, hot meals, teas, cakes, hot drinks. Light refreshments and snacks in gardens during peak times. Shop and plant centre selling local products and gifts. Freshly milled wholemeal flour available from the historic watermill. Second-hand bookshop.

Things to see and do: **Indoors** Hands-on activities and demonstrations in the house. **Outdoors** Self-led family activities. Weekday garden tours. **Dogs**: assistance dogs only. Downloadable dog walk in local area available.

Access: 🅿️ 🚽 🚻 🦽 🔛 ♿ 📷
Abbey and Lode Mill 🦽 🪑 **Grounds** 🦽 ➡️ 🚶 ♿
Parking: 50 yards.

Find out more: 01223 810080 or angleseyabbey@nationaltrust.org.uk

Anglesey Abbey		M	T	W	T	F	S	S
Garden, restaurant, shop and plant centre								
1 Jan–24 Mar	10–4:30	M	T	W	T	F	S	S
25 Mar–27 Oct	10–5:30	M	T	W	T	F	S	S
28 Oct–31 Dec	10–4:30	M	T	W	T	F	S	S
House								
1 Jan–24 Mar	11–4*	M	T	W	T	F	S	S
25 Mar–27 Oct	11–5*	M	T	W	T	F	S	S
28 Oct–31 Dec	11–4*	M	T	W	T	F	S	S
Lode Mill								
2 Jan–30 Dec	10:30–3:30**		T	W	T	F	S	S

Snowdrop season: 29 January to 4 March. *House: last entry one hour before closing. **Lode Mill open Bank Holiday Mondays and Mondays during school holidays. Everything closed 24 to 26 December.

Anglesey Abbey, Gardens and Lode Mill, Cambridgeshire: parts of the house date back to the 13th century

For centuries, visitors from pilgrims to picnickers have enjoyed Ashridge Estate in Hertfordshire

Ashridge Estate

near Berkhamsted, Hertfordshire

⚒ 🏛 ⚓ 1926

This special place has been enjoyed for centuries by everyone from pilgrims to picnickers. With its rich wildlife, diverse habitats and varied history, there is plenty to uncover at Ashridge. From the scent of the bluebells in spring, glorious birdsong and spectacular views from the chalk downland of the Pitstone Hills in summer, the rutting fallow deer in autumn and crisp walks on swathes of open common in winter, Ashridge has a landscape for every season. Waymarked trails and walks leaflets from the visitor centre. Wildwood Den natural play area for children. Climb the Bridgewater Monument for fantastic views. **Note**: toilets available only when café open.

Eat, shop, stay: our shop offers an ever-changing array of local and seasonal gifts, maps and books. The Brownlow Café (concession) serves homemade meals and snacks to eat in our outdoor courtyard.

Things to see and do: events and children's activities throughout the year. Why not visit Pitstone Windmill, also part of the Ashridge Estate, open Sundays and Bank Holiday Mondays from 27 May to 27 August?
Dogs: under close control at all times for the safety of wildlife and visitors.

Access: 🅿️ 🛗 🚻 ♿ 🚶 Visitor centre 🐕 Grounds 🐕 ➡️ 👶

Sat Nav: use HP4 1LT for the visitor centre and Bridgewater Monument (points to the end of the drive). **Parking**: at the visitor centre, Ivinghoe Beacon and many other parts of the estate.

Find out more: 01442 851227 or ashridge@nationaltrust.org.uk

Ashridge Estate		M	T	W		T	S	S
Estate								
Open all year	Dawn–dusk	M	T	W	T	F	S	S
Visitor centre, Brownlow Café and shop*								
1 Jan–28 Feb	10–4	M	T	W	T	F	S	S
1 Mar–31 Oct	10–5	M	T	W	T	F	S	S
1 Nov–31 Dec	10–4	M	T	W	T	F	S	S
Bridgewater Monument (weather dependent)								
31 Mar–28 Oct	11–4		M	T	W	T	F	S	S

*Visitor centre, café and shop closed 24 and 25 December. Café: March to October, opens 8 and closes 6; November to February, opens 8 and closes 4. Estate may close in very high winds.

Blakeney National Nature Reserve

near Morston, Norfolk

🏠 🏛 ♿ 🎨 🐕 ⛴ | 1912

At the heart of the Norfolk Coast Area of Outstanding Natural Beauty, Blakeney National Nature Reserve boasts wide open spaces and uninterrupted views of the beautiful North Norfolk coastline. The four-mile long shingle spit of Blakeney Point offers protection for Blakeney Harbour and provides a perfect habitat for the vast array of residential and migratory wildlife. Spectacular displays of the summer breeding tern colony and winter breeding grey seals will delight visitors all year round. Great for walkers, sightseers and wildlife enthusiasts alike, the internationally important reserve guarantees an inspiring and memorable visit no matter the season. **Note**: nearest toilets at Morston Quay and Blakeney Quay.

Eat, shop, stay: takeaway snacks, drinks and tasty treats available from our refreshment kiosk at Morston Quay. Nearby pubs and hotels (not National Trust) offering locally themed menus. Our holiday cottage, a simple lodge by Blakeney village, offers a romantic getaway for two.

Blakeney National Nature Reserve, Norfolk: the Old Lifeboat Station, above, and swathes of purple sea lavender, below

Things to see and do: information centres at Morston Quay and Lifeboat House on Blakeney Point. Extensive coastal walks on the Norfolk Coast Path. Guided walks available. Ferry trips (not National Trust) to Blakeney Point.
Dogs: some restrictions apply (particularly Blakeney Point), 1 April to 15 August.

Access: 🚽♿🎨📺♿ Information centre ♿♿ Lifeboat House ♿♿
Sat Nav: use NR25 7BH for Morston Quay.
Parking: at Green Way Stiffkey Saltmarshes, Morston Quay and Blakeney Quay.

Find out more: 01263 740241 or blakeneypoint@nationaltrust.org.uk

Blakeney		M	T	W	T	F	S	S
Refreshment kiosk (Morston Quay)								
6 Jan–4 Feb	11–2						S	S
10 Feb–18 Feb	11–3	M	T	W	T	F	S	S
24 Feb–25 Feb	11–2						S	S
1 Mar–31 Oct	10–4	M	T	W	T	F	S	S
3 Nov–16 Dec	11–2						S	S
19 Dec–31 Dec*	11–2	M	T	W	T	F	S	S
Lifeboat House (Blakeney Point)								
30 Mar–30 Sep	Dawn–dusk	M	T	W	T	F	S	S

*Closed 25 December. Morston Information Centre open around the tides. Nature Reserve open all year.

Blickling Estate

Blickling, Aylsham, Norfolk NR11 6NF

🏠 ✝ 🍴 ♿ 🐾 🛏 1940

You'll never forget your first sight of Blickling, as the breathtaking Jacobean mansion comes into view, flanked by magnificent yew hedging. This 1,821-hectare (4,500-acre) gift to the nation was bequeathed by the grace of its visionary owner, Lord Lothian, who wished his former home to be a place 'from which artistic endeavours go forth'. From May to October you'll see something very different at Blickling. Inspired by this special place and in response to the threats to our library and nationally important book collection, award-winning theatre company Les Enfants Terribles has created an immersive art installation using sound, light and theatrical design. This exciting and challenging experience invites you to question your perceptions of historic spaces and collections. **Note**: additional charges apply for some special events.

Eat, shop, stay: three cafés and a pub offering bed and breakfast (not National Trust). Large second-hand bookshop, stamp shop with extensive stock for collectors (donations welcome), gift shop, plant and garden centre and exhibition gallery. Nine holiday cottages on the estate.

Things to see and do: **Indoors** Nearly 400 years of history brought to life through sounds, stories and personal insights. New contemporary art project May to October. Nationally important book collection in the Long Gallery. Loft Gallery with local artists' work. Family games and trails. Living history performances. RAF museum.
Outdoors Magnificent garden offering three centuries of inspired planting. Daily tours. Walled garden regeneration project ongoing. Park offers waymarked cycling and walking trails (free guides). Pyramid mausoleum. Permit fishing June to March. Events throughout year, including summer music concerts, Festival of the Blues, special days leading up to Christmas.

Blickling Estate in Norfolk: the breathtaking Jacobean mansion, right, and discovering the treasures inside this magnificent house, below

Felbrigg Hall and Sheringham Park nearby.
Dogs: welcome in park and at Farmyard café.
Assistance dogs only elsewhere.

Access: 🅿🦽🏠🔦🔉🎨📹♿
House 🔦🏠🚻🚹♿ Gardens 🏠➡🔦♿
Parking: 400 yards.

Find out more: 01263 738030 or
blickling@nationaltrust.org.uk

Blickling Estate		M	T	W	T	F	S	S
House								
1 Jan–18 Mar	10:30–3	M	T	W	T	F	S	S
19 Mar–28 Oct*	12–5	M	T	W	T	F	S	S
30 Oct–31 Dec**	10:30–3	M	T	W	T	F	S	S
Garden, shops and cafés								
1 Jan–18 Mar	10–3:30	M	T	W	T	F	S	S
19 Mar–28 Oct	10–5:30	M	T	W	T	F	S	S
29 Oct–31 Dec**	10:30–3	M	T	W	T	F	S	S
Park								
Open all year	Dawn–dusk	M	T	W	T	F	S	S

*Closed 27 to 29 April. **Closed 24 and 25 December.
Last entry one hour before closing. Fishing all year, except
15 March to 16 June.

**A springtime stroll at Blickling Estate:
centuries of garden history to enjoy**

Bourne Mill

Bourne Road, Colchester, Essex CO2 8RT

🏠 1936

Bourne Mill, Essex: late Elizabethan playfulness

Picturesque watermill with working waterwheel
in tranquil grounds. A delightful piece of late
Elizabethan playfulness, used at different times
for banqueting, milling flour and 'fulling' wool
cloth. Large millpond, Tudor Physic Garden,
wildlife area with ponds and babbling stream.
Pond-dipping and garden games. Special
events and family activities.

Eat, shop, stay: light refreshments available.
Pond-side seating area. Shop selling a range
of National Trust products.

Things to see and do: you can view the mill's
workings, then explore the wildlife area and see
how many '50 things' activities you can tick off.
Dogs: welcome on leads.

Access: 🦽🔦🔉🔦📷🎨 Building 🔦🏠
Grounds 🔦🏠
Parking: on site (very limited), or on street.

Find out more: 01206 549799 or
bournemill@nationaltrust.org.uk

Bourne Mill		M	T	W	T	F	S	S
21 Mar–4 Nov	11–4:30			W	T	F	S	S

Open Bank Holiday Mondays, April to August.
Closes 4 from 29 October.

Brancaster Estate

near Brancaster, Norfolk

 1923

The Brancaster Estate comprises the beautiful endless sandy Brancaster Beach, perfect for summer sandcastles and winter walks, the intriguing Branodunum Roman Fort site and the traditional fishing harbour of Brancaster Staithe. The area is rich in wildlife and offers a memorable visit regardless of the time of year. **Note**: beach car park (not National Trust). Toilets at beach and harbour. Parking charges apply at Brancaster Beach (including members). Weekly and seasonal passes available.

Eat, shop, stay: stay at Brancaster Activity Centre, perfect for a large group and family getaways. Self-catering accommodation sleeping up to 48 in dorm-style bedrooms with *en-suite* facilities.

Things to see and do: walk along the Norfolk Coast Path and explore the coastline, taking in the panoramic views of the saltmarsh across to Brancaster Harbour and Scolt Head Island National Nature Reserve beyond.
Dogs: responsible dog owners welcome. Restrictions apply on Brancaster Beach (May to September).

Every season offers its own distinctive delights at Brancaster Estate, Norfolk, above and below

Access: 🚾
Sat Nav: use PE31 8AX (Beach Road); PE31 8BW (Brancaster Staithe). **Parking**: Beach Road, Brancaster (not National Trust), charge including members. Limited parking at Harbour Way, Brancaster Staithe. Both subject to tidal flooding.

Find out more: 01263 740241 or brancaster@nationaltrust.org.uk

Copt Hall Marshes

near Little Wigborough, Essex

 1989

Working farm on the remote and beautiful Blackwater Estuary – a fantastic birdwatching spot, important for overwintering species. **Note**: for Sat Nav use CO5 7RD.

Find out more: 01245 227662 or copthall@nationaltrust.org.uk

Danbury Commons and Blakes Wood

near Danbury, Essex

1953

Varied countryside, ranging from the lowland heath of Danbury Common to ancient woodland with stunning spring flowers at Blakes Wood. **Note**: sorry no toilets. Sat Nav: for Danbury Commons use CM3 4JH and for Blakes Wood use CM3 4AU. Danbury Commons main car park closes dusk.

Find out more: 01245 227662 or danbury@nationaltrust.org.uk

Darrow Wood

Darrow Green Road, Denton, Harleston, Norfolk IP20 0AY

 1990

Darrow Wood is a small, hedge-enclosed, lightly wooded pasture field containing earthworks, including a compact motte-and-bailey castle. **Note**: very limited roadside parking. Sorry no toilet.

Find out more: 01728 648020 (Dunwich Heath) or darrowwood@nationaltrust.org.uk

Dunstable Downs and the Whipsnade Estate

near Dunstable, Bedfordshire

 1928

The Downs have so much to offer all year round. The best kite-flying and picnicking site for miles around. A haven for wildlife; home to orchids, butterflies, birds and much more. Enjoy the ever-changing view from the

Two views of Dunstable Downs and the Whipsnade Estate, Bedfordshire: perfect for walks and kite-flying

Chilterns Gateway Centre with a refreshing drink or delicious meal. **Note**: Chilterns Gateway Centre is owned by Central Bedfordshire Council and managed by the National Trust.

Eat, shop, stay: shop selling a wide range of kites and Dunstable Downs branded products. The View Café serves light lunches, snacks, hot and cold drinks with the option to eat in or take away.

Things to see and do: events, including the annual Kite Festival in July. Nature trail and playscape in Chute Wood. Waymarked routes. History to discover and wildlife to spot.
Dogs: under close control, on leads in car parks, near livestock and ground-nesting birds.

Access: [icons] Dunstable Downs [icons]
Chilterns Gateway Centre [icons]
Sat Nav: use LU6 2GY (or LU6 2TA for older equipment). **Parking**: at Dunstable Downs, off B4541, and Bison Hill off the B4540.

Find out more: 01582 500920 or dunstabledowns@nationaltrust.org.uk

Dunstable Downs		M	T	W	T	F	S	S
Chilterns Gateway Centre								
1 Jan–11 Feb	9:30–4	M	T	W	T	F	S	S
12 Feb–28 Oct	9:30–5	M	T	W	T	F	S	S
29 Oct–31 Dec	9:30–4	M	T	W	T	F	S	S

Closed 24 and 25 December. Hot food served up to 30 minutes before Centre closes.

Dunwich Heath and Beach

Dunwich, Saxmundham, Suffolk

🛏️ 🏞️ 🐾 🛌 1968

A precious landscape on the Suffolk coast, Dunwich Heath offers a true sense of being at one with nature. Set in the very middle of an Area of Outstanding Natural Beauty, there is an abundance of wildlife to discover, including rare birds such as the Dartford warbler and nightjar. With a network of footpaths to explore, a walk on Dunwich Heath will rejuvenate you at any time of the year. Download our free app to help you make the most of your visit – search 'Dunwich Heath'. **Note**: opening hours may be adjusted during bad weather.

Eat, shop, stay: clifftop tea-room serving breakfast, lunch, cream teas, homemade cakes, scones and ice-cream. Enjoy views from the lookout or warm yourself by the log burner. Gift shop selling selected National Trust bestsellers. Enjoy a stay in our holiday apartments.

Feel at one with nature at Dunwich Heath and Beach, Suffolk, below and right

Things to see and do: self-guided walking trails. Family activities, including bug-hunting, den-building, geocaching and children's trails. Heath Barn discovery area and family beach. **Dogs**: welcome. On leads around heath March to end of August. 'Woof' walk/beach unrestricted.

Access: 🅿️ 🅳 ♿ ♿ ♿ **Grounds** ➡️ ♿
Sat Nav: use IP17 3DJ. **Parking**: on site.

Find out more: 01728 648501 or dunwichheath@nationaltrust.org.uk

Dunwich Heath and Beach		M	T	W	T	F	S	S
6 Jan–11 Feb	10–3						S	S
12 Feb–18 Feb	10–4	M	T	W	T	F	S	S
24 Feb–25 Feb	10–4						S	S
1 Mar–22 Jul	10–5	M	T	W	T	F	S	S
23 Jul–9 Sep	9:30–5	M	T	W	T	F	S	S
10 Sep–31 Oct	10–5	M	T	W	T	F	S	S
3 Nov–23 Dec	10–3						S	S
26 Dec–31 Dec	10–3	M		W	T	F	S	S

Open 1 January, 10 to 3. Opening times may be adjusted in line with weather conditions.

Elizabethan House Museum

4 South Quay, Great Yarmouth, Norfolk NR30 2QH

🏠 🔔 🍷 1943

A 16th-century quayside home, set out to reflect day-to-day domestic life from Tudor to Victorian times. **Note**: managed by Norfolk Museums Service. Open Monday to Friday and Sundays, 29 March to 31 October, 10 to 4.

Find out more: 01493 855746 or elizabethanhouse@nationaltrust.org.uk

Felbrigg Hall, Gardens and Estate

Felbrigg, Norwich, Norfolk NR11 8PR

🏠 ✝ ❖ ⛵ 🏠 | 1969 |

Home to eight generations, Felbrigg is a place of tranquillity and atmosphere. From family rooms to functional rooms, the Hall, which still contains its original collection, reflects the people who shaped it. There are also more than 400 years of family stories to discover. Set in extensive parkland with a working walled garden and dove-house, orangery, lake and miles of estate walks all framed by Norfolk skies, it's the perfect place to escape and relax.

Eat, shop, stay: Squire's Pantry serving a selection of sandwiches, light meals, snacks, cakes and drinks. Jester's trailer is open at peak times in the meadow. Shop and second-hand bookshop selling a selection of gifts and plants. Eight holiday cottages on the estate.

Things to see and do: **Indoors** Introductory talks and attics and cellars tours on most days (call property to confirm on day of visit). Children's trails. **Outdoors** Events throughout the year (see website for details).
Dogs: welcome in tea-room. On leads near livestock. Assistance dogs only in Hall and gardens.

Felbrigg Hall, Gardens and Estate, Norfolk: the walled garden, above, and house at sunrise, left

Access: 🅿️ 🚗 ♿ 🚻 🏞️ 🚶 ⚲ 📷 **Hall** ♿ ♿
Gardens ♿ ➡️ ♿ ♿
Sat Nav: use NR11 8PP. **Parking**: 100 yards. Electric vehicle charging point in main car park.

Find out more: 01263 837444 or felbrigg@nationaltrust.org.uk

Felbrigg Hall		M	T	W	T	F	S	S
House*								
10 Feb–23 Mar	12–3	M	T	W	T	F	S	S
24 Mar–28 Oct	12–5	M	T	W	T	F	S	S
Service Wing, garden, shop and tea-room*								
6 Jan–4 Feb	11–3	·	·	·	·	·	S	S
Service Wing*								
3 Nov–30 Dec	11–3	·	·	·	·	·	S	S
Garden, shop and tea-room								
10 Feb–23 Mar	11–3	M	T	W	T	F	S	S
24 Mar–28 Oct	11–5	M	T	W	T	F	S	S
1 Nov–30 Dec	11–3	·	·	·	T	F	S	S
Parkland								
Open all year	Dawn–dusk	M	T	W	T	F	S	S

*Last entry to Service Wing and house one hour before closing; Service Wing opens at 11, housing temporary exhibitions or installations. Garden, shop and tea-room: open 31 December, 11 to 3.

Flatford

East Bergholt, Suffolk CO7 6UL

 1943

Flatford lies at the heart of the Dedham Vale Area of Outstanding Natural Beauty. This charming hamlet was the inspiration for some of John Constable's most famous paintings, including *The Hay Wain, Boat Building* and *Flatford Mill*. Our fascinating exhibition gives you an insight into Constable's life and career whilst Bridge Cottage tells the story of the people who lived and worked at Flatford. You can explore the beautiful countryside on one of the circular walks or hire a boat and row along the River Stour. A visit to Flatford is a chance to walk in Constable's footsteps! **Note**: no public access inside Flatford Mill, Valley Farm and Willy Lott's House. £3.50 charge for guided tour (including members).

Eat, shop, stay: riverside tea-room serving a tempting range of homemade cakes and light lunches. The gift shop offers quality gifts, souvenirs and Constable merchandise.

Things to see and do: volunteer guides offer short walking tours taking in the views which inspired John Constable (April to October only). Waymarked circular walks and family trails around Flatford. **Dogs**: welcome, but please keep dogs on leads amongst livestock.

Dusk falls at Flatford, in the heart of Dedham Vale

Access: 🅿️ 🚻 ♿ 🧸 🔔 👶 🎣 📷 🅰️
Bridge Cottage 👣 ♿ **Grounds** 🚶 🐾 ♿
Parking: 100 yards.

Find out more: 01206 298260 or flatford@nationaltrust.org.uk

Flatford		M	T	W	T	F	S	S
1 Jan–5 Jan	10–3:30	M	T	W	T	F		
6 Jan–11 Feb	10–3:30						S	S
12 Feb–18 Feb	10–4:30	M	T	W	T	F	S	S
21 Feb–25 Mar	10–4:30			W	T	F	S	S
26 Mar–2 Nov	10–5	M	T	W	T	F	S	S
3 Nov–23 Dec	10–3:30			W	T	F	S	S
27 Dec–31 Dec	10–3:30	M			T	F	S	S

Willy Lott's Cottage at Flatford, Suffolk: the hamlet inspired some of John Constable's most famous paintings

Grange Barn

Grange Hill, Coggeshall, Colchester,
Essex CO6 1RE

🏠🔔🍽️ 1989

One of Europe's oldest timber-framed
buildings, Grange Barn stands as a lasting
reminder of the once-powerful Coggeshall
Abbey. With oak pillars soaring up to a
cathedral-like roof, bearing the weight of
centuries, it was saved and restored in the
1980s. This 13th-century building has truly
stood the test of time.

Eat, shop, stay: honey from Grange Barn's
beehives is available to buy in season, alongside
a limited range of souvenirs, second-hand
books, takeaway refreshments and ice-cream.
Coffee shop at nearby Paycocke's House and
Garden. Picnics welcome.

Massive oak pillars at Grange Barn in Essex

Things to see and do: exhibition on the life
and work of local woodcarver Bryan Saunders.
Events during the year. Circular walk taking in
Paycocke's House and Garden nearby.
Dogs: welcome on leads in grounds.

Access: 🅿️🚻 Building 🔄 Grounds 🔄
Parking: on site.

Find out more: 01376 562226 or
grangebarncoggeshall@nationaltrust.org.uk

Grange Barn		M	T	W	T	F	S	S
17 Mar–30 Sep	11–4	M	T	W	T	F	S	S
1 Oct–28 Oct	11–3	M	T	W	T	F	S	S

Closes occasionally for private events (check before visiting).

Hatfield Forest

near Bishop's Stortford, Essex

🏠🏛️🚲♿🐕🍽️ 1924

Red Poll cattle at Hatfield Forest in Essex

When Henry I established a Royal Hunting
Forest here in 1100, he could little have guessed
that almost a millennium later it would be the
best survivor of its kind in the world. The
ancient trees are managed using traditional
techniques, and the forest is home to more
than 3,500 species of wildlife, including fallow
deer descended from the original herd. Explore
the wide open plains, grazed by Red Poll cows,
or enjoy the shade of the coppice woodland.
With over 405 hectares (1,000 acres), there are
many places for imaginative play or a spot of
quiet relaxation.

Eat, shop, stay: café (outdoor-only dining
area) serving hot and cold refreshments,
ice-cream and drinks. Shop selling gifts,
guidebook and maps, plus Hatfield Forest
venison (when in season).

The lake at Hatfield Forest, above, and exploring with a canine friend, below

Things to see and do: events, including open-air theatre and WoodFest. Rowing boat hire available in the summer. Family activities in the summer holidays. **Dogs**: welcome under close control. On leads in lake area, boardwalk and near livestock.

Access:
Shell House **Forest**
Sat Nav: use CM22 6NE.
Parking: on site (limited in winter).

Find out more: 01279 874040 (Infoline). 01279 870678 or hatfieldforest@nationaltrust.org.uk

Hatfield Forest		M	T	W	T	F	S	S
Café								
1 Jan–16 Mar	10–3:30	**M**	**T**	**W**	**T**	**F**	**S**	**S**
17 Mar–28 Oct	9–5	**M**	**T**	**W**	**T**	**F**	**S**	**S**
29 Oct–31 Dec	10–3:30	**M**	**T**	**W**	**T**	**F**	**S**	**S**

Entrance car park open daily; Shell House and Elgin's car parks open 17 March to 28 October, 10 to 4:30, Monday to Friday, and 9 to 4:30, Saturday and Sunday (conditions permitting). Café and internal car parks closed 25 December.

Horsey Windpump

Horsey, Great Yarmouth, Norfolk NR29 4EE

1948

Horsey Windpump, Norfolk, shows off its new sails

Fully restored and once again standing proud over the broadland landscape, Horsey Windpump is complete with new cap and patent sails. Explore this historic building to discover its fascinating story and the connection between man and nature. There are fantastic views over Horsey Mere and beyond from the top. **Note**: surrounded by Horsey Estate – managed by the Buxton family. Horsey Gap car park, not National Trust (charge including members).

Eat, shop, stay: shop and tea-room (next to Horsey Windpump) serving snacks, drinks, tasty treats and small range of gifts. Stay in one of our converted barn holiday cottages nearby in Horsey village. Perfectly placed for exploring the Broads and Norfolk coast.

Things to see and do: great starting point for accessing the outdoors, with walking routes to Horsey Mere and the beach. Boat trips (not National Trust) across Horsey Mere (May to September). **Dogs**: welcome (on leads near wildlife and livestock).

Access: ⌷🅿🦽♿🔊📷🚽🛗🖊🅾
Windpump 🦽♿🦽 Grounds 🦽 ➡
Parking: on site. Alternatively, at Horsey Gap car park, 1 mile, not National Trust (charge including members).

Find out more: 01263 740241 or horseywindpump@nationaltrust.org.uk

Horsey Windpump		M	T	W	T	F	S	S
Windpump, shop and tea-room								
24 Mar–28 Oct	10–4:30	**M**	**T**	**W**	**T**	**F**	**S**	**S**

Car park and toilets open all year, dawn to dusk.

Houghton Mill and Waterclose Meadows

Houghton, near Huntingdon, Cambridgeshire PE28 2AZ

🏚🌲🛆🔔 1939

In a stunning riverside setting, surrounded by meadow walks, Houghton Mill is the oldest working watermill on the Great Ouse. There are hands-on activities for all the family, as well as milling demonstrations. You can buy our flour, ground in the traditional way on our French burr millstones.

Eat, shop, stay: riverside tea-room serving snacks, cakes and scones made with our traditional stoneground flour. Freshly ground flour and gifts for sale in our mill shop. Come and stay at our tranquil riverside camp/caravan site.

Houghton Mill and Waterclose Meadows, Cambridgeshire

Things to see and do: **Indoors** Milling demonstrations on Sundays. Baking days. Family events. **Outdoors** Open-air theatre. Children's trails, activities and summer holiday events. Access to surrounding meadows via public footpaths.
Dogs: assistance dogs only please in mill; all dogs welcome in grounds on leads.

Access: ⌷🅿🦽♿🔊📷🖥🎬🖊 Mill 🦽♿
Tea-room 🦽 Grounds ➡
Sat Nav: use PE28 2AZ. **Parking**: on site.

Find out more: 01480 499990 (property main line). 01480 466716 (campsite) or houghtonmill@nationaltrust.org.uk

Houghton Mill		M	T	W	T	F	S	S
Tea-room								
3 Jan–18 Mar	10:30–3:30	·	·	**W**	·	·	**S**	**S**
19 Mar–30 Sep	10:30–5	**M**	**T**	**W**	**T**	**F**	**S**	**S**
1 Oct–28 Oct	10:30–5	**M**	**T**	**W**	·	·	**S**	**S**
31 Oct–30 Dec	10:30–3:30	·	·	**W**	·	·	**S**	**S**
Mill								
17 Mar–28 Oct	11–5	·	·	·	·	·	**S**	**S**
19 Mar–25 Jul	1–5	**M**	**T**	**W**	·	·	·	·
30 Jul–31 Aug	1–5	**M**	**T**	**W**	**T**	**F**	·	·
3 Sep–24 Oct	1–5	**M**	**T**	**W**	·	·	·	·

Open Bank Holiday Mondays and Good Friday, 11 to 5. Waterclose Meadows Caravan and Campsite (National Trust): open 23 March to 28 October (01480 466716). Car park and riverside: close 8, or dusk if earlier.

Ickworth

The Rotunda, Horringer, Bury St Edmunds,
Suffolk IP29 5QE

🏠✝🔭🔀📷🚻 1956

An Italianate palace in the heart of Suffolk.
The Ickworth Estate reflects the Hervey family's
passion for everything Italian. The Rotunda is a
Neo-classical showcase, intended by the 4th
Earl of Bristol to display his impressive
treasures. Home to one of the finest silver
collections by Huguenot silversmiths, and
family portraits by artists such as
Gainsborough and Reynolds. In the basement,
1930s domestic service is brought to life
through the stories and memories of former
staff. The Italianate Garden mirrors the house
architecture, with clipped hedges and
Mediterranean planting, while an idiosyncratic
Victorian stumpery, planted with shade-loving
ferns, creates an air of mystery. Extensive
parkland walks and cycle routes offer space and
freedom to discover hidden pathways and
inspiring views. **Note**: accommodation

provided at The Ickworth hotel (part of the
Luxury Family Hotel Group), 01284 735350.

Eat, shop, stay: West Wing Café serving
seasonal lunches all year. Porter's Lodge
outdoor café. Squash Court Café open
weekends. Gift shop, plant and garden shop
offer a wide range of local goods. Five stunning
holiday cottages across the estate.

Things to see and do: Indoors Tours daily,
house exhibitions, 1930s Living History days
and children's crafts in the Gallery. Basement
servants' quarters, an extensive silver
collection, Regency furniture, historic books
and Italian porcelain, as well as paintings by
Titian, Vigée Le Brun and Kauffmann.
Outdoors Events and activities all year,
including Easter Egg trails, wildlife days,
summer open-air theatre and cinema, autumn
Wood Fair and family Christmas weekends.
Seasonal highlights include snowdrops,
lambing and Walled Garden seasonal flower
meadow. Extensive guided tours, waymarked
walks, cycle routes (all year), Hervey family
church, den-building, children's play area and
trim trail. **Dogs**: welcome on leads at all times.
Assistance dogs only in the Italianate Garden.

Baking the old-fashioned way at Ickworth: an Italianate palace in the heart of Suffolk

By shopping with us, you support special places – shop.nationaltrust.org.uk

Access: [icons]
House [icons] **West Wing** [icons]
Gardens/parkland [icons]
Sat Nav: may not direct you to main entrance. Access to Ickworth is through Horringer village.
Parking: on site.

Find out more: 01284 735270 or ickworth@nationaltrust.org.uk

Ickworth		M	T	W	T	F	S	S
House								
1 Jan–2 Mar*	11–3	M	T	W	T	F	S	S
3 Mar–28 Oct**	11–5†	M	T	W	T	F	S	S
29 Oct–31 Dec*	11–3	M	T	W	T	F	S	S
Gift shop and West Wing Café								
1 Jan–2 Mar	10:30–4	M	T	W	T	F	S	S
3 Mar–28 Oct	10:30–5	M	T	W	T	F	S	S
29 Oct–31 Dec	10:30–4	M	T	W	T	F	S	S
Porter's Lodge outdoor café								
6 Jan–25 Feb	10–4						S	S
3 Mar–28 Oct	10–5	M	T	W	T	F	S	S
29 Oct–31 Dec	10–4	M	T	W	T	F	S	S
Plant and garden shop								
3 Mar–28 Oct	10–5	M	T	W	T	F	S	S
3 Nov–30 Dec	12–3						S	S

*Tours only weekdays; servants' quarters free-flow only weekends. **Tours only, 11 to 12 and 4 to 5; free-flow 12 to 4. Last entry 3.15. †Sneak peek Wednesdays; see the house in a different way, check before visiting for details. Plant and garden shop and Porter's Lodge outdoor café may close earlier in winter and adverse weather. Italianate garden, parkland and children's play area: open daily, 9 to 5:30 (closes dusk if earlier). Children's play area may close if poor ground conditions. Everything closed 24 and 25 December.

Kyson Hill

Broomheath, Woodbridge, Suffolk

[icons] 1934

Diminutive Kyson Hill, with its grassy slopes, specimen trees and estuarine views, is a favourite destination for walking or relaxation. **Note**: sorry no toilet. Broomheath public car park, 546 yards (not National Trust). For Sat Nav use IP12 4DL. OS map reference is 197/212:TM264478.

Find out more: 01394 389700 (Sutton Hoo) or kysonhill@nationaltrust.org.uk

The Rotunda at Ickworth: a Neo-classical showcase

Lavenham Guildhall

Market Place, Lavenham, Sudbury, Suffolk CO10 9QZ

 1951

The Guildhall of Corpus Christi is a remarkable medieval survivor at the centre of the village of Lavenham, remaining a constant presence over the past 500 years. When you step inside this complex of fine timber-framed buildings, you'll feel the centuries melt away. You can discover the stories of the people who have lived and worked here, their highs and lows. From religious guild to workhouse, family home to nightclub, there is more than meets the eye. After your visit, why not explore the picturesque streets of Lavenham, lined with shops, galleries and more than 320 buildings of historic interest?

Step inside Lavenham Guildhall in Suffolk and feel the centuries melt away

Examining the bell at Lavenham Guildhall: a remarkable medieval survivor

Eat, shop, stay: tea-room serving light lunches, cream teas and hot and cold drinks. Shop selling local gifts, souvenirs, books and plants.

Things to see and do: **Indoors** Children's trails and dressing-up costumes. Changing exhibitions. **Outdoors** Guided walks and talks in summer.

Access: 🏛️♿️🦽🚻📷🖥️🚶‍♂️📱Ⓟ
Guildhall ♿️🦽 Garden ♿️🦽
Parking: in village (free) – no National Trust parking. Nearest car parks at Prentice Street (200 yards, 24 spaces), use CO10 9RD, and main car park Church Street (800 yards, 86 spaces), use CO10 9SA.

Find out more: 01787 247646 or lavenhamguildhall@nationaltrust.org.uk

Lavenham Guildhall		M	T	W	T	F	S	S
5 Jan–25 Feb	11–4	·	·	·	·	**F**	**S**	**S**
1 Mar–4 Nov	11–5	**M**	**T**	**W**	**T**	**F**	**S**	**S**
8 Nov–23 Dec*	11–4	·	·	·	**T**	**F**	**S**	**S**

*7 to 9 December: Lavenham Christmas fair only (admission free); shop and tea-room open as normal.

Melford Hall

Long Melford, Sudbury, Suffolk CO10 9AA

🏠♿️♿️ 1960

Melford Hall has had its fair share of trials and tribulations, from being ransacked during the Civil War to being devastated by fire in 1942. It is thanks to the many generations who have left their mark that it continues to survive. This year we will concentrate on two strong women, Countess Rivers and Ulla, Lady Hyde Parker, who transformed Melford Hall in the 17th and 20th centuries respectively. It is their stories, and those of Hyde Parker family life – from naval exploits to visits from their cousin Beatrix Potter – which make this house more than mere bricks and mortar.

Eat, shop, stay: small tea-room or Park Room serving sandwiches and cream teas. Gatehouse shop selling souvenirs, gifts, books, souvenir story books and plants.

Melford Hall in Suffolk, below and right, has faced many trials, from the Civil War to a major fire in the 1940s

Things to see and do: **Indoors** Taster tours and talks. Spot-it quiz for children under eight. **Outdoors** Garden tours and games. Walks, talks and family events. **Dogs**: welcome on leads in car park and park walk only.

Access: 🅿️♿🏠♿🔔📷📹♿🚻
Building ♿♿👥♿ **Grounds** ♿♿
Parking: on site.

Find out more: 01787 376395 (Infoline). 01787 379228 or melford@nationaltrust.org.uk

Melford Hall		M	T	W	T	F	S	S
21 Mar–28 Oct	12–5				W	T	F	S	S

House: 12 to 1, entry by short taster tour only; free-flow from 1. Open Bank Holiday Mondays and Good Friday.

Morven Park

Great North Road, Potters Bar, Hertfordshire

🏞️ 1928

On the site of the original Potters Bar, these eight hectares (20 acres) of parkland are over 150 years old. **Note**: sorry no toilet or on-site parking. For Sat Nav use EN6 1HS.

Find out more: 01582 873663 or morvenpark@nationaltrust.org.uk

Northey Island

near Maldon, Essex

🏠🏞️⛺🐕 1978

A peaceful retreat in the Blackwater Estuary, important for overwintering birds, Northey is also the oldest recorded battlefield in Britain. **Note**: causeway access is restricted by tides. To arrange a visit, please phone to book a permit. For Sat Nav use CM9 6PP (CM9 5JQ parking).

Find out more: 01621 853142 or northeyisland@nationaltrust.org.uk

Orford Ness National Nature Reserve

Orford Quay, Orford, Woodbridge, Suffolk IP12 2NU

🏠🏞️⛺🐕 1993

This is Suffolk's secret coast, only reached by National Trust ferry. Wild, remote and exposed, the 'Island' contains the ruined remnants of a disturbing past. Ranked among the most important shingle features in the world, rare and fragile wildlife thrives where weapons, including atomic bombs, were once tested and perfected. **Note**: limited tickets. Steep, slippery

Wild, remote and exposed, Orford Ness
National Nature Reserve in Suffolk

steps, long distances. Hazardous debris.
Limited access: 'pagodas' only on tours.
Charge for ferry crossing (including members).

Eat, shop, stay: shops, cafés and pubs in
village (none National Trust). Fresh fish
available at quay. Local smokehouses.

Things to see and do: trails lead through
coastal grazing marsh and vegetated shingle
habitats to the sea, taking in wildlife, ex-military
testing areas, buildings and displays.
Dogs: assistance dogs only.

Access: ⬚⬚⬚ **Buildings** ⬚⬚ **Trails** ⬚➡
Sat Nav: IP12 2NU. **Parking**: at Riverside
car park, Quay Street, not National Trust
(charge including members), 150 yards to
Trust Orford Quay office to buy ferry ticket.

Find out more: 01728 648024 (Infoline).
01394 450900 (office) or
orfordness@nationaltrust.org.uk

Orford Ness		M	T	W	T	F	S	S
31 Mar–23 Jun	10–2						S	
26 Jun–29 Sep	10–2		T	W	T	F	S	
6 Oct–27 Oct	10–2						S	

Access by National Trust ferry from Orford Quay. Boats cross
to the Ness every 20 minutes, 10 to 2 only, returning regularly
through day (last ferry back departs 5). Tickets limited,
only available on day. Main visitor trail (Red Route) always
available, other routes open seasonally.

Oxburgh Hall

Oxborough, near Swaffham, Norfolk PE33 9PS

⬚⬚⬚⬚⬚⬚ 1952

No one forgets their first sight of Oxburgh.
Built in 1482 by the Catholic Bedingfeld family,
it is the enduring legacy of their survival
through turbulent times. There are 500 years
of history to explore and hidden doors, rooftop
views and a secret priest's hole to discover.
Victorian Gothic interiors reflect a romantic
view of Oxburgh's medieval past. The
collections include embroideries worked by
Mary, Queen of Scots, and colourful wallpapers
from the mid-19th century. The moated hall is
surrounded by nearly 28 hectares (70 acres),
containing gardens with seasonal
interest, streams and woodland walks.
Note: scaffolding in the courtyard due to
important conservation work.

Eat, shop, stay: tea-room in old Kitchen and
Servants' Hall. The Pantry is a seasonal kiosk
serving light refreshments. Picnic in the
grounds or area by the car park. Gift shop
selling gifts, games and local products.
Plant sales. Second-hand bookshop.
Holiday cottage.

Oxburgh Hall, Norfolk: the moated house, left, and colourful herbaceous borders, above

Things to see and do: **Indoors** Introductory talks most days, March to October. Family trails. **Outdoors** Guided garden tours most days, March to October. Winter weekend snowdrop walks. Children's activities, including woodland den-building area. Year-round events. **Dogs**: on short leads in the gardens and countryside. Assistance dogs only indoors.

Access: 🅿️ ♿ 🚻 ♿ 🔊 📷 📹 🎧
Hall ♿ ♿ 🚻 ♿ Chapel ♿ Garden ♿ ➡️ ♿
Parking: on site.

Find out more: 01366 328258 or oxburghhall@nationaltrust.org.uk

Oxburgh Hall		M	T	W	T	F	S	S
House								
10 Feb–9 Mar	12–3	M	T	W	T	F	S	S
10 Mar–30 Sep	11–5*	M	T	W	T	F	S	S
1 Oct–4 Nov	11–4	M	T	W	T	F	S	S
10 Nov–25 Nov**	Tour						S	S
Garden, shop and tea-room								
6 Jan–11 Feb	11–4						S	S
12 Feb–9 Mar	11–4	M	T	W	T	F	S	S
10 Mar–30 Sep	10:30–5	M	T	W	T	F	S	S
1 Oct–4 Nov	10:30–4	M	T	W	T	F	S	S
10 Nov–22 Dec	11–4						S	S

*House: last entry at 4; access may be by guided tours only after 3, March to October. **Guided tours only at 12 and 2, places limited.

Paycocke's House and Garden

25 West Street, Coggeshall, Colchester, Essex CO6 1NS

🏠 ❋ 1924

Exquisitely carved half-timbered Tudor cloth merchant's house, with a beautiful and tranquil cottage garden. Visitors can follow the house's changing fortune and see how it was saved from demolition and restored to its former glory. You can discover five centuries of craftsmanship and conservation.

Eat, shop, stay: coffee shop serving cream teas, coffee, cakes and soft drinks (courtyard and garden). Picnics welcome. Shop selling gifts and local products. Plants for sale at our garden stall. Second-hand bookshop.

Two views of Paycocke's House and Garden in Essex: exquisite Tudor craftsmanship

Things to see and do: **Indoors** Events all year. Children's dressing-up costumes. **Outdoors** Relax or play garden games. Why not combine with visit to nearby Grange Barn and enjoy the circular walk? **Dogs**: welcome in garden only on a lead; assistance dogs only in house.

Access: ⬚⬚⬚⬚⬚ Building ⬚ Grounds ⬚⬚
Parking: at Coggeshall Grange Barn, ½ mile.

Find out more: 01376 561305 or paycockes@nationaltrust.org.uk

Paycocke's		M	T	W	T	F	S	S
17 Mar–28 Oct	11–5	**M**	**T**	**W**	**T**	**F**	**S**	**S**
Garden: open 10:30; closing time as house.								

Peckover House and Garden

North Brink, Wisbech, Cambridgeshire PE13 1JR

🏠✳️🏘️▲🍽️ 1943

While its riverside setting at Wisbech was popular among merchants, imposing Peckover House stood apart as an oasis of calm,

reflecting the Quaker way of life. The Peckovers were bankers and added a specially designed wing to the house; an exhibition tells its story. They also loved their garden; discover its delights as you explore the unexpected 0.8 hectare (two acres) of abundance. This year sees the 70th anniversary of the passing of the last Peckover and the property coming to the National Trust. Our Trust New Art project 'Transitions in Time' will explore this period of change for the property.

Eat, shop, stay: the Reed Barn is the ideal place for a light lunch or afternoon tea. Browse our gift shop, second-hand bookshop and our plant trolley. Stay a little longer in one of our holiday cottages – Wainman House or Coach House Loft.

Things to see and do: **Indoors** Grand piano to play, behind-the-scenes tours, handling collection, children's trails, exhibitions, Trust New Art project. **Outdoors** Garden tours, croquet/lawn games (summer). Octavia Hill's Birthplace House opposite (not National Trust). **Dogs**: assistance dogs only.

Access: ⬚⬚⬚⬚⬚⬚⬚
House ⬚⬚ Garden ⬚▶️⬚
Sat Nav: use PE13 1RG or PE13 2RA for nearest car parks. **Parking**: nearest at Chapel Road or Somers Road, 500 yards (not National Trust). Car parks occasionally used for town events and may not be in use – please check before journey.

Find out more: 01945 583463 or peckover@nationaltrust.org.uk

Peckover House and Garden		M	T	W	T	F	S	S
13 Jan–18 Feb	12–4*						**S**	**S**
24 Feb–25 Mar	11–4**	**M**	**T**	**W**	**T**		**S**	**S**
26 Mar–15 Apr	11–5¹	**M**	**T**	**W**	**T**	**F**	**S**	**S**
16 Apr–1 Jul	11–5¹	**M**	**T**	**W**	**T**		**S**	**S**
2 Jul–8 Jul	11–5¹	**M**	**T**	**W**	**T**	**F**	**S**	**S**
9 Jul–21 Oct	11–5¹	**M**	**T**	**W**	**T**		**S**	**S**
22 Oct–28 Oct	11–4¹	**M**	**T**	**W**	**T**	**F**	**S**	**S**
3 Nov–18 Nov	11–4¹						**S**	**S**
8 Dec–16 Dec	11–4²	**M**	**T**	**W**	**T**	**F**	**S**	**S**

*House open for conservation talk only at 2 (limited spaces, booking advisable). **House open by timed tours only weekdays; free-flow at weekends. ¹House open 12 to 4. ²Christmas Celebration.

Imposing Peckover House and Garden in Cambridgeshire: an oasis of calm

Pin Mill

near Chelmondiston, Suffolk

 1978

A woodland and heathland restoration site. A number of footpaths from the village with panoramic views over the River Orwell. **Note**: for Sat Nav use IP9 1JW. Parking in Pin Mill village, not National Trust (charge including members), or Chelmondiston.

Find out more: 01206 298260 or pinmill@nationaltrust.org.uk

Ramsey Abbey Gatehouse

Hollow Lane, Ramsey, Huntingdon, Cambridgeshire PE26 1DH

🏛️✝️ 1952

This fascinating medieval gatehouse, along with the Lady Chapel, are all that remain of the great Benedictine abbey at Ramsey. **Note**: in school grounds so no public access except on open days. Gatehouse and Lady Chapel open first Sunday of the month, April to September, 1 to 5.

Find out more: 01480 301494 or ramseyabbey@nationaltrust.org.uk

Rayleigh Mount

Rayleigh, Essex

🏛️ 1923

Medieval motte-and-bailey castle site, with adjacent windmill housing historical exhibition. **Note**: exhibition in windmill operated by Rochford District Council. For Sat Nav use SS6 7ED. Parking at Bellingham Lane –

adjacent to main entrance (not National Trust). Open daily, 1 January to 24 March and 28 October to 31 December, 7 to 4; 25 March to 27 October, 7 to 6. Opening times may vary, call 01268 775328 to check before visiting. Gates close 2 on Saturdays.

Find out more: 01284 747500 or rayleighmount@nationaltrust.org.uk

Sharpenhoe

Sharpenhoe Road, Streatley, Bedfordshire

🏛️♿👣 1939

Dominating the landscape, this steep chalk escarpment (above) is crowned with beech woodland and at the northern end traces of an Iron Age hill fort. Managed as a nature reserve, there is wildlife to discover all year around. **Note**: sorry no toilets.

Access: 🅿️♿
Sat Nav: use LU3 3PR.
Parking: on Sharpenhoe Road, Streatley.

Find out more: 01582 873663 or sharpenhoe@nationaltrust.org.uk

Shaw's Corner

Ayot St Lawrence, near Welwyn,
Hertfordshire AL6 9BX

🏠 ✤ 1944

Shaw's Corner, Hertfordshire, above and below:
an inspiration for one of England's greatest playwrights

George Bernard Shaw's peaceful rural home
and garden show what inspired this great
playwright. Pictures and sculpture reflect his
wide circle of friends in theatre and the arts.
See the writing hut where he created plays
which won the Nobel Prize, an Oscar
and the hearts of millions of admirers.
Note: access roads very narrow.

Eat, shop, stay: small gift shop. Second-hand
bookshop. Ice-cream and soft drinks available
in garden. Pre-1950s varieties of plants for sale.

Things to see and do: events, including
open-air performances of Bernard Shaw's
plays (summer). **Dogs**: assistance dogs only.

Access: 🅿️ 🖼️ ♿ 📷 🅰️ **House** 🔦 🔦 👥 ♿
Grounds 🔦 🔦 ♿
Sat Nav: use AL6 9BX (some routes might take
you through a ford and a route not signposted
to Shaw's Corner). **Parking**: very limited (not
suitable for large vehicles).

Find out more: 01438 821968 (Infoline).
01438 820307 or
shawscorner@nationaltrust.org.uk

Shaw's Corner		M	T	W	T	F	S	S
24 Mar–28 Oct	12–5		·	W	T	F	S	S
Open Bank Holiday Mondays.								

Sheringham Park

Upper Sheringham, Norfolk NR26 8TL

🔦 ✤ 🍴 🏛️ 🎏 1987

Using the undulating landscape laid down by
glaciers 430,000 years ago, Humphry Repton
created views of the North Norfolk coast that
can still be enjoyed today, 200 years after his
death. His 1812 design stated 'Sheringham Park
had more natural beauty and advantages than
any place he had ever seen'. The Upcher family

Eat, shop, stay: gift shop selling guidebooks, local gifts and souvenirs. Peat-free plant sales. Courtyard Café serving soup, sandwiches, cake and ice-cream. A range of gluten-free food also available. Picnics welcome. Five holiday cottages on site.

Things to see and do: self-guided trails and guided walks. From the gazebo tower you can see coastal views enjoyed since Napoleonic times. Events celebrating the life of Humphry Repton. Free children's Tracker Packs.
Dogs: welcome under control. Please keep on leads near livestock and visitor facilities.

Access: 🅿️ ♿ 🚻 🦽 🔊 ♿ •• 🖼️
Building 🅿️ ♿ Grounds 🅿️ ➡️ 🚴 ♿
Parking: 60 yards. Two electric vehicle charging points in car park.

Find out more: 01263 820550 or sheringhampark@nationaltrust.org.uk

added an extensive rhododendron collection to Repton's design, bringing an array of colour to the wild garden in the spring. A walk may be interrupted by the drumming of a woodpecker, the song of skylarks or the sound of a steam train travelling through the park.
Note: Sheringham Hall is privately occupied. April to September: limited access by written appointment with leaseholder.

Sheringham Park		M	T	W	T	F	S	S
Park								
Open all year	Dawn–dusk	M	T	W	T	F	S	S
Visitor Centre and Courtyard Café								
6 Jan–4 Mar	11–4						S	S
10 Mar–28 Oct	10–5	M	T	W	T	F	S	S
3 Nov–30 Dec	11–4						S	S

Courtyard Café opens 8:45 and Visitor Centre 9:30 on Saturdays. Visitor Centre and Courtyard Café: open daily, 10 to 5, 10 to 18 February; 11 to 4, 27 to 31 December; open to 6:30, 19 May, 26 May to 2 June and 9 June.

Sundon Hills Country Park

Harlington Road, Upper Sundon, Bedfordshire

🏞️ 🚶 2000

Wildlife-rich chalk grassland, beech woodland, open meadows and a picnic site with views north towards the Greensand Ridge.
Note: sorry no toilets. For Sat Nav use LU3 3PE.

Find out more: 01582 873663 or sundonhills@nationaltrust.org.uk

The glorious landscape, left, and rhododendrons, above, at Sheringham Park in Norfolk, are guaranteed to delight

Sutton Hoo

Tranmer House, Sutton Hoo, Woodbridge, Suffolk IP12 3DJ

🏠 🏛 ♿ 🚻 ⊤ 1998

Shortly before the outbreak of the Second World War, the ship burial of an Anglo-Saxon king and his extraordinary treasures were unearthed by archaeologist Basil Brown. These ancient graves kept their secrets for 1,300 years, but what was found here changed our perceptions of the past for ever. The atmospheric burial mounds, breathtaking replica treasures and reconstruction of the king's burial chamber bring this fascinating story to life. Edith Pretty's country house takes you back to that remarkable discovery, while relaxing in true 1930s style. Various walks across this Anglo-Saxon landscape offer impressive views over the River Deben. **Note**: closed from 30 September to early 2019 for completion of an exciting site transformation project.

Eat, shop, stay: café serving hot meals, snacks and cream teas with veranda looking out towards the River Deben. Gift shop. Second-hand bookshop. Three holiday apartments on the top floors of Tranmer House, all with stunning views.

Things to see and do: **Indoors** Exhibition – introductory video, audio recordings, dressing up, replica treasures, burial reconstruction, children's trail. Tranmer House – children's

Mist shrouds one of the Anglo-Saxon burial mounds at Sutton Hoo in Suffolk, below, while a young visitor is engrossed by the exhibition room, right

quiz, Basil's workshop. **Outdoors** Burial mound tours, circular walks, children's trails, play area. **Dogs**: welcome on leads in reception, shop, café and walks.

Access:
Buildings **Grounds**
Parking: on site.

Find out more: 01394 389700 or suttonhoo@nationaltrust.org.uk

Sutton Hoo		M	T	W	T	F	S	S
6 Jan–4 Feb	10:30–4	·	·	·	·	·	**S**	**S**
10 Feb–30 Sep	10:30–5	**M**	**T**	**W**	**T**	**F**	**S**	**S**

Open 1 January, 10:30 to 4. Estate walks: open daily, 9 to 6, January to September (except some Thursdays in January).

Theatre Royal Bury St Edmunds

Westgate Street, Bury St Edmunds, Suffolk IP33 1QR

1974

Grade I listed theatre, one of the country's most significant theatre buildings and the only surviving Regency playhouse in Britain. **Note**: managed by Bury St Edmunds Theatre Management Ltd. The theatre offers a vibrant, year-round programme of drama, music, dance and comedy. Admission charges apply to live shows. Selected guided tours are free for members. Please call before visiting, as opening times may vary.

Find out more: 01284 769505 or theatreroyal@nationaltrust.org.uk

Totternhoe Knolls

Castle Hill Road, Totternhoe, Bedfordshire

2000

The dramatic earthworks of a Norman castle rise from important chalk grassland habitat, sitting high above the surrounding landscape. **Note**: sorry no toilets. For Sat Nav use LU6 1RG.

Find out more: 01582 873663 or totternhoeknolls@nationaltrust.org.uk

West Runton and Beeston Regis Heath

near West Runton, Norfolk

1925

A lovely place to walk among heath and woods, with fine views of the North Norfolk coast. **Note**: sorry no toilets. For Sat Nav use NR27 9ND.

Find out more: 01263 820550 or westrunton@nationaltrust.org.uk

Whipsnade Tree Cathedral

Whipsnade, Dunstable, Bedfordshire

1960

Peaceful place with trees planted in shape of medieval cathedral. Created after the First World War to commemorate fallen comrades. **Note**: annual service second Sunday, June. Sat Nav use LU6 2LQ. Open daily, 1 January to 24 March and 25 October to 31 December, 9 to 4; 25 March to 24 October, 9 to 7.

Find out more: 01582 872406 or whipsnadetc@nationaltrust.org.uk

Wicken Fen National Nature Reserve, Cambridgeshire: the windpump, above, and exploring the wetlands, below

Wicken Fen National Nature Reserve

Lode Lane, Wicken, Ely, Cambridgeshire

🪧 ♿ ☕ 1899

With vast skies above flowering meadows, sedge and reed-beds, Wicken Fen is a window onto a lost fenland landscape. A wealth of wildlife is at home in this important wetland, including rarities such as hen harriers and bitterns, numerous dragonflies, moths and wildfowl. The landscape feels wild, though people have managed it for years, as revealed by the fenman's yard, windpump and cottage.

The Wicken Fen Vision, an ambitious landscape-scale conservation project, is opening up new areas for wildlife and for you to explore. Grazing herds of Highland cattle and

Places may occasionally close for events or bad weather

Konik ponies help create a diverse range of new habitats. **Note**: some paths are subject to seasonal closure.

Eat, shop, stay: shop in the visitor centre selling wildlife and outdoor books, local food and crafts. Café serving light lunches and afternoon teas. Picnics welcome.

Things to see and do: explore the heart of the Fen on foot, via the Boardwalk and longer paths. Seasonal boat trips available. Cycle across the wider reserve; we hire bikes, or bring your own. **Dogs**: welcome on leads on reserve and in visitor centre.

Access: 🅿️♿️🚹♿🛗🎨👁️🔍
Building ♿🅰️ **Grounds** ♿🅰️
Sat Nav: use CB7 5XP. **Parking**: 120 yards.

Find out more: 01353 720274 or wickenfen@nationaltrust.org.uk

Wicken Fen		M	T	W	T	F	S	S
Reserve, visitor centre and shop								
Open all year**	10–5*	M	T	W	T	F	S	S
Café								
1 Jan–11 Feb	10–4:30	M	T	W	T	F	S	S
12 Feb–28 Oct	10–5	M	T	W	T	F	S	S
29 Oct–31 Dec**	10–4:30	M	T	W	T	F	S	S

*Access to reserve dawn to dusk; visitor centre closes dusk in winter. **Closed 25 December.

Willington Dovecote and Stables

Willington, Church End, near Bedford, Bedfordshire MK44 3PX

✝️♿ 1914

These stunning remnants of Gostwick's show farm stand like two ancient warriors, the only survivors from the battle with time. **Note**: open last Sunday of the month April to September, 1 to 5. Dovecote and Stable can be viewed by appointment dependent on volunteer availability, contact Judy Endersby (01234 838278).

Find out more: 01480 301494 or willingtondovecote@nationaltrust.org.uk

Wimpole Estate

Arrington, Royston, Cambridgeshire SG8 0BW

🏛️✝️🎞️🖼️❄️🚻🔔🍽️ 1976

Wimpole Estate, Cambridgeshire: the impressive mansion

A unique working estate, with an impressive mansion at its heart. Discover Wimpole's acres of parkland, miles of walks, vibrant Walled Kitchen Garden and Home Farm. Explore the hall, where intimate rooms contrast with beautiful Georgian interiors. With its various owners driven by passion and purpose, Wimpole is both a place to escape to and a place to get involved. We continue the 3rd Earl of Hardwicke's passion for trail-blazing food production and design, celebrating the estate's past magnificence and echoing Elsie Bambridge's 20th-century revival. As owners changed, a roll-call of ingenious architects, artists and landscape designers shaped the estate. Wimpole is an 'all-year-round' place to visit, reflecting the changing seasons, with something to captivate and inspire all visitors.

Eat, shop, stay: choose from the Old Rectory Restaurant, Farm Café and Stables Café, serving produce from the Walled Garden and Home Farm. Stable shop with gifts and plants, Wimpole rare-breed meat, flour, apple juice and eggs. Second-hand bookshop, toy shop.

Why not share your pictures with us? #nationaltrust

Find out more: 01223 206000 or wimpole@nationaltrust.org.uk

Wimpole Estate		M	T	W	T	F	S	S
Garden, Old Rectory Restaurant and stable block								
1 Jan–9 Feb	11–4	M	T	W	T	F	S	S
10 Feb–28 Oct	10–5	M	T	W	T	F	S	S
29 Oct–31 Dec	11–4	M	T	W	T	F	S	S
Home Farm and Farm Café								
1 Jan–9 Feb	11–4	M				F	S	S
10 Feb–28 Oct	10:30–5	M	T	W	T	F	S	S
29 Oct–31 Dec	11–4	M				F	S	S
Hall								
10 Feb–28 Oct	11–5	M	T	W	T	F	S	S
Hall (guided tour)*								
1 Jan–9 Feb	11–3	M	T	W	T	F	S	S
3 Nov–25 Nov	11–3	M	T	W	T	F	S	S
4 Dec–20 Dec	11–3		T	W	T			
Farm (guided tour)*								
2 Jan–8 Feb	12–3			T	W	T		
30 Oct–20 Dec	12–3			T	W	T		

Car park: open 7:30 to 6:30. Home Farm: open 2 January and 27 to 31 December, 11 to 4. Estate: closed 25 and 26 December, although park and stable block (café and gift shops) open 26 December, 11 to 4. *Guided tours' route and content varies, bookable on day, please check with visitor reception.

Things to see and do: **Indoors** Explore the Hall at your own pace or try a bookable basement tour. Pop into the Gardener's Cottage to uncover our garden history. **Outdoors** Seasonal spectaculars, including daffodils, spring blossom, June Bloom, summer parterre, herbaceous borders and autumn trees. Free guided walks in the parkland and geocaching. Daily farm activities: grooming the donkey, meeting the Shire horse, rabbits, feeding the pigs and milking the cow. Lambing time. History festival, open-air theatre, '50 things to do before you're 11¾' and Christmas events. Sporting activities, including running and walking groups, cycle and running trails. **Dogs**: welcome on leads in park and anywhere near livestock.

Access: 🅿️♿🚻🍽🎧📷💻🎵📱 Hall ♿♿
Farm ♿♿ Gardens ♿➡♿♿
Sat Nav: entrance via A603, not A1198.
Parking: 275 yards.

Wimpole Estate, clockwise from above:
Home Farm, the 18th-century folly in the parkland and ornate gilt plasterwork in the hall's library

East Midlands

Ilam Park, Dovedale and the White Peak, Derbyshire
Competition entry from Kerry Morwood

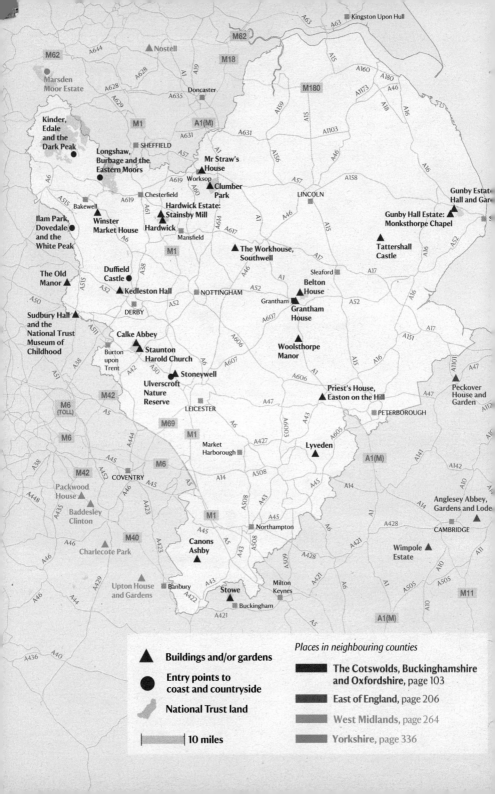

Kingston Upon Hull

Nostell

Marsden
Moor Estate

Kinder,
Edale
and the
Dark Peak

Longshaw,
Burbage and the
Eastern Moors

SHEFFIELD

Mr Straw's
House

Worksop

Clumber
Park

LINCOLN

Gunby Estate
Hall and Gar

Chesterfield

Hardwick Estate:
Stainsby Mill

Gunby Hall Estate:
Monksthorpe Chapel

Bakewell

Ilam Park,
Dovedale
and the
White Peak

Winster
Market House

Hardwick

Mansfield

Tattershall
Castle

The Workhouse,
Southwell

The Old
Manor

Duffield
Castle

Kedleston Hall

NOTTINGHAM

Sleaford

Belton
House

DERBY

Grantham

Grantham
House

Sudbury Hall
and the
National Trust
Museum of
Childhood

Calke Abbey

Burton
upon
Trent

Staunton
Harold Church

Woolsthorpe
Manor

Stoneywell

Ulverscroft
Nature
Reserve

LEICESTER

Priest's House,
Easton on the Hill

PETERBOROUGH

Peckover
House and
Garden

Market
Harborough

Lyveden

COVENTRY

Packwood
House

Baddesley
Clinton

Anglesey Abbey,
Gardens and Lode

CAMBRIDGE

Charlecote Park

Northampton

Wimpole
Estate

Canons
Ashby

Upton House
and Gardens

Banbury

Stowe

Milton
Keynes

Buckingham

Legend

▲ **Buildings and/or gardens**

● **Entry points to
coast and countryside**

National Trust land

|_____| **10 miles**

Places in neighbouring counties

**The Cotswolds, Buckinghamshire
and Oxfordshire,** page 103

East of England, page 206

West Midlands, page 264

Yorkshire, page 336

Belton House, Lincolnshire: this perfect house, full of superlative collections, sits elegantly in formal gardens

Belton House

Grantham, Lincolnshire NG32 2LS

🏠✝✿♻🔔🍷 1984

Sitting elegantly in formal gardens with views across Pleasure Grounds and an ancient deer-park, Belton is often cited as being the perfect example of an English country-house estate. Although built on a modest scale, it has a superlative collection of porcelain and silver, a world-renowned library, and architectural finesse which reflects the continued wealth and cultured tastes of its former owners, the Brownlow family. In more recent times, Belton has also become a popular destination for families in search of outdoor fun, with seasonal trails and the National Trust's largest open-air adventure playground. **Note**: stables building undergoing extensive restoration this year. Entry to house by timed ticket only.

Eat, shop, stay: Marquee restaurant serving hot meals (12 to 2), including Belton's award-winning venison (in season). Ride Play Café and Muddy Hands kiosk offer snacks and light meals. Large gift shop selling local produce, and second-hand bookshop which also offers seasonal plants.

Things to see and do: **Indoors** Learn more about the house with themed interpretation and guided tours. The 'below stairs' servant areas are open by guided tour all year. For young families, there's an indoor adventure play café and a discovery centre for weekend and school holiday activities. **Outdoors** Downloadable walks and seasonal trails. Open-air cinema and theatre in the summer. Extensive outdoor adventure playground. Family-focused events during the school holidays. Christmas lights and events. Woolsthorpe Manor, home of Sir Isaac Newton, is nearby. **Dogs**: welcome in parkland and stableyard on leads. Assistance dogs only in gardens, playground and mansion.

The Staircase Hall at Belton House, above, and exploring the adventure playground, below – the largest in the Trust

Access:

House **Grounds**

Sat Nav: use NG32 2LW. **Parking**: on site.

Find out more: 01476 566116 or belton@nationaltrust.org.uk

Belton House		M	T	W	T	F	S	S
House								
3 Mar–28 Oct	12:30–5		·	**W**	**T**	**F**	**S**	**S**
Shops, restaurant, Ride Play Café, adventure playground*								
Open all year	9:30–5:30	**M**	**T**	**W**	**T**	**F**	**S**	**S**
Basement**								
Open all year	Tour	**M**	**T**	**W**	**T**	**F**	**S**	**S**

*Close at 4 in winter. **Volunteer-led tours (subject to availability), 11 to 3; last tour at 2 in winter. Park and gardens: open as shops and restaurant. Bellmount Woods: open daily (access from separate car park). Everything closed 25 December. Entry to house by timed ticket only.

For other ways to get involved go to nationaltrust.org.uk/volunteer

Calke Abbey

Ticknall, Derby, Derbyshire DE73 7JF

🏠✝️📷✳️♿🥾🚐🍽️ 1985

With peeling paintwork and overgrown courtyards, Calke Abbey tells the story of the dramatic decline of a country-house estate. Faded garden buildings, such as the orangery, hint at former fortunes while grand rooms full of treasures tell tales of an eccentric family who never threw anything away. Many secrets are yet to be uncovered in the seemingly abandoned rooms of the mansion and often overlooked views of the estate, where hidden stories, collections and spaces are revealed for the first time. Beyond the house and garden, the historic and fragile habitats of Calke Park and its National Nature Reserve await discovery, together with the limeyards, wetlands, ancient trees and ponds.
Note: everyone requires admission tickets for house and garden (including members), available from the ticket office.

Eat, shop, stay: breakfast and main meals served daily in the restaurant with light refreshments available in the café at weekends and peak times. Barbecue offers estate-reared burgers (peak times). Large shop selling seasonal gifts, plants and local food. Five holiday cottages.

Things to see and do: **Indoors** Ground-floor taster visit every morning; full house open from 12:30 (timed-ticket entry). Introductory film. Stableyards, garden outbuildings and underground tunnels reveal the lives of Calke's past employees. Family activities in Squirt's Stable during weekends and school holidays (February to October). **Outdoors** Seasonal highlights, such as wallflowers, lambing and auricula theatre. Cycling and waymarked walks, including the Tramway Trail. Park play map and Tracker Packs for families exploring the parkland. Children's play areas. Broad events programme, including food and craft fairs, open-air cinema and autumnal favourites such as Apple Day and the Pumpkin Party. Stoneywell is nearby. **Dogs**: welcome on leads in parkland and stableyards; assistance dogs only in house and garden.

Calke Abbey, Derbyshire: faded grandeur on an epic scale

Letting off steam at Calke Abbey, above, and right, Sir Vauncey Harpur Crewe's little-changed bedroom

Access: 🅿️ 🚌 ♿ 🚻 🏪 📷 🎞️ 📺 ⏲️ 👓
House 🔉♿♿ Stables ♿♿ Grounds 🔉♿ ➡️
Sat Nav: use DE73 7JF. **Parking**: on site.

Find out more: 01332 863822 or
calkeabbey@nationaltrust.org.uk

Calke Abbey		M	T	W	T	F	S	S
Calke Park National Nature Reserve†								
Open all year	7:30–7	M	T	W	T	F	S	S
House*								
3 Mar–31 Oct	11–5	M	T	W	T	F	S	S
Garden								
3 Feb–31 Oct	10–5	M	T	W	T	F	S	S
Stables, restaurant and shop**								
Open all year	10–5	M	T	W	T	F	S	S

†Closes dusk, if earlier; closed 25 December. *House: ground-floor taster visit, 11 to 12:30; then open fully (admission by timed ticket). **Stables, restaurant and shop: close at 5 when house is open, March to October; at 4 all other times. Everything closed 25 December.

Canons Ashby

near Daventry, Northamptonshire NN11 3SD

🏠✝🏛♿❋♣ 1981

Ancient and peaceful, Canons Ashby is far removed from today's bustling lifestyle. Medieval canons built their priory near the little village of Ashby, but the Dissolution left a curiously truncated church, and the village was lost, leaving nothing but mounds in the landscape. Nearby, the Elizabethan Dryden family built their home, making few changes over their 450 years of occupation. Victorian Sir Henry Dryden's curiosity led him to record the detail of the mansion, with its quirky blend of architectural styles, mysterious wall-paintings, plasterwork and fine furnishings. Outside, lush gardens, parkland, lakes and ancient church offer space for tranquil contemplation. **Note**: admission by timed tickets on busy days.

Eat, shop, stay: Stables tea-room and pretty tea-garden offering light meals and freshly baked treats. Coach House shop selling home and garden gifts and Canons Ashby home-grown plants. Well-stocked second-hand bookshop (donations welcome).

Things to see and do: **Indoors** Discovery trails for families in the house and church. **Outdoors** Parkland and garden walks all year. Open-air theatre and croquet in summer. Family activities during school holidays.

Dogs: welcome on leads in car park, paddock, tea-garden and parkland only.

Access: 🅿♿♿♿♿🔍📷🎧📹🚗📷
Building 🔃🍴 Church 🔃 Grounds 🔃♿
Parking: 218 yards.

Find out more: 01327 861900 or canonsashby@nationaltrust.org.uk

Canons Ashby		M	T	W	T	F	S	S
Tea-room, shop, gardens, priory church and parkland*								
1 Jan–5 Jan	10–3	M	T	W	T	F	·	·
10 Feb–9 Mar	10–3:30	M	T	W	T	F	S	S
10 Mar–28 Oct	10–5	M	T	W	T	F	S	S
29 Oct–21 Dec	10–3:30	M	T	W	T	F	S	S
27 Dec–31 Dec	10–3	M	·	·	T	F	S	S
House*								
10 Feb–9 Mar	11–3	M	T	W	·	F	S	S
10 Mar–28 Oct†	1–5	M	T	W	·	F	S	S
3 Nov–2 Dec	11–3	·	·	·	·	·	S	S
8 Dec–16 Dec	11–3	M	T	W	T	F	S	S

†House: taster tours 11 to 1 (30 minutes, three rooms), tickets available on arrival. *Some parts of garden and house may close for conservation work in winter.

The ancient mansion at Canons Ashby in Northamptonshire, left, and kitchen, below

Clumber Park

Worksop, Nottinghamshire S80 3BE

✠ ✿ ♿ ☂ 1946

Carved out of the ancient forest of Sherwood, a space of playfulness and pleasure on a grand scale was created by the Dukes of Newcastle. Clumber Park is true to its spirit as a place of recreation, with 20 miles of cycle routes and 1,537 hectares (3,800 acres) of parkland, woodland and heathland to explore. The beauty of the Gothic Revival chapel, with its original stained-glass windows, reveals a rich historic past. The Pleasure Grounds frame the magnificent lake, making a perfect place to stroll or picnic. The Walled Kitchen Garden, with its National Collection of Rhubarb, provides a variety of fruit and vegetables to the café and colourful herbaceous borders during the summer.

Eat, shop, stay: café and garden tea-house serving hot meals, snacks, cream teas and a children's menu. Barbecue at peak times. Large gift shop and plant sales. Second-hand bookshop; cycle hire, servicing and sales. Picnics welcome and designated barbecue site.

Things to see and do: **Indoors** Year-round activities for all ages and interests, including art, history and wildlife exhibitions at the Discovery Centre. The glasshouse and Museum of Gardening Tools at the Walled Kitchen Garden, and Clumber chapel – a cathedral in miniature. **Outdoors** Seasonal highlights include the spring bluebells, rhododendrons and apple blossom, late-summer-flowering heathers and autumn tree colour. During your visit, tick off some of the '50 things to do before you're 11¾'. There are many downloadable walks, woodland play areas, a cycle hire centre and many outdoor activities. **Dogs**: welcome, some restrictions apply. Indoor refreshment area for dog walkers. Downloadable guide.

Access: ⛿♿🚻👁🗺🅿
Buildings ♿🚻 **Grounds** ♿➡🚲♿
Parking: 250 yards.

Find out more: 01909 476592 or
clumberpark@nationaltrust.org.uk

Clumber Park		M	T	W	T	F	S	S
Park								
Open all year	7–7	M	T	W	T	F	S	S
Visitor facilities, café, shop, Walled Kitchen Garden, chapel*								
1 Jan–24 Mar	10–4**	M	T	W	T	F	S	S
25 Mar–27 Oct	10–5**	M	T	W	T	F	S	S
28 Oct–31 Dec	10–4**	M	T	W	T	F	S	S

Park: open until dusk in summer. 25 March to 27 October:
visitor facilities (café, shop, Walled Kitchen Garden, chapel,
cycle hire centre, garden tea-house, Discovery Centre
and woodland play park) close at 6 at weekends and
Bank Holidays. Open daily, except 25 December.
*Chapel: 13 January to 15 March, closed for conservation.
**Café: opens at 9. Last cycle hire two hours before closing.

Three views of Clumber Park in Nottinghamshire:
the magnificent Clumber Lake, above and right,
and the Gothic Revival chapel, left

Duffield Castle

Duffield, Derbyshire

 1899

One of England's largest 13th-century castles – today you can see its foundations, imagine the stories and savour the views. **Note**: sorry no toilets. Steep steps. For Sat Nav use DE56 4DW.

Find out more: 01332 842191 or duffieldcastle@nationaltrust.org.uk

Grantham House

Castlegate, Grantham, Lincolnshire NG31 6SS

 1944

Handsome town house, one of the oldest buildings in Grantham, with a riverside walled garden. **Note**: leased by the National Trust and the lessee is responsible for arrangements and facilities. Open by appointment only with the lessee, Wednesdays and Thursdays, 4 April to 25 October, 2 to 5 (appointments not required in June). Entrance via gates opposite Church Street.

Find out more: 01476 564705 or granthamhouse@nationaltrust.org.uk

Gunby Estate, Hall and Gardens

Gunby, Spilsby, Lincolnshire PE23 5SS

1944

The Massingberd family home from 1700 until 1967, Gunby Hall still feels cherished and lived-in. Exploring three floors, you can easily imagine you'll bump into one of the family at any moment. Enjoy garden colour whatever the season: abundant spring flowers, summer roses, autumn borders and plentiful fruit and vegetables. **Note**: building works taking place all year.

Eat, shop, stay: courtyard tea-room offering cakes, sweet treats and pre-packed sandwiches. Well-stocked second-hand bookshop. Small gift shop, seasonal plants and produce. Choose from three holiday cottages: The Old Rectory and Whitegates Cottage in Bratoft or Orchard Cottage, nestled in the Gunby gardens.

Gunby Estate, Hall and Gardens in Lincolnshire

Things to see and do: events throughout year, from open-air theatre to Rose and Apple Days. Public footpaths run across the wider historic park and estate: ask for directions and maps at admissions. **Dogs**: welcome on leads in the gardens, courtyard tea-room terrace and grounds.

Access: House Grounds
Sat Nav: may misdirect – entrance is off roundabout (not beyond or before).
Parking: on site.

Find out more: 01754 890102 or gunbyhall@nationaltrust.org.uk

Gunby Estate		M	T	W	T	F	S	S
House*								
10 Feb–28 Oct	11–5	M	T	W			S	S
24 Nov–9 Dec	1–5:30	M	T	W	T	F	S	S
Gardens and tea-room**								
10 Feb–28 Oct	11–5	M	T	W	T	F	S	S
24 Nov–9 Dec	1–5:30	M	T	W	T	F	S	S
Parkland								
Open all year	11–5	M	T	W	T	F	S	S

*House: last admission one hour before closing (on busy days admission may be by timed ticket). **Tea-room: last service 4:30. May close dusk, or earlier.

Gunby Hall Estate: Monksthorpe Chapel

Monksthorpe, near Spilsby,
Lincolnshire PE23 5PP

✝ 2000

Monksthorpe Chapel, dated 1701, was made to look like a barn to avoid detection and features a rare open-air baptistry. **Note**: chapel open daily, 10 February to 28 October, 11 to 5. Grounds open every day all year, 11 to 5. Access by key, obtained from Gunby Hall tea-room (£20 refundable deposit required).

Find out more: 01754 890102 or monksthorpe@nationaltrust.org.uk

Hardwick

Doe Lea, Chesterfield, Derbyshire S44 5QJ

🏠 ✿ ♿ 🛏 🔔 ⚓ 🍴 1959

The Hardwick Estate is made up of stunning houses and beautiful landscapes that have been created by a cast of thousands. It was the formidable Bess of Hardwick who first built Hardwick Hall in the late 16th century, and in the centuries since then, gardeners, builders, decorators, embroiderers and craftsmen of all kinds have contributed and made Hardwick their creation. This year we'll be exploring the women of Hardwick, from the redoubtable Bess of Hardwick to the forgotten servants. **Note**: Old Hall owned by the National Trust and administered by English Heritage (01246 850431).

Hardwick in Derbyshire, above and below: so much to fascinate, both indoors and out

Eat, shop, stay: Great Barn Restaurant serving hot meals, seasonal specials (using garden produce) and cakes. Stables shop selling gifts and souvenirs. Outdoors shop and plant sales (many propagated in Hardwick's nursery). Picnic areas. Three holiday cottages (sleeping two, six and 12).

Things to see and do: Indoors Seasonal events, including Easter and Christmas. Outdoors Open-air films during the summer and themed tours and talks. You can see the garden highlights, including the stumpery and herbaceous borders. There are also walking trails around the estate and surrounding countryside. Family woodland trail and fun family activities during all school holidays. Stainsby Mill is nearby. Dogs: welcome on leads in Stableyard, park and car park. Assistance dogs only in gardens.

Access: 🅿♿🚻♿🔓🛗📷💷♿❓
Hall ♿♿♿ Restaurant ♿♿ Garden ➡♿
Sat Nav: use S44 5RW. Parking: 600-space car park.

Find out more: 01246 850430 or hardwick@nationaltrust.org.uk

Hardwick		M	T	W	T	F	S	S
Hall								
17 Feb–4 Nov	11–5[1]	.	.	W	T	F	S	S
24 Nov–23 Dec	11–3[2]	.	.	W	T	F	S	S
Park and restaurant								
Open all year*	9–6	M	T	W	T	F	S	S
Garden and shop								
Open all year*	10–6	M	T	W	T	F	S	S

*Park, garden, restaurant and shop: close at 5, November to February, or dusk if earlier. Closed 25 December.
[1]Hall also opens Bank Holiday Mondays, April to August.
[2]Christmas: ground and middle floors only open.

The Entrance Hall at Hardwick. Dating from the late 16th century, Hardwick Hall was built for Bess of Hardwick

Hardwick Estate: Stainsby Mill

Doe Lea, Chesterfield, Derbyshire S44 5RW

🏭 1976

Hardwick Estate: Stainsby Mill in Derbyshire

A fully operational Victorian flour mill giving an insight into the workplace of a 19th-century miller. There has been a mill on this site for hundreds of years, providing flour for the local villages and the Hardwick Estate. Flour is ground regularly showing the cogs and machinery in action. **Note**: nearest toilets and refreshments at Hardwick Hall.

Eat, shop, stay: you can learn more about the mill from our guides and pick up recipes to try at home. Restaurant and gift shop at nearby Hardwick Hall.

Things to see and do: why not start your day at Stainsby Mill, with its children's trail and activity sheets? Visitors are welcome to have a go grinding flour on the hand quern. **Dogs**: welcome on leads in Hardwick Park.

Access: 📷 🖥 🎨 👓 🗺 Building 🦽 Grounds 🦽🦼
Parking: limited on-road parking (not National Trust).

Find out more: 01246 856522 or stainsbymill@nationaltrust.org.uk

Hardwick Estate: Stainsby Mill	M	T	W	T	F	S	S
17 Feb–4 Nov*	10–4		·	W	T	F	S	S

*Open Bank Holiday Mondays. 26 May to 2 September, open 10 to 5.

Ilam Park, Dovedale and the White Peak

Ilam, Ashbourne, Derbyshire

🏠 ✝ 🏛 🚲 ❄ 🚶 🐾 🛝 1906

The Stepping Stones at Dovedale lead to a riverside walk through a dramatic valley full of caves and pinnacles, rich in wildlife and fossils. A mile and a half walk links Dovedale and Ilam Park, a tranquil parkland nestled beneath steep-sided hills on the bank of the River Manifold. The park is dotted with majestic mature trees and offers views across to the rugged backdrop of Thorpe Cloud and Bunster Hill. Short, circular woodland and parkland routes make this a popular choice for families and dog walkers. The densely wooded Manifold Valley offers a largely traffic-free cycling route. **Note**: Ilam Hall is let to the Youth Hostel Association.

Ilam Park, Dovedale and the White Peak, Derbyshire

Eat, shop, stay: Manifold tea-room at Ilam Park, with views towards Dovedale. Peak season accessible grab-and-go counter in stableyard. Shops at Ilam Park and Dovedale Barn offering maps, gifts and information. Café at Wetton Mill (tenant-run) on River Manifold.

Exploring the dramatic valley at Dovedale

Kedleston Hall

near Quarndon, Derby, Derbyshire DE22 5JH

🏠✝♣🏋🛏🔔⛱ 1987

Designed by architect Robert Adam as 'a temple of the arts', Kedleston is one of the grandest, most perfectly finished houses and locations for entertainment. Discover the grandeur of this 1760s mansion, which was designed as a show palace with lavish décor, paintings, furniture and sculpture, and lived in over the centuries by the Curzon family. Set in beautiful naturalistic parkland, blending seamlessly into the surrounding countryside, the 332 hectares (820 acres) are perfect for walks, picnics and spotting wildlife, as well as being home to more than 100 ancient trees. **Note**: medieval All Saints Church, containing many family monuments, run by the Churches Conservation Trust.

Things to see and do: school holiday family trails. Summer play across river in Hinkley Hollow. See the orchard area developing next to the tea-room. Free Monday and Friday walks all year (no booking needed). **Dogs**: under close control; on leads spring and summer (ground-nesting birds), and near livestock.

Access: 🅿♿♿♿♿♿
Ilam Park stableyard ♿♿♿
Ilam Park grounds ♿♿♿➡♿
Sat Nav: use DE6 2AZ. **Parking**: at Ilam Park 119:132507 and Dovedale, not National Trust (charge including members).

Find out more: 01335 350503 or peakdistrict@nationaltrust.org.uk

Ilam Park		M	T	W	T	F	S	S
Dovedale Barn								
24 Mar–30 Sep	11–5	M	T	W	T	F	S	S
Tea-room and shop*								
1 Jan–16 Feb	10:30–4	M	T	W	T	F	S	S
17 Feb–4 Nov	10:30–5	M	T	W	T	F	S	S
5 Nov–31 Dec	10:30–4	M	T	W	T	F	S	S

*Shop: opens 11. Tea-room and shop: closed 24 and 25 December. Ilam bunkhouse: open all year (0344 335 1296). Darfar and Redhurst holiday cottages: available to let all year (0344 800 2070). Ilam Hall: available for overnight accommodation via the Youth Hostel Association (01335 350212).

Eat, shop, stay: Old Kitchen Restaurant serving hot and cold lunches, cakes, ice-cream and afternoon tea. Refreshments available from kiosk (peak times). Gift shop, plant sales and second-hand bookshop. Luxurious Park House holiday cottage sits on the edge of Kedleston Park.

Why not share your pictures with us? #nationaltrust

Things to see and do: **Indoors** Explore the completed State Floor with recently restored state bed, an 18th-century masterpiece. **Outdoors** Four waymarked walks. Talks and tours. Family crafts and activities. Hermitage on the long walk. **Dogs**: welcome on leads in park and Pleasure Grounds.

Access: ⚹⚹⚹⚹⚹⚹⚹⚹⚹⚹
Ground floor ⚹⚹ State floor ⚹⚹ Grounds ⚹▶
Sat Nav: for main entrance use DE22 5JD.
Parking: 200 yards.

Find out more: 01332 842191 or kedlestonhall@nationaltrust.org.uk

Kedleston Hall		M	T	W	T	F	S	S
Park and Pleasure Grounds								
1 Jan–9 Feb	10–4	M	T	W	T	F	S	S
10 Feb–4 Nov	10–6	M	T	W	T	F	S	S
5 Nov–31 Dec	10–4	M	T	W	T	F	S	S
Hall*								
24 Feb–4 Nov	12–5	M	T	W	T	·	S	S
30 Nov–23 Dec	11–3	·	·	·	·	F	S	S
Restaurant and shop								
1 Jan–9 Feb	10–3:30	M	T	W	T	F	S	S
10 Feb–4 Nov	10–5	M	T	W	T	F	S	S
5 Nov–31 Dec	10–3:30	M	T	W	T	F	S	S

*Hall: introductory talk at 11:30. Open Good Friday. Everything closed 25 December and occasionally for events.

Kedleston Hall in Derbyshire: the 1760s mansion was designed as a show palace

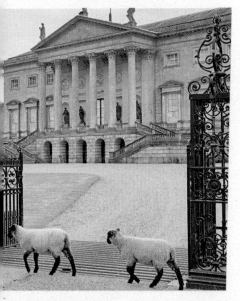

Kinder, Edale and the Dark Peak

near Hope Valley, Derbyshire

🏛️🔥♿👥 1936

Biking at Kinder, Edale and the Dark Peak, Derbyshire

The Dark Peak, including Kinder, the Vale of Edale and along the Snake moors to the Derwent edges, offers exhilarating walks across heather moors, high gritstone edges and monumental windswept tors. Stories and wild nature abound amid the ancient peat bogs and quiet wooded cloughs. You can follow the route of the 1932 Mass Trespass onto Kinder Scout National Nature Reserve, retracing the steps of those early champions of access to wild places. Alternatively, a short walk up the steps of Mam Tor rewards you with panoramic views from this ancient hilltop fortress.
Note: nearest toilets in villages and visitor centres (not Trust) at Ladybower Reservoir, Edale and Castleton.

Eat, shop, stay: Penny Pot in Edale, serving cooked breakfasts, soup, sandwiches, cakes, tea and coffee. Seating and bike racks outside. Find us next to Edale railway station.

Things to see and do: guided walks, help the rangers at Muck In days. Downloadable walking and cycling routes. **Dogs**: on leads near livestock and throughout spring and summer (ground-nesting bird breeding season).

Access:
Sat Nav: use S33 8WA. **Parking:** at Mam Nick National Trust car park 110:SK124832. Also non-National Trust parking at Edale, Castleton, Bowden Bridge, Hayfield, Sett Valley, Hayfield and Upper Derwent Valley (charge including members).

Find out more: 01433 670368 or peakdistrict@nationaltrust.org.uk

Kinder, Edale and the Dark Peak		M	T	W	T	F	S	S
Penny Pot Café								
5 Jan–18 Feb	10–4					F	S	S
19 Feb–4 Nov	10–4:30	M	T	W	T	F	S	S
28 Apr–30 Sep	8:30–4:30						S	S
9 Nov–30 Dec	10–4					F	S	S

Closed 24 to 26 December. Information shelters open all year: Lee Barn (110:SK096855) and Dalehead (110: SK101843) in Edale; South Head (SK060854) at Kinder; Edale End (SK161864); Grindle Barns above Ladybower Reservoir (SK189895). Mam Nick car park (SK123832) and Dalehead bunkhouse (0344 3351296) open all year.

Longshaw, Burbage and the Eastern Moors

Longshaw, near Sheffield, Derbyshire

[icons] 1931

A countryside haven on Sheffield's doorstep, Longshaw, Burbage and the Eastern Moors has a network of footpaths and bridleways you can explore within a typical Peak District landscape of skies and silhouettes. Here you'll find long views, with scooping shapes of rocks and hills and gorges where water tumbles through ancient woods and over mossy boulders. A diverse range of wildlife lives peacefully here among abandoned millstones and packhorse routes of the past. The designed landscape

Longshaw, Burbage and the Eastern Moors, Derbyshire, left and above: typical Peak District landscape

around Longshaw Lodge, a former grouse-shooting estate, offers a warm and friendly starting point for your adventure.
Note: National Trust/RSPB manage Eastern Moors for Peak District National Park Authority; Burbage for Sheffield County Council.

Eat, shop, stay: Longshaw café serving soup, scones, cakes and dishes made using produce plucked straight from the kitchen garden. Shop selling outdoor and wildlife-themed products, maps and guides. Outdoor seats provide views across the valley to Burbage and Higger Tor.

Things to see and do: accessible woodland walks, natural play, bridleways and waymarked walks. Kitchen garden behind tea-room. Regular trails, outdoor activity and nature conservation-themed Muck In events. Free guided walks (Wednesdays and Sundays).
Dogs: on leads near livestock and throughout spring and summer (ground-nesting bird breeding season).

Access: [icons]
Building [icons] **Grounds** [icons]
Sat Nav: use S11 7TZ (follow brown signs).
Parking: at Woodcroft car park (110: 266800), Wooden Pole and Haywood for Longshaw and at Curbar Gap, Birchen Edge and Shillito Wood for the Eastern Moors. Additional car parks at Surprise View and Burbage, not National Trust (charge including members).

Find out more: 01433 637904 (Longshaw). 0114 289 1543 (Eastern Moors) or peakdistrict@nationaltrust.org.uk

Longshaw, Burbage, Eastern Moors		M	T	W	T	F	S	S
Tea-room and shop								
1 Jan–16 Feb	10:30–4	M	T	W	T	F	S	S
17 Feb–4 Nov	10:30–5	M	T	W	T	F	S	S
5 Nov–31 Dec	10:30–4	M	T	W	T	F	S	S

Tea-room: last orders 30 minutes before closing. Closed 24 and 25 December. White Edge Lodge: available as holiday cottage all year (0344 800 2070). Longshaw Lodge: not open to public.

Lyveden

Harley Way, near Oundle,
Northamptonshire PE8 5AT

 1922

Deep in the Northamptonshire countryside lies a mysterious garden. Begun by Sir Thomas Tresham in 1595 but never completed, Lyveden stands as testament to his Catholicism. Moats and terraces surround an enigmatic building rich in religious symbolism. The intriguing story of Tresham's design is revealed in the audio guide.

Eat, shop, stay: small traditional Northamptonshire cottage tea-room, serving homemade cakes and cream teas. Ice-cream available from visitor reception. Picnics welcome.

Things to see and do: free audio guide. Children's activities in the Family Den. Numerous public footpaths and bridleways within easy reach for exploring further afield. **Dogs**: welcome on leads only.

Access: [icons] Building [icon] Grounds [icon]
Parking: 100 yards.

Find out more: 01832 205158 or lyveden@nationaltrust.org.uk

Lyveden		M	T	W	T	F	S	S
6 Jan–25 Feb	11–4*						S	S
26 Feb–28 Oct	10:30–5**	M	T	W	T	F	S	S
3 Nov–30 Dec	11–4*						S	S

*Tea-room: last orders 3:30. ** Tea-room: last orders 4. Last audio guide issued one hour before closing.

The mysterious garden of Lyveden, Northamptonshire

Mr Straw's House

5–7 Blyth Grove, Worksop,
Nottinghamshire S81 0JG

[icons] 1990

Mr Straw's House, Nottinghamshire: 1920s time capsule

Within the Sanderson-papered walls of this middle-class home, the family lived thriftily, installing few modern conveniences since 1923. A large and intriguing collection of everyday objects and personal papers has survived alongside traces of the occasional indulgence. The lovingly tended garden and orchard include a cacti collection and fruit trees.
Note: to help you enjoy your visit we operate timed tickets, please telephone to book.

Eat, shop, stay: small shop selling a range of souvenirs, plants, jams, books and gifts. Tea and coffee area.

Things to see and do: changing exhibitions, family activities, events and guided town walks all year. **Dogs**: assistance dogs only.

Access: [icons] 5 Blyth Grove [icons]
7 Blyth Grove [icons] Gardens [icon]
Parking: on site, in orchard opposite property.

Find out more: 01909 482380 or mrstrawshouse@nationaltrust.org.uk

Mr Straw's House		M	T	W	T	F	S	S
1 Mar–3 Nov*	Tour		T	W	T	F	S	

*Admission by timed ticket (please telephone in advance to book).

The Old Manor

Norbury, Ashbourne, Derbyshire DE6 2ED

 1987

Medieval hall featuring a rare king post, Tudor door and 17th-century Flemish glass. **Note**: parking limited (cars only). Open 23 March to 27 October, Fridays, 11 to 1, and Saturdays, 1 to 3 (next to National Trust holiday house, please respect the occupants' privacy).

Find out more: 01283 585337 or oldmanor@nationaltrust.org.uk

Priest's House, Easton on the Hill

38 West Street, Easton on the Hill, near Stamford, Northamptonshire PE9 3LS

🏠 1966

Delightful small late 15th-century building, with interesting local architecture and museum exploring Easton on the Hill's industrial and mining heritage. **Note**: open daily, 10 to 5. Unmanned. Access from neighbouring keyholders (details on property noticeboard).

Find out more: 01832 205158 or priestshouse2@nationaltrust.org.uk

Staunton Harold Church

Staunton Harold Estate, Ashby-de-la-Zouch, Leicestershire LE65 1RW

✠ 1954

One of the few churches built between the outbreak of the English Civil War and the Restoration period. **Note**: nearest toilet 500 yards (not National Trust). Parking not National Trust; Staunton Harold Estate, charges apply (including members). Open weekends, 7 April to 28 October and Wednesdays to Sundays, 6 June to 2 September, 1 to 4:30. Church open Good Friday and Bank Holidays. Services are normally held Easter to December, second and fourth Sundays.

Find out more: 01332 863822 or stauntonharold@nationaltrust.org.uk

Stoneywell

Whitcroft's Lane, Ulverscroft, Leicestershire LE67 9QE

🏠 ❋ 2012

Stoneywell, Leicestershire: Arts and Crafts vision

Zigzagging from its rocky outcrop, Stoneywell is the realisation of one man's Arts and Crafts vision within a family home. Original furniture and family treasures fill the cottage's quirky rooms and, outside, every turn conjures childhood memories of holiday excitement – one way to the fort, another to the woods beyond. **Note**: booking essential (including members).

Eat, shop, stay: Stables tea-room (for use by booked visitors only) serving light lunches, homemade cakes and cream teas. Small range of Arts and Crafts-inspired gifts, seasonal plants and second-hand books available. Picnics welcome in grounds.

Things to see and do: **Indoors** Guided tours, events and family activities reveal stories of life at Stoneywell. **Outdoors** The garden and woodland are great for exploring, with seasonal highlights, including daffodils, bluebells and rhododendrons. **Dogs**: assistance dogs only.

Access: 🅿️🚐🚾♿🦽🖐️🔁♫📳◉
Stables 🚹🛗 Cottage ♿🛗 Gardens ♿➡️
Parking: for booked visitors only.

Find out more: 01530 248040 (Infoline). 01530 248048 (bookings) or stoneywell@nationaltrust.org.uk

Stoneywell		M	T	W	T	F	S	S
1 Feb–30 Nov	Tour	**M**	**T**	**W**	**T**	**F**	S	S

Sudbury Hall and the National Trust Museum of Childhood, Derbyshire, above and below: two unique experiences in one location

Sudbury Hall and the National Trust Museum of Childhood

Sudbury, Ashbourne, Derbyshire DE6 5HT

🏛️❄️🔔☕ 1967

A complete day out, with two unique experiences in one location. The Hall has one of the most surprising, light and beautiful long galleries in England and is the result of George Vernon's aspirations to create a perfect new home. Get a glimpse of life 'below stairs' in the kitchen and basement, and picture yourself at home in some of the smaller family rooms. The museum is a place of fun and fascination for all ages. View childhood from the Victorian period to the present day; send your little one up a chimney, play with our hands-on toys and games and experience the Victorian Schoolroom.

Uncle Bruin teddy bear at the Museum of Childhood

Eat, shop, stay: tea-room serving light lunches and homemade cakes. Additional refreshments available at peak times. Gift shop, plant sales, sweets, ice-cream and toys.

Things to see and do: **Indoors** Hands-on toys in the museum and family crafts during most school holidays. Themed Hall tours, including the chance to explore areas not normally open to visitors. **Outdoors** Trails and fun activities for all the family. Spot wildlife from the boathouse and younger visitors can find adventure in the woodland play area.

Access:
Hall **Museum** **Grounds**
Parking: 500 yards.

Find out more: 01283 585337 or sudburyhall@nationaltrust.org.uk

Sudbury Hall		M	T	W	T	F	S	S
Museum, tea-room and shop*								
10 Feb–23 Mar	10:30–5	·	·	W	T	F	S	S
24 Mar–4 Nov	10:30–5	M	T	W	T	F	S	S
8 Nov–30 Dec	10:30–4**	·	·	·	T	F	S	S
Hall								
10 Feb–4 Nov	1–5	·	·	W	T	F	S	S
1 Dec–30 Dec	1–6	·	·	·	T	F	S	S
Hall tours								
27 Mar–30 Oct	11:30–2:30	·	T	·	·	·	·	·

*Museum: opens 11. **Tea-room and shop: close 6 in December. Extended opening during school holidays. Open Bank Holiday Mondays.

Tattershall Castle

Sleaford Road, Tattershall, Lincolnshire LN4 4LR

1925

Rising proudly from the flat Lincolnshire fens, Tattershall Castle was designed to display wealth, position and power. Built by Lord Ralph Cromwell, Treasurer of England, the Great Tower is one of the earliest and finest surviving examples of English medieval brickwork. Dramatically saved from being dismantled and exported, the castle and its huge Gothic fireplaces were restored from ruin by Lord Curzon of Kedleston between 1912 and 1914. Imagine the splendour of this once-palatial private residence as you wander through the vast echoing chambers. Ascend the spiral staircase from basement to battlements and take in spectacular views of the Lincolnshire countryside. **Note**: access to the tower via a spiral staircase only (149 steps). Loose gravel paths throughout.

Eat, shop, stay: Guardhouse shop selling gifts, plants, souvenirs, second-hand books and a limited catering offer (hot and cold drinks, wrapped cakes and ice-cream). Picnics welcome in the grounds.

Tattershall Castle in Lincolnshire was designed to display wealth, position and power

Tattershall Castle		M	T	W	T	F	S	S
10 Feb–4 Nov	11–5	M	T	W	T	F	S	S
10 Nov–2 Dec	11–4*						S	S
3 Dec–9 Dec	11–4*	M	T	W	T	F	S	S
10 Dec–16 Dec**	11–4*	M	T	W	T	F	S	S

Last entry one hour before closing. Last multimedia guides issued one hour before closing. Some areas may temporarily close for weddings. *May close earlier due to light levels. **Open for Christmas activities (booking required).

Things to see and do: **Indoors** Multimedia guides (adult and family versions), children's trails, medieval games. **Outdoors** Year-round events for all ages and interests, including the Easter Hunt, re-enactment weekends, open-air theatre and Christmas market. **Dogs**: welcome on leads in the grounds only.

Access: 🅿️♿🏠🖼️📷♨️👁️ **Castle** 🪜
Sat Nav: LN4 4LR. **Parking**: 150 yards from entrance.

Find out more: 01526 342543 or tattershallcastle@nationaltrust.org.uk

The Great Tower at Tattershall Castle, above and below, rises proudly above the flat Lincolnshire fens, dominating the surrounding landscape

Ulverscroft Nature Reserve

near Copt Oak, Loughborough, Leicestershire

🏞️ 1945

Nestled in the ancient Charnwood Forest, a rich variety of wildlife thrives in the heathland and woodland habitats of Ulverscroft.
Note: assistance dogs only. Sorry no toilet. For Sat Nav use LE67 9QE. Limited parking along Whitcroft's Lane adjacent to the reserve. Access by permit only from The Secretary, Leicestershire and Rutland Wildlife Trust, The Old Mill, 9 Soar Lane, Leicester, LE3 5DE (0116 262 9968). Please allow a week to receive permit.

Find out more: 01332 863822 or ulverscroftnaturereserve@nationaltrust.org.uk

Winster Market House

Main Street, Winster, Matlock, Derbyshire DE4 2DJ

🏠 1906

A small listed 16th-century Market House with displays upstairs – the first Derbyshire place acquired by the Trust, costing £50.
Note: Winster Market House is unstaffed. Open daily, 24 March to 4 November, 11 to 5.

Find out more: 01335 350503 or winstermarkethouse@nationaltrust.org.uk

Woolsthorpe Manor

Water Lane, Woolsthorpe by Colsterworth, near Grantham, Lincolnshire NG33 5PD

🏠 ❀ 1943

Without Isaac Newton, this small manor would be just another Lincolnshire farmhouse – however, in 1665 the plague sent him back here, to his birthplace. For 18 months Newton worked in solitude, experimenting obsessively, laying foundations for a scientific revolution which changed the world. Here he split white light into colours with a prism, and an apple fell from a tree to inspire his theory of gravity. Newton's genius still resonates through our world, and for more than 300 years people have come to Woolsthorpe to walk in his footsteps and be inspired by his story.
Note: potential building works this year.

Eat, shop, stay: Newton's Barn coffee shop. Small shop in ticket office with local and Newton-specific gifts. Small second-hand bookshop.

Things to see and do: **Indoors** Hands-on Science Centre and family activities. Science fairs and volunteer-led 'Tales from Woolsthorpe' and 'pop-up' science. Film. Family events. **Outdoors** The apple tree which inspired Newton's theory of gravity.
Dogs: welcome in car park only.

Access: [icons] Grounds [icons]
House [icons] Science Centre [icons]
Parking: 50 yards.

Find out more: 01476 860338 or woolsthorpemanor@nationaltrust.org.uk

Woolsthorpe Manor

Please visit website for details of opening times. Manor house: closed Tuesdays and Tuesday to Thursday in winter.

Sir Isaac Newton's birthplace, Woolsthorpe Manor in Lincolnshire, above and below, offered refuge from the plague and allowed Newton the solitude to lay the foundations for a scientific revolution

The Workhouse, Southwell

Upton Road, Southwell,
Nottinghamshire NG25 0PT

🏠 ✿ 2002

Things to see and do: **Indoors** 'Re-imagining The Workhouse' updates our story through art, music, photography and innovative technology. Regular activities, including living history days, family events and exhibitions. **Outdoors** Re-created Victorian vegetable garden. **Dogs**: assistance dogs only in house and garden. Dogs on leads in front field.

Access: 🅿️🔄🔼🔽🌀🖼️📺🎧👓🎨
Workhouse 🔼🔼🍴🔽 Firbeck 🔼🔼
Grounds 🔄➡️🔽
Sat Nav: use NG25 0QB. **Parking**: 200 yards.

Find out more: 01636 817260 or
theworkhouse@nationaltrust.org.uk

The Workhouse, Southwell		M	T	W	T	F	S	S
10 Feb–4 Nov	12–5*		M	T	W	T	F	S	S

*Café: open 10:30 to 4. Guided tour of the outside and other buildings at 11 (places limited, book on arrival only). House: open Bank Holidays from 11; last admission one hour before closing; may close earlier due to light levels.

The Workhouse, Southwell in Nottinghamshire, clockwise from top left: a last resort for the desperate, this austere building was used as temporary housing in the 1970s. Today a young visitor plays at the pump

Walking up the paupers' path towards The Workhouse it is easy to imagine how the Victorian poor might have felt as they sought refuge here. This austere building, the most complete workhouse in existence, was built in 1824 as a place of last resort for the destitute. Its architecture was influenced by prison design and its harsh regime became a blueprint for workhouses throughout the country. The stories of people who lived and worked here over the years help tell the history of the building's evolution and prompt reflection on how society has tackled social welfare through time. **Note**: please expect some disruption as we embark on our creative presentation and building works programme.

Eat, shop, stay: café offering hot drinks, soup, sandwiches, cakes and snacks. Shop selling gifts, ice-cream and traditional toys. Picnic benches in the garden.

Birmingham Back to Backs, West Midlands

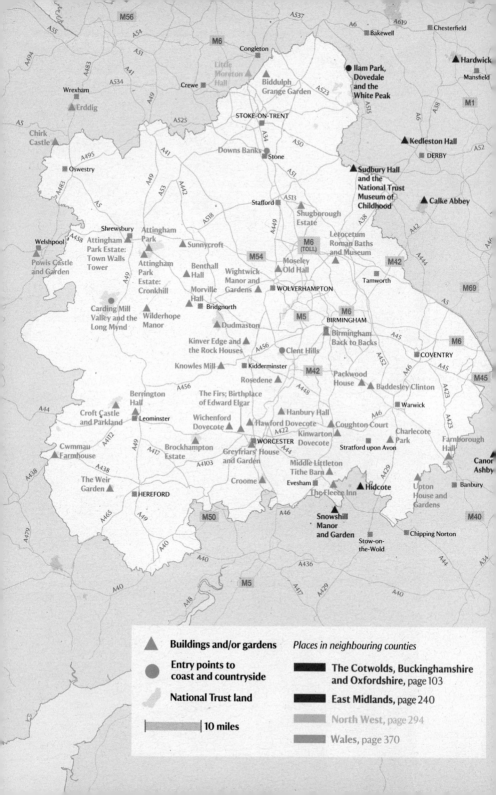

Legend:

▲ Buildings and/or gardens

● Entry points to coast and countryside

National Trust land

⊢————⊣ 10 miles

Places in neighbouring counties

The Cotwolds, Buckinghamshire and Oxfordshire, page 103

East Midlands, page 240

North West, page 294

Wales, page 370

Map labels:

M56, A55, A54, A51, M6, A537, A6, A619, Bakewell, Chesterfield

Congleton, ▲ Hardwick, Mansfield, M1

Little Moreton Hall, Biddulph Grange Garden, A523, ● Ilam Park, Dovedale and the White Peak, A515, A38

Wrexham, A483, A534, Crewe, STOKE-ON-TRENT, A525, A34, A50, A6, A52

▲ Erddig, A5, A495, A41, Downs Banks, Stone, ▲ Kedleston Hall, DERBY

Chirk Castle, A483, A5, Oswestry, A49, A53, A42, Stafford, A513, ▲ Sudbury Hall and the National Trust Museum of Childhood, ▲ Calke Abbey, A42

Welshpool, A458, Shrewsbury, Attingham Park, A518, A449, Shugborough Estate, A38, Letocetum Roman Baths and Museum, M42, A444

Powis Castle and Garden, Attingham Park Estate: Town Walls Tower, ▲ Sunnycroft, M54, M6 (TOLL), Moseley Old Hall, Tamworth, M69

Attingham Park Estate: Cronkhill, ▲ Benthall Hall, Wightwick Manor and Gardens, ▲ WOLVERHAMPTON

Carding Mill Valley and the Long Mynd, ▲ Morville Hall, ▲ Wilderhope Manor, Bridgnorth, ▲ Dudmaston

Kinver Edge and the Rock Houses, A456, ● Clent Hills, Birmingham Back to Backs, BIRMINGHAM, A45, M6

Knowles Mill, Kidderminster, Rosedene, M42, Packwood House, ▲ Baddesley Clinton, COVENTRY, A45, M45

A456, A448, A452, A6, M6

Berrington Hall, The Firs; Birthplace of Edward Elgar, ▲ Hanbury Hall, A46, Warwick, A423

Croft Castle and Parkland, Leominster, Wichenford Dovecote, Hawford Dovecote, Coughton Court, Charlecote Park, Farnborough Hall

Cwmmau Farmhouse, A412, Brockhampton Estate, A4103, ▲ WORCESTER, A422, Kinwarton Dovecote, Stratford upon Avon, A429, Canon Ashby

The Weir Garden, A438, Greyfriars' House and Garden, ▲ Croome, A44, Middle Littleton Tithe Barn, Evesham, ▲ Hidcote, Upton House and Gardens, Banbury, M40

HEREFORD, A465, A49, M50, The Fleece Inn, A46, Snowshill Manor and Garden, Stow-on-the-Wold, Chipping Norton

A40, M5, A48, A417, A429, A436, A40

(Various road numbers: A5, A41, A49, A51, A38, A442, A53, A518, A422, A4103, A44, A412, A438, A465, etc.)

Attingham Park

Atcham, Shrewsbury, Shropshire SY4 4TP

🏛️ ✣ ♿ 🍴 | 1947 |

Attingham inspires a sense of beauty, space and awe. The imposing entrance, glimpses of the vast mansion against silhouettes of cedars and expansive parkland, epitomise classical design and Italian influence. The completeness of its survival exemplifies the rise and decline, love and neglect of great country-house estates. Discovering the Berwicks' estate with acres of parkland, miles of walks, the huge organic walled garden, large playfield and welcoming mansion is a full day out. There's so much to see and do at Attingham, whether you're a family looking for activities, both inside and out, or simply in search of a traditional visit to a historic house and parkland. Full of life and locally loved, there's something for everyone all year round.

Attingham Park in Shropshire, inside and out, inspires a sense of beauty, space and awe

Eat, shop, stay: range of catering experiences available – main courtyard café open daily offering three serveries, including takeaway, light meals/cake and hot food counters. Takeaways from Greedy Pig catering in playfield. Courtyard shopping includes Stables shop and second-hand bookshop.

Things to see and do: **Indoors** 'Attingham Re-discovered' project of conservation and restoration continues. Themed tours. Attingham '1940s Christmas' daily in December. **Outdoors** Park open daily from 8. Summer late opening (to 7). Seasonal spectaculars, including winter snowdrops, spring bluebells, summer blossom and autumn tree colour. Year-round events for all ages and interests, including family activities during local school holidays, annual classic car rally and theatre evenings. Sporting activities to help you get active, including regular run groups and major events/competitions. Walled Garden and Pleasure Grounds projects continue to transform and restore Attingham.

Exploring the extensive parkland, above, and organic walled garden, below, at Attingham Park

Sunnycroft, a fabulous local Edwardian suburban villa, is nearby in Wellington. **Dogs**: welcome in grounds on leads (with some identified off-lead areas). Dog walkers' guide available.

Access: 🅿️🚏🚌🐕🍼📷📖🎫📱📷
Mansion 🔊♿️🎫♿️ Café 🔊 Grounds ♿️➡️🔊♿️
Parking: 25 to 200 yards.

Find out more: 01743 708123 (Infoline).
01743 708162 or
attingham@nationaltrust.org.uk

Attingham Park		M	T	W	T	F	S	S
Park, Field of Play and Carriage House Café[1]								
1 Jan–16 Feb	8–5*	M	T	W	T	F	S	S
17 Feb–25 May	8–6	M	T	W	T	F	S	S
26 May–2 Sep	8–7	M	T	W	T	F	S	S
3 Sep–4 Nov	8–6	M	T	W	T	F	S	S
5 Nov–31 Dec	8–5*	M	T	W	T	F	S	S
Walled Garden								
Open all year	9–5*	M	T	W	T	F	S	S
Mansion								
5 Jan–11 Feb[2]	11–3					F	S	S
17 Feb–4 Nov	11–4:30	M	T	W	T	F	S	S
1 Dec–23 Dec[3]	10–3	M	T	W	T	F	S	S

[1]Carriage House Café: opens 9 and closes one hour before park. [2]Entry by tour (booking required). [3]Entry by timed tickets (booking required). *Park, Field of Play and Walled Garden: closes 5, or dusk if earlier. Field of Play catering: open from 11 weekends, daily during Shropshire school holidays (weather permitting). Stables shops: open daily from 10. 24 December: mansion closed; site closes 3. Everything closed 25 December.

Attingham Park Estate: Cronkhill

near Atcham, Shrewsbury, Shropshire SY5 6JP

🏠🌼 1947

Delightful picturesque Italianate hillside villa designed by Regency architect John Nash, with beautiful views across the Attingham Estate. **Note**: house ground floor, garden and stables open as part of visit. Property contents belong to tenant. Open Fridays and Sundays, 11 and 13 May, 20 and 22 July, 14 and 16 September, 11 to 4 (admission by booked timed tickets).

Find out more: 01743 708162 or
cronkhill@nationaltrust.org.uk

Attingham Park Estate: Town Walls Tower

Shrewsbury, Shropshire SY1 1TN

🏠 1930

This last remaining 14th-century watchtower sits on what were once the medieval fortified, defensive walls of Shrewsbury. **Note**: sorry no toilet or car parking and 40 extremely steep, narrow steps to top floor. Open weekends, 28 and 29 April, 9 and 10 June, 18 and 19 August and 6 and 7 October, 10:30 to 3:30 (admission by booked timed tickets).

Find out more: 01743 708162 or
townwallstower@nationaltrust.org.uk

Baddesley Clinton

Rising Lane, Baddesley Clinton,
Warwickshire B93 0DQ

🏠✝️🌼🦽🍴 1980

The Great Hall at Baddesley Clinton, Warwickshire

The magic of Baddesley Clinton comes from its secluded, timeless setting deep within its own parkland. From refuge to haven, this atmospheric moated manor house has been a

Swathes of wisteria and clematis drape the walls at Baddesley Clinton, above, while visitors discover the peaceful gardens, below

sanctuary since the 15th century. Discover Baddesley's late medieval, Tudor and 20th-century histories and uncover its stories, from hiding persecuted Catholics in its priest's holes, to the history of the Ferrers family who lived at Baddesley for more than 500 years. This year find out about some of Baddesley's strong female characters and their intriguing stories. The peaceful gardens include fish pools, walled garden and a lakeside walk, perfect for a tranquil stroll.

Eat, shop, stay: Barn Restaurant serving hot meals, drinks and snacks and The Stables offering light refreshments. Picnics welcome. Shop selling seasonal gifts, local foods and plants. Second-hand bookshop.

Things to see and do: **Indoors** Discover Baddesley's story, from medieval farmstead to modest Georgian status symbol and Victorian retreat. Seasonal children's trails. House dressed for Christmas throughout December. **Outdoors** Natural Play around the estate all year. Outdoor games in school holidays. Welcome talks and garden tours, plus walking trails around the estate and surrounding countryside. Packwood House and Coughton Court are nearby. **Dogs**: welcome on leads in car park and estate public footpaths. Assistance dogs only beyond visitor reception.

Access: 🅿️ 🏚️ ♿ 📷 📺 🎵 👓
Building 🏠 🏠 ♿ Grounds 🏠 ➡️ ♿
Parking: 100 yards.

Find out more: 01564 783294 or baddesleyclinton@nationaltrust.org.uk

Baddesley Clinton		M	T	W	T	F	S	S
1 Jan–16 Feb	9–4*	M	T	W	T	F	S	S
17 Feb–28 Oct	9–5*	M	T	W	T	F	S	S
29 Oct–31 Dec	9–4*	M	T	W	T	F	S	S

30 March to 2 April and 25 to 27 August: admission by bookable tickets only, limited (including members).
*House: opens 11; admission by timed ticket (available from reception, not bookable). Closed 24 and 25 December.

Benthall Hall

Broseley, Shropshire TF12 5RX

1958

Benthall Hall, Shropshire, high above the River Severn

Within this fine stone house, discover the history of the Benthall family from the Saxon period to the present day. Outside, the garden includes a beautiful Restoration church, a restored plantsman's garden with pretty crocus displays in spring and autumn, and an old kitchen garden.

Eat, shop, stay: tea-room serving drinks, cakes and ice-cream.

Things to see and do: **Indoors** Informative guides, children's trail. **Outdoors** Elizabethan skittle alley. Circular walks through the park and woodland. **Dogs**: in park and woodland only.

Access:
House **Church**
Parking: 100 yards.

Find out more: 01952 882159 or benthall@nationaltrust.org.uk

Benthall Hall		M	T	W	T	F	S	S
3 Feb–28 Feb	1–4*	·	·	·	·	·	S	S
1 Mar–31 Oct	1–5*	·	T	W	·	·	S	S

Open Bank Holiday Mondays and Good Friday. Tea-room: last orders 30 minutes before house closes. *Garden and church: open and close 30 minutes earlier and later than stated times, apart from February when they open at 1.

Berrington Hall

near Leominster, Herefordshire HR6 0DW

1957

Standing proud and strong, this fine Georgian mansion sits within 'Capability' Brown's final garden and landscape. Find out about the walled garden and Pleasure Grounds restoration project with a visit to the Georgian-inspired, pineapple-shaped pavilion, created by internationally renowned artists Heather and Ivan Morison. Follow the parkland walk to discover Brown's ingenious design for the landscape. In the house, there are jewel-like interiors, designed by Henry Holland and home to the Harley, Rodney and Cawley families, and you can experience some of the extremes of the 18th century in the wig-and-bum shop, then discover the hidden 'below stairs'.

Eat, shop, stay: shop selling gifts, local products and preserves made from our fruit. Tea-room serving light lunches, afternoon tea

Berrington Hall in Herefordshire: jewel-like interiors

Berrington Hall sits within 'Capability' Brown's final garden

Biddulph Grange Garden

Grange Road, Biddulph, Staffordshire ST8 7SD

❀ 1988

Biddulph Grange Garden is a remarkable survival, a formal Victorian horticultural masterpiece and a quirky, playful paradise full of intrigue and surprise. Created by its visionary owner, James Bateman, the garden and Geological Gallery express his attempts to reconcile his religious convictions and his passion for botany and geology. His plant and fossil collections come from all over the world – a visit takes you on a journey from an Italian terrace to an Egyptian pyramid, via a Himalayan glen and Chinese garden, hidden by tunnels, hedges and rockwork. The collection includes rhododendrons, Wellingtonias and the oldest golden larch in Britain. **Note**: there are 400 steps in the garden.

and cakes, made using produce from the garden. Stables café selling grab-and-go. Triumphal Arch holiday cottage.

Things to see and do: **Indoors** Exhibitions. Costume collection on view. Family trails, games and dressing-up. Servants' quarters to explore. **Outdoors** Stables, welcome centre and walled garden to discover. Play area. Waymarked estate walks. **Dogs**: welcome on leads in parkland and in parts of garden.

Access: 🅿️🅿️♿♿♿♿♿
Building ♿♿ Grounds ♿▶♿♿
Parking: 30 yards.

Find out more: 01568 615721 or berrington@nationaltrust.org.uk

Berrington Hall		M	T	W	T	F	S	S
1 Jan	10–4	M	·	·	·	·	·	·
6 Jan–11 Feb	10–4	·	·	·	·	·	S	S
17 Feb–4 Nov	10–5	M	T	W	T	F	S	S
10 Nov–23 Dec	10–4	·	·	·	·	·	S	S
27 Dec–31 Dec	10–4	M	·	·	T	F	S	S

Mansion and shop open at 11. Last admission one hour before closing.

Eat, shop, stay: self-service tea-room. Gift shop. Plant centre. Picnics only in the paddock area beside the car park.

Things to see and do: talks, guided tours, events and children's trails all year. Summer activities. **Dogs**: assistance dogs only in garden.

Access: 🅿️🅿️♿🔖🎫🚹 Garden 🔖
Parking: 50 yards.

Find out more: 01782 517999 or biddulphgrange@nationaltrust.org.uk

Biddulph Grange Garden		M	T	W	T	F	S	S
1 Jan–16 Feb	10–3:30	M	T	W	T	F	S	S
17 Feb–11 Mar	10–4:30	M	T	W	T	F	S	S
12 Mar–28 Oct	10–5:30	M	T	W	T	F	S	S
29 Oct–4 Nov	10–4:30	M	T	W	T	F	S	S
5 Nov–24 Dec	10–3:30	M	T	W	T	F	S	S
27 Dec–31 Dec	10–3:30	M			T	F	S	S

Closes dusk if earlier. Closed 25 and 26 December.

The temple in the Chinese-inspired garden at Biddulph Grange Garden in Staffordshire: a formal Victorian horticultural masterpiece

Birmingham Back to Backs

55-63 Hurst Street/50-54 Inge Street, Birmingham, West Midlands B5 4TE

🏠🔖 2004

Immerse yourself in the life of residents at Birmingham's last surviving court of back to backs. The evocative guided tour will give you an insight into how people lived from the 1840s to 1970s. With privies, coal fires, candlelight and cramped spaces, you'll get a real taste of back-to-back life. **Note**: booking essential. Eight flights of steep, winding stairs. Ground-floor tours (booking required). Sorry no café.

Birmingham Back to Backs, West Midlands

Eat, shop, stay: traditional sweetshop selling childhood favourites and a small gift shop. Vintage holiday cottages (booked via National Trust Holidays).

Things to see and do: events all year.

Access: 🅿️♿🔖🎫📺🚹💺🚻 Building 🔖♿🚻
Parking: nearest at Arcadian Centre, Bromsgrove Street, Hurst Street (none National Trust).

Find out more: 0121 666 7671 (booking line). 0121 622 2442 (office) or backtobacks@nationaltrust.org.uk

Birmingham Back to Backs		M	T	W	T	F	S	S
30 Jan–21 Dec	Tour		T	W	T	F	S	S

Admission by timed, guided tour only (booking essential).
Closed 3 to 7 September. Open Bank Holiday Mondays (but closed next day). Term-time tours from 1, Tuesdays, Wednesdays and Thursdays. Last tour times vary in winter due to low light levels.

Brockhampton Estate, Herefordshire: the chapel and moat, above, and gatehouse, below

Brockhampton Estate

Bringsty, near Bromyard,
Herefordshire WR6 5TB

[icons] 1946

Brockhampton is set in the tranquil Herefordshire countryside at the heart of a 688-hectare (1,700-acre) ancient rural estate. The medieval moated manor house tells the stories of the families that lived here from the 15th to the 20th centuries. Estate walks cross rolling parkland, wooded dingles, traditional orchards and working farmland. Keep an eye out for wildlife – you may even hear the rare lesser spotted woodpecker.
Note: challenging terrain with extremely steep slopes and muddy areas.

Eat, shop, stay: Granary shop and refreshment kiosk open all year. Priority seating available. Tea-room open weekends from February half-term and seven days during school holidays. Second-hand bookshop. Three holiday cottages on the estate – sleeping three, five and ten.

Things to see and do: Indoors Year-round family activities, demonstrations, exhibitions and historical re-enactments. **Outdoors** Countryside event days, family trails and games. Natural play trail, orienteering and waymarked walks. Picnics welcome.
Dogs: Welcome across the estate – on leads in grounds. Dog waste bins in car parks.

Access: [icons]
Building [icons] **Grounds** [icons]
Parking: 100 yards and 1 mile.

Find out more: 01885 482077 (Infoline) or brockhampton@nationaltrust.org.uk

Brockhampton Estate		M	T	W	T	F	S	S
Estate								
Open all year	10–5	**M**	**T**	**W**	**T**	**F**	**S**	**S**
House and Granary shop*								
6 Jan–11 Feb	11–4	·	·	·	·	·	**S**	**S**
12 Feb–4 Nov	11–5	**M**	**T**	**W**	**T**	**F**	**S**	**S**
10 Nov–30 Dec	11–4	·	·	·	·	·	**S**	**S**
Old Apple Store tea-room*								
10 Feb–4 Nov**	10–5	·	·	·	·	·	**S**	**S**

*House, grounds, Granary shop and Old Apple Store tea-room close 30 minutes before the estate. **Open every day during Herefordshire school holidays.

Carding Mill Valley and the Long Mynd

near Church Stretton, Shropshire

🏛️🌿♿👷🍵 1965

At Carding Mill Valley (below) you are suddenly in the heart of wild countryside. Here families can enjoy playing in the stream, a variety of walks and exploring. From the valley, head up to the top of the Long Mynd and be rewarded with views of Shropshire and beyond.

Eat, shop, stay: Chalet Pavilion tea-room and roof terrace in Carding Mill Valley serving hot lunches, afternoon teas, drinks and ice-cream. Shop selling gifts, souvenirs, maps and pond nets.

Things to see and do: courses and family-friendly events all year. Free walks cards available in Carding Mill Valley.
Dogs: under close control and in sight (grazing livestock and ground-nesting birds).

Access: 🅿️♿♿♿♿♿ Building ♿
Sat Nav: use SY6 6JG. **Parking**: 50 yards.

Find out more: 01694 725000 or cardingmill@nationaltrust.org.uk

Carding Mill Valley		M	T	W	T	F	S	S
Tea-room								
1 Jan–16 Feb	10–4	M	T	W	T	F	S	S
17 Feb–4 Nov	10–5	M	T	W	T	F	S	S
5 Nov–31 Dec*	10–4	M	T	W	T	F	S	S
Shop**								
1 Jan	11–4	M	·	·	·	·	·	·
6 Jan–28 Jan	10–4	·	·	·	·	·	S	S
29 Jan–16 Feb	11–4	M	T	W	T	F	S	S
17 Feb–4 Nov	11–5	M	T	W	T	F	S	S
5 Nov–31 Dec*	11–4	M	T	W	T	F	S	S

*Tea-room and shop: closed 25 December.
**Shop: opens 10 at weekends.

Charlecote Park

Wellesbourne, Warwick,
Warwickshire CV35 9ER

🏛️🌿♿👷🍵🏠 1946

Charlecote Park, Warwickshire: a picture of peace

The scene of Shakespeare's reputed poaching exploits, Charlecote Park was already in its middle age by the time Elizabeth I arrived, along the carriage drive through the Gatehouse and on to the welcoming red-brick mansion. Generations of the Lucy family have left their mark on the buildings, gardens and parkland where visitors are intrigued to this day by the family's continuing presence. Charlecote presents a picture of peace and repose, protected by the rivers Dene and Avon and by its distinctive cleft-oak paling fences. It is a park where people picnic, play, walk and wander. Look out for the Jacob sheep and fallow deer which still roam across the 'Capability' Brown landscape.

Eat, shop, stay: variety of catering facilities across the site, serving a range of meals and snacks. Servants' Hall gift shop selling a range of Charlecote specific, locally sourced produce and seasonal plant sales. Picnics welcome. Stay at Turret holiday flat (sleeps six).

Things to see and do: **Indoors** Hands-on activities help bring the Victorian kitchen to life. You can explore the carriage houses, brew house and laundry and learn more in the introductory Gatehouse room. The house is festively decorated during December. **Outdoors** Why not take a walk through the wider parkland? There are guided park walks, talks and seasonal trails for all ages. **Dogs**: welcome on a short lead at all times (on a designated route only).

Access: ♿ symbols
Building ♿ symbols **Grounds** ♿ symbols
Parking: 300 yards.

Find out more: 01789 470277 or charlecotepark@nationaltrust.org.uk

Protected by the rivers Dene and Avon, the gardens and park at Charlecote Park are prefect for play, picnics, walks or just having a good long chat

Charlecote Park		M	T	W	T	F	S	S
Park and garden								
1 Jan–16 Feb	9–4	M	T	W	T	F	S	S
17 Feb–4 Nov	9–6†	M	T	W	T	F	S	S
5 Nov–31 Dec	9–4	M	T	W	T	F	S	S
House								
17 Feb–4 Nov[1]	11–3:30[2]	M	T	W	T	F	S	S
10 Nov–16 Dec	11–3:30[2]						S	S
17 Dec–23 Dec	11–3:30[2]	M	T	W	T	F	S	S
Tea-room and shop*								
1 Jan–16 Feb	10–4	M	T	W	T	F	S	S
17 Feb–4 Nov	10–5	M	T	W	T	F	S	S
5 Nov–31 Dec	10–4	M	T	W	T	F	S	S

*Shop: opens 10:30. [1]House: Wednesdays by guided tours only (places limited); [2]admission by non-bookable timed tickets. †Park and garden: close at 6, 17 February to 4 November; everything closes at dusk if earlier. Everything closed 24 and 25 December.

Places may occasionally close for events or bad weather

Clent Hills

near Romsley, Worcestershire

🏛️🎣 1959

Clent Hills, Worcestershire: perfect for family adventures

Set on the edge of Birmingham and the Black Country, this green oasis with panoramic views is the perfect place for a refreshing walk or a picnic on a sunny day. Families can create their own adventures – building dens, hunting for geocaches or simply getting closer to nature. **Note**: nearest facilities at Nimmings Wood entrance.

Eat, shop, stay: café (not National Trust) at Nimmings Wood car park serving light meals and refreshments.

Things to see and do: regular guided rambles and family activities. Natural play area and play trail. **Dogs**: welcome, but please be considerate to other visitors.

Access: 🅿️🔊♿💧➡️
Sat Nav: use B62 0NL for Nimmings Wood entrance. **Parking**: at Nimmings Wood; additional parking at Adam's Hill and Walton Hill.

Find out more: 01562 712822 or clenthills@nationaltrust.org.uk

Clent Hills

Nimmings Wood car park: open 8:30 to 5 (to 4, November to March). Closed 25 December.

Coughton Court

Alcester, Warwickshire B49 5JA

🏠✝️🌸🔔📷☕ 1946

Coughton has been home to the Throckmorton family for over 600 years. Facing persecution for their Catholic faith, they were willing to risk everything. You can discover their story and find out about a family's ingenuity, resilience and resolve, including their link to the infamous Gunpowder Plot. Coughton is very much a family home with an intimate feel. The Throckmorton family still live here and they created and manage the gardens, including a riverside walk, bog garden and beautiful display of roses in the walled garden.

Coughton Court, Warwickshire: still a family home

Eat, shop, stay: Coughton Café serving lunch and teas. Drinks and ice-cream available from the Stableyard Coffee Bar. Coach House shop selling local food and seasonal gifts. Throckmorton family plant sales. Second-hand bookshop.

Things to see and do: Indoors Children's trail. **Outdoors** Wide selection of talks. Walking trails around the estate and surrounding countryside. Natural Play and outdoor games.

Croft Castle and Parkland

Yarpole, near Leominster, Herefordshire HR6 9PW

The rose labyrinth in Coughton Court's walled garden

🏠🖼️✝️🏛️❄️🦮🌳🏕️🍽️ 1957

This intimate house became the Croft family home before the Domesday Book. There are many compelling 20th-century stories to uncover, including the impact of the First World War and Croft during the 1950s. This year we share the story of the remarkable women of Croft, as we mark the 100-year anniversary of the suffrage movement. You can also explore the walled garden, its working vineyard and historic glasshouse, and stroll into the picturesque Fishpool Valley or go in search of Croft Ambrey, the Iron Age hill fort, discovering the historic wood pasture and many ancient trees along the way.

Eat, shop, stay: tea-room (licensed) serving food made using fresh garden produce – hot lunches, cakes and ice-cream. Children's lunchboxes and half portions. Shop selling gifts, plants, home and garden products.

Baddesley Clinton and Packwood nearby.
Dogs: welcome on leads in car park and public footpaths. Assistance dogs only in gardens.

Access: 🅿️♿🚻♿🔦📷♿📖♿
House ♿♿♿ Grounds ♿➡️♿
Parking: 150 yards.

Find out more: 01789 400777 or coughtoncourt@nationaltrust.org.uk

Coughton Court		M	T	W	T	F	S	S
House, shop and café*								
8 Mar–25 Mar	11–5	·	·		T	F	S	S
House, shop, café and grounds**								
28 Mar–30 Sep	11–5	·	·	W	T	F	S	S
4 Oct–4 Nov	11–5	·	·		T	F	S	S
House, shop and café†								
24 Nov–2 Dec	11–4	M	T	W	T	F	S	S

*Grounds closed. Open Bank Holiday Mondays. Everything closed Good Friday, plus 8 and 9 September. House and walled garden: admission by timed ticket on weekends and busy days. **Walled garden: opens at 12. Taster tours and talks (not bookable) subject to availability.
†Coughton Winter Festival, grounds closed.

Why not share your pictures with us? #nationaltrust

Second-hand bookshop. Picnic area. Garden and Ambrey holiday cottages for a longer stay.

Things to see and do: **Indoors** Games, interactive memorabilia and dressing-up. **Outdoors** Family activities, living history, open-air theatre, seasonal events. Natural and castle-inspired play areas. Walks, dog-walking, bird hide, information barn and orienteering. **Dogs**: welcome on leads in gardens, parkland and glazed area of tea-room only.

Access: ⓟ ⓓ ⏚ ⏚ ⏚ ⏚ ⏚
Castle ⏚ ⏚ ⏚ Grounds ⏚ ➡ ⏚ ⏚
Sat Nav: use HR6 0BL. **Parking**: 100 yards.

Find out more: 01568 780246 or croftcastle@nationaltrust.org.uk

Croft Castle and Parkland		M	T	W	T	F	S	S
Tea-room, garden, shop and parkland								
1 Jan	10–4	M	·	·	·	·	·	·
27 Dec–31 Dec	10–4	M	·	·	T	F	S	S
Castle, tea-room, garden, shop and parkland								
6 Jan–11 Feb	10–4	·	·	·	·	·	S	S
17 Feb–4 Nov	10–5	M	T	W	T	F	S	S
10 Nov–16 Dec	10–4	·	·	·	·	·	S	S

Castle and shop: open 11. Play area: open as parkland.

Croft Castle and Parkland, Herefordshire: from the time of the Domesday Book to today, there is so much to discover

Croome

near High Green, Worcester, Worcestershire WR8 9DW

🏠 ✝ ❀ ♨ 🔔 1996

Croome, Worcestershire: grandest of English landscapes

There's more than meets the eye at Croome. A secret wartime airbase, now a visitor centre and museum, was once a hub of activity for thousands of people. Outside is the grandest of English landscapes, 'Capability' Brown's masterful first commission, with commanding views over the Malverns. The parkland, nearly lost but now restored, is great for walks and adventures with a surprise around every corner. At the heart of the park lies Croome Court, once home to the Earls of Coventry. The 6th Earl was an 18th-century trendsetter, and today Croome follows his lead using artists and craftspeople to tell the story of its eclectic past in inventive ways. Explore four floors of the mansion, perfect for making new discoveries. **Note**: Walled Gardens, privately owned (admission charge towards their restoration, including members), open days throughout the year.

Eat, shop, stay: 1940s-style restaurant, gift shop, Gardener's Bothy plant shop and second-hand bookshop at the Visitor Centre. Kitty Fisher's Coffee House serving light lunches in Croome Court's basement.

Entry is still possible at most places up to 30 minutes before closing

Things to see and do: **Indoors** Contemporary exhibitions, including select pieces from the collection and creative installations. All four floors of the house are open, some areas by guided tour. RAF Defford Museum at the Visitor Centre. **Outdoors** Acres of parkland to explore. Regular guided tours of the park and outer eye-catcher open days. Special family trails around park every school holiday. RAF-themed playground, natural play area and bird hide close to the Visitor Centre. Walled Gardens to explore. **Dogs**: welcome on short fixed leads. Assistance dogs only in house, RAF museum, restaurant and shop.

The church and Chinese Bridge at Croome, left, while above, visitors come to the end of a fun day exploring the extensive grounds, 'Capability' Brown's masterful first commission

Access:
House 🄿🄿🄿 Park ➡🄿🄿
Sat Nav: follow signs from main road, not Sat Nav. **Parking**: on site.

Find out more: 01905 371006 or croome@nationaltrust.org.uk
Croome National Trust Visitor Centre, near High Green, Severn Stoke WR8 9DW

Croome		M	T	W	T	F	S	S
House								
1 Jan–16 Feb	11–4	M	T	W	T	F	S	S
17 Feb–4 Nov	11–4:30	M	T	W	T	F	S	S
5 Nov–23 Dec	11–4	M	T	W	T	F	S	S
26 Dec–31 Dec*	Tour	M		W	T	F	S	S
Park, restaurant and shop								
1 Jan–16 Feb	10–4	M	T	W	T	F	S	S
17 Feb–4 Nov**	9–5	M	T	W	T	F	S	S
5 Nov–23 Dec	10–4	M	T	W	T	F	S	S
26 Dec–31 Dec	10–4	M		W	T	F	S	S

*House: open for timed tours only. **Shop: opens at 10.

Cwmmau Farmhouse

Brilley, Whitney-on-Wye, Herefordshire HR3 6JP

🏠 ❀ ♨ ↩ 1965

Located on the Herefordshire and Welsh border with stunning views, this 17th-century timbered farmhouse has many original features to explore. **Note**: open daily, 22 to 28 June, 11:30 to 4:30.

Find out more: 01568 780246 or cwmmaufarmhouse@nationaltrust.org.uk

Downs Banks

Washdale Lane, Oulton Heath, near Stone, Staffordshire

♨ 1950

A little wilderness of woodlands and heath, with easy access walks, in the heart of the Midlands. **Note**: sorry no toilets. Some steep paths.

Find out more: 01889 881388 or downsbanks@nationaltrust.org.uk

Dudmaston

Quatt, near Bridgnorth, Shropshire WV15 6QN

🏠 ❀ ♨ ↩ 1978

Set within the South Shropshire countryside, Dudmaston remains today what it has been for 875 years: a much-loved and lived-in family home. The estate, shaped as much by modern thinking, tastes and culture as it is by its ancient heritage, is steeped in history, and the wooded parkland and sweeping garden contain a few surprises. There are garden sculptures and a woodland playground to discover, or you could go exploring, find a tranquil spot and

enjoy the views. Soak up the family history in the Hall and the contrasting Modern Art Galleries, created by the last owner, Lady Labouchere. **Note**: the family home of Mr and Mrs Mark Hamilton-Russell.

Eat, shop, stay: Orchard tea-room offering lunches and a selection of freshly made cakes. Also a seasonal ice-cream parlour and Apple Store Snacks café. Shop selling seasonal gifts, locally sourced items and plants. Second-hand bookshop. Holiday cottage and bunkhouse available for rent.

Things to see and do: **Indoors** Historical family rooms, as well as modern, Spanish and botanical art collections, with weekly art tours. **Outdoors** Walk maps and garden tours. Family trails and crafts, and woodland playground.

Dogs: welcome on leads in parkland and orchard only.

Access: 🅿️♿🏬🔄📷🖼️📠🦯👁️🌀
Building 🔣🔣♿ Grounds 🔣➡️
Parking: on site or at The Old Sawmill and Hampton Loade.

Find out more: 01746 780866 or dudmaston@nationaltrust.org.uk

Dudmaston		M	T	W	T	F	S	S
Park, tea-room and shop								
17 Feb–25 Feb*	11–4	.	.	.	.	.	S	S
18 Mar–29 Mar	11–4:30	M	T	W	T	.	.	S
1 Apr–30 Sep	11–5	M	T	W	T	.	.	S
1 Oct–28 Oct	11–4:30	M	T	W	T	.	.	S
3 Nov–25 Nov	11–4	.	.	.	.	.	S	S
Galleries								
18 Mar–28 Oct	12:30–4	M	T	W	T	.	.	S
Hall and galleries								
1 Apr–30 Sep	12:30–4:30	M	T	W	T	.	.	S
Garden and second-hand bookshop **								
18 Mar–28 Oct	11:30–4:30	M	T	W	T	.	.	S

No entry to the car park before opening time.
*Restricted park access – Dingle walks only.
**1 April to 30 September: garden and second-hand bookshop close at 5. Closed Good Friday.

The lawns and lake, above and below, at Dudmaston in Shropshire, offer endless opportunities for family days out

Farnborough Hall

Farnborough, near Banbury,
Warwickshire OX17 1DU

🏠🌸♿ 1960

Carolean house with exquisite plasterwork and grand stairway. Set in landscaped gardens with a mile-long terrace walk and parkland views. **Note**: occupied and administered by the Holbech family. House open by booked guided tours only (please email or call). Open Wednesdays and Saturdays, 1 April to 30 September, 2 to 5:30. Also open 6 and 7 May.

Find out more: 01295 690002 or farnboroughhall@nationaltrust.org.uk

The Firs – Birthplace of Edward Elgar

Crown East Lane, Lower Broadheath,
Worcester, Worcestershire WR2 6RH

🏠🌸♈ 2017

Family treasures tell the story of Sir Edward Elgar's humble beginnings in the family cottage. Outside, the cottage garden is the perfect place to sit and reflect on the life of this great composer and his works. **Note**: nearest toilet at Visitor Centre.

The Firs – Birthplace of Edward Elgar, Worcestershire

Eat, shop, stay: new tea-room with outdoor area within the Visitor Centre (near car park). Small shop in the tea-room. Picnic spaces around the Visitor Centre.

Things to see and do: 'All you need to write a symphony' exhibition. Visitor Centre, cottage and garden. **Dogs**: welcome on leads in garden.

Access: 🅿🅿🗄🔔🏷🎦📺🚪 **Garden** 🐾➡♿
Visitor Centre 🐾🐾♿ **Cottage** 🐾🐾🍴♿
Parking: on site.

Find out more: 01905 333330 or thefirs@nationaltrust.org.uk

The Firs		M	T	W	T	F	S	S
Open all year	10–5	**M**	.	.	.	**F**	**S**	**S**

Admission by timed ticket. Closed 24 December.

The Fleece Inn

Bretforton, near Evesham,
Worcestershire WR11 7JE

🏠🍷🌸🔔🍷 1978

Medieval half-timbered longhouse, now a traditional village inn, with barn and orchard. Known for folk music, Morris dancing and asparagus. **Note**: open daily, 10 to 11 (reduced opening 25 December).

Find out more: 01386 831173 or fleeceinn@nationaltrust.org.uk

Greyfriars' House and Garden

Friar Street, Worcester,
Worcestershire WR1 2LZ

🏠🌸🔔 1966

Set in the heart of historic Worcester, Greyfriars is a charming timber-framed house – perfect for getting away from the hustle and bustle. This unique property was rescued by two extraordinary people in the 20th century

Greyfriars' House and Garden, Worcestershire

with a vision to revive this medieval gem and create a peaceful home and garden.

Eat, shop, stay: light refreshments served in the walled garden or in Elsie's tea-room (in house) in colder weather. Small gift shop and second-hand bookshop.

Things to see and do: **Indoors** Themed events throughout the year, including house tours. Children's trails. **Outdoors** Garden games and geocaching. **Dogs**: welcome in garden.

Access: 🖥️ 🅿️ House 👣 👣 👪 👣
Parking: none on site. Nearest at Corn Market, King Street and Cathedral Plaza, not National Trust (charge including members).

Find out more: 01905 23571 or greyfriars@nationaltrust.org.uk

Greyfriars		M	T	W	T	F	S	S
13 Feb–24 Mar	11–4*	·	T	W	T	F	S	·
27 Mar–27 Oct	11–5*	·	T	W	T	F	S	·
30 Oct–15 Dec	11–4*	·	T	W	T	F	S	·

*House: taster tours only from 11 to 1 (last tour 12:30), tour places allocated on arrival; free-flow access from 1. Open Bank Holiday Mondays.

Hanbury Hall

School Road, Hanbury, Droitwich Spa, Worcestershire WR9 7EA

🏠 ❄️ 🍴 🧺 📶 1953

A country retreat in the heart of Worcestershire. The house and garden, originally a stage-set for summer parties, offer a glimpse into life at the turn of the 18th century. Don't miss the original wall-paintings by Sir James Thornhill. Full of drama and politics, they show the birth of Georgian society. The original formal gardens, designed by George London, have been faithfully re-created and complement the relaxed later gardens, with orangery, orchards and walled garden. If you venture further afield, our walks leaflet will help you find George London's visionary Semicircle in the parkland – the beginning of the landscape movement. **Note**: trialling new ways of opening the house, please call for details.

Hanbury Hall, Worcestershire: the house and garden, right, and Painted Staircase, below

Eat, shop, stay: Servants' Hall tea-room serving meals and cakes made using seasonal Hanbury-grown produce. Chambers tea-room serving traditional afternoon teas. Plants and produce from the walled garden for sale. Make Hanbury a home from home in one of two holiday cottages.

Things to see and do: spend perfect days picnicking and playing on sweeping lawns, surrounded by rolling Worcestershire countryside. For those seeking a more adventurous day, enjoy estate walks or 10k runs through the parkland. **Dogs**: welcome on leads in parkland and in the stableyard. Assistance dogs only in gardens.

Access: 🅿️🅳️♿🎦📷🎨♿🚫
Building ♿♿♿ **Grounds** ♿♿➡️♿
Parking: 150 yards.

Find out more: 01527 821214 or hanburyhall@nationaltrust.org.uk

Hanbury Hall		M	T	W	T	F	S	S
1 Jan–25 Feb*	10–4**	M	T	W	T	F	S	S
26 Feb–28 Oct	10–5**	M	T	W	T	F	S	S
29 Oct–31 Dec*	10–4**	M	T	W	T	F	S	S

*Closed 24/25 January and 24/25 December.
**House: entry by timed ticket on busy days.

Hawford Dovecote

Hawford, Worcestershire WR3 7SG

 1973

Picturesque dovecote, which has survived virtually unaltered since the late 16th century, retaining many nesting boxes. **Note**: sorry no toilet or tea-room. Please park carefully to one side of lane. Open daily, dawn to dusk.

Find out more: 01527 821214 or hawforddovecote@nationaltrust.org.uk

Kinver Edge and the Rock Houses

Holy Austin Rock Houses, Compton Road, Kinver, near Stourbridge, Staffordshire DY7 6DL

🏠🏚️🎎⛲ 1917

The Holy Austin Rock Houses, inhabited until the 1960s, have no equivalent in the whole of England. Discover how a few extraordinary people carved themselves homes in this imposing sandstone ridge. A walk in the surrounding woodland of Kinver Edge leads to open heath with dramatic views across three counties.

Eat, shop, stay: quirky tea-room inside a Rock House serving homemade savoury food, cakes and drinks.

Things to see and do: **Indoors** Traditional toys, working range and free guided tours on weekdays. **Outdoors** Natural woodland play trail and family activities all year. **Dogs**: welcome on leads in grounds of Rock Houses. Assistance dogs only inside buildings.

Access: 🅿️♿ Restored Rock Houses ♿
Tea-room and toilets ♿ Gardens ♿
Parking: by Warden's Lodge, Comber Road, for the Edge, and Compton Road or Kingsford Lane overflow car park for the Rock Houses.

Kinver Edge and the Rock Houses, Staffordshire, were inhabited until the 1960s

Find out more: 01384 872553 or kinveredge@nationaltrust.org.uk

Kinver Edge and the Rock Houses	M	T	W	T	F	S	S
17 Feb–4 Nov	11–4				**T**	**F**	**S**	**S**
10 Nov–9 Dec	11–4						**S**	**S**

Open every day during Staffordshire school holidays. Gardens and tea-room: open to 4:30.

Kinwarton Dovecote

Kinwarton, near Alcester, Warwickshire B49 6HB

 1958

Rare 14th-century circular dovecote with metre-thick walls, hundreds of nesting holes and original rotating ladder. **Note**: stock may be grazing. Sorry no toilet. Limited parking (not National Trust). Open daily, 1 March to 28 October, 9 to 6.

Find out more: 01789 400777 or kinwartondovecote@nationaltrust.org.uk

Knowles Mill

Dowles Brook, Bewdley, Worcestershire DY12 2LX

 1938

Dating from the 18th century, the mill retains much of its machinery, including the frames of an overshot waterwheel. **Note**: Mill Cottage not open to visitors (please respect the resident's privacy). Sorry no toilets or tea-room. No parking at Mill Cottage. Open daily, dawn to dusk.

Find out more: 01527 821214 or knowlesmill@nationaltrust.org.uk

Letocetum Roman Baths and Museum

Watling Street, Wall, near Lichfield, Staffordshire WS14 0AW

1934

Open-air remains of a once-important Roman staging post and settlement, including *mansio* (Roman inn) and bathhouse. **Note**: in the guardianship of English Heritage. Baths accessible all year, dawn to dusk. Museum open last weekend of month, March to October. Additional openings during August and for some Bank Holidays.

Find out more: 0370 333 1181 (English Heritage) or letocetum@nationaltrust.org.uk

Middle Littleton Tithe Barn

Middle Littleton, Evesham, Worcestershire WR11 8LN

 1975

The largest and finest restored 13th-century tithe barn in the country. **Note**: sorry no toilets. Guided tours available on request. Open daily, 1 April to 31 October, 2 to 5 (guided tours available).

Find out more: 01905 371006 or middlelittleton@nationaltrust.org.uk

Morville Hall

Morville, near Bridgnorth, Shropshire WV16 5NB

🏠 ✿ ♿ | 1965 |

Elizabethan gem with a Georgian makeover. Enchanting gardens spill down to the Mor Brook against the backdrop of Shropshire hills. **Note**: property contents are a mix of items on loan and tenant's own. Open Fridays and Saturdays, 11 and 12 May, 8 and 9 June, 6 and 7 July and 7 to 8 September, 12 to 5. Dower House and gardens opened independently by Dr K. Swift (telephone 01746 714407 for details).

Find out more: 01746 780866 (Dudmaston Hall) or morvillehall@nationaltrust.org.uk

Moseley Old Hall

Moseley Old Hall Lane, Fordhouses, Wolverhampton, Staffordshire WV10 7HY

🏠 🔥 ✿ ♿ | 1962 |

Moseley Old Hall, Staffordshire: a house of many secrets

This atmospheric farmhouse, built *circa* 1600, holds many secrets. Charles II hid here after escaping the 1651 Battle of Worcester. Inside, a log fire crackles as 17th-century domestic life surrounds you. Outside, explore the walled garden, containing herbs and vegetables, the orchard and knot garden. Beyond is King's Walk Wood.

Eat, shop, stay: tea-room serving soup, one-pots and seasonal specials. Cakes and scones are baked here throughout the day. Shop selling gifts and plants. Second-hand bookshop.

Things to see and do: **Indoors** Guided tours, have-a-go sessions and re-creations of 17th-century life all year. **Outdoors** Children's activities, including two-level tree house, den-building, rope swings, trails and activity packs. Wightwick Manor nearby. **Dogs**: welcome on leads in garden and grounds.

Access: 🅿️ 🅳 ⬚ ⬚ ⬚ ⬚ 🖥 📱 ⬚
House ⬚ ♿ **Garden and woodland** ⬚ ⬚ ➡️ ♿
Parking: on site.

Find out more: 01902 782808 or moseleyoldhall@nationaltrust.org.uk

Moseley Old Hall		M	T	W	T	F	S	S
15 Feb–16 Mar	10–4	M	T	W	T	F	S	S
17 Mar–4 Nov	10–5	M	T	W	T	F	S	S
5 Nov–24 Dec	10–4	M				F	S	S

House: opens 11; entry on Bank Holiday weekends and very busy times by timed ticket; February, March, November and December: access to top floor may be limited for safety; last entry one hour before closing.

Packwood House

Packwood Lane, Lapworth, Warwickshire B94 6AT

🏠 ✿ ♿ 🍽 | 1941 |

Surrounded by beautiful gardens and countryside, Packwood was described by a guest in the 1930s as 'a house to dream of, a garden to dream in'. Lovingly restored at the beginning of the 20th century by Graham Baron Ash, you can discover the detail behind the man, his passion for collecting and his

collection. The gardens include brightly coloured, 'mingled style' herbaceous borders, famous sculpted yews and an 18th-century gentleman's kitchen garden.

Eat, shop, stay: Garden Kitchen Café serving hot food, soup, salads, sandwiches, cakes and snacks. Shop selling seasonal gifts, local foods and plants, many grown in our own nursery. Picnics welcome by the lakeside and in the picnic area by the car park.

Things to see and do: Indoors Children's trail. **Outdoors** Welcome and garden talks, countryside walks and Natural Play. Baddesley Clinton and Coughton Court nearby. Areas of the gardens may be closed, please call before travelling. **Dogs**: welcome in car park, park footpaths and café terrace. Assistance dogs only in gardens.

Access: [icons]
House [icons] **Grounds** [icons]
Parking: 150 yards.

Packwood House, Warwickshire: bright 'mingled style' borders, above, and visitors exploring inside, below

Find out more: 01564 782024 or packwood@nationaltrust.org.uk

Packwood House		M	T	W	T	F	S	S
1 Jan–16 Feb	9–4†	M	T	W	T	F	S	S
17 Feb–28 Oct	9–5*	M	T	W	T	F	S	S
29 Oct–31 Dec	9–4†	M	T	W	T	F	S	S

30 March to 2 April and 25 to 27 August, admission by bookable tickets only, limited (including members). *House: formal gardens and gift shop open at 11; admission by timed ticket (not bookable). †House, formal gardens and gift shop: open 11 to 3. Access to house by guided tour, subject to availability. Closed 24 and 25 December.

Rosedene

Victoria Road, Dodford, near Bromsgrove, Worcestershire B61 9BU

[icons] 1997

Restored 1840s cottage with an organic garden and orchard, illustrating the mid-19th-century Chartist Movement. **Note**: available to hire as a 'back to basics' holiday cottage. Admission by guided tour on the first Sunday of month, March to December (booking essential).

Find out more: 01527 821214 or rosedene@nationaltrust.org.uk

Shugborough Estate

Milford, near Stafford, Staffordshire ST17 0XB

🏛️ 🖼️ 🔊 ✳️ 🐾 🚻 1966

Join us on a journey as we revive and reunite the Shugborough Estate over the next ten years. Home to the Anson family since 1624 and with a legacy of exploration and innovation, it was once described as 'a perfect paradise'. You can explore sweeping parkland, ancient woodland and a landscape peppered with monuments, then discover Park Farm, created at the cutting-edge of agricultural reforms. In the Georgian mansion, unearth prized treasures and experience life 'below stairs', then enter a world of glamour and royalty in the apartments of Patrick Lichfield, 5th Earl and fashion photographer.

Eat, shop, stay: delicious treats and meals on offer at the mansion tea-room and Park Farm café, using produce from the Walled Garden. Why not visit the shop or plant centre and pick up the perfect gift?

Shugborough Estate, Staffordshire: the garden, above, and west front of the Georgian mansion, below

Things to see and do: **Indoors** There are stories of adventure, travels and triumphs to discover in the mansion. **Outdoors** New estate walks to explore and wonderful views from the Triumphal Arch to enjoy plus explorers' wood natural play area for children. **Dogs**: on leads in formal gardens and parkland.

Access: 🅿♿♿♿♿♿♿
Building ♿♿♿♿ **Grounds** ♿➡
Parking: 25 yards from reception.

Find out more: 01889 881388 or shugborough@nationaltrust.org.uk

Shugborough Estate		M	T	W	T	F	S	S
Park, gardens and Park Farm*								
1 Jan–16 Feb	9–4	M	T	W	T	F	S	S
17 Feb–4 Nov	9–6	M	T	W	T	F	S	S
5 Nov–31 Dec	9–4	M	T	W	T	F	S	S
Park Farm Café								
1 Jan–16 Feb	9–3:30	M	T	W	T	F	S	S
17 Feb–4 Nov	9–5:30	M	T	W	T	F	S	S
5 Nov–31 Dec	9–3:30	M	T	W	T	F	S	S
Mansion, Lichfield apartments and servants' quarters**								
17 Feb–4 Nov	11–5†	M	T	W	T	F	S	S
1 Dec–23 Dec	10–3	M	T	W	T	F	S	S
Mansion tea-room and shop								
1 Jan–16 Feb	11–3:30	M	T	W	T	F	S	S
17 Feb–4 Nov	10–5:30††	M	T	W	T	F	S	S
5 Nov–31 Dec	11–3:30¹	M	T	W	T	F	S	S

*Walled Garden and visitor reception: open as park, gardens and Park Farm. **Some areas of mansion accessible by timed ticket or booking only. †Last admission one hour before closing. ††Mansion tea-room closes at 5. ¹Mansion tea-room opens at 10, 1 December to 23 December. Closed 25 December.

The River Sow on the Shugborough Estate, below, and playing badminton at Sunnycroft, Shropshire, right

Sunnycroft

200 Holyhead Road, Wellington, Telford, Shropshire TF1 2DR

🏠❄ 1999 ·

Hidden down an avenue of towering redwoods is an oasis in the middle of suburbia. Designed to emulate the upper classes, this rare middle-class Victorian survival is a mini estate. Built to last, little was thrown away and the life of a family home envelops you as you enter.

Eat, shop, stay: small tea-room in house, with doors leading onto the veranda, serving light lunches, cakes, scones and slices, ice-cream and drinks. Picnics welcome. Shop selling gifts, plants, produce and second-hand books.

Things to see and do: **Indoors** Introductory talks, guided tours, workshops, family activities and trails reveal the stories of life at Sunnycroft. **Outdoors** Family trails, garden games on lawn, seasonal events and garden tours. **Dogs**: welcome on leads in grounds only.

Access: 🅿♿♿♿♿ **Building** ♿ **Grounds** ♿➡
Sat Nav: use TF1 2DP (exit 7 from M54).
Parking: 150 yards from front of house.

Find out more: 01952 242884 or sunnycroft@nationaltrust.org.uk

Sunnycroft		M	T	W	T	F	S	S
6 Jan–11 Feb	10:30–3	·	·	·	·	·	S	S
17 Feb–26 Mar	10:30–4	M	·	·	·	F	S	S
30 Mar–16 Apr	10:30–5	M	T	·	·	F	S	S
20 Apr–23 Jul	10:30–5	M	·	·	·	F	S	S
27 Jul–3 Sep	10:30–5	M	T	·	·	F	S	S
7 Sep–4 Nov	10:30–5	M	·	·	·	F	S	S
1 Dec–23 Dec	10:30–4	M	T	·	·	F	S	S

Entry by timed tickets. Last admission to house one hour before closing. Last service in tea-room 30 minutes before closing. Optional ten-minute introductory talk, then free-flow.

The Long Gallery at Upton House and Gardens in Warwickshire

Upton House and Gardens

near Banbury, Warwickshire OX15 6HT

🏠 ❖ 🛏 🔔 ♨ 🍷 1948

Sold! This year you are invited to a very special house viewing. Purchased in 1927 by the 2nd Viscount Bearsted, Upton had great potential but was in need of modernisation. Be inspired by the Bearsteds' house and garden renovations; see how they created a made-to-measure family home to showcase a world-class art collection, including fine porcelain and works by Bosch, Stubbs and El Greco. Every ideal home needs a spectacular feature garden. Lady Bearsted's passion for plants bloomed, with early spring bulbs, herbaceous planting and productive kitchen garden, all reflected in the Mirror Pool.

Eat, shop, stay: restaurant (licensed) serving lunches and freshly baked cakes; gluten-free and vegetarian options always available. Shop selling gifts, art prints, plants and mementoes of your visit. Two holiday cottages; one with 1930s décor and one overlooking the gardens.

Things to see and do: **Indoors** Topical house tours, hands-on displays, changing exhibitions, design-themed activities and workshops. **Outdoors** Woodland adventure and activities, local walks, seasonal planting schemes. Jazz music and garden chats. **Dogs**: assistance dogs only in grounds.

Access: 🅿 ♿ ♿ ♿ ♿ ♿ ♿ 🖼 🎵
House and gallery 👟 ♿ ♿ Grounds 👟 ♿ ♿
Sat Nav: follow brown signs to car park once you arrive at postcode location.
Parking: 300 yards.

Find out more: 01295 670266 or uptonhouse@nationaltrust.org.uk

Upton House and Gardens		M	T	W	T	F	S	S
Gardens, restaurant and shop*								
6 Jan–4 Feb	12–4	·	·	·	·	·	S	S
10 Feb–28 Oct	11–5	M	T	W	T	F	S	S
29 Oct–23 Dec	12–4	M	·	·	·	F	S	S
26 Dec–31 Dec	12–4	M	·	W	T	F	S	S
House**								
6 Jan–4 Feb	12–4	·	·	·	·	·	S	S
10 Feb–28 Oct	1–5	M	T	W	T	F	S	S
29 Oct–23 Dec	12–4	M	·	·	·	F	S	S

*November to March: gardens open by winter walk only.
**Timed tickets operate daily. 10 February to 28 October: themed tours 11 to 1, places limited.

The Weir Garden

Swainshill, Hereford, Herefordshire HR4 7QF

🏛️❄️♿ 1959

Whatever the season, the natural beauty of this riverside garden is completely captivating. During spring, the ground beneath the ancient trees is carpeted with bulbs; then, in summer, a picnic by the river while watching the wildlife is irresistible. Autumn brings an abundance of seasonal produce in the walled garden.
Note: sturdy footwear recommended.

The Weir Garden, Herefordshire, in spring

Eat, shop, stay: self-service tea and coffee available. Picnics welcome. Small selection of children's toys, gifts, maps and seasonal gifts available in the shop.

Things to see and do: events, including walks and talks. Historical secrets to discover, from giant fish to Roman remains. Natural play area and family trails during school holidays.
Dogs: assistance dogs only (dogs allowed in car park).

Access: 🚾 Grounds ♿🦽
Parking: on site.

Find out more: 01981 590509 or theweir@nationaltrust.org.uk

The Weir Garden		M	T	W	T	F	S	S
20 Jan–28 Jan	10:30–4						S	S
29 Jan–4 Nov	10:30–4:30	M	T	W	T	F	S	S
10 Nov–9 Dec	10:30–4						S	S

Wichenford Dovecote

Wichenford, Worcestershire WR6 6XY

🏠 1965

Small but striking 17th-century half-timbered dovecote at Wichenford Court.
Note: no access to Wichenford Court (privately owned). Sorry no toilet or tea-room. Please consider local residents when parking. Open every day all year, dawn to dusk.

Find out more: 01527 821214 or wichenforddovecote@nationaltrust.org.uk

Wightwick Manor and Gardens

Bridgnorth Road, Wolverhampton, West Midlands WV6 8BN

🏛️❄️ 1937

A place where liberal dreams for the future mix with a love for unfashionable art. The Mander family's political ideals inspired them to share their home with the nation and fill it with art for visitors to enjoy. Their belief in women's rights, fairness for their employees and

Wightwick Manor and Gardens, West Midlands: left and above, the house is filled with works of art collected for the nation to enjoy, while the gardens offer numerous horticultural gems to delight visitors

confronting fascism is the story behind a home bursting with works by the greatest artists of the Pre-Raphaelite and Arts and Crafts movements. A house of colour and comfort; a garden of yew and roses; and a gallery of De Morgan treasures – the legacy of one remarkable family and their friends.

Eat, shop, stay: specialist shop selling William Morris and Arts and Crafts-inspired ranges with plant centre. Tea-room serving breakfast, light lunches, sandwiches and sweet treats.

Things to see and do: **Indoors** World-class art collection, interactive servants' rooms, specialist talks and tours all year. Malthouse gallery with De Morgan Collection exhibition. **Outdoors** Family orienteering map and trails, self-led activities. **Dogs**: welcome on leads in garden.

Access: [icons]
Manor [icons] Malthouse [icons]
Gardens [icons]
Parking: entrance off A454.

Find out more: 01902 761400 (Infoline) or wightwickmanor@nationaltrust.org.uk
Wightwick Bank, Wolverhampton,
West Midlands WV6 8EE

Wightwick Manor and Gardens		M	T	W		T	F	S	S
1 Jan–16 Mar*	10–4**	M	T	W		T	F	S	S
17 Mar–28 Oct	10–5**	M	T	W		T	F	S	S
29 Oct–31 Dec	10–4**	M	T	W		T	F	S	S

*House: closed Tuesdays, January to March; reduced number of rooms open in January, February and March.
**House: opens 11 and entry by tour only, 11 to 12; free-flow from 12. Shop and gallery: open 10:30. Last entry to house one hour before closing. Closed 25 and 26 December.

Wilderhope Manor

Longville, Much Wenlock, Shropshire TF13 6EG

[icons] 1936

Charming Elizabethan manor house with commanding views across a secluded valley with many original features inside and lovely walks outside. **Note**: Youth Hostel, access may be restricted. Open 2 to 4, Sundays, 7 January to 25 March and 7 October to 23 December; Wednesdays and Sundays, 4 April to 30 September.

Find out more: 01694 771363 (Hostel Warden YHA) or wilderhope@nationaltrust.org.uk

Legend

▲ **Buildings and/or gardens**

● **Entry points to coast and countryside**

National Trust land

Places in neighbouring counties

East Midlands, page 240
West Midlands, page 264
The Lakes, page 313
Yorkshire, page 336
Wales, page 370

|———————| 10 miles

A685

A591
● Kendal
▲ **Sizergh**

● **Fell Foot**

A590
■ Ulverston

Arnside and Silverdale

A687

■ Barrow-in-Furness

▲ Morecambe
A683

Heysham Coast
■ **LANCASTER**

A65
■ Settle

M6

A59
A56
A629

■ East Riddlesden Hall ▲

■ Blackpool
M55

▲ **Gawthorpe Hall** ■ Burnley

Hardcastle Crags ▲

■ Preston
A6
M65
A666
A56

M62

■ Todmorden ■

■ Southport ▲ **Rufford Old Hall**

A365
M61

■ Rochdale ■
M66

● **Formby**
■ Bolton

M58
■ Wigan A58

A580

M60

Salford ■ ● **MANCHESTER**

A570
A59

M67

The Hardmans' House
LIVERPOOL ■
M62
The Beatles' Childhood Homes
▲ Dunham Massey ■ Sale

■ Warrington
A57
Stockport ■

Kinder, Edale and the Dark Peak ●

M53
A56
M56
▲ **Quarry Bank**
A523 Lyme ▲
A6

Longshaw, Burbage and the Eastern Moors ●

Speke Hall ▲
▲ **Tatton Park**
Nether Alderley Mill ▲ ▲ **Hare Hill**

A41
A49

Alderley Edge and Cheshire Countryside
Macclesfield ■

Bakewell ■

A537

A55
A534

■ **CHESTER**
A51
A530
M6
Congleton ■
A53

Ilam Park, Dovedale and the White Peak ●

A494
A534

Little Moreton Hall ▲
A534

■ Crewe

Biddulph Grange Garden ▲
A523

A49
A525

▲ **Erddig**
A483

A495
A53

Alderley Edge and Cheshire Countryside

Nether Alderley, Macclesfield, Cheshire

🏛️🦯 1946

The dramatic red sandstone escarpment of Alderley Edge has far-reaching views over the Cheshire Plain and towards the Peak District. Numerous paths meander through open pasture and mature pine and beech woodland. The site, designated a Site of Special Scientific Interest for its geology and history of copper mining dating back to the Bronze Age, is also noted for its wizard myth, which inspired the novel *The Weirdstone of Brisingamen*. There's more Cheshire countryside to explore: Bickerton, Bulkeley and Helsby Hills on the Sandstone Ridge, Thurstaston Common on the Wirral, and The Cloud and Mow Cop on the Staffordshire border. **Note**: toilets at Alderley Edge car park only.

Eat, shop, stay: Alderley Edge: Wizard Tea-room (Tuesday to Sunday and Bank Holidays) and Wizard Inn (neither National Trust). Ice-cream vendor (when weather is fine). Picnic area close to car park.

Things to see and do: guided walks provide an insight into the industrial archaeology, geology and legends at Alderley Edge. Waymarked walking routes. Three orienteering courses. Ancient copper mine tours: Derbyshire Caving Club, twice yearly. **Dogs**: under close control. On leads near livestock and ground-nesting birds.

Access: 🅿️♿️♿️ **Grounds** ▶️
Sat Nav: for Alderley Edge use SK10 4UB; for Mow Cop ST7 3PA; for Bickerton SY14 8LN.
Parking: at Alderley Edge, Mow Cop ST7 3PA and Bickerton SY14 8LN (plus roadside elsewhere).

Find out more: 01625 584412 or alderleyedge@nationaltrust.org.uk

Alderley Edge	
Car park	
Open every day all year	8–5*

*1 April to 31 October, closes at 8.

Cheshire Countryside: Thurstaston Common on the Wirral with views over the Dee Estuary, below, and a young naturalist zooms in for a magnified view, above

Arnside and Silverdale

near Arnside, Cumbria

🏛🏖🦋🏊 1929

The toposcope on Arnside Knott in Cumbria

With a wildlife-rich mosaic of limestone grassland, pavement, woodland and meadows, this coastal countryside offers miles of footpaths and fine views over Morecambe Bay. Arnside Knott and Eaves Wood are home to butterflies and flowers; Jack Scout's cliffs are perfect for watching the setting sun or migrant birds passing through.

Eat, shop, stay: variety of small shops, galleries and cafés in and around Arnside and Silverdale villages (not National Trust). Nearest National Trust café at Sizergh.

Things to see and do: toposcope (landmark orientation map) viewpoint (short uphill from Arnside Knott car park). With lots of footpaths, Silverdale is perfect for strolls to the cove or the Silverdale village heritage walk.
Dogs: welcome under control (on leads where stock grazing).

Access: 🦽
Sat Nav: use LA5 0BP for Arnside Knott; LA5 0UG for Eaves Wood (Silverdale), both nearby. **Parking**: at Arnside Knott (signposted from Arnside Promenade) and Eaves Wood, Silverdale. Also in Silverdale village (not National Trust).

Find out more: 01524 701178 or arnsidesilverdale@nationaltrust.org.uk

The Beatles' Childhood Homes

Woolton and Allerton, Liverpool

🏠 2002

A combined tour to Mendips and 20 Forthlin Road, the childhood homes of John Lennon and Paul McCartney respectively, is your only opportunity to see inside the houses where The Beatles met, composed and rehearsed many of their earliest songs. You can walk through the back door into the kitchen and imagine John's Aunt Mimi cooking him his tea, or stand in the spot where Lennon and McCartney composed 'I Saw Her Standing There'. The custodians take you on a fascinating trip down memory lane in these two atmospheric period houses, so typical of Liverpool life in the 1950s.
Note: handbags, cameras and recording equipment must be left in secure facilities at both houses. Access is by National Trust minibus tour only from Liverpool city centre and Speke Hall (depending on time). Admission charge applies to all, including members.

Eat, shop, stay: guidebooks and postcards available at the houses and Speke Hall shop. Speke Hall's Home Farm restaurant serves regional specialities, such as Scouse and Wet Nelly.

Things to see and do: departures from convenient pick-up points (city centre and Speke Hall). Our comfortable minibus and easy online booking service allow you to relax, as we take the strain out of visiting.

Access: 🅿️🗺️🏠🎧👓📷 **Building** ♿
Parking: numerous car parks near collection point (not National Trust) for tours from city centre, or at Speke Hall for tours departing from there.

Find out more: 0151 427 7231 (booking line) or thebeatleshomes@nationaltrust.org.uk

The Beatles' Childhood Homes		M	T	W	T	F	S	S
1 Mar–3 Jun	Tour*			W	T	F	S	S
4 Jun–4 Nov	Tour*	M	T	W	T	F	S	S
7 Nov–25 Nov	Tour*			W	T	F	S	S

*Admission by guided tour only. Times and pick-up locations vary (please visit website or call for details and tickets).

The Beatles' Childhood Homes, Liverpool:
20 Forthlin Road, Paul McCartney's childhood home

Dunham Massey

Altrincham, Greater Manchester WA14 4SJ

🏠✝️🖼️❀♿🍽️ 1976

Dunham Massey, Greater Manchester: a green haven

A green haven encircled by a wall of red brick, Dunham Massey park is at the heart of a 1,200-hectare (3,000-acre) estate. Inside the park, you'll spot fallow deer as you walk along the tree-lined avenues leading to the Georgian house, also of warm red brick. The house is filled with a large collection of beautiful and useful objects amassed by a family that never threw anything away. With more than 400 years' worth of history, there are many fascinating stories to uncover: this year focuses on women's history. The gardens must be some of the finest in the North, with the largest winter garden in the UK and colourful swathes of planting all year round. **Note**: everyone (including members) requires a house and garden ticket (available from reception on the day).

Eat, shop, stay: large shop selling food, locally sourced gifts and a wide range of plants. Café with indoor and outdoor seating; Stables Restaurant serving hot lunches and The Parlour offering drinks and treats, including ice-cream (hours vary).

Things to see and do: at least one free guided tour every day with a range of options in the house, garden and park. Visit the stables and motor house to find out about the importance of horses and then the motorcar for this country estate. Turn on the waterwheel and see the old sawmill in action. Map available for walks, runs and cycle routes on the wider estate. Events all year, including open-air theatre and garden parties. Family activities during school holidays. Cycling in the deer-park for under-fives only.
Dogs: welcome on leads in the park. Assistance dogs only in the house and garden.

Access:
House **Garden and park**
Parking: 200 yards.

Find out more: 0161 942 3989 (Infoline). 0161 941 1025 or dunhammassey@nationaltrust.org.uk

Dunham Massey		M	T	W	T	F	S	S
House, stables and mill*								
10 Feb–4 Nov	11–5**	M	T	W	·	·	S	S
Garden, café, restaurant and shop								
1 Jan–9 Feb	10:30–4†	M	T	W	T	F	S	S
10 Feb–4 Nov	10:30–5†	M	T	W	T	F	S	S
5 Nov–31 Dec	10:30–4†	M	T	W	T	F	S	S
Park								
1 Jan–9 Feb	8–6	M	T	W	T	F	S	S
10 Feb–4 Nov	8–8	M	T	W	T	F	S	S
5 Nov–31 Dec	8–6	M	T	W	T	F	S	S

*10 February to 21 March: house entry by guided tour only (booking not necessary); mill opening times vary. **House: closes dusk, if earlier; last entry one hour before closing. Mill: open 12 to 4. †Shop, café and restaurant: open 10. Garden: closes at dusk if earlier. Restaurant: closes one hour earlier.

Bluebells brighten a corner of the estate at Dunham Massey, below, while a family meets the deer, right

Formby

near Formby, Liverpool

🏛️ 🛏️ 🏞️ 👤 1967

Formby near Liverpool: sculpted sands and surging tides

Formby's shifting sands create ever-changing dunes sculpted by the wind and squeezed by surging tides. Sea views over Liverpool Bay to the hills of North Wales can be enjoyed from the wide sandy beaches. Footprint trails 5,000 years old sometimes reappear as the sea erodes ancient mudflats. Pinewood walks with red squirrels lead to open fields and the Formby Asparagus Trail. Formby is a place for the simple pleasures of a family day out, for healthy exercise, fresh air and relaxation, and for a seaside picnic in the perfect spot. **Note**: toilets open when car park is staffed.

Eat, shop, stay: ice-cream, soft drinks, coffee and confectionery available from mobile vans (not National Trust). A favourite place for picnics. Safe barbecue area is available at the family picnic site.

Gawthorpe Textile Collection, including needlework, lace and embroidery. Outside, dog walkers will enjoy the woodland walks. **Note**: financed and run in partnership with Lancashire County Council.

Eat, shop, stay: tea-room serving light snacks.

Things to see and do: **Indoors** Guided tours, talks and exhibitions. Events all year, including Victorian Christmas. **Outdoors** Open-air theatre in July and other events, including some for children. **Dogs**: under close control in grounds.

Access: ⊞⊞⊞⊡⊡⊡ Building ⧖
Grounds ⧖⧖⧖➡
Sat Nav: use BB12 8SD then follow brown signs. **Parking**: 150 yards, narrow access road (passing places).

Find out more: 01282 771004 or gawthorpehall@nationaltrust.org.uk

Gawthorpe Hall		M	T	W	T	F	S	S
Hall								
28 Mar–4 Nov	12–5*		·	W	T	F	S	S
Tea-room								
28 Mar–4 Nov	11–5**		·	W	T	F	S	S
Grounds								
Open all year	8–7	M	T	W	T	F	S	S

Hall and tea-room: open Bank Holidays. *Hall: last entry 4:15.
**Tea-room: last orders 4:30. Opening times subject to change.

Things to see and do: self-guided trails, including the Formby Asparagus Trail and the Asparagus Cycle Trail. Guided walks. Circular and longer walks linked to the Sefton Coastal Path. Orienteering and geocaching. **Dogs**: on leads on Squirrel Walk and under close control elsewhere (vulnerable wildlife).

Access: ⊞⊞⊞⊡⊡⊡ Grounds ⧖➡
Sat Nav: use L37 1LJ for Victoria Road car park; L37 2EB for Lifeboat Road. **Parking**: on site.

Find out more: 01704 878591 or formby@nationaltrust.org.uk

Formby		M	T	W	T	F	S	S
Car park								
1 Jan–4 Feb	9–4	M	T	W	T	F	S	S
5 Feb–25 Mar	9–4:45	M	T	W	T	F	S	S
26 Mar–30 Sep	9–5:15	M	T	W	T	F	S	S
1 Oct–25 Nov	9–4:45	M	T	W	T	F	S	S
26 Nov–31 Dec	9–4	M	T	W	T	F	S	S

Closed 25 December.

Gawthorpe Hall

Burnley Road, Padiham, near Burnley, Lancashire BB12 8UA

⌂⧖ 1972

This Elizabethan house, in the heart of urban Lancashire, contains opulent 19th-century interiors by Sir Charles Barry (of the Houses of Parliament and 'the real Downton Abbey' fame). The Hall displays textiles from the

Walking through the pinewoods at Formby, left, and Elizabethan Gawthorpe Hall in Lancashire, below

The Hardmans' House

59 Rodney Street, Liverpool, Merseyside L1 9ER

🏠 2003

The studio with equipment and props at The Hardmans' House, Liverpool

Step inside the sophisticated life of a 1950s society photographer in the heart of Liverpool. The handsome Georgian house – both glamorous workplace and modest, cluttered home for Edward Chambré Hardman and his talented wife Margaret – is a time capsule of life and creativity, packed with vintage treasures and fascinating photography. **Note**: admission by guided tour only – booking advised. Entrance on Pilgrim Street at rear of property.

Eat, shop, stay: small shop selling unique photographic prints, postcards, guidebooks and hot drinks. The nearest café (not National Trust) is just a short walk away at the Anglican Cathedral.

Things to see and do: tours (book your place to avoid disappointment). Family trail. Virtual tour of the house. Walking trails of Hardman's Liverpool available online.

Access: 🖼️🖐️🔌🎦📹🎧📷🅿️ Building ♿
Parking: none on site. Car parks at Anglican Cathedral and Slater Street, not National Trust (charge including members).

Find out more: 0151 709 6261 or thehardmanshouse@nationaltrust.org.uk

The Hardmans' House	M	T	W	T	F	S	S
14 Mar–27 Oct 11–3:30	·	·	**W**	**T**	**F**	**S**	·

Admission by timed ticket only, booking advisable (places limited). Open Bank Holiday Mondays.

Hare Hill

Over Alderley, Macclesfield, Cheshire SK10 4PY

❈ 🐾 1978

Hare Hill is a place to refresh the senses and the soul. Set within tenanted farmland, this woodland is full of twists, turns and surprises, wooden hares and hidden paths and ponds. At its heart is the stunning walled White Garden offering an oasis of tranquillity.

Eat, shop, stay: external catering at weekends and Bank Holidays only. Picnics welcome in the garden. Small shop in car park and plants for sale. Second-hand bookstall.

Things to see and do: trail of carved wooden hares through the woodland and bird-spotting in the hide. Why not relax in the walled garden with a book? Explore the changing woodland in all seasons. **Dogs**: assistance dogs only in garden and woodland.

Hare Hill, Cheshire: refreshment for the senses and soul

Access: 🔤 🎵 ♿ **Grounds** ♿
Sat Nav: use SK10 4PY to take you 109 yards west of car park. **Parking:** car park on site.

Find out more: 01625 827534 or harehill@nationaltrust.org.uk .

Hare Hill		M	T	W	T	F	S	S
10 Feb–4 Nov	10:30–5	**M**	**T**	**W**	**T**	**F**	**S**	**S**

Last admission one hour before closing. Car park: closes 5.

Heysham Coast

Heysham, near Morecambe, Lancashire

✝ 🏛 ♿ 🖼 1996

A sandstone headland with a beautiful walk through grassland and woodland, passing a ruined Saxon chapel and unusual rock-cut graves. **Note**: nearest facilities in village (not National Trust); park in the main village car park. For Sat Nav use LA3 2RW.

Find out more: 01524 701178 or heysham@nationaltrust.org.uk

Little Moreton Hall

Congleton, Cheshire CW12 4SD

🏠 ✝ 🏛 ❖ 1938

Moated Little Moreton Hall in Cheshire, above and left, was built to impress more than 500 years ago

While modern life rushes by on the busy road outside, Little Moreton Hall, encircled by a moat, survives as a Tudor fantasy, transporting visitors in seconds back to another time. Built to impress by craftsmen's hands more than 500 years ago, the hall continues to exude an inimitable quirky charm and homely intimacy. With its crooked walls and uneven floors, it seems at once fragile and resilient. Outside is the manicured knot garden, plus herbs and vegetables used in Tudor cooking and medicine. This remarkable survivor inspires reflection on the ups and downs of a simpler way of life.

Eat, shop, stay: the Little Tea-room (with outdoor seating) and Mrs Dale's Tea-room serve delicious homemade food produced in the on-site bakery. Ice-cream kiosk (open on sunny days) and large shop in the car park selling gifts, plants and local products.

Things to see and do: Indoors Free guided tours and family trails. Tudor displays and activities most days. Costumes to try on. Contemporary exhibition programme. **Outdoors** Summer open-air theatre and Tudor festivals throughout the year. **Dogs**: on leads in car park and front lawn only.

Access: 🅿️ symbols

Hall symbols **Reception** symbols
Grounds symbols ➡️
Parking: 100 yards.

Find out more: 01260 272018 or
littlemoretonhall@nationaltrust.org.uk

Little Moreton Hall		M	T	W	T	F	S	S
10 Feb–28 Oct*	11–5**			W	T	F	S	S
8 Dec–16 Dec	11–4**	M	T	W	T	F	S	S

Open Bank Holiday Mondays. *10 to 18 February,
2 to 15 April, 28 May to 3 June, 30 July to 2 September and
20 to 28 October: open daily. **Upper floors may close early
if light levels are poor.

Lyme

Disley, Stockport, Cheshire SK12 2NR

symbols 1947

If you had to conjure up the ultimate grand
English country house, you'd picture
something like Lyme. The imposing mansion,
which sits in 570 hectares (1,400 acres) of
deer-park, with glorious views across
Manchester and the Cheshire Plain, was the
much-loved home of the Legh family for more
than 600 years. Its lavish interiors reflect the
life of a great estate, from its earliest
beginnings to its Regency heyday, when
Thomas Legh brought Lyme back to its full
glory. You may recognise Lyme as 'Pemberley'
from the BBC adaptation of *Pride and Prejudice*,
starring Colin Firth. Lyme's ever-changing
gardens, with the Reflection Lake, Orangery
and Rose Garden, are an ideal place to stroll
and relax. **Note**: owned and managed by the
National Trust, but partly financed by
Stockport Metropolitan Borough Council.

Eat, shop, stay: choice of café and tea-rooms
serving light snacks and lunches. Salting Room
Tea Parlour and Garden offers afternoon tea
(booking essential). Timber Yard shop for
gardening/outdoors products. Gift and book
shop. East Lodge holiday cottage in deer-park
with stunning views.

**Lyme in Cheshire: the imposing mansion across the
Reflection Lake, sits within a vast estate**

Wood Playscape for five- to twelve-year-olds. Events include Easter trails, summer holiday activities, Hallowe'en and Christmas celebrations. **Dogs**: under close control in park; leads near livestock and vehicles; selected days in garden.

Access: ⬚⬚⬚⬚⬚⬚⬚⬚⬚⬚⬚
House ⬚⬚⬚ Garden ⬚⬚⬚⬚⬚
Sat Nav: use SK12 2NR. **Parking**: 200 yards.

Find out more: 01663 762023 or lyme@nationaltrust.org.uk

Lyme		M	T	W	T	F	S	S
House								
10 Feb–24 Jul*	11–5	M	T	·	·	F	S	S
26 Jul–30 Aug*	11–5	M	T	·	T	F	S	S
31 Aug–4 Nov*	11–5	M	T	·	·	F	S	S
23 Nov–24 Dec**	11–3	M	·	·	·	F	S	S
Garden, shop and tea-room								
6 Jan–4 Feb	11–3†	·	·	·	·	·	S	S
10 Feb–4 Nov	11–5†	M	T	W	T	F	S	S
10 Nov–30 Dec	11–3†	·	·	·	·	·	S	S
Estate								
Open all year	8–6††	M	T	W	T	F	S	S
Timber Yard shop and café								
1 Jan–24 Mar	10–4	M	T	W	T	F	S	S
25 Mar–28 Oct	10–5	M	T	W	T	F	S	S
29 Oct–31 Dec	10–4	M	T	W	T	F	S	S

*Last entry one hour before closing. **Parts of house open for Christmas events. †Garden: opens 10:30. ††10 February to 4 November: estate closes at 8 or dusk when earlier. Gates locked at closing. Lyme closed 25 December.

Things to see and do: **Indoors** Activities, such as reading in the Library, home to the 15th-century *Lyme Missal* – a rare Caxton prayer book; dressing-up in Regency costume; experiencing the beautiful sounds of Regency musical instruments; or discovering more about Thomas Legh, Lyme's very own Indiana Jones, and the fascinating women who helped shape Regency Lyme. **Outdoors** Regular Saturday parkruns, family orienteering course (changes every month), self-led woodland and moorland walks, adventurous play in Crow

Filming 'Secrets of the National Trust' in the Library, below, and playtime, above, at Lyme

Places may occasionally close for events or bad weather

Nether Alderley Mill

Congleton Road, Nether Alderley,
Macclesfield, Cheshire SK10 4TW

 1950

Learning about Nether Alderley Mill, Cheshire

Concealed under the long sloping roof of this medieval building is a fully restored, working corn mill. Inside, as the waterwheels turn, huge millstones grind the flour. On the guided tours, centuries-old graffiti can be spotted and you can discover more about the life of a miller. **Note**: view by guided tour only. Uneven floor, steep stairs and low ceilings throughout. Limited parking.

Eat, shop, stay: small range of souvenirs available. Sorry no toilets or food outlets at this property. Nearest National Trust facilities at nearby Alderley Edge.

Things to see and do: at nearby Quarry Bank, you can continue your industrial adventures at one of England's earliest cotton mills, experiencing the lives of the apprentices and workers who powered the Industrial Revolution.

Access: ⓟ🏠🚻 Mill ♿🚹
Parking: limited.

Find out more: 01625 527468 or netheralderleymill@nationaltrust.org.uk

Nether Alderley Mill		M	T	W	T	F	S	S
31 Mar–30 Sep	1–4:30	·	·	·	T	·	S	S

Access by guided tour only. Last tour 3:45.

Quarry Bank

Styal, Wilmslow, Cheshire SK9 4LA

🏠🖼️❄️🛏️🔔🍽️ 1939

As the Industrial Revolution dawned, the tranquillity of the river valley at Quarry Bank gave way to the clatter and bustle of an industrial community at work. The people here, from the mill-owning Greg family in Quarry Bank House, to the workers living in Styal village, were at the forefront of an era that changed the world. You can soak up the atmosphere in Quarry Bank House, the garden, a worker's cottage and, later this year, the mill. As part of a Heritage Lottery Funded project, there'll be building works in the mill to install a lift to allow all visitors to access every floor for the first time. **Note**: mill closed for building works until full reopening in summer (check for exact reopening date).

Eat, shop, stay: mill and garden shops selling gifts, including fabric and glass cloths produced at Quarry Bank. Mill café serving hot lunches and afternoon tea. Garden café offering light lunches and snacks. Drinks and ice-cream available from the Pantry. Picnic areas.

Catmint edges a garden path at Quarry Bank in Cheshire

Things to see and do: **Indoors** Guided tours of the Apprentice House and the two-up-two-down worker's cottage in Styal village reveal the home lives of the mill workers and the community that they built together. Quarry Bank will host the National Trust Children's Book Festival from 23 to 24 June (limited availability for tours). **Outdoors** Wander through the picturesque gardens for scenic views of Quarry Bank House and the mill.

Quarry Bank: the mill owner's house, above, and terraced workers' cottages in Styal village, below

In the restored glasshouse, you can marvel at the exotic plants and fruit that reflect those grown in the early 19th century by Quarry Bank's gardeners. **Dogs**: welcome under close control on estate. On leads in garden, mill yard and meadow.

Access: 🅿️🚻♿🚽🔍📷📱👓🔦
Mill 🚶♿♿🚻🍴♿ **Apprentice House** ♿🚶
Grounds ♿♿➡️🐕
Parking: car park improvements until spring (expect minor disruptions).

Find out more: 01625 527468 or quarrybank@nationaltrust.org.uk

Quarry Bank		M	T	W	T*	F	S	S
1 Jan–7 Jan	10:30–4	M	T	W	T	F	S	S
24 Jan–9 Feb*	10:30–4	·	·	W	T	F	S	S
10 Feb–4 Nov	10:30–5	M	T	W	T	F	S	S
7 Nov–30 Dec	10:30–4	·	·	W	T	F	S	S
Estate								
Open all year	8–6	M	T	W	T	F	S	S

Everything closed 8 to 21 January for annual maintenance. Open 31 December to 6 January 2019. Garden: closes dusk if earlier. Mill: closed until summer for lift installation.
*Mill shop and café: closures during January (garden shop and café remain open).

Rufford Old Hall

200 Liverpool Road, Rufford, near Ormskirk, Lancashire L40 1SG

🏠 ✥ 🔔 1936

This black-and-white Tudor building, with its contrasting mellow red-brick Jacobean wing, hunkers in the low-lying mosslands of south-west Lancashire. More than 500 years old, this family home has many stories to tell about the intriguing Heskeths, which we will be revealing throughout the year. You can delve into tales of a travelling baronet, an American heiress, or the housekeeper who helped care for Rufford. The children can get closer to nature with our bug-hunting and wild-art kits, while you unwind in our Victorian-style garden and grounds with colourful seasonal displays – carpets of bluebells in spring and golden leaves in autumn.

Eat, shop, stay: you can experience local tastes with Lancashire tea in the Victorian tea-room. The shop offers special treats, including Lancashire sauce, Lancashire crisps and plenty of gifts to keep memories of Rufford Old Hall fresh.

Fun at Rufford Old Hall, Lancashire, above and below

Things to see and do: Indoors Daily house talks and seasonal children's trail. Christmas events. **Outdoors** Guided garden tours. Events, including open-air theatre. Seasonal family trails and games. **Dogs:** welcome on leads in courtyard and woodland only.

Access: 🅿️ 🎫 ♿ 🖐️ 📷 🔄 📷 📱 🖼️
Building ♿ ♿ ♿ 🚻 ♿ **Grounds** ♿ ♿ ♿ ➡️ ♿
Parking: on site.

Find out more: 01704 821254 or ruffordoldhall@nationaltrust.org.uk

Rufford Old Hall		M	T	W	T	F	S	S
10 Feb–1 Apr	11–4	M	T	W	·	·	S	S
2 Apr–30 Sep*	11–5**	M	T	W	·	·	S	S
1 Oct–4 Nov*	11–4	M	T	W	·	·	S	S
10 Nov–25 Nov	11–4	·	·	·	·	·	S	S
29 Nov–16 Dec	11–4	·	·	·	T	F	S	S

*April, 31 May, 1 June, August, 25 and 26 October: also open Thursdays and Fridays. **4 June to 2 September: gardens, shop and tea-room open 10:30. Car park: closes 30 minutes after times above. Tudor Great Hall occasionally closed until 1 for weddings.

Speke Hall

Speke, Liverpool L24 1XD

🏠 ❀ ♿ 🐾 🔔 ⊤ 1944

Speke Hall is a cherished Tudor mansion – an oasis of beauty, atmosphere and surprise. Built by the Catholic Norris family during the unsettled Tudor period, the house has several hidden security features, including a priest's hole and eavesdrop (a hole above the entrance, for listening to visitors' conversation before letting them in). Following years of neglect (including a spell when it was used as a

Speke Hall, Liverpool, this page and opposite: from the servants' bells to inviting gardens and woodland, this cherished Tudor mansion, overflowing with beauty and atmosphere, is sure to surprise

cowshed), interiors were revived in a cosy Arts and Crafts style during the Victorian push for improvement. Today you can relax in inviting gardens and woodland, with seasonal displays of rhododendrons and bluebells. The adjacent coastal reserve, along the shore of the River Mersey, is perfect for bracing strolls and wildlife walks.

Eat, shop, stay: Home Farm Restaurant serving regional specialities, including Scouse and Wet Nelly. Stable Tea-room offering hot drinks and homemade cakes. Locally sourced gifts, as well as plants and books available in the gift shop.

Things to see and do: **Indoors** Costumed guided tours; a chance to play Victorian billiards; families can solve a tricky trail. **Outdoors** Formal and kitchen gardens and the recently restored Secret Garden. The coastal and woodland walks are great to explore and spot wildlife whatever the weather. Families can lose themselves in the Victorian maze, ride the zip wire or explore our woodland play trails. Exciting range of sports activities for all abilities. Join us every school holidays for great family events. Seasonal events, such as Easter Egg hunts, Tudor May Day, open-air theatre in the summer and Christmas festive fun. **Dogs**: welcome on leads in the woodland and on signed estate walks.

Access: [icons]
Hall [icons] Grounds [icons]
Parking: on site.

Find out more: 0151 427 7231 or spekehall@nationaltrust.org.uk

Speke Hall		M	T	W	T	F	S	S
House								
10 Feb–22 Jul	11–5*			W	T	F	S	S
24 Jul–2 Sep	11–5*		T	W	T	F	S	S
5 Sep–4 Nov	11–5*			W	T	F	S	S
23 Nov–9 Dec	11–4*					F	S	S
Gardens, catering and retail								
Open all year†	10:30–5**	M	T	W	T	F	S	S

*House: entry before 12:30 by guided tour only (places limited), tickets available from reception on day; free-flow from 12:30. **Shop: opens at 11. †13 March, 20 November and 24 to 26 December: everything closed. Access and closing times subject to change in winter (check at reception on arrival). Car park: closes 30 minutes after all times stated.

Tatton Park

Knutsford, Cheshire WA16 6QN

Tatton Park is the perfect example of a grand country estate, set in 400 hectares (1,000 acres) of historic deer-park. The Egerton family acquired an impressive collection of fine art, books and furnishings that can be seen in the Neo-classical mansion, which also houses the servants' quarters. There is a medieval Old Hall and 20 hectares (50 acres) of award-winning gardens, including a 100-year-old Japanese Garden to enjoy. New 'Field to Fork' developments at the farm include opening up the 18th-century agricultural mill, guided tours, demonstrations of machinery and traditional skills along with rare-breed animals. **Note**: managed/financed by Cheshire East Council. £7 vehicle entry and charges for Old Hall, farm (with 50% discount), tours and special events, including Christmas and RHS Flower Show, apply to members.

Eat, shop, stay: Stables self-service restaurant and award-winning Gardener's Cottage offer afternoon tea. Speciality shops include the Housekeeper's Store, offering local and estate-reared meat and produce. Gift, garden, farm and tuck shops too. None of the catering or retail outlets is National Trust.

Things to see and do: **Indoors** You can visit the mansion, Old Hall, farm, shops and restaurants. Learning activities and events. **Outdoors** Gardens, parkland, farm, adventure playground and stableyard. Events and learning activities. **Dogs**: on leads at farm and under close control in park only.

Access:
Building **Grounds**
Sat Nav: use WA16 6SG. **Parking**: park vehicle entry charge £7 (including members).

Find out more: 01625 374400 or tatton@cheshireeast.gov.uk tattonpark.org.uk

Tatton Park		M	T	W	T	F	S	S
Parkland, gardens and restaurant*								
2 Jan–23 Mar**	10–5†		T	W	T	F	S	S
24 Mar–28 Oct	10–7†	M	T	W	T	F	S	S
30 Oct–30 Dec	10–5†		T	W	T	F	S	S
Mansion								
24 Mar–30 Sep††	1–5		T	W	T	F	S	S
2 Oct–4 Nov	12–4		T	W	T	F	S	S
Farm*								
6 Jan–18 Mar[1]	11–4						S	S
24 Mar–28 Oct[2]	12–5		T	W	T	F	S	S
29 Oct–4 Nov	11–4	M	T	W	T	F	S	S
10 Nov–30 Dec	11–4						S	S
Shops*								
2 Jan–23 Mar**	12–4		T	W	T	F	S	S
24 Mar–28 Oct	11–5	M	T	W	T	F	S	S
30 Oct–30 Dec	12–4		T	W	T	F	S	S

*Open 1 January. **Also open 19 February. †Gardens and restaurant: close one hour earlier. ††Open Bank Holiday Mondays; guided mansion tours at 12, Tuesday to Sunday (small charge including members). Mansion: open for Christmas event. [1]Farm: also open 19 to 23 February. [2]Open Bank Holiday Mondays; farm closed during July RHS Flower Show. Old Hall special opening arrangements and charge. Parkland, mansion, farm and garden last entry one hour before closing. Everything closed 25 December.

With its impressive mansion and deer-park, Tatton Park, Cheshire, is every inch the grand country estate

Additional coastal and countryside car parks in the North West

Coast

Arnside Knott	LA5 0BP
Eaves Wood (Silverdale)	LA5 0UG

Countryside

Mow Cop	ST7 3PA
Bickerton	SY14 8LN
Formby (Lifeboat Road)	L37 2EB

The Lakes

Buttermere Valley, Cumbria

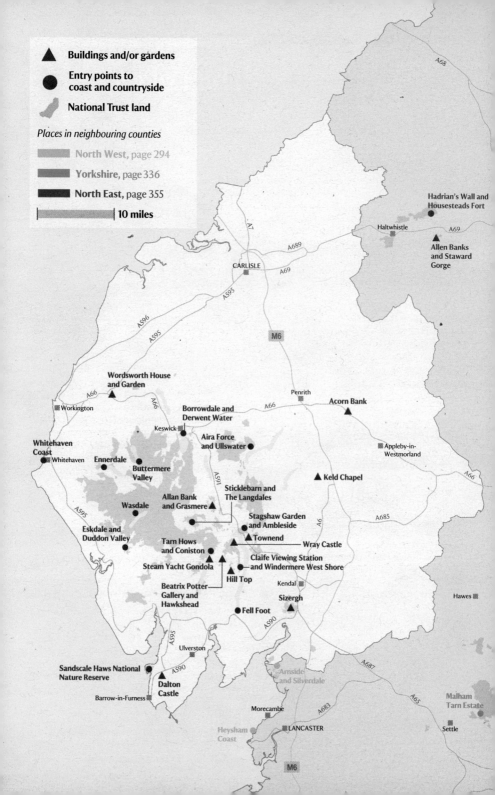

Buildings and/or gardens

Entry points to coast and countryside

National Trust land

Places in neighbouring counties

North West, page 294

Yorkshire, page 336

North East, page 355

10 miles

A68

Hadrian's Wall and Housesteads Fort

Haltwhistle

A69

Allen Banks and Staward Gorge

A7

CARLISLE

A689

A69

A595

M6

A596

A595

Wordsworth House and Garden

A66

A66

Penrith

Acorn Bank

Workington

Borrowdale and Derwent Water

Keswick

Aira Force and Ullswater

Appleby-in-Westmorland

Whitehaven Coast

Whitehaven

Ennerdale

Buttermere Valley

Keld Chapel

A66

Wasdale

Allan Bank and Grasmere

Sticklebarn and The Langdales

A591

Stagshaw Garden and Ambleside

A685

A595

Eskdale and Duddon Valley

Tarn Hows and Coniston

Townend

A6

Wray Castle

Steam Yacht Gondola

Claife Viewing Station and Windermere West Shore

Beatrix Potter Gallery and Hawkshead

Hill Top

Kendal

Sizergh

Hawes

Fell Foot

A595

Ulverston

A590

Sandscale Haws National Nature Reserve

A590

Dalton Castle

Arnside and Silverdale

A687

A683

A65

Malham Tarn Estate

Barrow-in-Furness

Morecambe

A590

Settle

Heysham Coast

LANCASTER

M6

Acorn Bank

Temple Sowerby, near Penrith,
Cumbria CA10 1SP

🏠🖼️❄️🛏️🚲 1950

At the heart of the Eden Valley, with views to the Lake District and Howgill Fells, Acorn Bank is a tranquil haven with a rich history. The walled gardens shelter a medicinal herb garden and traditional orchards as well as herbaceous borders, stone steps, grass pathways and a lily-filled pond. Woodland walks, loved for the springtime daffodils, reveal a half-hidden story of gypsum mining and a working watermill with a medieval past. The estate frames a 17th-century sandstone manor, once owned by indomitable writer Dorothy Una Ratcliffe. This unfurnished house is partially open to visitors while under restoration. **Note**: access to fragile grass paths may be restricted after wet weather.

Acorn Bank in Cumbria: pond-dipping among the lilies, above, and playing dominoes at the front of the house, left

Eat, shop, stay: tea-room uses seasonal homegrown garden produce (courtyard tables available). Shop sells plants, flour milled on-site and national products. Sandwath and Bank Wood, spacious holiday apartments (sleeping two to three), allow you to enjoy the estate after hours.

Things to see and do: watermill machinery operates most weekend afternoons during the summer. Wild play area in the woods and secret places for children to discover. **Dogs**: welcome in the woodland. Assistance dogs only in the gardens and house.

Access: 🅿️♿🔊📷📱🎧🖼️ **Watermill** 🚶♿ **House** 🚶♿♿ **Grounds** 🚶♿♿➡️♿ **Parking**: large car park.

Find out more: 017683 61893 or acornbank@nationaltrust.org.uk

Acorn Bank		M	T	W	T	F	S	S
23 Mar–28 Oct	10–5*	M	T	W	T	F	S	S
3 Nov–16 Dec	11–4	.	.	.	.	.	S	S

House: partially open; guided tours twice a day (places limited). *Tea-room: open 10:30 to 4:30.

Aira Force and Ullswater

near Watermillock, Penrith, Cumbria

🔲 1906

Aira Force is a showcase for the power and beauty of nature; it's a place to escape the ordinary. For 300 years visitors have been drawn here, where rainwater runs from the fells into Aira Beck and thunders in one 65-foot leap over the falls. Yet Aira Force is much more than an impressive waterfall. A network of trails weaves its way from Ullswater lakeshore to Gowbarrow summit, passing the falls, towering Himalayan firs, rare red squirrels, woodland glades, picnic spots and views out across Ullswater. You can start your day in Glenridding and arrive by boat, taking in the sights of Ullswater Valley along the way, then stroll back to Glenridding through Glencoyne Park and along the lakeshore. **Note**: boat rides on Ullswater operated by Ullswater 'Steamers' (not National Trust).

Eat, shop, stay: tea-room serving light lunches, cakes, ice-cream and hot and cold drinks. Shop selling gifts, ice-cream, souvenirs and maps. Takeaway kiosk serving hot drinks and snacks. Picnics welcome.

Things to see and do: follow the red squirrel trail and play at the natural play area. Arrive early for your best chance of spotting a red squirrel. Bring a picnic. Stroll through ancient woodland and landscaped glades. Follow the tree trail to find out more about the varied species of tree you can spot. Launch a canoe at Glencoyne Bay. Try pebble-skimming at Aira Green or take a boat ride with Ullswater 'Steamers' and return on foot from Aira Force to Glenridding. Walk to Gowbarrow summit, the best spot for panoramic views across the Lakeland fells. **Dogs**: welcome on a lead.

Access: 🅿️ 🚇 🚻 🅿️ **Grounds** 🅿️
Sat Nav: use CA11 0JS for Aira Force; CA11 0NQ for Glencoyne Bay. **Parking**: at Aira Force, Aira Force High Cascades, Aira Force Park Brow and Glencoyne Bay.

Find out more: 017684 82067 or ullswater@nationaltrust.org.uk

Aira Force and Ullswater	
Tea-room and shop	
Open every day all year*	10:30–4**

*Tea-room and shop: closed 22 to 26 December.
**Tea-room: closes 4:30. Opening times may vary during low season.

Aira Force and Ullswater, Cumbria: exploring the Ullswater lakeshore, below, and Aira Force waterfall, right. This is an ideal place to escape the ordinary and appreciate the power and beauty of nature

The Lakes

Allan Bank and Grasmere

near Ambleside, Cumbria LA22 9QB

🏚 🏛 ❖ ♨ 1920

Make yourself at home at Allan Bank, where views of Grasmere's valley unfold from picture windows and woodland grounds. Once home to National Trust founder Canon Rawnsley, it's now only partially decorated and not your typical National Trust experience. Have something to eat in the homely kitchen; help yourself to a cup of tea; watch red squirrels as you read by the fire in the study or picnic on the lawn; or paint and draw. Secret hideaways, such as the Victorian viewing tunnel, create an air of mystery. William Wordsworth was inspired here – and there's even more to discover today. **Note**: designated parking only on site. Follow directions on foot from Miller Howe Café in village.

Relaxing in the garden of Allan Bank in Grasmere, Cumbria

Eat, shop, stay: at Allan Bank, snacks and tasty cakes are available from the kitchen. Picnics welcome in the gardens. National Trust Church Stile shop in Grasmere selling unusual gifts, local books and maps in Grade II listed 17th-century building.

Relaxing with the papers at Allan Bank

Things to see and do: **Indoors** Drawing, painting, board games, children's activities. Read the papers or borrow a book from the library or binoculars for wildlife-spotting. **Outdoors** Deckchairs, kitchen garden, woodland trail, wild play area. **Dogs**: welcome indoors and out, on a lead.

Access: 📷 🎧 ♿ 🔊 🏠 ♿ 📷 Countryside ♿ 📷
Sat Nav: use LA22 9TA for nearest car park.
Parking: nearest in village, not National Trust (charge including members).

Find out more: 015394 35143 or allanbank@nationaltrust.org.uk

Allan Bank and Grasmere		M	T	W	T	F	S	S
Allan Bank								
10 Feb–26 Feb	10:30–4	M	T	W	T	F	S	S
2 Mar–30 Mar	10:30–4					F	S	S
31 Mar–4 Nov	10:30–5	M	T	W	T	F	S	S
9 Nov–16 Dec	10:30–4					F	S	S
Grasmere shop								
1 Jan–5 Jan	11–4	M	T	W	T	F		
17 Feb–4 Nov	10–5	M	T	W	T	F	S	S
5 Nov–31 Dec*	11–4	M	T	W			S	S

*Grasmere shop: closed 25, 26 and 27 December; opening times may vary during the low season.

Beatrix Potter Gallery and Hawkshead

Main Street, Hawkshead, Cumbria LA22 0NS

🏠 1944

The Beatrix Potter Gallery displays original items from our collection in this year's exhibition 'The Right Sort of Woman'. For anyone who has ever been enchanted by Beatrix's endearing characters, this is the place to go to marvel at these miniature masterpieces. The gallery is in a 17th-century building which Beatrix's solicitor husband used as his office. Hawkshead village is an excellent base for exploring the countryside that inspired Beatrix and many other artists, authors and poets. Her home, Hill Top (also National Trust), which she bought with the proceeds of her first book, is just two miles away. **Note**: nearest toilet 300 yards in main village car park (not National Trust).

Eat, shop, stay: small gallery shop selling Beatrix Potter items. Hawkshead corner shop stocks local products and gifts. Stay nearby in one of our holiday cottages, like The Summer House or Rose Castle Cottage, or camp at Low Wray.

Beatrix Potter Gallery and Hawkshead, Cumbria: the gallery, above, and picturesque village, below

Things to see and do: Indoors Original Beatrix Potter artwork on display. **Outdoors** Miles of walking: to Hill Top, Tarn Hows and Wray Castle. The nearby Courthouse has an interesting history (collect key from shop). **Dogs**: assistance dogs only.

Access: 📷🚫🖼️📲 Gallery ♿🚻 **Parking**: 300 yards, not National Trust (charge including members).

Find out more: 015394 36355 (gallery). 015394 36471 (shop) or beatrixpottergallery@nationaltrust.org.uk

Beatrix Potter Gallery/Hawkshead		M	T	W	T	F	S	S
Gallery								
10 Feb–28 Oct	10:30–4	M	T	W	T	F	S	S
Shop								
10 Feb–25 May	10–4	M	T	W	T	F	S	S
26 May–2 Sep	10–5	M	T	W	T	F	S	S
3 Sep–31 Dec	10–4*	M	T	W	T	F	S	S

At busy periods, timed entry system in operation.
*Closed 24 to 26 December. Medieval Hawkshead Courthouse: open 24 March to 28 October (access by key from National Trust shop in Hawkshead).

Borrowdale and Derwent Water

near Keswick, Cumbria

🏠🍴🏛🏊🚶 1902

Looking south over Derwent Water, Cumbria

Running down to Derwent Water, Borrowdale has dramatic fells and crags, accessible lake shores, waymarked walks and traditional hamlets. You can lap up iconic Lakes landscapes on scenic drives or short strolls while never being far from a cup of tea. In the valley, the Trust cares for Watendlath, Bowder Stone, Friar's Crag, Ashness Bridge and Derwent Water, where five days a year Derwent Island House is open to visitors. From Keswick to Seathwaite there are eight car parks to explore from: call in to our Keswick lakeside shop for ideas such as a 10-mile walk round Derwent Water. **Note**: charges apply to members on Force Crag Mine and Derwent Island House open days.

Eat, shop, stay: Keswick lakeside shop offers local knowledge to help you plan your visit, plus souvenirs, cold drinks and ice-cream. Tenant-run cafés serving local treats. Watendlath Bothy (sleeps six) and Millbeck Towers (sleeps 12) provide perfect holiday bases.

Things to see and do: open five days a year, the quirky Force Crag Mine is hidden in the stunning Coledale Valley: book your seat in our 4x4 for an intriguing historic tour. **Dogs**: very welcome, but please keep them under close control at lambing time.

Access: 🚾📷 Derwent Island 🚶
Force Crag Mine 🚶🍴 Derwent Water foreshore ♿➡
Sat Nav: use CA12 5DJ for Keswick lakeside shop and CA12 5XN for Seatoller (at foot of Honister Pass). **Parking**: at Great Wood, Ashness Bridge, Surprise View, Watendlath, Kettlewell, Bowder Stone, Rosthwaite, Seatoller and Honister Pass.

Find out more: 017687 74649 or borrowdale@nationaltrust.org.uk

Borrowdale and Derwent Water		M	T	W	T	F	S	S
Shop and visitor centre								
12 Feb–28 Oct	10–5	M	T	W	T	F	S	S
29 Oct–25 Nov	10–4	M				F	S	S
1 Dec–30 Dec	10–4						S	S

Shop: open weekends, 5 January to 10 February 2019. For open days at Derwent Island House and Force Crag Mine, check 'What's on' page online.

Force Crag Mine, Borrowdale: the last working metal mine in the Lake District

Buttermere Valley

near Cockermouth, Cumbria

🏛🏊🚶🏕 1935

Peaceful Buttermere Valley in Cumbria

Buttermere Valley has some satisfyingly adventurous ridgeline walking, as well as low-level lakeshore walks on accessible footpaths. Whether you start your day at Buttermere, Crummock Water or Loweswater, high fells, rolling lakeside landscape and cascading waterfalls will make for impressive backdrops to your holiday snaps.
Note: toilets at Buttermere only.

Eat, shop, stay: pubs and cafés in Buttermere and Loweswater hamlets (not National Trust). You can stay in comfort at Watergate Farm, with fishing, swimming and walking from your doorstep, or choose simplicity at Holmewood Bothy, a camping barn on Loweswater's shore.

Things to see and do: deer, red squirrels, birds, fish, otters and other wildlife to spot. Buttermere and Crummock Water are Special Areas of Conservation. Tick off waterfalls, walk, climb, stroll or try wild swimming.
Dogs: welcome throughout the valley (under close control at lambing time please).

Access: ♿ Lakeshore path ➡️
Sat Nav: use CA13 9UZ for Buttermere; CA13 0RT for Crummock Water; CA13 0RU for Loweswater. **Parking**: at Honister Pass, Buttermere village, Rannerdale, Cinderdale, Lanthwaite Green, Lanthwaite Wood near Crummock Water and Maggie's Bridge at Loweswater.

Find out more: 01768774649 or buttermere@nationaltrust.org.uk

Claife Viewing Station and Windermere West Shore

near Far Sawrey, Cumbria LA22 0LW

🏛🏊🚶🚶 1962

Early 18th-century tourists would take to the water from Bowness to seek out this picturesque spot. You can now do the same, taking the ferry to the restored Claife Viewing Station. The first-floor platform gives impressive panoramic views of Windermere and the Lakeland fells – views that were hidden for years. With 4 miles of lakeshore path towards Wray Castle to explore on bike or on foot, the western shore of Windermere is perfect for a car-free adventure. You can walk from here through the landscape that inspired Beatrix Potter, to Hill Top house and Hawkshead village. **Note**: toilets at nearby Ferry House, none at the Viewing Station. Boats (not National Trust) run by Windermere Lake Cruises.

A bike boat picks up on Windermere, Cumbria

Eat, shop, stay: cosy café in the courtyard at Claife Viewing Station (not National Trust) serving light lunches, drinks and cakes. Picnics welcome on lakeshore. Stay at nearby High and Low Strawberry Gardens – holiday cottages with England's largest lake on your doorstep.

Claife Viewing Station: viewpoint framed by coloured glass

Things to see and do: coloured glass panels frame two of the viewpoints, which could inspire some adventurous photographs. Share your photos using #claife, then walk along the lakeshore or take to the water. **Dogs**: allowed in countryside, under close control.

Access: Viewing Station 🚻 Café 🚻 🚻
Sat Nav: use LA22 0LP for Ash Landing; LA22 0LR Harrowslack; LA22 0JH Red Nab (all nearby). **Parking**: at Ash Landing and Harrowslack, near Windermere lakeshore, for Claife Viewing Station and at Red Nab.

Find out more: 015394 41456 or claife@nationaltrust.org.uk

Dalton Castle

Market Place, Dalton-in-Furness, Cumbria LA15 8AX

🏛 1965

Formerly the manorial courthouse of Furness Abbey, this eye-catching 14th-century tower was built to assert the Abbot's authority. **Note**: opened on behalf of the National Trust by the Friends of Dalton Castle. Parking in Dalton town centre (not National Trust). Open Saturdays, 31 March to 29 September, 2 to 5.

Find out more: 015395 60951 or daltoncastle@nationaltrust.org.uk

Ennerdale

Cleator, Cumbria

🏛 👥 1927

Ennerdale is Lakeland's quiet side: 30 miles of traffic-free tracks and paths, and home of the Wild Ennerdale partnership. **Note**: nearest toilets at Ennerdale Bridge. For Sat Nav use CA23 3BA for Ennerdale Bridge; CA23 3AS for Bleach Green; and CA23 3AU for Bowness Knott.

Find out more: 017687 74649 or ennerdale@nationaltrust.org.uk

Eskdale and Duddon Valley

Eskdale, near Ravenglass; Duddon Valley, near Broughton in Furness, Cumbria

🏛 👥 🐾 🛏 1926

Eskdale is a valley of contrasts. Upper Eskdale leads to the high mountains, including Scafell and Bowfell: the valley floor has meandering

Blea Tarn overlooking Eskdale, Cumbria

riverside and woodland paths, including the Eskdale Trail, for walkers and cyclists. Across high mountain passes lies the Duddon Valley, with meadows, woodlands, mountains, hill farms and rivers.

Eat, shop, stay: pubs at Eskdale Green, Boot and Seathwaite; shops at Eskdale Green, Boot and Ulpha; café and shop at Dalegarth station (none National Trust). Picturesque Bird How and Thrang holiday cottages have spectacular walks from their front doors.

Things to see and do: walks from 'La'al Ratty' railway running through Eskdale. Woodland and riverside paths in the Duddon Valley. Upland walks to Harter Fell and Seathwaite Tarn. Hardknott Roman Fort (English Heritage). **Dogs**: well-behaved dogs welcome. Please follow local and seasonal guidance.

Access: 🐾
Parking: in lay-bys, along roadsides and at some small village car parks (not National Trust).

Find out more: 019467 26064 or eskdaleandduddon@nationaltrust.org.uk

Fell Foot

Newby Bridge, Windermere, Cumbria

🏠🦮🍴 1948

Sitting on the southern tip of Windermere with views across the lake to the mountains, this family-friendly park has extensive lawns rolling down to the water and is a great place for playing, picnics or barbecues. It's a good spot for exploring: just a stroll along the lakeshore is one of the best ways of soaking up Windermere in all its beauty. With its network of paths and easy lake access, the park is ideal for running, paddling, swimming and boating. Newly open Active Base offers boats and kayaks for hire, changing rooms and launching facilities. **Note**: facility improvements under way: building works possible. Launch and new changing facilities available for wide range of craft (charges including members). Rowing boats, canoes/kayaks for hire April to October. Additional charges apply.

Eat, shop, stay: Boathouse Café serving hot and cold drinks, soup and snacks, homemade cakes and pastries. A selection of children's toys, gifts, maps, picnic rugs and seasonal goods available in the Boathouse Shop. Picnics welcome on the lawns.

Things to see and do: seasonal rowing boat hire (daily, weather permitting) and canoe/kayak hire (weekends, school holidays). Events year-round. Adventure playground and lake access with 'beach' for paddling. Quiet spots and easy meadow walk. **Dogs**: welcome on leads.

Access: 🅿️🐕🚻🚽♿ Grounds ♿🚶
Sat Nav: use LA12 8NN. **Parking**: two large car parks on site.

Find out more: 015395 31273 or fellfoot@nationaltrust.org.uk

Taking a boating selfie at Fell Foot in Cumbria

The Lakes

Hill Top

Near Sawrey, Hawkshead, Ambleside, Cumbria LA22 0LF

🏠 ✳ 🛏 1944

Beatrix Potter's beloved Hill Top is more than just the inspiration for her little white books. Full of her precious things, Hill Top encapsulates her passion that went on to dominate her life – preserving the landscape and culture of the Lakes. From traditional Lakeland furniture, to trophies for her prize-winning Herdwick sheep, Hill Top represents her legacy. The colourful garden is just as she knew it. Today, we continue in Beatrix's footsteps, working in a changing world to conserve the Lake District for ever, for everyone. The house can be very busy and visitors occasionally have to wait to enter. **Note**: timed-ticket entry system for the house. Tickets not needed for garden and shop.

Eat, shop, stay: shop selling Beatrix Potter books and collectables, including exclusive items. Nearby holiday cottages include High or Low Strawberry Gardens on Windermere's shore. Eat in the heart of Beatrix Potter country at Sawrey House Hotel or Tower Bank Arms (both tenant-run).

Getting active at Fell Foot

Fell Foot		M	T	W	T	F	S	S
Park								
1 Jan–30 Mar	9–5	M	T	W	T	F	S	S
31 Mar–2 Sep	8–6*	M	T	W	T	F	S	S
3 Sep–31 Dec	9–5	M	T	W	T	F	S	S
Active Base launch**								
26 Mar–4 Nov	8–6†	M	T	W	T	F	S	S
Café and shop								
10 Feb–18 Feb	11–4††	M	T	W	T	F	S	S
24 Feb–25 Mar	11–4††						S	S
26 Mar–2 Sep	10–5††	M	T	W	T	F	S	S
3 Sep–4 Nov	11–4	M	T	W	T	F	S	S

*Last entry at 6. **Active Base changing rooms: open as launch/slipway; also open daily, 5 November to 31 December (excluding 25 December), 9 to 5. †Entry outside these times can be arranged. ††Café: opens 9 on Saturdays. Boat hire available daily, April to October (weather permitting).

Things to see and do: tours and talks. Visit Beatrix Potter Gallery (2 miles) to see original artwork or walk less than a mile to Moss Eccles Tarn, where Beatrix and her husband went boating. **Dogs**: assistance dogs only.

Access: 🅿️🖼️🖵🚶♿📷 House ♿♿
Shop ♿ Garden ♿➡️
Parking: limited and for visitors to Hill Top only.

Find out more: 015394 36269. 015394 36801 (shop) or hilltop@nationaltrust.org.uk

Hill Top		M	T	W	T	F	S	S
House, shop and garden*								
10 Feb–24 May**	10–4:30	M	T	W	T	.	S	S
26 May–2 Sep	10–5:30	M	T	W	T	F	S	S
3 Sep–28 Oct**	10–4:30	M	T	W	T	.	S	S
Shop and garden								
2 Nov–23 Dec	10–3:30	.	.	.	.	F	S	S

*House: entry by timed ticket (places limited); free entry to garden. **Shop and garden also open Fridays. Small car park.

Keld Chapel

Keld Lane, Shap, Cumbria CA10 3NW

✠ 1918

With rustic stone floor and walls, this 16th-century chapel is thought to have been the chantry for Shap Abbey. **Note**: sorry no facilities. For Sat Nav use CA10 3NW. Open every day all year, dawn to dusk (for key, please see notice on chapel door).

Find out more: 017683 61893 or keldchapel@nationaltrust.org.uk

Sandscale Haws National Nature Reserve

near Barrow-in-Furness, Cumbria

🏖️ 🦅 1984

This beach has wild, grass-covered dunes and Lakeland mountain views: it's the perfect habitat for rare wildlife, including natterjack toads. **Note**: toilets (not National Trust). For Sat Nav use LA14 4QJ. New welcome hut serving light refreshments. Welcome hut open weekends, 6 January to 4 February, 24 February to 25 March and 10 November to 23 December, 11 to 4; open daily, 10 to 18 February, 11 to 4; 26 March to 2 September, 11 to 5; 3 September to 4 November and 24 December to 31 December, 11 to 4. Closed 25 December. Also open 1, 5 and 6 January 2019. Car park open all year (height restriction 2.1 metres).

Find out more: 01229 462855 or sandscalehaws@nationaltrust.org.uk

Two young Beatrix Potter fans at Hill Top, Cumbria, left, and the colourful garden in the summer, above

Sizergh

Sizergh, near Kendal, Cumbria LA8 8DZ

🏯 🍴 🏛 ❖ 🦽 � 1950

With more than 750 years of history and centuries-old portraits sitting alongside modern family photographs, this medieval house is still home to the Strickland family. Inside, the impressive wood panelling culminates in the exquisite patterned panels of the Inlaid Chamber. The house is surrounded by rich gardens and a 647-hectare (1,600-acre) estate, combining a newly created wetland, limestone pastures, orchards and semi-natural woodland, all inhabited by a rich variety of wildlife, including the rare hawfinch. There is a unique and very special limestone rock garden, where colours change with the seasons, and its timeless atmosphere makes this the perfect place to relax. Sizergh has many tales to tell and is an ideal place to start discovering the Lakes. **Note**: some opening restrictions apply. Separate admission charges may apply for tours or special events.

Eat, shop, stay: contemporary licensed café serving drinks, meals, snacks and cakes. Shop selling local products, home accessories, gifts, toys and plants. Strickland Arms pub (tenant-run) nearby. You can make Sizergh your holiday destination and stay at rustic Holeslack Farmhouse or Courtyard Cottage.

Things to see and do: **Indoors** Exhibitions, virtual and guided tours, and significant Elizabethan carved furniture and panelling. Important collection of portraits of members of the exiled Stuart court. **Outdoors** Working organic kitchen garden containing bees and hens. Of great horticultural significance are four National Collections of Hardy Ferns, some showcased in new stumpery. Orchard featuring more than 50 apple varieties, some rare and local. A walk through Brigsteer Wood leads to a newly created wetland area and bird hide at Park End Moss. Network of footpaths, guided walks and orienteering available in the wider estate. Children can enjoy a natural play trail and quizzes. **Dogs**: welcome on estate footpaths (on leads where stock grazing). House/garden: assistance dogs only.

Access: 🅿️ 👶 ♿ 🔦 📷 🎧 📺 ♿
Building 🔦 🍴♿ ♿ Grounds ♿ ➡️ 🛴 ♿
Sat Nav: use LA8 8DZ. **Parking**: 250 yards. Parking for cars and bikes only.

Find out more: 015395 60951 or sizergh@nationaltrust.org.uk

Sizergh		M	T	W	T	F	S	S
House*								
17 Mar–28 Oct	12–3:30		T	W	T	F	S	S
Garden, café and shop								
20 Jan–16 Mar**	10–4	M	T	W	T	F	S	S
17 Mar–28 Oct	10–5	M	T	W	T	F	S	S
29 Oct–31 Dec**	10–4	M	T	W	T	F	S	S
Estate								
Open all year	9–6†	M	T	W	T	F	S	S

*Guided house tours (excluding Saturdays): at 11 and 11:20 (approximately 45 minutes, places limited, £1 per person; tickets obtained from reception at least 15 minutes before tour). House: open Bank Holiday Mondays. **Garden: parts closed in January, February, November and December. †1 January to 16 March and 29 October to 31 December: closes 4:30. Car park: open as estate. Closed 25 December.

Sizergh, Cumbria: clockwise from right, examining a portrait, the fascinating fern garden and looking across the lake towards the castle

Why not share your pictures with us? #nationaltrust

Stagshaw Garden and Ambleside

near Windermere, Cumbria

🏠 🏛 ✿ 🛥 | 1927

On the edge of Windermere, Stagshaw Garden bursts into life with azaleas and rhododendrons. Rising behind, Skelghyll Woods are home to Cumbria's tallest trees; in front, Jenkin's Field is great for a lakeshore picnic and paddle. A mile north, the town of Ambleside, on Windermere's northern tip, has many attractions. **Note**: Ambleside Roman Fort (see below) owned by English Heritage, run by the National Trust.

Eat, shop, stay: plenty of places to eat and drink in Ambleside (none National Trust). Nearest National Trust café at Wray Castle. National Trust shop in Grasmere, 4 miles.

Stagshaw Garden and Ambleside, Cumbria: playing in Skelghyll Woods

Things to see and do: Bridge House, Ambleside's smallest building, built on a bridge over a beck. Tall Tree Trail at Skelghyll Woods. The remains of Ambleside Roman Fort (free) on Ambleside's edge. Townend nearby. **Dogs**: welcome, on a lead.

Access: Bridge House 🦽 Stagshaw Garden 🦽 🏔 **Sat Nav**: use LA22 0HE for Stagshaw Garden and Skelghyll Woods; LA22 9AN for Bridge House. **Parking**: small car park at Stagshaw Garden. Several car parks in Ambleside, not National Trust (charge including members).

Find out more: 015394 46402 or stagshawgarden@nationaltrust.org.uk

Stagshaw Garden				M	T	W		F	S	S
Stagshaw Garden*										
Open all year		Dawn–dusk		M	T	W	T	F	S	S
Bridge House										
30 Mar–4 Nov		11:30–4:15		M	T	W	T	F	S	S

*Stagshaw Garden is at its best April to July.

Steam Yacht Gondola

Coniston Pier, Lake Road, Coniston, Cumbria LA21 8AN

🛥 🔔 🍽 | 1980

This steam yacht was rebuilt by the National Trust from the original 1859 *Gondola*: today's passengers can experience the nostalgia of a steam-driven cruise on Coniston Water as enjoyed by the Victorians. Based on the design of a Venetian 'Burchiello' boat, Steam Yacht Gondola cuts silently through the water, with the majestic figurehead of Sid the golden sea serpent at the bow of her streamlined hull. You can watch the steam engine in action at close quarters, explore the boat and listen to the crew's commentary on her long history on the lake and her association with *Swallows and Amazons*. **Note**: cruises depart from Coniston Pier (subject to weather conditions). Sorry no toilet on scheduled sailings. Steam Yacht Gondola is an historic ship and extremely costly to run. Charge for members, although a small member discount applies on scheduled round-trip cruises.

Eat, shop, stay: small shop on board selling souvenirs. Gift experiences available online. Bluebird Café at Coniston Pier and coffee house/restaurant at Brantwood (neither National Trust). Catering available for private charters. Rose Castle Cottage above Tarn Hows is a perfect base for ramblers.

Things to see and do: 'Steam and Cream' and 'Engineer for the Day' gift experiences. Themed events. Grand Victorian Circular Tour package for small groups. Downloadable walks from Gondola's jetties. Joint tickets with partner attractions. **Dogs**: welcome in outside areas only.

Stately Steam Yacht Gondola
on Coniston Water, Cumbria

Sticklebarn and The Langdales

near Ambleside, Cumbria

🎭🏛️🏊📧🏕️🔔🍵 1925

The barn-turned-pub, Sticklebarn sits at The Langdales' heart: with fresh food, real ale and roaring fires, this is the perfect place to relax after a day on the fells. The great Lakes guidebook author, Alfred Wainwright, said 'no mountain profile arrests and excites the attention more than that of the Langdale Pikes'. With miles of walking, cycling and climbing routes, Langdale is a natural playground. The ambitious can tackle the dramatic peaks, but it's not all about high-level scrambling. The route around Blea Tarn is easily accessible, with views of Little and Great Langdale. Nearby High Close Estate and Arboretum offers 4.5 hectares (11 acres) of tranquillity with more than 100 years of fascinating history and trees from around the globe.

The sun rises over Sticklebarn
and The Langdales in Cumbria

Access: 🅿️♿🚽🅰️👓🚫 Gangway 👨‍🦽♿
Parking: at Coniston Pier, 50 yards, not National Trust (charge including members).

Find out more: 015394 32733 or sygondola@nationaltrust.org.uk
Booking Office, The Hollens, Grasmere, Cumbria LA22 9QZ

Steam Yacht Gondola		M	T	W	T	F	S	S
Head of Lake Cruise								
26 Mar–31 Oct	11–11:45	M	T	W	T	F	·	·
26 Mar–31 Oct	12–12:45	M	T	W	T	F	·	·
26 Mar–31 Oct	1–1:45	M	T	W	T	F	S	S
24 Mar–28 Oct	2:30–3:15	·	·	·	·	·	S	S
24 Mar–28 Oct	3:30–4:15	·	·	·	·	·	S	S
Full Lake Cruise								
26 Mar–31 Oct	2:30–4:15	M	T	W	T	F	·	·
Walkers/Full Lake Cruise								
24 Mar–28 Oct	11–12:45	·	·	·	·	·	S	S

All sailings depart Coniston Pier. You can 'hop off/hop on' at other piers: Monk Coniston and Parkamoor, plus Lake Bank and Brantwood (not National Trust). Cruises subject to weather conditions.

Sticklebarn and The Langdales: Great Langdale Campsite, above, and relaxing at the pub, left

Eat, shop, stay: Sticklebarn serves freshly prepared hot food and a range of drinks, including Cumbrian real ales. Outdoor eating on the terrace. Café at High Close. Lovely options for camping or staying at Silverthwaite cottage (sleeps eight) in Langdale valley.

Things to see and do: Indoors Sticklebarn is the perfect place to relax in all weather: read a book by the fire, play a board game and catch a family movie in the Hayloft or simply catch up over a drink. **Outdoors** Walking and climbing in the Lakeland fells. Guided gyhll scrambling, guided rock-climbing and bike hire from Great Langdale Campsite. Off-road cycle trail from Skelwith Bridge to Sticklebarn. Take a riverside ramble from Elterwater or explore the tree trail at High Close. Why not finish your day on the terrace at Sticklebarn with occasional live music? Sleep under the stars at Great Langdale Campsite. **Dogs**: welcome indoors and out, on a lead.

Access: ♿ 🚻 🍴 Sticklebarn ♿ ♿ Grounds ♿ ♿
Sat Nav: use LA22 9JU for Sticklebarn; LA22 9PG for Blea Tarn; LA22 9HP for Elterwater; LA22 9HJ for High Close Estate. **Parking**: at Stickle Ghyll, Old Dungeon Ghyll, Blea Tarn, Elterwater village and High Close Estate.

Find out more: 015394 37356 (Sticklebarn) or sticklebarn@nationaltrust.org.uk

Sticklebarn and The Langdales		M	T	W	T	F	S	S
Sticklebarn								
1 Jan–5 Jan	11–9	M	T	W	T	F	.	.
3 Feb–31 Dec*	11–9**	M	T	W	T	F	S	S
Great Langdale Campsite†								
Open all year		M	T	W	T	F	S	S

*Sticklebarn closed 24 and 25 December. **Bar: open until late in high season. †For detailed opening times and bookings please visit ntlakescampsites.org.uk or call 015394 32733.

Tarn Hows and Coniston

near Coniston, Cumbria

🦽 🛏 ♿ 1943

Tarn Hows offers an accessible circular walk (1¾ miles) through beautiful countryside with majestic mountain views, which change depending on the weather and seasons. We have off-road mobility scooters available for less-able visitors. The area around Tarn Hows and Coniston village is a great place to begin your Lakes adventure. **Note**: nearest toilets in main car park.

Eat, shop, stay: refreshments available most days. Picnics welcome. Numerous catering options nearby in Coniston and Hawkshead (none National Trust) plus National Trust gift shop in Hawkshead. The enchanting Rose Castle Cottage, with views across Tarn Hows, is a perfect holiday hideaway.

Things to see and do: why not theme your day around water? Start with a leisurely Steam

Tarn Hows and Coniston, Cumbria:
the circular walk, below, and Tarn Hows, above

Yacht Gondola cruise on Coniston Water, then walk through Monk Coniston Hall's grounds to Tarn Hows. **Dogs**: welcome on leads (stock grazing).

Access: 🅿️ ♿ 🚻 Grounds 🦽 ♿
Sat Nav: use LA22 0PP for Tarn Hows or LA21 8DP for Glen Mary (both nearby).
Parking: on site at Tarn Hows, also at Glen Mary nearby. Parking available in Coniston (not National Trust).

Find out more: 015394 41456 or tarnhows@nationaltrust.org.uk

Tarn Hows and Coniston	M	T	W	T	F	S	S
Hoathwaite Campsite*							
23 Mar–17 Sep	**M**	**T**	**W**	**T**	**F**	**S**	**S**

*For detailed opening times and bookings please visit ntlakescampsites.org.uk or call 015394 32733.

Townend

Troutbeck, Windermere, Cumbria LA23 1LB

🏠 ❄️ 1948

History comes to life in the
Library at Townend in Cumbria

Townend is a little Lake District farmhouse with a big history. The Brownes were a simple farming family, but their home and belongings bring to life more than 400 years of extraordinary stories. Recipes written into a book in 1699 have been passed down through generations and today are still made on a Thursday. Throughout the house, intricately

The cottage-style garden at Townend

carved furniture provides a window into the personality of George Browne. The family's well-used collection of books includes 45 that are the only remaining copies in the world. Outside, the colourful cottage-style garden is a lovely place to while away some time. **Note**: unfortunately we cannot accept card payments.

Eat, shop, stay: picnics welcome. Tea-room in Troutbeck village (not National Trust).

Things to see and do: **Indoors** Guided tours at 11 and 12 (places limited). 'A Taste of Townend', living-history cooking demonstrations on Thursdays. Children's trail. **Outdoors** Garden trail for children. Traditional games.

Access: [P][D][symbols] **Building** [symbol] **Grounds** [symbol]
Parking: 300 yards.

Find out more: 015394 32628 or townend@nationaltrust.org.uk

Townend		M	T	W	T	F	S	S
10 Mar–28 Oct	1–5*		·	**W**	**T**	**F**	**S**	**S**

*11 to 1: entry by guided tour only at 11 and 12 (places limited). Open Bank Holiday Mondays. May close early due to poor light.

Wasdale

near Gosforth, Cumbria

[symbols] [1920]

At the foot of the high mountains of Wasdale is England's deepest lake, Wastwater, with the screes sweeping down from the top of Illgill Head creating ever-changing reflections in the water. Towards the southern end of the lake and Nether Wasdale, winding paths weave through woodland. This year we are commemorating the end of the First World War. The mountain memorials, including Great Gable and Scafell Pike, are looked after by the National Trust in memory of those who were killed during the war: we will continue our work on the footpaths and rebuild the Scafell Pike summit cairn. **Note**: limited toilet facilities (construction to improve facilities is expected to start this year).

Eat, shop, stay: with numerous camping options – tents, campervans, pods, Nordic tipis – and pastoral cosy cottages, Wasdale is a

perfect place for digital detox holidays. Campsite shop. Pub and shop at Wasdale Head; pubs in Nether Wasdale and Santon Bridge (none National Trust).

Things to see and do: walking and climbing in England's highest mountains. Lakeside, riverbank and woodland rambles. Wild swimming and paddling in Wastwater and rivers. Herdwick sheep graze in fields and on fells. **Dogs**: well-behaved dogs welcome. Please follow local and seasonal guidance.

Access: 🏠
Sat Nav: use CA20 1EX. **Parking**: at Lake Head CA20 1EX; Overbeck CA20 1EX (limited space); Nether Wasdale CA20 1ET (limited space).

Find out more: 019467 26064 or wasdale@nationaltrust.org.uk

Wasdale	
Wasdale Campsite*	
Open every day all year	

*For detailed opening times and bookings please visit ntlakescampsites.org.uk or call 015394 32733.

England's deepest lake, Wastwater in Wasdale, Cumbria, sits surrounded by high mountains

Whitehaven Coast

Whitehaven, Cumbria

🏠 📈 2008

This post-industrial coastline is teeming with wildlife. Enjoy clifftop walks, the Georgian harbour and views to the Isle of Man.
Note: sorry no toilets. For Sat Nav use CA28 9BG for clifftop car park and CA28 7LY for Whitehaven Harbour.

Find out more: 017687 74649 or whitehavencoast@nationaltrust.org.uk

Wordsworth House and Garden

Main Street, Cockermouth, Cumbria CA13 9RX

🏠 ❄ 🔔 ⊤ 1938

Step back to the 1770s at the childhood home and garden that inspired William to become a poet. Hands-on rooms give a feel for middle-class Georgian life – there's even a rope bed to try. Costumed servants cook in the kitchen, gossip and tell tales on selected days in term-time and throughout school holidays. Guided and audio tours reveal the happiness and heartache experienced by the Wordsworths and other occupants, while in the cellar, household 'ghosts' share their stories. New exhibition, 'Where Poppies Blow', shines a light on the men who fought for Britain's rural heart in the First World War.

Wordsworth House and Garden in Cumbria

Heritage flowers in the garden at Wordsworth House

Eat, shop, stay: browse through Wordsworth and local souvenirs in the shop. A light lunch or cream tea in the cosy café makes the perfect end to a visit. Takeaway option available and picnics welcome. Second-hand books for sale.

Things to see and do: replica costumes, toys and games. Evocative and atmospheric animations related to the Wordsworths showing in some rooms. Holiday activities. A relaxing spot, the garden has heritage flowers, vegetables and trees. **Dogs**: on leads in front garden only. Free biscuits for your pooch!

Access: [icons]
Building [icons] Grounds [icons]
Parking: in town centre car parks, none National Trust (charge including members). Please note long-stay car park signposted as coach park, 300 yards, Wakefield Road.

Find out more: 01900 820884 (Infoline). 01900 824805 or wordsworthhouse@nationaltrust.org.uk

Wordsworth House and Garden		M	T	W	T	F	S	S
10 Mar–28 Oct	11–5*	M	T	W	T	·	S	S

*Café: open 10:30 to 4:30. Last entry to house one hour before closing (timed tickets may operate on busy days). Open selected Fridays in holidays (please telephone for information).

Wray Castle

Low Wray, Ambleside, Cumbria LA22 0JA

[icons] 1929

If you take a regular lake cruise from Ambleside, you can arrive at Wray Castle in style. Or a gentle walk or cycle is a relaxed start to a visit. With turrets and towers, a Gothic Revival interior and dramatic views to the fells, there's lots to explore and enjoy. We don't have any of the original contents, so it is more informal and child-friendly. The Peter Rabbit Adventure is a great spot for creative play for younger visitors, while older children might like dressing-up or building their own castle. Join one of our guided tours, which run most of the year, to find out more about this fascinating building. Plus, there's loads to do outdoors in the grounds. **Note**: limited car parking. Shopping vouchers for visitors arriving by boat.

Eat, shop, stay: simple café serving hot and cold drinks, snacks and cakes. Picnics welcome in the grounds. Shop offering family games, gifts and souvenirs. Camp or glamp nearby at Low Wray or stay on the castle estate in The Summer House.

Things to see and do: **Indoors** The informal atmosphere and family-friendly activities –

Arriving by boat at Wray Castle, Cumbria

Wray Castle sits on the less-developed west shore of Windermere

including crafts, dressing-up and castle-building – mean that you can discover the house your way. Guided tours unearth the Castle's hidden past and help you learn more about this quirky building. **Outdoors** Arrive in style by boat. Miles of lakeside walks and trails, as well as a woodland adventure play area with tree house and rope swings. Seasonal activities throughout the year. Wray Castle is a great stop on a walk or cycle ride along the lakeshore from Claife Viewing Station or the path from Hawkshead. **Dogs**: welcome in the grounds on leads, assistance dogs only in Castle.

Access: [icons] **Castle** [icons]
Parking: restricted car parking. Please come by boat, bike or boot to avoid disappointment.

Find out more: 015394 33250 or wraycastle@nationaltrust.org.uk

Wray Castle		M	T	W	T	F	S	S
Castle								
10 Feb–23 Mar*	10–4	M	T	W	T	F	S	S
24 Mar–28 Oct	10–5	M	T	W	T	F	S	S
3 Nov–25 Nov	10–4						S	S
Grounds								
Open all year	8–8	M	T	W	T	F	S	S
Low Wray Campsite**								
23 Mar–28 Oct		M	T	W	T	F	S	S
3 Nov–30 Dec							S	S

*26 February to 2 March: castle open by guided tour only, places limited, booking optional (call 015394 33250).
**For detailed opening times and bookings please visit ntlakescampsites.org.uk or call 015394 32733.

Additional countryside car parks in The Lakes

Borrowdale and Derwent Water		**Buttermere Valley**		**The Langdales**	
Great Wood	CA12 5UP	Honister Pass	CA12 5XJ	Blea Tarn	LA22 9PG
Kettlewell	CA12 5UN	Lanthwaite Wood	CA13 0RT	Old Dungeon Ghyll	LA22 9JY
Ashness Bridge	CA12 5UN	**Ullswater**		Stickle Ghyll	LA22 9JU
Surprise View	CA12 5UU	Glencoyne Bay	CA11 0NQ	Elterwater	LA22 9HP
Watendlath	CA12 5UW	High Cascades	CA11 0JY	High Close	LA22 9HJ
Bowderstone	CA12 5XA	Park Brow	CA11 0JY	**Coniston**	
Rosthwaite	CA12 5XB	**Wasdale**		Glen Mary	LA21 8DP
Seatoller	CA12 5XN	Lake Head	CA20 1EX	**Windermere West Shore**	
		Overbeck	CA20 1EX	Red Nab	LA22 0JH
		Nether Wasdale	CA20 1ET	Harrowslack	LA22 0LR
				Ash Landing	LA22 0LP

Yorkshire

Treasurer's House, York, North Yorkshire

Buildings and/or gardens

Entry points to coast and countryside

National Trust land

H **Historic House Hotel**

Places in neighbouring counties

East Midlands, page 240

North West, page 294

10 miles

Beningbrough Hall, Gallery and Gardens, North Yorkshire: in partnership with the National Portrait Gallery

Beningbrough Hall, Gallery and Gardens

Beningbrough, York,
North Yorkshire YO30 1DD

🏠 ❄ 🐕 🛏 🍽 1958

A 20-year-old's trip to Italy inspired the grand style of Beningbrough Hall: completed in 1716, it has been shaped by its many occupants since. The house has intriguing stories to tell, from the wealthy teenager who inherited the estate, through the Hall's use as an RAF base in the Second World War, to its reinvention as a country-house gallery, in partnership with the National Portrait Gallery. The architectural grandeur of the rooms is a perfect setting for many 18th-century portraits of people who have influenced British history and culture. In the garden, the story continues with Italian, Victorian and even horse-racing influences. Traditional herbaceous borders contrast with sweeping lawns, formal gardens and beds, wildlife areas, and a working walled garden.

Eat, shop, stay: the Walled Garden Restaurant serves hot lunches, sandwiches and snacks. You can choose from plants and extensive home and garden ranges in the shop. A holiday apartment above the Victorian laundry provides exclusive out-of-hours access to the gardens.

Things to see and do: Indoors You can get creative in the hands-on interactive galleries and discover history and portraiture from a new perspective, including sitting for your own virtual 18th-century portrait which you can email to friends and family. Glimpse servant life in the Victorian laundry. A programme of family activities is on offer throughout the year. **Outdoors** Got a little more time to spare? Then why not get off the beaten track on riverside paths, or relax in the easily accessible garden and pause to enjoy the parkland views? Families can let off steam in the wilderness play area. **Dogs**: welcome on leads in parkland. Assistance dogs only in gardens, buildings and restaurant.

A tempting doorway in the walled garden at Beningbrough

Head over heels in the garden at Beningbrough

Access: 🅿️🚻♿🚆🔛🎦🚜🅿️ Stable block ♿🚻
Hall ♿🚻♿🛗🍴🚻 **Gardens** 🚻➡♿🚻
Parking: on site.

Find out more: 01904 472027 or beningbrough@nationaltrust.org.uk

Beningbrough Hall		M	T	W	T	F	S	S
6 Jan–11 Feb	11–3:30*	·	·	·	·	·	S	S
13 Feb–18 Feb	11–3:30*	·	T	W	T	F	S	S
24 Feb–25 Feb	11–3:30*	·	·	·	·	·	S	S
3 Mar–30 Jun	10:30–5**	·	T	W	T	F	S	S
1 Jul–31 Aug	10:30–5**	M	T	W	T	F	S	S
1 Sep–4 Nov	10:30–5**	·	T	W	T	F	S	S
10 Nov–30 Dec	11–3:30*	·	·	·	·	·	S	S

Open Bank Holidays, except 25 December. *Hall: parts closed, remaining areas open at 11:30. **Hall and shop: open at 12.

Braithwaite Hall

East Witton, Leyburn, North Yorkshire DL8 4SY

🏠♿🏚 1941

This beautiful 17th-century tenanted farmhouse lies in the heart of Coverdale. Explore the surrounding woodland and River Cover. **Note**: sorry, no toilet. Parts of the Hall are open in June, July and August (by arrangement in advance with the tenant).

Find out more: 01969 640287 or braithwaitehall@nationaltrust.org.uk

Bridestones, Crosscliff and Blakey Topping

near Pickering, North Yorkshire

 1944

On the North York Moors, the Bridestones are geological wonders – rock formations with moorland vistas, woodland walks and grassy valleys. **Note**: nearest toilets at Low Staindale car park. For Sat Nav use YO18 7LR. Road access is via Dalby Forest Drive starting 2½ miles north of Thornton le Dale: toll charges payable (including members) to Forestry Commission.

Find out more: 01723 870423 or bridestones@nationaltrust.org.uk

Brimham Rocks

Summerbridge, Harrogate, North Yorkshire HG3 4DW

 1970

These eye-catching rocks have been sculpted by 320 million years of ice, wind and continental movement. The panoramic views across Nidderdale inspire artists to capture the landscape in all seasons. Brimham is a haven for climbers, walkers, picnickers and nature spotters, as well as families looking for freedom to explore. **Note**: nearest toilets 600 yards from car park. Charges (including members) may apply in overflow car park when busy.

Eat, shop, stay: shop selling books, gifts and the popular locally made bilberry jam. Hot pies, cold drinks, ice-cream and more available from our stone-built kiosk, with picnic tables outside with views of the rocks. Additional seating inside the visitor centre.

Things to see and do: regular guided walks, events, family activities, geocaching trails and climbing days. Visitor centre exhibition space illustrates the story of the rocks and explains our conservation work. **Dogs**: welcome on leads.

Access: 🅿️ 💧 ♿ 🔄 📷 🚶
Visitor centre/shop 🔋 ♿ Countryside ➡️ ♿
Parking: on site.

Find out more: 01423 780688 or brimhamrocks@nationaltrust.org.uk

Brimham Rocks		M	T	W	T	F	S	S
Countryside								
Open all year	Dawn–dusk*	M	T	W	T	F	S	S
Visitor centre, kiosk and shop**								
6 Jan–4 Feb†	11–3						S	S
10 Feb–18 Feb	11–4	M	T	W	T	F	S	S
24 Feb–25 Mar	11–4						S	S
30 Mar–4 Nov	11–5	M	T	W	T	F	S	S
10 Nov–23 Dec	11–4						S	S
26 Dec–31 Dec	11–4	M		W	T	F	S	S

*Main gate: closes 9, or dusk if earlier. **Also open 1 January.
†Shop: closed 6 January to 4 February.

Sculptural Brimham Rocks in North Yorkshire

There are plenty of places to explore and hidden secrets to discover at East Riddlesden Hall in West Yorkshire

East Riddlesden Hall

Bradford Road, Riddlesden, Keighley,
West Yorkshire BD20 5EL

🏠 ❄ 🏋 🔺 🍽 1934

Hundreds of years ago this home was a thriving farming estate: today we're taking it back to its roots and rediscovering how it once held the community together. The jigsaw puzzle of a house offers a taste of life in the past; imposing oak beams in the Great Barn show the markings of proud craftsmen; and the gardens and grounds, with their explosions of colour, provide great spaces to relax in year-round. There's plenty of unexpected places to explore, hidden secrets to discover, and lots of reasons why this is the perfect place to spend half a day. **Note**: closed Thursdays in July and August.

Eat, shop, stay: a converted bothy is home to a shop selling gifts, books, homeware, gardenware, plants and ice-cream. On the first floor the tea-room sells seasonal light meals, sandwiches, cakes and drinks. Accessible tables are available on the ground floor.

Things to see and do: Indoors Ceramic, textile and furniture collections in the house, plus the Great Barn to explore. Trails and family activities. **Outdoors** Walks, intimate gardens, bird hide, children's natural play areas.

Dogs: welcome on the lower fields and riverside. Assistance dogs only in house and gardens.

Access: 🅿 🅳 ♿ 🔊 👁 📖 ♿ ⋮ 📷
House, shop and tea-room 🐾 ♿ 👌 Gardens ♿ ♿ 👌
Parking: 250 yards.

Making friends with the ducks at East Riddlesden Hall

Find out more: 01535 607075 or eastriddlesden@nationaltrust.org.uk

East Riddlesden Hall		M	T	W	T	F	S	S
House, tea-room, shop and garden								
10 Feb–18 Feb	10:30–4:30	M	T	W	T	·	S	S
24 Feb–18 Mar	10:30–4:30	·	·	·	·	·	S	S
19 Mar–4 Nov*	10:30–4:30	M	T	W	T	·	S	S
10 Nov–25 Nov**	10:30–3:30	·	·	·	·	·	S	S
Tea-room, shop, garden								
1 Dec–16 Dec	10:30–3:30	·	·	·	·	·	S	S

Tea-room: last entry 15 minutes before closing.
*Open Good Friday; closed Thursdays in July and August.
**House: entry by timed guided tours (please check for timings); some rooms may be closed due to winter conservation work.

Fountains Abbey and Studley Royal Water Garden

near Ripon, North Yorkshire HG4 3DY

1983

Hidden in the secluded valley of the River Skell is a World Heritage Site of sculpted water gardens, natural landscapes and awe-inspiring, atmospheric ruins. Fountains Abbey was established by Cistercian monks in 1132, and the walls echo with centuries-old stories. A riverside walk leads to the elegantly impressive Studley Royal Water Garden, created by the socially ambitious John Aislabie in the 18th century. You can while away hours wandering through the Georgian landscape of mirror-like ponds and canals, taking in statues, follies and rushing cascades. You'll discover surprising new artworks in the garden this year, with fantastical creations to feast your eyes on. Beyond the lake lies Studley Royal deer-park, with ancient lime avenues and red, fallow and sika deer. **Note**: cared for in partnership with English Heritage.

Eat, shop, stay: restaurant serving daily specials and Sunday lunch. Lighter bites at Abbey and Studley tea-rooms, with lake views/terrace. Picnics welcome. Large shop and plant stall. Stay in a cosy cottage, a grand house in the park or the Jacobean Fountains Hall.

Fountains Abbey and Studley Royal Water Garden, North Yorkshire: a World Heritage Site

Things to see and do: **Indoors** You can find out about the ancient Abbey's history in the Porter's Lodge, see the mill created by the skilful monks, step into the Jacobean Fountains Hall and admire St Mary's Church, a Victorian Gothic masterpiece in the deer-park.
Outdoors Families can have fun at Swanley Grange, with a new vegetable garden, sheep, hens, beehives and crafts, as well as a new play area. There are miles of walks in the deer-park and Water Garden and a herb garden to enjoy, plus art installations among the follies.

Free guided tours. **Dogs**: welcome on leads. Fresh water bowls and dog-friendly eating areas outside restaurant and tea-rooms.

Access: 🅿️🏛️♿🚽🍼🔍📷🚻♿
Fountains Abbey 🚶♿♿ Fountains Hall 🚶
Water Garden 🚶➡️♿♿
Parking: on site at visitor centre. Electric vehicle charging point available. Accessible parking at West Gate car park and Studley Lakeside.

Find out more: 01765 608888 or fountainsabbey@nationaltrust.org.uk

Fountains Abbey		M	T	W	T	F	S	S
Abbey and Water Garden, visitor centre restaurant, shop								
1 Jan–28 Feb*	10–5**	M	T	W	T	F	S	S
1 Mar–26 Oct	10–6**	M	T	W	T	F	S	S
27 Oct–31 Dec*	10–5**	M	T	W	T	.	S	S
Deer-park								
Open all year	6–6	M	T	W	T	F	S	S

Last admission one hour before closing. *Closed Fridays in January, plus 24 and 25 December. **Visitor centre restaurant and shop close one hour earlier. Check opening times before visit for Hall, mill, tea-rooms, Studley Royal shop and St Mary's Church.

Autumn colours at Fountains Abbey and Studley Royal Water Garden, above, and intrepid adventurers, left

Goddards House and Garden

27 Tadcaster Road, Dringhouses, York, North Yorkshire YO24 1GG

🏠❀⊤ 1984

Discover the Terry family's story and confectionery history (think Chocolate Orange) at their former house and garden. A warm Arts and Crafts building, full of memories, Goddards invites you to make yourself at home in the drawing-room with a sherry. Meander through garden 'rooms', discovering fragrant borders and hidden corners.

Eat, shop, stay: lunch is served in the Terry's dining-room. You can take coffee or afternoon tea in the drawing-room, or a slice of chocolate-orange cake on the terrace, enjoying views of the Arts and Crafts garden.

Things to see and do: Indoors Curl up by the fire on chilly days. Family trails and nostalgic displays of chocolate boxes, remembering old favourites. **Outdoors** Beautifully restored Arts and Crafts garden with outdoor games. **Dogs**: welcome on leads in garden.

Access: 🅿️♿♿📷📷🔊
House 🔊♿🔊 Garden 🔊➡️
Sat Nav: enter 27 Tadcaster Road, Dringhouses, York, not postcode.
Parking: accessible parking only on site (car park used by regional office staff).

Goddards House and Garden, North Yorkshire

Please use city centre car parks (1 to 2 miles) or park on nearby Knavesmire Road (off A1036) by York racecourse.

Find out more: 01904 771930 or goddards@nationaltrust.org.uk

Goddards		M	T	W	T	F	S	S
1 Mar–4 Nov	10:30–5			**W**	**T**	**F**	**S**	**S**
16 Nov–16 Dec	10:30–4					**F**	**S**	**S**

Open spring and summer Bank Holiday Mondays.

Hardcastle Crags

near Hebden Bridge, West Yorkshire

🏠♿🛏️🔔⊤ 1950

Home to deep ravines, tumbling streams and waterfalls, this enchanted wooded valley in the South Pennines is a walker's paradise. There are 25 miles of footpaths waiting to be explored, with Gibson Mill lying at its heart. This former

Exploring Hardcastle Crags in West Yorkshire

cotton mill and popular Edwardian entertainment emporium makes a perfect stop for refreshments. You can also explore the building, learn about its history and discover what it means to be #OffTheGrid. The mature woodland surrounding the Mill is rich in wildlife with something new every season – from seas of bluebells in late spring, to carpets of golden leaves in autumn. **Note**: steep paths and rough terrain. Nearest toilets at Gibson Mill, 1 mile from car parks.

Eat, shop, stay: Weaving Shed Café serving drinks, sandwiches, soup, ice-cream and cakes – around a log stove in cooler weather. Shop

Pond-dipping near Gibson Mill, Hardcastle Crags

Maister House

160 High Street, Hull, East Yorkshire HU1 1NL

🏠 1966

A merchant family's tale of fortune and tragedy is intertwined with the intriguing history of the 18th-century Maister House. **Note**: staircase and entrance hall only on show. Sorry no toilet. Due to a change in circumstances we are unable to confirm opening arrangements at the time of going to print. Please visit website for opening details.

Find out more: 01904 472027 (Beningbrough Hall) or maisterhouse@nationaltrust.org.uk

Malham Tarn Estate

Waterhouses, Settle, North Yorkshire

🛏️ 🏕️ 📷 🚻 1946

Peaceful Malham Tarn Estate in North Yorkshire

High up in the Dales, with views across rolling fields, limestone pavements and the tarn, this National Nature Reserve is perfect for enjoying the peace of the great outdoors. With walking and cycling routes, and a 'Tramper' (scooter) for hire, you can explore on foot, or two or four wheels. **Note**: nearest toilet at Malham National Park Centre car park or Orchid House learning centre.

selling books, gifts, sweets. Stay longer at The Lodge (at the site's entrance), or the converted Widdop Gate Barn overlooking the valley.

Things to see and do: **Indoors** Learn about the Mill's history and the #OffTheGrid technology while finding out more about the local area. Occasional exhibitions. **Outdoors** Walking trails, guided walks, picnics, wildlife and family activities. **Dogs**: welcome under close control at all times.

Access: 🅿️ 🚪 ♿ 🔦 📷 🪑 ••
Mill ♿ ⬆️ 🚹 Countryside ♿
Sat Nav: for Midgehole car park use HX7 7AA; Clough Hole car park HX7 7AZ. **Parking**: at Midgehole car park, 1 mile to Gibson Mill, or Clough Hole car park, ¾ mile (steep walk).

Find out more: 01422 844518 (weekdays). 01422 846236 (weekends) or hardcastlecrags@nationaltrust.org.uk

Hardcastle Crags		M	T	W	T	F	S	S
Gibson Mill and Weaving Shed Café								
6 Jan–18 Feb	11–3						S	S
19 Feb–25 Feb	11–3	M	T	W	T	F	S	S
3 Mar–18 Mar	11–3						S	S
19 Mar–4 Nov	11–4	M	T	W	T	F	S	S
10 Nov–30 Dec*	11–3						S	S

*Open 26 December, 11 to 3.

Eat, shop, stay: tea-rooms, pubs and facilities in Malham village (none National Trust). To stay longer, Darnbook Cottage (sleeps five) has fine views of the surrounding dales of Malham Moor and stands at the base of Fountains Fell. Picnics welcome.

Things to see and do: guided walks and family events during holidays. Accessible boardwalk. Cycle trails. Exhibitions at Orchid House and Town Head Barn. Walking routes for all abilities. **Dogs**: welcome on leads (livestock roaming).

Access: Town Head Barn 🖿 Grounds 🖿 ➡ ⟨⟩
Sat Nav: use BD24 9PT. **Parking**: off-road at Waterhouses and at Watersinks car park, south side of Malham Tarn.

Find out more: 01729 830416 or malhamtarn@nationaltrust.org.uk

Marsden Moor Estate, West Yorkshire: the Buckstones

Marsden Moor Estate	
Exhibition Centre	
Open every day all year*	9–5

*Closed 25 December.

Marsden Moor Estate

Marsden, Huddersfield, West Yorkshire

🏛 🖿 🖿 1955

As you explore this open moorland with views across the South Pennines and Peak District National Park, you're on a Site of Special Scientific Interest steeped in history. There are more than 2,300 hectares (5,700 acres) of moors, teeming with wildlife and rare plants, and miles of footpaths. **Note**: sorry, no toilet.

Eat, shop, stay: tea-rooms, restaurants and shops in Marsden village (none National Trust). Plant sales in spring and summer.

Things to see and do: walking routes – downloadable or paper versions – available (OS map required) from the Exhibition Centre at the Estate Office. Guided walks throughout the year. **Dogs**: welcome on leads.

Access: Exhibition Room 🖿 Countryside 🖿
Sat Nav: use HD7 6DH for Marsden village.
Parking: at Marsden village (not National Trust), Buckstones and Wessenden Head.

Find out more: 01484 847016 or marsdenmoor@nationaltrust.org.uk

Middlethorpe Hall Hotel, Restaurant and Spa

Bishopthorpe Road, York, North Yorkshire YO23 2GB

🏛 ❄ 🖿 🛏 🔔 🍴 2008

Middlethorpe Hall is an elegant house just outside York, built in 1699 of mellow red brick in the reign of William III and set in eight hectares (20 acres) of parkland. Furnished with antiques and fine paintings, Middlethorpe retains the look and ambiance of a well-kept, well-furnished private house. The charming bedrooms are complemented by handsome public rooms, such as the drawing-room and the wood-panelled dining-room, where imaginative cuisine is served. The garden includes a rose garden, a walled garden and a romantic meadow leading to a tree-ringed lake. In the spa, which has a swimming pool and sauna, the trained therapists use Decléor and Neom Organics products. **Note**: access is for paying guests of the hotel, including for luncheon, afternoon tea and dinner. Children over the age of six welcome.

Find out more: 01904 641241. 01904 620176 (fax) or info@middlethorpe.com middlethorpe.com

Moulton Hall

Moulton, Richmond, North Yorkshire DL10 6QH

🏠 ⚙️ 1966

Elegant 17th-century tenanted manor house with a beautiful carved staircase, set in a pretty garden with stone paths and borders. **Note**: sorry no toilet. Visit by arrangement in advance with the tenant (please give as much notice as possible).

Find out more: 01325 377227 or moultonhall@nationaltrust.org.uk

Mount Grace Priory, House and Gardens

Staddle Bridge, Northallerton, North Yorkshire DL6 3JG

🏠 ✝️ 🏛️ ⚙️ 1953

Woodland-set, well-preserved Carthusian (hermit-like, contemplative monks) priory. Explore ruins, reconstructed cell, garden and Arts and Crafts-style manor house rooms. **Note**: operated by English Heritage; National Trust members free, except on event days. Open weekends, 6 January to 31 March and 3 November to 31 December, 10 to 4; open daily, 1 April to 30 September, 10 to 6 and 1 to 31 October, 10 to 5.

Find out more: 01609 883494 or mountgracepriory@nationaltrust.org.uk

Nostell

Doncaster Road, Nostell, near Wakefield, West Yorkshire WF4 1QE

🏠 ✝️ ⚙️ 🌳 🔔 ⊤ 1954

Nostell in West Yorkshire: cycling heaven

Created in the 18th century by master craftsmen, Nostell is a grand house built to impress. The greatest architects of the time designed the exquisite rooms, and England's foremost furniture-maker, Thomas Chippendale, furnished them. All year, events and exhibitions celebrate the 300th anniversary of Chippendale's birth. As well as more than 100 objects crafted by him, you can see his letters and unravel the stories within Nostell's bespoke Chippendale interiors. Home to a rich variety of wildlife, the surrounding 121-hectare (300-acre) estate is a colourful tapestry of parkland, lakes, meadows, working kitchen garden and the secluded Menagerie Garden. Cycling along the woodland trails, swinging in the outdoor play area and getting creative in the workshop are all firm family favourites.

Eat, shop, stay: Courtyard Café serving hot food and refreshments. Shop selling gifts, souvenirs and plants. Second-hand bookshop and kiosk offering snacks and drinks open at peak times. Picnics welcome in the park and gardens.

Things to see and do: Indoors Enjoy Nostell's design, craftsmanship and art through temporary exhibitions and events and learn a new skill in artist-led sessions for adults in the workshop. Families can follow the trail for little

explorers and join in creative activities on selected days in term-time and every school holiday. **Outdoors** Join regular running, walking and cycling groups and explore the woodland cycle trails and all-weather tracks in Obelisk Park. There are led family activities every school holiday: geocaching, den-building,

orienteering, nature trails and the outdoor play area available all year round. **Dogs**: assistance dogs only: gardens and house. Under close control, on leads when requested: park.

Access: 🅿️🅳🖼️♿🚻🔆📷♿👓🔍
House ♿⬆️♿ Grounds ♿♿➡️👓♿
Parking: 650 yards.

Find out more: 01924 863892 or nostell@nationaltrust.org.uk

Nostell		M	T	W	T	F	S	S
House*								
3 Mar–28 Oct	1–5	·	·	W	T	F	S	S
1 Dec–16 Dec	10–4	·	·	·	·	·	S	S
Gardens, shop and café**								
1 Jan–2 Mar	10–4	M	T	W	T	F	S	S
3 Mar–28 Oct	10–5	M	T	W	T	F	S	S
29 Oct–31 Dec	10–4	M	T	W	T	F	S	S
Parkland								
Open all year	7–7†	M	T	W	T	F	S	S

*House: check additional opening arrangements before visit. Last admission 45 minutes before closing. Open Bank Holidays, 11 to 5. **Rose Garden may close for private functions. †Parkland: last entry 6, or dusk if earlier. Closed 25 December.

Chippendale desk in the Library at Nostell, above, and admiring the colourful garden flowers, left

Nunnington Hall

Nunnington, near York,
North Yorkshire YO62 5UY

🏠 ❀ 1953

This welcoming and friendly home, with its
enchanting house and gardens, is cradled in a
beautiful Yorkshire setting. You can learn about
the Fife family, owners of Nunnington Hall in
the 1920s and – if you're brave enough – listen
to the Hall's ghostly tales. In spring, the
wildflower meadows in the organic gardens
bloom. In summer, the lawn is perfect for
relaxing and picnicking by the meandering
River Rye. In autumn, the orchards are
bountiful with produce. Whatever the weather,
whatever the season, Nunnington Hall, within
easy reach of York and Scarborough, is a
perfect day out for all the family.

The south front of Nunnington Hall from the orchard

Access: 🅿 ♿ 🔊 Building ♿ ♿ ♿ Grounds ♿ ♿
Parking: on site.

Find out more: 01439 748283 or
nunningtonhall@nationaltrust.org.uk

Eat, shop, stay: atmospheric, licensed
waitress-service tea-room in the main part of
the house, serving homemade lunch and cakes.
Outdoor garden kiosk (available during peak
times) with seating next to the River Rye. Shop
on the third floor, selling gifts and souvenirs.

Nunnington Hall		M	T	W	T	F	S	S
10 Feb–4 Mar	10:30–4	·	T	W	T	F	S	S
6 Mar–1 Jul	10:30–5	·	T	W	T	F	S	S
2 Jul–9 Sep	10:30–5	M	T	W	T	F	S	S
11 Sep–4 Nov	10:30–5	·	T	W	T	F	S	S
17 Nov–16 Dec	10:30–4	·	·	·	·	·	S	S

Last entry 45 minutes before closing. Open Mondays during
school holidays and Bank Holiday Mondays.

Things to see and do: **Indoors** 'Carlisle
Collection' of 22 miniature rooms, art
exhibitions, concerts and seasonal events.
Family activities. **Outdoors** Garden games,
mud-pie kitchen, bird-spotting, quoits,
pooh-sticks, giant chess and croquet.
Dogs: welcome on leads in the garden.

A froth of alchemilla at Nunnington Hall, North Yorkshire

Ormesby Hall

Ladgate Lane, Ormesby, near Middlesbrough,
Redcar & Cleveland TS3 0SR

🏠 ❀ ♨ 🔔 🍽 1962

Now a tranquil oasis on Middlesbrough's
doorstep, Ormesby Hall was not always so! The
last owners, Jim and Ruth Pennyman, put
Ormesby on the national stage with an eclectic
mix of revolutionary theatre, tradition and
socialism. Their spirit pervades parts of the
Georgian mansion, Victorian formal garden
and sprawling parkland.

Eat, shop, stay: Servants' Hall tea-room
serving barista-style coffee and a range of hot
and cold drinks, soup, sandwiches, cakes,
scones, ice-cream and snacks. Gift shop selling

National Trust products, children's toys and plants. Second-hand bookshop. Picnics welcome in the garden.

Things to see and do: **Indoors** New theatre room, family room, model railway layouts, living history days and family activities. **Outdoors** New natural wild play area, mud-pie kitchen, '50 things' trail, garden games and croquet. **Dogs**: welcome on leads in parkland, courtyard, lawn. Assistance dogs only in house and garden.

Ormesby Hall, Redcar & Cleveland: enjoying the garden, above, and helping in the kitchen, below

Access: ⬛🅿️🅳🅼🆂🆗🆘🅰️🆎🅾️
House 🅰️🆎🅶 **Grounds** 🆎➡️🅶
Parking: 200 yards.

Find out more: 01642 324188 or ormesbyhall@nationaltrust.org.uk
Church Lane, Ormesby, Middlesbrough TS7 9AS

Ormesby Hall		M	T	W	T	F	S	S
4 Feb–29 Mar	11–4	M	T	W	T	·	·	S
1 Apr–4 Nov	11–5	M	T	W	T	·	·	S
25 Nov–17 Dec	11–4	M	·	·	·	·	·	S

Last entry 45 minutes before closing. Additionally open for model railway weekends. 29 April: closed for Brides Up North WEDFEST18.

Rievaulx Terrace

Rievaulx, Helmsley, North Yorkshire YO62 5LJ

⬛❄️♿ 1972

Enchanting Rievaulx Terrace in North Yorkshire

Designed primarily for promenading and dining in style, Rievaulx Terrace was created by the Duncombe family and finished *circa* 1757. It maintains a feeling of grandeur and tranquillity. Walking through the woods is a perfect start to your visit, with tantalising glimpses of the terrace and the views beyond. When you leave the woods and walk down the terrace, spectacular views of Rievaulx Abbey and the valley beyond appear across banks of wild flowers through man-made vistas. At one end is the Tuscan Temple; at the other, the Ionic Temple, where the family dined under the magnificent painted ceiling. **Note**: no access from Rievaulx Terrace to Rievaulx Abbey (English Heritage).

Eat, shop, stay: pre-packed snacks, ice-cream, hot and cold drinks available. Picnics welcome. Shop selling gifts and souvenirs.

The Ionic Temple at Rievaulx Terrace: the Duncombe family dined under its magnificent painted ceiling

Roseberry Topping

near Newton-under-Roseberry, North Yorkshire

 1985

Affectionately known as 'Yorkshire's Matterhorn', Roseberry Topping has woodland walks and wildlife on its slopes and views from its summit. **Note**: nearest parking at Newton-under-Roseberry, not National Trust (charge including members). Nearest toilets also in this car park. For Sat Nav use TS9 6QR.

Find out more: 01723 870423 or roseberrytopping@nationaltrust.org.uk

Treasurer's House, York

Minster Yard, York, North Yorkshire YO1 7JL

🏛️ ✳️ 🐾 🍴 1930

Tucked behind York Minster, Treasurer's House is not as it first appears. In 1897, Frank Green (the grandson of a wealthy industrialist)

Things to see and do: furnished Ionic Temple opens at intervals throughout the day. Woodland natural play area for children including den-building, rope swing, balance beam, log-scotch, quoits and stepping stones. Family trails and activities. **Dogs**: welcome on leads.

Access: 🅿️📶♿🅿️🎵 Visitor centre ♿
Temples 🔦 Grounds ♿➡️♿♿
Parking: 100 yards.

Find out more: 01439 798340 (summer). 01439 748283 (winter) or rievaulxterrace@nationaltrust.org.uk

Rievaulx Terrace		M	T	W	T	F	S	S
10 Feb–4 Mar	10–4	M	T	W	T	F	S	S
5 Mar–30 Sep	10–5	M	T	W	T	F	S	S
1 Oct–4 Nov	10–4	M	T	W	T	F	S	S

Last entry one hour before closing.

bought the property and created an opulent show home, grand enough to impress Edward VII during his visit. Frank Green was passionate about history and indulged this by saving Treasurer's House and other buildings in York. He built a large collection of fine antiques, art and furniture, and even placed studs in the floor to show where they should go. The award-winning garden is an oasis of calm, to relax in and enjoy unrivalled views of York Minster.

Treasurer's House, York, North Yorkshire: admiring the collection, above, and the award-winning garden, below

Eat, shop, stay: the Below Stairs Café serves morning coffee, lunch and afternoon tea. Around the corner, on Goodramgate, is the Trust's large high-street shop selling a wide selection of gifts. Stay a little longer in Minstergate, the city-centre holiday apartment.

Things to see and do: Indoors Family trails, plus hard-hat tours on selected days (five years plus) to the cellar – the site of York's most famous ghost story. **Outdoors** Lawn games and wildlife-watching. **Dogs**: welcome in the garden on leads.

Access: 🏠🏛️🖼️🎧📷🖨️
House ♿🏛️🚻 **Garden** ♿
Parking: nearest at Lord Mayor's Walk (not National Trust). Park and ride from city outskirts recommended.

Find out more: 01904 624247 or treasurershouse@nationaltrust.org.uk

Treasurer's House		M	T	W	T	F	S	S
1 Mar–4 Nov*	11–4:30	M	T	W	T	F	S	S
15 Nov–16 Dec	11–4:30				T	F	S	S

*On selected days access is by guided tour only.

Upper Wharfedale

near Buckden, North Yorkshire

  1989

This Dales landscape – with fields full of sheep and cows, wildflower meadows in early summer and characteristic dry-stone walls and barns – is a wonderful place to relax and enjoy the great outdoors. Weave your way along the river and through woodland valleys by foot or by bike.

Eat, shop, stay: village tea-rooms, shops, pubs and farm shops (none National Trust). Nestling in the heart of Buckden, we have The Old Smithy, a tiny and cosy holiday cottage (sleeps two), and Town Head Bunkhouse (sleeps 13) to rent.

Things to see and do: guided walks, events, workshops and activities. Family events during school holidays. **Dogs**: welcome on leads due to livestock.

Upper Wharfedale in the North Yorkshire Dales

Access: [P♿][♿] Town Head Barn [♿] Grounds [➡]
Sat Nav: use BD23 5JA. **Parking**: in Kettlewell and Buckden, pay and display, not National Trust (charge including members).

Find out more: 01729 830416 or
upperwharfedale@nationaltrust.org.uk

Wentworth Woodhouse

Cortworth Lane, Wentworth, Rotherham,
South Yorkshire S62 7TQ

[♿][❄][♨][🔔][☂] [2017]

Stately Wentworth Woodhouse in South Yorkshire

Large Palladian-style country house. Saved for the nation by Wentworth Woodhouse Preservation Trust – working to restore the house and increase access. **Note**: operated by Wentworth Woodhouse Preservation Trust. National Trust members receive 50 per cent discount on all tours. Admission by booked guided tour only (call for details). State rooms only open.

Find out more: 01226 351161 or
info@wentworthwoodhouse.org.uk

Yorkshire Coast

near Ravenscar, North Yorkshire

[♿][♨][🚲][🐾][🛏] [1976]

The coastline from Saltburn to Filey has sea views, clifftop walks, cycling routes and sandy bays with excellent rock-pooling and fossil-hunting. Ravenscar Visitor Centre can give you ideas to make the most of your visit and there's also a coastal exhibition at the Old Coastguard Station, Robin Hood's Bay.

Eat, shop, stay: Old Coastguard Station shop selling gifts, books, maps and toys. Ravenscar Visitor Centre offering a limited selection of drinks and snacks. With ever-changing sea views, holiday cottages at Ravenscar and Boatman's Loft, Robin Hood's Bay, are great places to stay.

Things to see and do: Indoors Exhibitions at the Old Coastguard Station. **Outdoors** Family events, geocaching, wildlife activities and guided walks from Ravenscar and the Old Coastguard Station. **Dogs**: welcome, on leads around livestock and most events. Old Coastguard Station: assistance dogs only.

Access: [♿][♿][♿][♿] Old Coastguard Station [♿]
Sat Nav: for Ravenscar use YO13 0NE.
Parking: on roadside at Ravenscar. Pay and display at Saltburn, Runswick Bay and Robin Hood's Bay, not National Trust (charge including members).

Find out more: 01723 870423 or
yorkshirecoast@nationaltrust.org.uk

Yorkshire Coast		M	T	W	T	F	S	S
Old Coastguard Station and Ravenscar Visitor Centre								
1 Jan–7 Jan	10–4	M	T	W	T	F	S	S
13 Jan–4 Feb	10–4	.	.	.	.	.	S	S
10 Feb–18 Feb	10–4	M	T	W	T	F	S	S
24 Feb–25 Mar	10–4	.	.	.	.	.	S	S
30 Mar–2 Nov	10–5	M	T	W	T	F	S	S
3 Nov–23 Dec	10–4	.	.	.	.	.	S	S
28 Dec–31 Dec	10–4	M	.	.	.	F	S	S

The glorious Yorkshire Coast, North Yorkshire

North East

St Cuthbert's Cave, near the Northumberland Coast
Competition entry from Jules Hammond

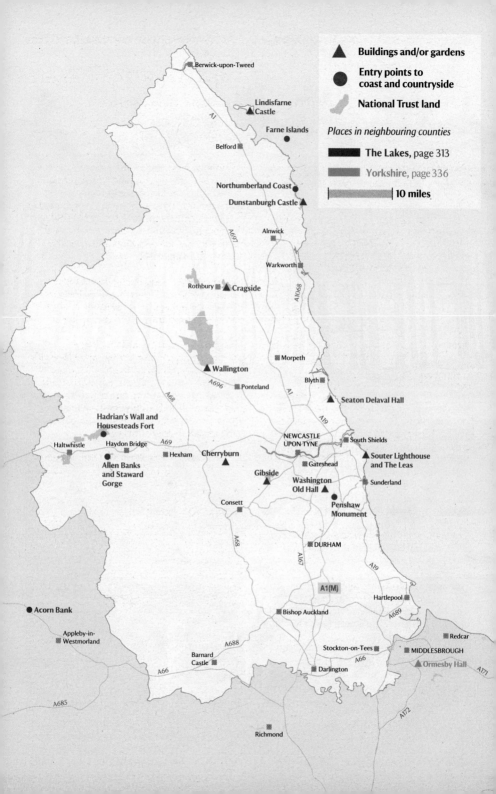

Buildings and/or gardens

Entry points to coast and countryside

National Trust land

Places in neighbouring counties

The Lakes, page 313

Yorkshire, page 336

10 miles

Berwick-upon-Tweed

Lindisfarne Castle

Farne Islands

Belford

Northumberland Coast

Dunstanburgh Castle

Alnwick

A1

A697

Warkworth

A1068

Rothbury ▲ Cragside

Morpeth

Blyth

▲ Wallington

A696 Ponteland

A1

▲ Seaton Delaval Hall

A68

A19

Hadrian's Wall and Housesteads Fort

Haltwhistle

Haydon Bridge

A69 Hexham

NEWCASTLE UPON TYNE

South Shields

▲ Souter Lighthouse and The Leas

Allen Banks and Staward Gorge

▲ Cherryburn

Gateshead

Gibside

Washington Old Hall ▲

Sunderland

Consett

A68

Penshaw Monument

A167

■ DURHAM

A1(M)

A19

Hartlepool

● Acorn Bank

Appleby-in-Westmorland

A688

Bishop Auckland

A689

Redcar

Barnard Castle

A66

Stockton-on-Tees

MIDDLESBROUGH

A171

Darlington

A66

▲ Ormesby Hall

A685

A172

Richmond

Allen Banks and Staward Gorge

near Ridley Hall, Bardon Mill, Hexham,
Northumberland NE47 7BP

🏠 🏛 🌿 1942

Allen Banks and Staward Gorge in Northumberland

With its deep gorge created by the River Allen,
this 250-hectare (617-acre) site provides the
perfect setting for an adventure. The largest
area of ancient semi-natural woodland in
Northumberland, it has miles of waymarked
walks, paths up to treetop views and a wide
array of wildlife and fungi. **Note**: site suffered
severe storm damage in 2015: check for open
sections and routes before visiting.

Eat, shop, stay: picnics welcome at the
numerous beauty spots in the woodland
and kitchen garden.

Things to see and do: events and things to
look out for include Easter Egg hunts,
woodland walks, wildlife spotting, ornamental
tarn and medieval pele-tower. **Dogs**: welcome
under close control.

Access: 🚻 ♿ Grounds ♿
Sat Nav: postcode directs to Ridley Hall – turn
left at Ridley Hall gates for Allen Banks car
park. **Parking**: at Allen Banks.

Find out more: 01434 321888 or
allenbanks@nationaltrust.org.uk

Cherryburn

Station Bank, Mickley, Stocksfield,
Northumberland NE43 7DD

🏠 🌿 ✿ T 1991

Set in a tranquil garden with views across the
Tyne Valley, this unassuming Northumbrian
farmstead is the birthplace of famous artist
and naturalist Thomas Bewick. Cherryburn is
surrounded by the natural world that inspired
his work. Explore the museum with Bewick's
pioneering wood engravings and meet the
friendly farm animals.

Eat, shop, stay: shop selling books and a
selection of original Bewick prints. Hot and
cold drinks and ice-cream available in house.
Farmyard picnic area.

Things to see and do: **Indoors** Regular
printing demonstrations. Museum of Bewick's
life and prints. Original birthplace cottage.
Outdoors Tranquil gardens. Family trail and
mini-adventure play area and activities.
Paddock walk and farmyard with animals.
Dogs: welcome on short leads in garden and
grounds (animals in farmyard).

A Thomas Bewick print at Cherryburn, Northumberland

Access: 📶🅿️♿🔲🔱🎫🚭🅿️📷

Birthplace ♿♿♿ **Café and museum** ♿♿🚻

Grounds ♿♿♿➡️

Sat Nav: some misdirect. **Parking**: 100 yards.

Find out more: 01661 843276 or
cherryburn@nationaltrust.org.uk

Cherryburn		M	T	W	T	F	S	S
10 Feb–1 Apr	11–5	M	T	W	T	F	S	S
2 Apr–2 Sep	10–5	M	T	W	T	F	S	S
3 Sep–4 Nov	11–5	M	T	W	T	F	S	S

Cragside

Rothbury, Morpeth, Northumberland NE65 7PX

🏠❄️🛏️🏡 1977

Trip the light fantastic to the home where
modern living began. Victorian engineering
supremo William Armstrong used his wealth,
art and science in an ingenious way. Cragside
was the first house in the world to be lit by
hydroelectricity, making it a wonder of the
Victorian age. What began as a modest country
retreat for Lord and Lady Armstrong became

'Magician of the North', a Perspex model of an
electrical discharge at Cragside in Northumberland

the most technologically advanced house of its
time, including every home comfort imaginable
and evolving into an Arts and Crafts
masterpiece. Outside, they were equally
ambitious with the garden and grounds,
engineering the landscape and experimenting
with plants on a spectacular scale. Rocky crags,
tumbling water, tranquil lakes, towering
North American conifers and great drifts of
rhododendrons create changing scenery.
Note: challenging terrain and distances
(stout footwear essential) outside.

Eat, shop, stay: tea-room serving hot meals,
sandwiches, hand-made treats and cream teas.
Kiosks at the house and play area. Shop selling
souvenirs, gifts, local food, crafts and plants.
Two holiday cottages in the formal garden plus
bunkhouse sleeping up to 16 people.

Cragside: a wonder of the Victorian age

Things to see and do: **Indoors** Among Armstrong's vast collection of British art and furniture sits the intriguing Electrical Room, where fascinating experiments were performed. Victorian baking events, specialist conservation demonstrations, exhibitions, events and family activities throughout the year. **Outdoors** Rugged landscape featuring spectacular rhododendron displays, trickling burns and open lakes. Six-mile carriage drive through woodland. Numerous footpaths with trails and walks for all abilities. Idyllic formal garden with seasonal planting and views across Northumberland. Engineering features include Archimedes Screw and Power House. Family highlights include labyrinth, adventure play area, den-building, barefoot walk and Young Engineers' Zone. Free shuttle bus between main features. **Dogs**: welcome outdoors on leads.

Access: ⃞⃞⃞⃞⃞⃞⃞⃞⃞⃞⃞⃞⃞
House ⃞⃞ Visitor centre ⃞⃞⃞ Estate ⃞➡
Parking: nine car parks on estate.

Find out more: 01669 620333 or cragside@nationaltrust.org.uk

Cragside		M	T	W	T	F	S	S
Gardens and woodland								
5 Jan–4 Feb*	10–3**	·	·	·	·	F	S	S
9 Feb–4 Nov	10–5**	M	T	W	T	F	S	S
5 Nov–31 Dec†	10–3**	M	T	W	T	F	S	S
House**								
9 Feb–4 Nov	11–5††	M	T	W	T	F	S	S

*Also open 1 January, 10 to 3. **Last admission at gate one hour before closing. Carriage Drive closes at 5:30, or sunset if earlier. †Whole estate closed 24 and 25 December. ††House: last entry one hour before closing; there may be queues at busy times.

Dunstanburgh Castle

Craster, Alnwick, Northumberland NE66 3TT

 1961

This castle ruin occupies a dramatic position on the Northumberland coastline a mile from Craster and towering over Embleton Bay. **Note**: managed by English Heritage. National Trust members admitted free. Sorry no toilets – closest at Craster car park. Parking at Craster, pay and display, not National Trust (charge including members). Call English Heritage on 01665 576231 or visit english-heritage.org.uk for opening times. Closed 1 January and 24 to 26 December.

Find out more: 01665 576231 or dunstanburghcastle@nationaltrust.org.uk

Farne Islands

Northumberland

✝ 🏛 👤 ♿ 1925

One of the UK's best wildlife experiences. An exhilarating boat trip, landing April to October, takes you into the world of 23 nesting seabird species, including thousands of puffins (May to July), Arctic terns and guillemots. Each autumn, more than 1,000 pups are born to the grey seal colony. **Note**: Inner Farne island: basic toilets, easy access boardwalk. Staple island: challenging terrain and no toilets. Access by boat from Seahouses – separate charge applies (including members). Please show your membership card at harbour trailer – there is no facility to validate membership.

Eat, shop, stay: Seahouses shop selling wide range of goods, local produce and toy puffins. Some souvenirs available on islands. Small shop in Inner Farne Information Centre. Why not stay longer in one of our cottages at nearby Low Newton and Holy Island?

Things to see and do: nature-spotting paradise. Bring a hat – terns will dive-bomb! On Inner Farne: St Cuthbert's Chapel, with vibrant stained-glass, Victorian lighthouse and visitor centre. Lindisfarne Castle and Northumberland Coast nearby. **Dogs**: sorry, not allowed (including assistance dogs) due to extremely sensitive nature of the colony.

Access: 🚹 Staple Island 🚹 Inner Farne 🚹 **Sat Nav**: use NE68 7RQ. **Parking**: in Seahouses, not National Trust (charge including members).

A boat trip, below, round the Farne Islands, off the coast of Northumberland. The islands are home to 23 nesting seabird species, including puffins, right

Find out more: 01665 721099. 01289 389244 (Lindisfarne Castle) or farneislands@nationaltrust.org.uk

Farne Islands		M	T	W	T	F	S	S
Inner Farne Island								
30 Mar–30 Apr	10:30–5:30	M	T	W	T	F	S	S
1 May–31 Jul	1:15–5:45	M	T	W	T	F	S	S
1 Aug–31 Oct	10:30–5:30	M	T	W	T	F	S	S
Staple Island								
1 May–31 Jul	10–1:30	M	T	W	T	F	S	S
Shop								
3 Jan–28 Feb	11–4			W	T	F	S	S
1 Mar–31 Oct	10–5*	M	T	W	T	F	S	S
1 Nov–31 Dec**	10–4	M	T	W	T	F	S	S

Landings on Inner Farne and Staple Island only. Landings on Staple are subject to Rangers' discretion to ensure visitor safety. Seahouses Information Centre: open all year, 10 to 5. *Seahouses shop: open to 5:30, July and August. **Closed 25 and 26 December.

Gibside

near Rowlands Gill, Gateshead, Tyne & Wear NE16 6BG

🏛️ 🍴 ❄️ ♿ ⛺ 🔔 🍽️ ⎡1974⎤

One of the few surviving 18th-century designed landscapes, Gibside was fashioned with two things in mind: spectacular views and 'wow' moments. The estate, commissioned by coal baron George Bowes, offers a glimpse into the past and the compelling story of heiress Mary Eleanor Bowes. Escape the hustle and bustle of modern life at a peaceful Neo-classical chapel and grand ruin nestled in 243 hectares

(600 acres) of gardens, woodland, country and riverside – a wildlife haven on the edge of urban Tyneside. There's also the family-friendly Gibside Pub (open late Fridays and Saturdays), and Strawberry Castle play area, perfect for adventure.

Eat, shop, stay: café/pub, shop selling plants and gifts, twice-monthly markets offering local and handmade produce in the Market Place. Stables Courtyard contains Carriage House Coffee Shop and Renwick's second-hand books. Room hire and bunkhouse group accommodation. Refreshments kiosk at play area (weekends/holidays).

Things to see and do: **Indoors** Palladian chapel with unique three-tier pulpit. Gibside story and wildlife interpretation at the Stables. **Outdoors** Miles of estate footpaths. Look out for wildlife. Walks and events. Play areas. **Dogs**: welcome on leads. Assistance dogs only in Strawberry Castle play area.

Access: 🅿️ 🚹 ♿ 🏛️ 🔲 📷 ♿ ⊙ 🅰️ **Stables** ♿ ⬍ **Chapel** ♿ ♿ ♿ **Garden** ♿ ♿ ♿ ➡️ ♿ ♿ **Parking**: 382 yards from café and shop (uphill walkway).

Fun in the adventure play area, below, and a view of the avenue from the chapel, bottom, at Gibside, Tyne & Wear

Whin Sill escarpment, this epic structure kept the unwanted out and the welcome safe. There are invigorating walks and breathtaking landscapes. The fort offers insights into Roman soldiers' lives. **Note**: fort National Trust-owned, English Heritage-managed. Half-mile uphill walk from visitor centre. Parking charges (including members).

Eat, shop, stay: visitor centre offering sandwiches, snacks, ice-cream and drinks. Shop selling books, cards, gifts, souvenirs and plants. Picnics welcome. Holiday accommodation – set in spectacular landscapes, ideal for walkers and stargazers – includes a bothy, a farmhouse and a cottage.

The Column to Liberty at Gibside

Find out more: 01207 541820 or gibside@nationaltrust.org.uk

Gibside		M	T	W	T	F	S	S
Garden, woodlands, shop and café/pub								
1 Jan–28 Feb	10–4*	M	T	W	T	F	S	S
1 Mar–31 Oct	10–6*	M	T	W	T	F	S	S
1 Nov–31 Dec	10–4*	M	T	W	T	F	S	S
Chapel								
6 Jan–25 Feb	10–4						S	S
1 Mar–31 Oct	10–5	M	T	W	T	F	S	S
3 Nov–30 Dec	10–4						S	S

*Garden, woodlands and café: open 9:30 at weekends; pub closes 9, Friday and Saturday. Whole estate closed 24 and 25 December.

Hadrian's Wall and Housesteads Fort

near Bardon Mill, Hexham, Northumberland NE47 6NN

🏛️ ♿ ⛺ 1930

A UNESCO World Heritage Site, Hadrian's Wall is the Roman Empire's best-preserved outpost in northern Europe. Making use of the natural

Sycamore Gap at Hadrian's Wall, Northumberland; the best-preserved Roman outpost in northern Europe

Things to see and do: **Indoors** Museum (not National Trust) with dressing-up and video presentation. **Outdoors** Fort to explore. Walk along wall to Milecastle 37 and Sycamore Gap. Play area. Periodic activities, including rock-climbing, stargazing. **Dogs**: welcome on leads.

Access: 🅿️ 🅿️ 🚻 ♿ 🐕 🏠 🚶
Visitor centre ♿ ♿ Museum ♿
Parking: at Housesteads, Steel Rigg and Cawfields, not National Trust (charge including members).

Find out more: 01434 344525 or housesteads@nationaltrust.org.uk

Hadrian's Wall and Housesteads Fort

Housesteads Fort: open daily, except some days over Christmas; opening hours vary by season (please check before visiting).

Lindisfarne Castle

Holy Island, Berwick-upon-Tweed,
Northumberland TD15 2SH

🏰 ✳ 🚂 🐕 🛏 1944

Lindisfarne Castle, one of the UK's most recognisable castles, presides over Holy Island, reached via a causeway at low tide. The Tudor fort was converted into a holiday home for *Country Life* Editor Edward Hudson by architect Edwin Lutyens in 1903. Now reopening after a major conservation project, this is an unusual opportunity to experience the castle in a whole new way. The stripped-back spaces will be atmospheric and revealing and there'll be surprises in every room. Don't miss the summer-flowering Gertrude Jekyll walled garden, discover the grandeur of the lime kilns and visit the National Trust shop.
Note: reopening after major conservation project. Unfurnished rooms. Limited toilet facilities. Island accessed via tidal causeway.

Eat, shop, stay: National Trust shop in village with large range of homeware and gardenware. There are two holiday cottages on the island: Lutyens-designed St Oswald's with castle views (dog-friendly) and Glen House in the village. Refreshments in the village (not National Trust).

Gertrude Jekyll designed her Arts and Crafts walled garden, below, to bloom for summer guests at Lindisfarne Castle, Northumberland. This wild coastline is perfect for rock-pooling, above

Lindisfarne Castle silhouetted against a darkening sky

Things to see and do: Indoors Interior to explore. **Outdoors** Upper Battery views. Castle Point walk, with shoreline, lime kilns and small walled garden by Lutyens' collaborator Gertrude Jekyll. Farne Islands (boats from Seahouses) nearby. **Dogs**: welcome on leads.

Access: [icons] Castle [icons] Lime kilns [icon]
Parking: at main island car park, 1 mile, not National Trust (charge including members). Shuttle bus to Castle.

Find out more: 01289 389244 or lindisfarne@nationaltrust.org.uk

Lindisfarne Castle	
Garden	
Open every day all year	

Lindisfarne Castle is due to reopen in spring (please check before visiting for confirmation of dates/times). For access to Holy Island please check tide times.

Northumberland Coast

Northumberland

[icons] 1935

From Lindisfarne to Druridge Bay, you'll find wide open skies, golden sands and blue seas. This unspoilt coastline is rich in pretty fishing villages, castles, wildlife and deserted beaches with excellent rock pools. Look out for seals, dolphins, wading shorebirds and nesting terns at Long Nanny Estuary on Beadnell Bay. **Note**: public car parks only (charge including members).

Eat, shop, stay: shops on Holy Island and in Seahouses. Cafés, pubs and shops in coastal towns and villages (none National Trust). Holiday cottages with extraordinary views: two on Holy Island; three at Low Newton, including on the green at Newton-by-the-Sea.

Golden sands on the Northumberland Coast

Things to see and do: Long Nanny little tern breeding colony (June to August), access from High Newton. Events, '50 things' and spotting wildlife. Bird hides at Newton Pool. Farne Islands and Lindisfarne Castle nearby.
Dogs: welcome, some local restrictions may apply. On leads at Long Nanny tern site.
Sat Nav: for Low Newton use NE66 3EH; Druridge Bay NE61 5EG; St Aidan's Dunes NE68 7SH. **Parking**: limited at Druridge Bay. Also at Holy Island, Seahouses, Beadnell, Newton-by-the-Sea and Craster, none National Trust (charge including members).

Find out more: 01289 389244 or northumberlandcoast@nationaltrust.org.uk

Penshaw Monument

near Penshaw, Tyne & Wear DH4 7NJ

🏠 🏛 ♿ 1939

This Wearside landmark can be seen from miles around, but the temple is worth closer inspection for views and walks. **Note**: sorry no toilets. Walking routes nearby. Tours to the top of the monument on Saturdays, Sundays and Bank Holidays, 31 March to 30 September.

Find out more: 0191 416 6879 or penshaw.monument@nationaltrust.org.uk

Seaton Delaval Hall

The Avenue, Seaton Sluice, Northumberland NE26 4QR

🏠 ❀ ♿ 2009

Dramatic (in more ways than one) Seaton Delaval Hall was designed by Sir John Vanbrugh (Castle Howard, Blenheim Palace) and home to the larger-than-life Delaval family. The Central Hall bears the scars of fierce fires which almost condemned it to ruin 200 years ago: moments of striking theatre can be found in the house, gardens and surrounding landscape, which act as the stage for a tale of changing fortunes. The property is currently undergoing work to secure the Hall and bring to life the story of the colourful Delaval family, so you can see more changes in progress. **Note**: access to some areas may be restricted (please check before your visit).

Spiral staircase at Seaton Delaval Hall, Northumberland

The Rose Garden at Seaton Delaval Hall

Eat, shop, stay: café serving hot and cold drinks, snacks and sweet treats all year. In fine weather refreshments are served from the summerhouse. Shop in the ticket hut selling souvenirs, gifts and plants.

Things to see and do: **Indoors** Vanbrugh's architecture, including 18th-century stables. Great Hall with fire-damaged interior and original statues. Paintings and furniture in west wing. **Outdoors** Formal gardens, walks and coastal landscape. Events and activities. **Dogs**: welcome on leads outdoors.

Access: 🅿️🚻♿📷📹✏️ Hall ♿ Stables ♿ Grounds ➡️
Parking: 500 yards.

Find out more: 0191 237 9100 or seatondelavalhall@nationaltrust.org.uk

Seaton Delaval Hall		M	T	W	T	F	S	S
Central Hall, stables and gardens								
6 Jan–25 Feb*	11–3	·	·	·	·	·	S	S
26 Feb–18 Jul*	11–5	M	T	W	·	·	S	S
21 Jul–2 Sep	11–5	M	T	W	T	F	S	S
3 Sep–31 Oct*	11–5	M	T	W	·	·	S	S
3 Nov–30 Dec	11–3	·	·	·	·	·	S	S
West Wing								
26 Feb–28 Oct	11–5	M	T	W	·	·	S	S

*10 to 18 February, 26 March to 15 April, 28 May to 3 June, and 22 to 28 October: also open Thursdays and Fridays. Last admission 45 minutes before closing. **West Wing also open Thursday and Friday in school holidays.

Souter Lighthouse and The Leas

Coast Road, Whitburn, Sunderland, Tyne & Wear SR6 7NH

🏠❄️♿🐕🛏️🍴 1990

Scale the heights of a lighthouse which was truly modern for its time – the first purpose-built to be lit by electricity. Imagine what the views are like at the top. The Engine Room and Keeper's Cottage give a flavour of life in a working lighthouse. To the north stretches The Leas, dotted with wildflower meadows of bee orchids, yellow rattle and red clover. To the south is Whitburn Coastal Park, cared for by our rangers and great for wildlife: its nature reserve provides water and rest for birds making their way across the sea and along the coast. **Note**: Whitburn Coastal Park owned by South Tyneside Council, leased and managed by the National Trust.

Souter Lighthouse and The Leas, Tyne & Wear: the groundbreaking lighthouse was the first in the world built to run on electricity

Eat, shop, stay: Lighthouse Café serving light lunches, soup, cakes and refreshments. Local dishes Panackelty and Singin' Hinnies are a must-try. Shop stocking coastal gifts and Souter souvenirs. Picnic area. Extend your visit and stay in the picturesque, clifftop Lighthouse Keeper's cottages.

Things to see and do: events and activities, including seashore safaris, bug-hunting, nature walks, birdwatching, holiday crafts and car-boot sales. Self-led family activity packs available. Play area. Fog-horn demonstrations, wildlife and sensory gardens. **Dogs**: welcome on leads outdoors.

Access: ⚓ 🅿️ 🚻 ♿ 🅿️ 🚪
Building 🏠 ♿ **Grounds** 🏠 🚶 ♿
Parking: on site.

Find out more: 0191 529 3161 or souter@nationaltrust.org.uk

Souter Lighthouse and The Leas		M	T	W	T	F	S	S
Lighthouse								
3 Feb–4 Nov	11–5	M	T	W	T	F	S	S
5 Nov–30 Nov	11–4	M	T	W	T	F	S	S
Café and shop								
6 Jan–28 Jan	10–4						S	S
3 Feb–4 Nov	10–5	M	T	W	T	F	S	S
5 Nov–2 Dec	10–4	M	T	W	T	F	S	S
8 Dec–16 Dec	10–4						S	S

Wallington

Cambo, near Morpeth,
Northumberland NE61 4AR

🏠 🐕 ♿ 🛏️ 🅿️ 1941

Wallington is a 5,260-hectare (13,000-acre) working estate gifted to you by Sir Charles Philips Trevelyan, socialist MP and 'illogical Englishman'. The woodland gardens are full of wildlife and ancient trees; visit the hide to spot red squirrels or take the river walk where you may see otters or crayfish. There are lots of walks, or, using the family-friendly cycle trail, you can explore the wider estate. The three outdoor play spaces capture the spirit of the adventurous Trevelyan children. Throughout the year the walled garden and Edwardian conservatory are bursting with colour. The Trevelyans' informal home is full of treasured collections and curiosities: make yourself at home and find out about this unconventional family.

Soaking up the sun at Wallington, Northumberland

Eat, shop, stay: Clocktower Café offers hot and cold refreshments throughout the day. The seasonal kiosks in the courtyard, Walled Garden and West Wood serve drinks and snacks. Wide range of gifts for sale in our shops and plant centre. Bunkhouse accommodation available.

Things to see and do: Indoors Soak up the atmosphere in the Trevelyans' home and admire the Pre-Raphaelite paintings around the Central Hall, telling the history of Northumberland. Regular activities, including conservation in action, cookery demonstrations, family activities in the indoor

Why not share your pictures with us? #nationaltrust

The colonnaded Central Hall at Wallington, left, and exploring the Walled Garden, above

play space and Christmas events in December. **Outdoors** Enjoy heady fragrances in the Edwardian conservatory in the Walled Garden. Seasonal displays of snowdrops and crocuses. Choose from one of our many walks; there's miles and miles of footpaths and trails to explore. Family-friendly Dragon Cycle Trail, wildlife hide, adventure playground, play train and fort. Regular guided walks and family activities during school holidays. **Dogs**: welcome on leads outdoors and on all walks.

Access: 🅿️ 🅿️ ♿ 🚻 🅻 🎨 📷 🎵
House 🦽 🚶 ↕️ ♿
Garden and grounds 🦽 🚶 🚶 ➡️ 🚲 ♿
Parking: on site.

Find out more: 01670 773600 or wallington@nationaltrust.org.uk

Wallington		M	T	W	T	F	S	S
Walled Garden, woodland and estate*								
Open all year	10–6	M	T	W	T	F	S	S
House								
10 Feb–28 Oct	12–5	M	T	W	T	F	S	S
Shops and café**								
1 Jan–9 Feb	10:30–4:30	M	T	W	T	F	S	S
10 Feb–28 Oct	10:30–5:30	M	T	W	T	F	S	S
29 Oct–31 Dec	10:30–4:30	M	T	W	T	F	S	S

*Walled Garden: closes 7 in summer; 4 in winter. Woodland and estate: open 10 to dusk. **Shops and café: closed 24 to 26 December. Café: last orders 30 minutes before closing.

Washington Old Hall

The Avenue, Washington Village, Washington, Tyne & Wear NE38 7LE

🏠 ❄️ 🔔 🍽️ 1956

A little gem with a big story. This is the original medieval home of George Washington's ancestors: without Washington Old Hall the capital of the US wouldn't share the name. The small manor house overlooks tranquil gardens and a 'Nuttery' – a haven for wildlife and nature (and humans wanting quiet).

Eat, shop, stay: light refreshments available in the café – hot and cold drinks, cakes and scones. Small seating areas indoors and outside.

Things to see and do: **Indoors** 17th-century hall, Washington room, tenement rooms (the house was once split into cramped flats). Christmas events. **Outdoors** Wildlife-spotting, bird hide, beehives, play area, Fourth of July ceremony. Open-air theatre. **Dogs**: welcome on leads in garden only.

Access: 🅿️ 🚌 ♿ 🎨 🎵 🦽 📷 🚫
Building 🦽 🚶 Grounds 🦽 🚶 ➡️
Parking: on site (additional unrestricted parking on The Avenue).

Find out more: 0191 416 6879 or washingtonoldhall@nationaltrust.org.uk

Washington Old Hall		M	T	W	T	F	S	S
Hall and garden								
10 Feb–31 Mar	10–4	M	T	W	T	F	S	S
1 Apr–31 Oct	10–5	M	T	W	T	F	S	S
1 Nov–24 Dec	10–4	M	T	W	T	F	S	S
Café								
10 Feb–24 Dec	10–4	M	T	W	T	F	S	S

Geometric hedges at Washington Old Hall, Tyne & Wear

Cymru Wales

Sugar Loaf, Brecon Beacons, Powys
Competition entry from Suzannah Duggan

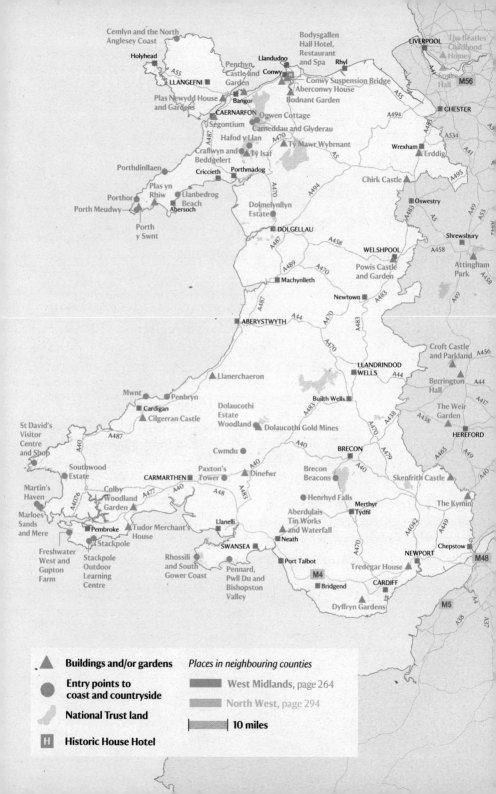

Cemlyn and the North
Anglesey Coast

Holyhead

LLANGEFNI

A55

Penrhyn
Castle and
Garden

Plas Newydd House
and Gardens

Bangor

CAERNARFON

Ségontium

Hafod y Llan

Crafnwyn and
Beddgelert

Ty Isaf

Porthdinllaen

Plas yn
Rhiw

Porthor

Porth Meudwy

Llanbedrog
Beach

Abersoch

Criccieth

Porthmadog

Porth
y Swnt

Bodysgallen
Hall Hotel,
Restaurant
and Spa

Llandudno

Conwy

Conwy Suspension Bridge

Aberconwy House

Bodnant Garden

Ogwen Cottage

Carneddau and Glyderau

Ty Mawr Wybrnant

Dolmelynllyn
Estate

DOLGELLAU

A487

A470

A494

A458

Machynlleth

A489

A470

Rhyl

LIVERPOOL

The Beatles'
Childhood
Homes

M56

Speke
Hall

CHESTER

A494

A534

A483

Wrexham

Erddig

A41

Chirk Castle

Oswestry

A483

A5

A49

A53

A483

Shrewsbury

A458

Attingham
Park

A458

WELSHPOOL

Powis Castle
and Garden

Newtown

A483

A49

A458

ABERYSTWYTH

A44

A470

A483

Croft Castle
and Parkland

A456

LLANDRINDOD
WELLS

A44

Berrington
Hall

A44

A417

The Weir
Garden

HEREFORD

Llanerchaeron

Mwnt

Penbryn

Cardigan

Cilgerran Castle

St David's
Visitor
Centre
and Shop

Southwood
Estate

Martin's
Haven

Marloes
Sands
and Mere

Pembroke

Freshwater
West and
Gupton
Farm

Stackpole

Stackpole
Outdoor
Learning
Centre

Colby
Woodland
Garden

Tudor Merchant's
House

A4076

A477

A487

A40

Builth Wells

Dolaucothi
Estate
Woodland

Dolaucothi Gold Mines

Cwmdu

Paxton's
Tower

Dinefwr

CARMARTHEN

A40

A48

A483

Llanelli

Rhossili
and South
Gower Coast

SWANSEA

Pennard,
Pwll Du and
Bishopston
Valley

Port Talbot

M4

Bridgend

Neath

A483

A40

BRECON

Brecon
Beacons

Henrhyd Falls

Aberdulais
Tin Works
and Waterfall

Merthyr
Tydfil

A465

A470

A479

A438

A438

Skenfrith Castle

A465

A49

A40

The Kymin

A4042

A449

Chepstow

Tredegar House

NEWPORT

M48

CARDIFF

Dyffryn Gardens

M5

A48

A38

A37

Aberconwy House

Castle Street, Conwy LL32 8AY

 1934

This is the only medieval merchant's house in Conwy to have survived the turbulent history of the walled town over seven centuries. Furnished rooms and helpful volunteers bring different periods in its history alive. **Note**: nearest toilets 50 yards. Steps to all parts of property.

Eat, shop, stay: gift shop.

Things to see and do: Easter events.
Dogs: assistance dogs only.

Access: Building
Parking: none on site.

Find out more: 01492 592246 or aberconwyhouse@nationaltrust.org.uk

Aberconwy House		M	T	W	T	F	S	S
House								
8 Mar–4 Nov	10–5	M	T	W	T	F	S	S
10 Nov–23 Dec	11–4						S	S
Shop								
2 Jan–28 Feb	11–5		T	W	T	F	S	S
1 Mar–31 Dec	10–5	M	T	W	T	F	S	S

House and shop: closed 25 December.

Aberconwy House, Conwy: seven centuries of turbulence

Aberdulais Tin Works and Waterfall

Aberdulais, Neath, Neath Port Talbot SA10 8EU

 1980

If you like archaeology, you'll love some of the secrets that have been uncovered here at Aberdulais – one of Britain's oldest tin works.

Aberdulais Tin Works and Waterfall, Neath Port Talbot

As you wander through the site, you'll find yourself at the very heart of the earliest industry in Britain. You'll also discover how Aberdulais played its part in shaping the world as we know it today. If you think you've seen Aberdulais before, think again – we've made new discoveries and we're dying to share them with you. We aim to enthral and fascinate all ages… Whoever thought history could be so much fun? **Note**: waterwheel and turbine subject to water levels and conservation work.

Eat, shop, stay: Old Schoolhouse tea-room serving light lunches, soup, cakes and refreshments. Gift shop and second-hand bookshop.

Picturesque Aberdulais Tin Works and Waterfall

Things to see and do: programme of activities throughout the year, including exhibitions, talks and tours as well as seasonal events such as Easter and Victorian Christmas.
Dogs: welcome on leads and inside buildings. Assistance dogs only in the Schoolhouse tea-room.

Access: 🅿️🅿️♿️♿️♿️♿️ **Grounds** ♿️♿️♿️➡️♿️
Stable and Tin Exhibition ♿️♿️♿️
Turbine House ♿️♿️♿️♿️♿️
Sat Nav: follow brown signs. **Parking**: 50 yards.

Find out more: 01639 636674 or aberdulais@nationaltrust.org.uk

Aberdulais		M	T	W	T	F	S	S
6 Jan–4 Feb	10:30–3	·	·	·	·	·	S	S
10 Feb–16 Feb	10:30–4	M	T	W	T	F	S	S
17 Feb–29 Mar	10:30–3	M	T	W	T	F	S	S
30 Mar–15 Apr	10–5	M	T	W	T	F	S	S
16 Apr–25 May	10:30–4	M	T	W	T	F	S	S
26 May–3 Jun	10–5	M	T	W	T	F	S	S
4 Jun–24 Jul	10:30–4	M	T	W	T	F	S	S
25 Jul–2 Sep	10–5	M	T	W	T	F	S	S
3 Sep–28 Oct	10:30–3	M	T	W	T	F	S	S
29 Oct–4 Nov	10:30–4	M	T	W	T	F	S	S
9 Nov–23 Dec	11–3	·	·	·	·	F	S	S

Tea-room: opening times vary (call for details).

Bodnant Garden

Tal-y-Cafn, near Colwyn Bay, Conwy LL28 5RE

🏠❄️🔔 1949

In Snowdonia's foothills this 32-hectare (80-acre) garden features scenery, plant collections and horticultural styles from formal to pastoral, and wild to exotic. One family's vision, the garden was established in 1874 by Victorian entrepreneur Henry Pochin, who transformed the landscape with rare trees and shrubs from around the world. Enjoy Italianate terraces with roses, herbaceous beds and parterres, shaded shrub borders and the drama of The Dell, with its waterfalls and towering conifers. Every season brings new delights – magnolias and rhododendrons in spring, roses and water lilies in summer, rich leaf colour in autumn and frosted landscapes in winter. You can also explore the Winter Garden, Old Park meadow, Yew Dell and Far End, plus Furnace Wood and Meadow.

Eat, shop, stay: two tea-rooms, as well as two open-air refreshment kiosks. Picnic areas. Shop. Neighbouring garden centre and craft units (not National Trust).

Things to see and do: events all year, including guided walks with a gardener, family trails and holiday activities for children. **Dogs**: welcome daily January to March, October to December. Also Wednesday evenings, April to September.

Access: 🅿️🐕♿️🚻🔄📷♿️ Grounds 🏛️➡️♿️
Parking: 150 yards. Electric vehicle charging point opposite café.

Find out more: 01492 650460 or bodnantgarden@nationaltrust.org.uk

From formal to pastoral and wild to exotic, there is a style to suit every taste at Bodnant Garden, Conwy. Clockwise from left, the Pin Mill, arboretum and satisfied visitors

Bodnant Garden		M	T	W	T	F	S	S
1 Jan–28 Feb	10–4	M	T	W	T	F	S	S
1 Mar–30 Apr*	10–5	M	T	W	T	F	S	S
1 May–30 Jun*	9–5	M	T	W	T	F	S	S
1 Jul–31 Oct*	10–5	M	T	W	T	F	S	S
1 Nov–31 Dec**	10–4	M	T	W	T	F	S	S

Pavilion tea-room: open from 9 daily. *Garden: open to 8 on Wednesdays, April to end September. **Garden and tea-room: closed 24 to 26 December.

Bodysgallen Hall Hotel, Restaurant and Spa

The Royal Welsh Way, Llandudno, Conwy LL30 1RS

🏠 ❄ 💪 ⛩ 🔆 ⊤ 2008

This Grade I listed 17th-century house, set within 89 hectares (220 acres) of parkland, has the most spectacular views towards Conwy Castle and Snowdonia. The romantic gardens, which have won awards for their restoration, include a rare parterre filled with sweet-smelling herbs, as well as several follies, a cascade, walled garden and formal rose gardens. Beyond, the hotel's parkland offers miles of stunning walks and views to the coastline. **Note**: access is for paying guests of the hotel, including for luncheon, afternoon tea and dinner, and the spa. Children over the age of six welcome.

Find out more: 01492 584466.
01492 582519 (fax) or info@bodysgallen.com
bodysgallen.com

Brecon Beacons

Powys

🏠 🏛 💪 1936

The Brecon Beacons, Sugar Loaf and Skirrid have captivated visitors for hundreds of years with their soaring mountain peaks and tranquil valleys. With lush farmland, ancient woodlands and southern Britain's highest mountain, Pen y Fan, they are perfect for hill-walking and exploring hidden streams and valleys. By contrast, Clytha Estate is a great place to have a picnic or take a short walk, meandering through parkland with views of Clytha House and Castle. In the heart of Wales you can discover the vast, remote moorlands of Abergwesyn Commons or ramble over the Begwns with panoramic views of the Brecon Beacons. **Note**: only toilets at Pont ar Daf car park in the Brecon Beacons (not National Trust).

For hundreds of years, the soaring peaks and tranquil valleys within the Brecon Beacons, Powys, left and above, have captivated visitors

Things to see and do: Indoors Bunkhouse near Pen y Fan. **Outdoors** Family activities during school holidays, including Wild Wednesdays at Sugar Loaf and Skirrid. Visit nearby Henrhyd Falls or Aberdulais Tin Works and Waterfall. **Dogs**: welcome on leads.

Access: 🦽
Sat Nav: use LD3 8NL. **Parking**: main car park at Pont ar Daf, off A470; alternatives not all National Trust.

Find out more: 01874 625515 or brecon@nationaltrust.org.uk

Carneddau and Glyderau

Nant Ffrancon, Bethesda, Gwynedd

[icons] 1951

This 8,498-hectare (21,000-acre) mountainous area includes Cwm Idwal National Nature Reserve, renowned for its geology and Arctic-Alpine plants, such as the rare Snowdon lily. There are eight tenanted upland farms here and nine peaks over 3,000 feet, including the famous Tryfan, where Edmund Hilary trained for his ascent of Everest. The area is home to a variety of wildlife, including otters, feral ponies and rare birds, such as dotterel and peregrine. The 60 miles of footpaths attract 500,000 walkers each year, while the bleak, photogenic landscapes have proved popular with artists.
Note: mountainous and difficult terrain – please come well equipped and check the weather. Charges apply in the National Park car parks.

Eat, shop, stay: Ogwen has a café and ranger base, as well as a warden centre run in partnership with Snowdonia National Park and Natural Resources Wales. There are two holiday cottages in Dyffryn Mymbyr, and one near Llyn Ogwen.

Things to see and do: you can walk to Cwm Idwal and enjoy dramatic mountain views, following in the footsteps of Charles Darwin (who 'discovered' glaciation here). Visit Ogwen ranger base for more information.
Dogs: on a lead at all times.

Access: [icon]
Sat Nav: use LL57 3LZ. **Parking**: at Ogwen Lake (not National Trust).

Find out more: 01248 605739 or carneddau@nationaltrust.org.uk

Carneddau and Glyderau, Gwynedd, above and below. The many miles of footpaths are irresistible to walkers of all ages

Cemlyn and the North Anglesey Coast

Cemaes Bay, Anglesey

✝ ⛪ 🏛 ♿ 🛏 🏔 👜 ➰ | 1971 |

Part of Anglesey's Area of Outstanding Natural Beauty, the north-west coast has a ruggedly beautiful coastline of rocks, small bays and headlands and is a delight for walkers. Cemlyn is a North Wales Wildlife Trust Nature Reserve and a Site of Special Scientific Interest. Renowned for its breeding colony of Sandwich, common and Arctic terns, Cemlyn Bay is a hive of seabird activity in spring and summer.

Headland paths offer dramatic land and seascapes during autumn and winter. The brackish lagoon is separated from the sea by a remarkable shingle ridge. **Note**: nearest toilets in Cemaes Bay, 3 miles (not National Trust).

Things to see and do: numerous footpaths and downloadable walks to help you explore. Events, including pram walks and walking festival. Summer fair at Swtan, a restored whitewashed cottage nearby (LL65 4EU). **Dogs**: welcome under control near livestock.

Access: 🦽
Sat Nav: use LL67 0DY.
Parking: at Bryn Aber car park, Cemlyn.

Find out more: 01248 714795 or cemlyn@nationaltrust.org.uk

Cemlyn and the North Anglesey Coast, Anglesey: with small bays and rocky headlands, this ruggedly beautiful coast is a delight for walkers

Chirk Castle

Chirk, Wrexham LL14 5AF

🏠🅿♿🐕🍴📷🛏🔔⛛ 1981

Completed by Marcher Lord Roger Mortimer in 1310, Chirk is the last Welsh castle from the reign of Edward I still inhabited today. You can explore medieval towers and dungeons, visit the 17th- and 18th-century rooms of the Myddelton family home, including the historic laundry, and discover the story of influential 20th-century tenant and polymath Lord Howard de Walden. The prized gardens contain clipped yews, herbaceous borders and rock gardens. A terrace gives stunning views over the Cheshire and Shropshire plains, while the large estate, divided by King Offa's Dyke, provides habitat for rare invertebrates, wild flowers and veteran trees.

Eat, shop, stay: café serving hot and cold food, drinks and cakes. Seasonal kiosk at Home Farm selling hot and cold drinks and snacks. Gift shops in Home Farm and courtyard, with plant sales and second-hand books. Two holiday cottages on the estate.

Things to see and do: Indoors Medieval fortress and dungeon, Myddelton family home, Servants' Hall and Victorian laundry to explore. **Outdoors** There are the formal gardens and a 194-hectare (480-acre) estate to discover. **Dogs**: welcome on leads. Assistance dogs only in formal gardens and Pleasure Ground wood.

Access: 🅿♿🖼🎧🔦📷📹🎨 ..:
State rooms 🦽🪜 **Adam Tower** 🦽🧗
Gardens 🦽🪜➡♿

Parking: at Home Farm by ticket office, 200 yards (steep hill) to castle. Two electric vehicle charging points at Home Farm.

Find out more: 01691 777701 or chirkcastle@nationaltrust.org.uk

Chirk Castle		M	T	W	T	F	S	S
Estate								
Open all year††	7–7	M	T	W	T	F	S	S
Garden, Adam's Tower, shop and café								
3 Feb–23 Mar	10–4	M	T	W	T	F	S	S
24 Mar–30 Sep	10–5	M	T	W	T	F	S	S
1 Oct–4 Nov	10–4	M	T	W	T	F	S	S
10 Nov–2 Dec	10–4						S	S
8 Dec–23 Dec	10–4	M	T	W	T	F	S	S
State rooms								
3 Feb–9 Mar*	10–4	M	T	W	T	F	S	S
10 Mar–23 Mar**	12–4	M	T	W	T	F	S	S
24 Mar–30 Sep**	12–5	M	T	W	T	F	S	S
1 Oct–4 Nov**	12–4	M	T	W	T	F	S	S
10 Nov–2 Dec†	12–4						S	S
8 Dec–23 Dec	11–4	M	T	W	T	F	S	S

*East wing only. **Guided tours: 11:15 and 11:30 (places limited). †Access by guided conservation tour only, timed tickets available on day (places limited). ††Estate open to 9, June to August.

Dating from 1310, Chirk Castle in Wrexham, above and below, is still inhabited today. As well as towers and dungeons, historic rooms and prized gardens to explore, there are so many stories to discover and views to enjoy

Cilgerran Castle

near Cardigan, Pembrokeshire SA43 2SF

 1938

13th-century castle overlooking the Teifi Gorge – the perfect location to repel attackers. Walk the walls and admire the stunning views. **Note**: in the guardianship of Cadw – Welsh Government's historic environment service. Dogs welcome on leads. Open daily, 2 January to 27 March, 10 to 4; 28 March to 31 October, 10 to 5; 1 November to 31 December, 10 to 4 (closed 24 to 26 December).

Find out more: 01239 621339 or cilgerrancastle@nationaltrust.org.uk

Colby Woodland Garden

near Amroth, Pembrokeshire SA67 8PP

 1980

A short walk from the beach, this hidden wooded valley, with its secret garden and industrial past, is a place for play. There are fallen trees to climb, rope swings and playful

Colby Woodland Garden, Pembrokeshire: this hidden wooded valley, above and below, is a place for play

surprises everywhere. Spring brings bluebells, camellias, rhododendrons and azaleas, while the walled garden gives year-round colour, peace and seclusion. There are woodland walks, meandering streams and ponds with stepping stones and log bridges in the wildflower meadow, and the whole valley teems with wildlife. Fun learning activities and exploration packs are available, and there are picnic and campfire spots in the meadow and free games to borrow. **Note**: house not open.

Eat, shop, stay: shop, plant sales and second-hand books. Bothy tea-room (concession). Picnics welcome. Three holiday cottages nearby.

Things to see and do: have fun with rope swings, pond-dipping and duck-racing. Children's exploration packs and games equipment available from the shop. Seasonal activities include Easter trails, wildlife walks and holiday events. **Dogs**: welcome on leads in woodland garden and meadow.

Access: ⓟ🅳🅴🏵🦽📷🎦📱🛗
Grounds 🏞➡🦽
Parking: 50 yards.

Find out more: 01834 811885 or colby@nationaltrust.org.uk

Colby Woodland Garden		M	T	W	T	F	S	S
Woodland and walled gardens*								
6 Jan–9 Feb	10–3	M	T	W	T	F	S	S
10 Feb–4 Nov	10–5	M	T	W	T	F	S	S
5 Nov–23 Dec	10–3	M	T	W	T	F	S	S
Shop								
10 Feb–4 Nov	10–5	M	T	W	T	F	S	S
Tea-room								
24 Mar–4 Nov	10–4:30	M	T	W	T	F	S	S

*Car park and bothy exhibition open as woodland and walled gardens. Closed 24 to 31 December.

Conwy Suspension Bridge

Conwy LL32 8LD

 1965

The tiny toll-keeper's cottage at Conwy Suspension Bridge, Conwy

Designed in the 1820s by Thomas Telford, this graceful bridge with its beautifully restored tiny toll-keeper's house has stunning views over the Conwy Estuary. Kept open by a husband and wife at a time when trade and travel brought Conwy to life, it never closed, whatever the weather. **Note**: sorry no toilet.

Eat, shop, stay: why not bring a picnic to enjoy on the grassed area?

Things to see and do: superb views of the river and castle. '50 things' activities for families and games. **Dogs**: allowed.

Access: Building 🏛 Grounds 🏞
Parking: none on site.

Find out more: 01492 573282 or conwybridge@nationaltrust.org.uk

Conwy Suspension Bridge
Open 8 March to 4 November. Toll House opening times available at Aberconwy House (01492 592246).

Craflwyn and Beddgelert

near Beddgelert, Gwynedd

 1994

The 81-hectare (200-acre) Craflwyn Estate is set in the heart of beautiful Snowdonia, within a landscape steeped in history and legend. There's a network of paths and woodland walks to explore and tumbling waterfalls to discover. At Craflwyn you can learn about the Princes of Gwynedd, before venturing up to nearby Dinas Emrys, legendary birthplace of the red dragon of Wales. Within a couple of miles of Craflwyn, there are great walks for all abilities – from a village stroll at pretty Beddgelert to the rugged Fisherman's Path down the spectacular Aberglaslyn Pass. **Note**: Craflwyn Hall is run and managed by HF Holidays (surrounding land open to the public).

Craflwyn and Beddgelert, Gwynedd, in Snowdonia

Eat, shop, stay: picnics welcome at Craflwyn. Local crafts on offer in Tŷ Isaf shop in Beddgelert. The village also has a selection of restaurants, cafés, taverns and hotels (not National Trust). Holiday cottage, chalet and campsite at Hafod y Llan.

Things to see and do: you can learn about Prince Llywelyn's legendary faithful hound by visiting Gelert's Grave. Children's adventure packs, maps and guides available from Tŷ Isaf shop in the centre of the village. **Dogs**: welcome, but on a lead near livestock.

Craflwyn and Beddgelert offers walks for all abilities

Access: 🔣
Sat Nav: use LL55 4NG. **Parking:** in Craflwyn.

Find out more: 01766 510120 or
craflwyn@nationaltrust.org.uk

Cwmdu

Llandeilo, Carmarthenshire

🔣🔣🔣 1991

Georgian terrace with pub, post office, chapel and vestry. Representing a rural Welsh village of the past. **Note:** pub and shop run by community. For Sat Nav use SA19 7DY. Shop and post office open Tuesday to Saturday, 2 January to 29 December, 9:30 to 1:30 (close 12:30 on Saturdays). Inn open Wednesday to Saturday, 3 January to 29 December, 7 to 11. Restaurant open selected Saturdays.

Find out more: 01558 685088 or
cwmdu@nationaltrust.org.uk

Dinefwr

Llandeilo, Carmarthenshire SA19 6RT

🔣🔣🔣🔣🔣🔣🔣🔣🔣🔣🔣🔣 1990

A place of legends and folklore, Dinefwr's long history has featured power, glory, downfall and loss. There is even a direct link with the past through our iconic White Park cattle, which have been kept here for 1,000 years. Walks lead through ancient woods, with gnarled veteran trees, and you can seek the inhabitants of the Bogwood and Mill Pond and walk in the footsteps of medieval princes – viewing 'your kingdom' from the castle on the hill. After exploring the tranquil countryside, you can continue your adventure in atmospheric Newton House, discovering the many changes the years have wrought. **Note:** Dinefwr Castle is owned by the Wildlife Trust and is in the guardianship of Cadw.

Eat, shop, stay: Billiard Tea-room (fully licensed). Castle Walk Café serving simple fare to parkland walkers (dogs welcome). Inner courtyard with a gift shop and plant sales. Pre-loved bookshop. Holiday cottages.

Places may occasionally close for events or bad weather

Things to see and do: **Indoors** Daily 'hidden house' tours. **Outdoors** Seasonal tours of parkland National Nature Reserve. Tractor trailer tours of estate and White Park cattle (summer). School holiday and family activities. **Dogs**: welcome in outer park on leads (cattle/sheep grazing). Not permitted in the deer-park.

Dinefwr, Carmarthenshire: Newton House, above and left, sits in the midst of ancient parkland

Access: 🅿️🅿️♿🦽🔊🖼️♨️🅰️ Castle 🦽🚶
Newton House 🦽♿⬆️🚶♿ Parkland 🦽🦽➡️
Sat Nav: enter Dinefwr. **Parking**: 50 yards. Electric vehicle charging point at Home Farm on 'The Granary'.

Find out more: 01558 824512 or dinefwr@nationaltrust.org.uk

Dinefwr		M	T	W	T	F	S	S
Parkland and tea-room*								
1 Jan–31 Mar	11–4	M	T	W	T	F	S	S
1 Apr–2 Nov	11–5†	M	T	W	T	F	S	S
3 Nov–31 Dec	11–4	M	T	W	T	F	S	S
Newton House and shop**								
6 Jan–30 Mar	11–4	·	·	·	·	F	S	S
31 Mar–4 Nov	11–6	M	T	W	T	F	S	S
9 Nov–30 Dec	11–4	·	·	·	·	F	S	S

*Boardwalk and deer-park: close one hour earlier. Newton House: last admission one hour before closing; house and shop open daily during school holidays. **Billiard Tea-room: last orders 30 minutes after last house admission; †Parkland: closes 6. Cadw manages Dinefwr Castle and may alter opening times. Everything closed 24 and 25 December.

Dolaucothi Estate Woodland

near Pumsaint, Llanwrda, Carmarthenshire

🏠🍴🏛️♿🅰️ 1944

Hours of woodland walks and a multi-user trail with route information in Dolaucothi Gold Mine visitor reception. **Note**: for Sat Nav use SA19 8US.

Find out more: 01558 650809 or dolaucothi@nationaltrust.org.uk

Dolaucothi Gold Mines

Pumsaint, Llanwrda, Carmarthenshire SA19 8US

🏠🍴🏛️♿🅰️ 1941

Hands-on at Dolaucothi Gold Mines, Carmarthenshire

Not your average National Trust visit, this hidden gem reveals the story of the quest for gold more than 2,000 years ago. You too can try your luck by panning for gold, and anything you find you keep. Or you can venture on an overground tour of the Roman archaeology, go underground to experience the harsh

Dolaucothi Gold Mines: an underground tour

conditions of Victorian times and listen to what 1930s miners had to say in their very own words about their final efforts to search for gold. Why not join us for the ultimate adventure and discover centuries of stories in just one day? **Note**: steep slopes, stout enclosed footwear essential. Minimum height 95cm, no carried children on underground tours. Caravan site adjacent; pitch charges (including members).

Eat, shop, stay: tea-room (concession) offering light refreshments. Shop specialising in Welsh gold jewellery and gifts. Dolaucothi Arms (tenant-run) offering food and accommodation. Picnic tables in the mine yard. Dolaucothi caravan and motor-home site adjacent.

Things to see and do: **Outdoors** Underground guided tours throughout the day and overground self-guided audio tour of Roman workings. 1930s machinery sheds. Children's trails. Walks around woodland estate.
Dogs: welcome on leads, although not on guided tours.

Access: 🅿️🅳♿🔼🔽🖊️🚶 Tea-rooms ♿
Machinery sheds ♿ Mine yard ♿ ➡️
Parking: on site; overflow car park opposite main entrance.

Find out more: 01558 650809 or dolaucothi@nationaltrust.org.uk

Dolaucothi Gold Mines		M	T	W	T	F	S	S
16 Mar–20 Jul	10:30–5	M	T	W	T	F	S	S
21 Jul–31 Aug	10–6	M	T	W	T	F	S	S
1 Sep–4 Nov	10:30–5	M	T	W	T	F	S	S

Shop: opens 11. Caravan site: open daily, dawn to dusk, 16 March to 4 November. Last tour leaves 90 minutes before closing.

Dolmelynllyn Estate

near Dolgellau, Gwynedd

🔲🔲🔲 1936

A 696-hectare (1,719-acre) estate, including woodland, two tenanted farms and Grade II-listed Dolmelynllyn Hall, with ornamental lake and parkland. Dinas Oleu, the first parcel of land donated to the Trust by Mrs Fanny Talbot in 1895, is a short (12-mile) drive away at Barmouth. **Note**: Dolmelynllyn Hall is a privately run hotel, not a pay-to-enter property.

Tumbling waterfall on the Dolmelynllyn Estate, Gwynedd

Eat, shop, stay: four holiday cottages nearby. Two National Trust-owned but tenanted hotels on the estate offering refreshments and light meals. Picnic site.

Things to see and do: you can explore the network of footpaths in the area – highlights include Rhaeadr Ddu waterfall, Cefn Coch gold mines and wildlife-rich oak woodlands.
Dogs: welcome on leads.

Access: ♿
Sat Nav: use LL40 2TF. **Parking**: on site.

Find out more: 01341 440238 or dolmelynllyn@nationaltrust.org.uk

Dyffryn Gardens

St Nicholas, Vale of Glamorgan CF5 6SU

🏛️ ❄️ 2013

A garden for all seasons, Dyffryn is celebrated for its botanical collection and is among the best in Wales. Meandering through the gardens, you will discover intimate garden rooms, formal lawns and an extensive arboretum. The reinstated glasshouse in the kitchen garden houses an impressive collection of rare cacti and orchids. Designed by the eminent landscape architect Thomas Mawson, the gardens are the early 20th-century vision of Reginald Cory. Standing at the heart of Dyffryn is a unique Victorian mansion. The Grade II* listed Dyffryn House is an ongoing conservation project and has been partly furnished, but with a difference. The house is used as a canvas to interpret the gardens and Cory family history.

Eat, shop, stay: Gardens Café nestled by the Nant Bran stream at reception and The Gallery café within the gardens, connected to Dyffryn House. A large portion of produce comes directly from the kitchen gardens. Shop selling plants and gifts.

The unique Victorian mansion, above and below, standing at the heart of Dyffryn Gardens in the Vale of Glamorgan, is used as a canvas to interpret the gardens and the history of the Cory family – who built the present house

Dyffryn Gardens: a herbaceous border at its prime in July

Things to see and do: network of garden rooms and champion trees in the arboretum to discover. Family events and play area. Tredegar House nearby. **Dogs**: welcome in gardens on short leads.

Access: 🅿️♿♿♿ House ♿🔼
Grounds ♿♿➡️♿♿
Parking: on site. Electric vehicle charging point in main car park beside play area.

Find out more: 02920 593328 or dyffryn@nationaltrust.org.uk

Dyffryn Gardens		M	T	W	T	F	S	S
Gardens, shop and café								
1 Jan–25 Feb	10–4	M	T	W	T	F	S	S
26 Feb–25 Mar	10–5	M	T	W	T	F	S	S
26 Mar–30 Sep	10–6	M	T	W	T	F	S	S
1 Oct–4 Nov	10–5	M	T	W	T	F	S	S
5 Nov–31 Dec*	10–4	M	T	W	T	F	S	S
House								
1 Jan–25 Feb	12–3:30	M	T	W	T	F	S	S
26 Feb–4 Nov	12–4	M	T	W	T	F	S	S
5 Nov–31 Dec*	12–3:30	M	T	W	T	F	S	S

Last entry to gardens: 60 minutes before site closes.
Gardens Café: 10 until 30 minutes before closing
(last food orders 3:30). *Closed 25 and 26 December.

Erddig

Wrexham LL13 0YT

🏠✝🏛️✳️🧺 1973

High above the winding Clywedog river, Erddig stands tall – an unexpected survivor. Bankruptcy and decline foretold Erddig's ruin, but the cherished home avoided the fate of many British country houses. Discover the story of a family's unique relationship with its servants, where saw and spade are as treasured as silver and silk. A large collection of servants' portraits and carefully preserved rooms capture their lives in the early 20th century. Upstairs is a treasure trove of fine furniture and textiles, while outdoors is a fully restored 18th-century garden. The landscape pleasure park, designed by William Emes, is a haven of peace and natural beauty. Discover the 'cup and saucer' cylindrical cascade or the earthworks of a Norman motte-and-bailey castle.

Eat, shop, stay: you can enjoy lunch in the Hayloft restaurant, light bites in the café and tea-garden, or fresh coffee in Wolf's Den on busy days. Don't forget to visit our second-hand bookshop and gift shop before leaving.

Things to see and do: Indoors Discover how generations of the Yorke family took an almost curatorial attitude to their possessions, bequeathing one of the largest, most diverse and fragile collections in the National Trust. **Outdoors** Year-long programme, including spring displays, atmospheric open-air theatre

evenings, Christmas and Easter trails, garden tours, orienteering and guided estate walks. Regular sporting activities on the estate include Nordic walking, beginner running groups and parkruns. Children can let off steam in the Wolf's Den natural play area and fly on the rope swing, climb the obstacles or enjoy building dens. **Dogs**: welcome in country park and tea-garden, but not house, garden, stables and play area.

Erddig in Wrexham: the house, above, contains a treasure trove of fine furniture and textiles, while the garden, below, has been fully restored to its 18th-century glory. Left, letting off steam

Access: 🅿️🚻♿️🚽🪑🏠📺🚗♿️
Building ♿️🏠 **Grounds** ♿️🏠♿️
Sat Nav: do not use, follow brown signs.
Parking: on site, 200 yards from ticket office. Electric vehicle charging point available in the car park.

Find out more: 01978 355314 or erddig@nationaltrust.org.uk

Erddig		M	T	W	T	F	S	S
House								
10 Feb–23 Mar*	11:30–2:30	M	T	W	T	F	S	S
24 Mar–26 Oct	12:30–3:30	M	T	W	T	F	S	S
27 Oct–31 Dec*	11:30–2:30	M	T	W	T	F	S	S
Garden, restaurant and shop**								
1 Jan–23 Mar	11–4	M	T	W	T	F	S	S
24 Mar–26 Oct	10–5	M	T	W	T	F	S	S
27 Oct–31 Dec	11–4	M	T	W	T	F	S	S

*Ground-floor servants' quarters only. Hourly tours weekdays and self-guided during school holidays and weekends.
**Natural play area open as garden, but closed weekdays, 2 January to 9 February. Closed 25 December. Timed tickets operate on Bank Holidays and during busy periods.

Freshwater West and Gupton Farm

Freshwater West and Gupton Farm,
Castlemartin, Pembrokeshire SA71 5HW

🏠🌲♿🏕🅰 1976

Things to see and do: uncover the story of this special place at our visitor information hub. Follow walking trails, go wildlife-watching and try watersports at the beach with a local activity provider (concession).
Dogs: welcome under close control.

Access: ♿🅰
Sat Nav: for Gupton Farm use SA71 5HW.
Parking: on site.

Find out more: 01646 661640 or freshwater@nationaltrust.org.uk

Freshwater West and Gupton Farm	M	T	W	T	F	S	S
Campsite							
27 Apr–30 Sep		M	T	W	T	F	S	S

Farmhouse open every day all year.

Freshwater West and Gupton Farm, Pembrokeshire

Freshwater West is a wild stretch of coast that's great for watersports and sandy adventures. Beyond the beach, discover Gupton Farm, our brand new campsite, farmhouse accommodation and visitor hub. A rustic escape for adventurous souls and nature lovers; go wildlife-watching, follow walking trails, make the most of the coast and sleep easy under the stars.

Eat, shop, stay: farmhouse accommodation and campsite at Gupton Farm; advanced booking advised, contact the farm for availability. Picnics welcome, seasonal catering also available at Freshwater West (concession).

Hafod y Llan

near Beddgelert, Gwynedd

🌲♿🛏🅰 1998

Hafod y Llan, in the beautiful Nantgwynant Valley, is the largest farm run by the National Trust, part of which is designated a National Nature Reserve and a Site of Special Scientific Interest. It extends from the valley floor to the summit of Snowdon and visitors are free to

Hafod y Llan in Gwynedd: the Trust's largest farm

Hafod y Llan: this unique landscape is open to all

wander the many paths which cross this unique landscape. **Note**: as this is a working farm, access to the farmyard is on foot only.

Eat, shop, stay: holiday cottage, chalet and campsite on the farm. Refreshments available at nearby Caffi Gwynant (not National Trust).

Things to see and do: a network of paths cross Hafod y Llan, including a low-level adventure trail. At the farm entrance the Watkin Path leads to the summit of Snowdon.
Dogs: welcome on leads.

Access: 🐾
Sat Nav: use LL55 4NQ. **Parking**: on farm for campsite only. Car park near farm entrance for the Watkin Path (not National Trust). Electric vehicle charging point available when staying at the campsite.

Find out more: 01766 890473 or hafodyllan@nationaltrust.org.uk

Henrhyd Falls

Coelbren, Powys

 1947

Henrhyd Falls, South Wales's highest waterfall, plunges 90 feet into the wooded Graig Llech Gorge – a haven for damp-loving wildlife. **Note**: steep descent into Graig Llech Gorge along uneven paths. Sorry no toilets.

Find out more: 01874 625515 or henrhydfalls@nationaltrust.org.uk

The Kymin

Monmouth, Monmouthshire NP25 3SF

🏠 👥 🔔 🍷 1902

Lord Nelson and Lady Hamilton were delighted with this Georgian banqueting house and Naval Temple when they visited in 1802. The Kymin is still a great spot from which to enjoy panoramic views of the Brecon Beacons and Wye Valley. The woods and pleasure grounds are also perfect for picnics. **Note**: access via steep winding single lane with passing places.

Eat, shop, stay: cold drinks and snacks available when the Round House is open. Picnics welcome.

Things to see and do: **Indoors** Our friendly guides offer a taste of a Georgian gentleman's picnic club. **Outdoors** Self-guided walks, featuring bluebells in spring. Children's nature quiz and special events throughout the year. **Dogs**: welcome in the Round House and grounds.

The Round House at The Kymin, Monmouthshire

Access: 🅿️ 🚻 🔺 Round House 🐾 ♿
Naval Temple ♿ Grounds ➡️
Parking: limited (narrow lane, single-lane traffic with passing places).

Find out more: 01600 719241 or kymin@nationaltrust.org.uk

The Kymin		M	T	W	T	F	S	S
Round House*								
31 Mar–29 Oct	11–4	M	·	·	·	·	S	S
Grounds								
Open all year	7–9	M	T	W	T	F	S	S

*Open Good Friday. Car park: open daylight hours only.

Llanbedrog Beach

Llanbedrog, Gwynedd

🏛 2000

Best known for its colourful beach huts, this wonderful stretch of sand has been enjoyed by generations. Its sheltered waters, fantastic views over Cardigan Bay and adjacent wooded and craggy landscape make this a real gem of Llŷn. **Note**: toilet (not National Trust).

Eat, shop, stay: shops and cafés at Llanbedrog and at nearby Pwllheli and Abersoch (not National Trust).

Things to see and do: events during summer months. Children's adventure packs, maps and guides available at second-hand bookshop. Beach huts available to hire. **Dogs**: welcome, but please be mindful of other beach users.

Access: 🧑‍🦽
Sat Nav: use LL53 7TT. **Parking**: on site. Electric vehicle charging point beside visitor welcome hut.

Find out more: 01758 740561 or llanbedrog@nationaltrust.org.uk

With its golden sands and sheltered waters, Llanbedrog Beach in Gwynedd, has been enjoyed by generations of families

Llanerchaeron

Ciliau Aeron, near Aberaeron,
Ceredigion SA48 8DG

🏛️🔥❄️⚒️🌳🍵 [1989]

A self-sufficient 18th-century Welsh minor gentry estate. The villa, designed in the 1790s, is the most complete example of the early work of John Nash. It has its own service courtyard with dairy, laundry, brewery and salting house, giving a full 'upstairs, downstairs' experience. The walled kitchen gardens, pleasure grounds, ornamental lake and parkland offer peaceful walks, while the Home Farm complex has an impressive range of traditional, atmospheric outbuildings. The working farm has Welsh Black cattle, Llanwenog sheep and rare Welsh pigs as well as chickens, geese and doves. Woodland walks available.

Eat, shop, stay: café serving light meals and cakes (not National Trust). Picnic site. Fresh garden produce and plants, farm meat, local crafts, art, gifts and books for sale. Second-hand bookshop. Two holiday cottages nearby.

Things to see and do: family activities during local school holidays, including the Servants' Trail, crafts, gardening, nature activities and self-led trails. Special events days. Cycle hire.

Dogs: welcome on the woodland walks and in the parkland on leads.

Access: 🅿️♿📷♿🦽📖📺♿🚻 Villa ♿🦽♿
Visitor building 🦽♿ Grounds 🦽➡️♿
Parking: 50 yards. Electric vehicle charging point in front of visitor reception/café.

Find out more: 01545 570200 or llanerchaeron@nationaltrust.org.uk

Llanerchaeron		M	T	W	T	F	S	S
Whole property								
17 Feb–25 Feb	11:30–3:30	M	T	W	T	F	S	S
17 Mar–4 Nov*	10:30–5:30	M	T	W	T	F	S	S
Farm and shop**								
6 Jan–11 Feb	11:30–3:30						S	S
26 Feb–16 Mar	11:30–3:30	M	T	W	T	F	S	S
5 Nov–31 Dec†	11:30–3:30	M	T	W	T	F	S	S

Last admission one hour before closing. *Villa: opens 11:30 and closes 4. **Garden: open as farm. †Closed 24 to 26 December. Geler Jones Rural Life Collection: open 12 to 4, Wednesday and Friday, 21 March to 2 November. Parkland and woodland walks: open daily.

Home Farm, above, at Llanerchaeron in Ceredigion, and the villa, below, designed by John Nash in the 1790s

Marloes Sands and Mere

Marloes, Pembrokeshire

1941

Marloes Sands and Mere, Pembrokeshire

A hidden gem, this long sandy stretch of coast is perfect for making a splash, spotting marine life on the shore and gorgeous walks. Just inland you'll find Marloes Mere, a wetland bustling with birdlife. Bring along the binoculars and get closer to nature at our on-site bird hides. **Note**: nearest toilets by Runwayskiln farm, alongside track from the car park to Marloes Mere.

Eat, shop, stay: information point at Martin's Haven. Tea-room at Runwayskiln (concession) and shop, café and pub in nearby Marloes village (not National Trust).

Things to see and do: for rock-pooling, birdwatching and getting closer to nature why not pick up a nature discovery Tracker Pack (available from the car park)? **Dogs**: welcome under close control.

Access:
Sat Nav: use SA62 3BH. **Parking**: on site.

Find out more: 01348 837860 or marloessands@nationaltrust.org.uk

Martin's Haven

near Marloes, Pembrokeshire

1981

The gateway to Skomer Island and a fabulously wild headland with fine panoramic views of St Bride's Bay. For a really varied and exciting day, why not combine spotting marine wildlife with discovering traces of ancient settlements? **Note**: nearest toilets by the slipway.

Eat, shop, stay: information point at Martin's Haven. Tea-room at Runwayskiln (concession) and shop, café and pub in nearby Marloes village (not National Trust).

Things to see and do: nature discovery Tracker Packs available from car park, for rock-pooling, birdwatching and getting closer to nature. **Dogs**: welcome under close control.

Martin's Haven in Pembrokeshire, right and below: perfect for beach-combing or wildlife-spotting

For other ways to get involved go to nationaltrust.org.uk/volunteer

mountaineering and adventure, a tradition we're maintaining by providing outdoor learning experiences on site in partnership with The Outward Bound Trust.

Eat, shop, stay: café. Maps and guides available at the Ogwen ranger base. Two holiday cottages at Dyffryn Mymbyr (7 miles), and one at Tal y Braich (3 miles).

Things to see and do: **Indoors** Visit the ranger base for advice about the area. **Outdoors** Range of rock-climbing and mountain-walking routes available, as well as the National Cycle Network's Lon Las Ogwen. **Dogs**: on leads only.

Access: ⓑ Ranger base ⓐ
Sat Nav: use LL57 3LZ. **Parking**: at Ogwen Lake (not National Trust).

Access: ⓑ ⓕ ➡
Sat Nav: use SA62 3BJ. **Parking**: on site.

Find out more: 01348 837860 or martinshaven@nationaltrust.org.uk

Mwnt

near Cardigan, Ceredigion

✝ ♨ ⋈ 1963

Beautiful secluded bay with a sandy beach – perfect for spotting dolphins, seals and other amazing wildlife. **Note**: small café and shop (not National Trust). Steep steps to beach. For Sat Nav use SA43 1QF.

Find out more: 01545 570200 or mwnt@nationaltrust.org.uk

Ogwen Cottage

Nant Ffrancon, Bethesda, Gwynedd LL57 3LZ

♨ 2014

Ogwen Cottage is nestled between the dramatic Carneddau and Glyderau mountain ranges, at the starting point for numerous walking routes in the area. It includes a base for our local ranger team and an information point for walkers exploring nearby Cwm Idwal, Tryfan, Y Glyderau and Y Carneddau. This iconic building has long been associated with

Long associated with adventure, Ogwen Cottage, Gwynedd, is the starting point for many walking routes

Find out more: 01248 605739 or ogwen@nationaltrust.org.uk

Ogwen Cottage		M	T	W	T	F	S	S
Café								
28 Mar–8 Apr	10–5			W	T	F	S	S
14 Apr–22 Jul	10–5						S	S
25 Jul–2 Sep	10–5			W	T	F	S	S
8 Sep–30 Sep	10–5						S	S

Opening times may vary (call for details).

Paxton's Tower

Llanarthne, near Dryslwyn, Carmarthenshire

 1965

Known as 'Golwg y Byd' (Eye of the World), Paxton's Tower is said to offer views of seven counties. **Note**: sorry no toilet. Nearest National Trust facilities at Dinefwr in Llandeilo. For Sat Nav use SA32 8HX.

Find out more: 01558 823902 or paxtonstower@nationaltrust.org.uk

Penbryn

near Sarnau, Cardigan, Ceredigion

 1967

One of Ceredigion's best-kept secrets, this beautifully secluded sandy cove lies down leafy lanes, edged with flower-covered banks. **Note**: café serving a selection of snacks and drinks (not National Trust). For Sat Nav use SA44 6QL. Electric vehicle charging point. Open daily, Easter weekend to end October (weekends only during winter).

Find out more: 01545 570200 or penbryn@nationaltrust.org.uk

Pennard, Pwll Du and Bishopston Valley

near Southgate, Swansea

 1954

Spectacular cliffs, caves where mammoth remains have been found, rare birds, an underground river, bat roosts, silver-lead mining, ancient woodland, smuggling and limestone quarrying are just a few of the wonders of this area. There are also numerous archaeological features and two important caves – Bacon Hole and Minchin Hole. **Note**: due to dangerous rip tides, swimming in Three Cliffs Bay is not advised.

Eat, shop, stay: coffee shop, village stores, tea-rooms and a pub in Pennard (none National Trust). Picnics welcome.

Things to see and do: Pennard provides a great starting point for a variety of walks, on which you can enjoy wild flowers and spot rare birds, such as choughs and Dartford warblers. **Dogs**: welcome, but please be aware livestock graze freely across Pennard Burrows.

Pennard, Pwll Du and Bishopston Valley, Swansea: Pennard Cliffs

Access: 🅿️
Sat Nav: use SA3 2DH.
Parking: at Southgate car park.

Find out more: 01792 390636 or pennard@nationaltrust.org.uk

Penrhyn Castle and Garden

Bangor, Gwynedd LL57 4HT

 1951

Penrhyn Castle is a vast neo-Norman castle with many different stories to tell. Extensive grounds and parkland include a Victorian walled garden, industrial Railway Museum and large Victorian kitchens. However, the castle's dominating stone façade hides more than just its internal red-brick construction. The unique architecture and opulent interiors sit alongside a darker history of slavery and a bitter industrial dispute that changed Penrhyn's relationship with the local community for ever. Over the coming years Penrhyn will be exploring these difficult stories and presenting them in new and exciting ways. **Note**: during this period of change, opening arrangements and tour availability may vary.

Eat, shop, stay: enjoy hot meals in the castle café or a lighter bite in the Stables. Browse through a range of National Trust and local products in our shop and find a bargain in our second-hand bookshop.

Things to see and do: **Indoors** Climb aboard an engine in the Railway Museum or see what life was like in the Victorian kitchens.

Outdoors Find peace in Walter Speed's famous walled garden. **Dogs**: welcome on leads in grounds. Assistance dogs only in the castle and walled garden.

Access: 🅿️🅳♿🚻♿🦽🖐️🖼️🅰️Ⓓ
Castle ♿♿♿ **Stable block** ♿♿ **Grounds** ♿♿
Parking: 500 yards. Electric vehicle charging point in main car park, just below visitor reception.

Find out more: 01248 353084 or penrhyncastle@nationaltrust.org.uk

Penrhyn Castle and Garden		M	T	W	T	F	S	S
Castle								
3 Mar–4 Nov†	12–5	M	T	W	T	F	S	S
1 Dec–16 Dec	11–4						S	S
Garden, parkland and Railway Museum								
1 Jan–9 Feb*	11–3	M	T	W	T	F	S	S
10 Feb–4 Nov	10:30–5	M	T	W	T	F	S	S
5 Nov–31 Dec**	11–3	M	T	W	T	F	S	S
Victorian kitchens, café and shop								
10 Feb–4 Nov	10:30–5	M	T	W	T	F	S	S
10 Nov–30 Dec	11–3						S	S

†Tours: daily, 10:30 to 12. *Excludes Railway Museum.
**Railway Museum open weekends only. Closed 25 December.

Penrhyn Castle and Garden, Gwynedd, above and below. Behind the castle's dominating stone façade and grand interiors, lies a dark history of slavery and bitter industrial dispute – difficult stories which visitors can explore over the coming years

Plas Newydd House and Gardens, Anglesey. Visitors enjoy the splendours of the Gothic hall, below, while outside, above, the house enjoys breathtaking views of Snowdonia from its fabulous position on the Menai Strait

Plas Newydd House and Gardens

Llanfairpwll, Anglesey LL61 6DQ

🏛️🏚️🍴🥤🎨 1976

The ancestral home of the Marquess of Anglesey sits majestically on the shores of the Menai Strait, enjoying breathtaking views of Snowdonia. The surrounding gardens are great for exploring and include an Australasian arboretum, Italianate terrace garden and extensive woodland walks. There's plenty for little explorers too, including a hand-built tree house, nine-hole Frisbee™ golf course, and adventure playground – you might even meet one of the resident red squirrels! This family home houses a Waterloo-inspired military museum, works of art, regular exhibitions and, at its heart, Rex Whistler's famous 58-foot fantasy landscape painting. **Note**: due to major reservicing works, opening arrangements and tour availability may vary.

Eat, shop, stay: the Mansion café serves hot and cold lunches. Light bites and cakes available from the Old Dairy and local ice-cream from the Sun Room. The Old Dairy Shop, Siop Newydd and second-hand bookshop are the perfect place for gifts.

Things to see and do: **Indoors** Learn about family life at Plas Newydd and the secrets behind Rex Whistler's masterpiece.
Outdoors Enjoy regular walks and talks with the gardeners and a full calendar of events.
Dogs: welcome on short leads. Assistance dogs only in the mansion and terraced gardens.

Access: 🅿♿🚻♿🚹♿📷📹:👓🖐
Building 🔸♿🔹 Grounds 🔹➡️
Parking: 400 yards from main entrance. Electric vehicle charging point in upper staff car park, beside the north wing.

Find out more: 01248 714795 or plasnewydd@nationaltrust.org.uk

Plas Newydd		M	T	W	T	F	S	S
Mansion								
10 Feb–4 Nov	11–4:30	M	T	W	T	F	S	S
Gardens, shop and café								
6 Jan–4 Feb	11–3	·	·	·	·	·	S	S
10 Feb–4 Nov	10:30–5	M	T	W	T	F	S	S
5 Nov–30 Dec	11–3	M	T	W	T	F	S	S

Opening times may vary due to major reservicing project (please call for updated times). Rhododendron garden at best April to June. Coronation Meadow open May to August. Everything closed 25 to 28 December.

Plas yn Rhiw

Rhiw, Pwllheli, Gwynedd LL53 8AB

 1952

Beautiful 16th-century Plas yn Rhiw in Gwynedd

Nestled on a hillside overlooking Cardigan Bay, Plas yn Rhiw is a beautiful 16th-century manor house with Georgian additions. The house was rescued from neglect and lovingly restored by the three Keating sisters, who bought the property in 1938. The views from the grounds and gardens across the bay are among the most spectacular in Britain. The garden contains many beautiful flowering trees and shrubs, with beds framed by box hedges and grass paths – a real joy to explore and stunning whatever the season.

Eat, shop, stay: tea-room serving a selection of fresh sandwiches, soup, cakes, drinks and ice-cream; picnics also available to take out. Shop selling gifts, plants, books and prints of Honora Keating's landscape watercolours. Three holiday cottages within walking distance.

Things to see and do: Indoors Virtual tour available on iPad and guided tours available by arrangement. **Outdoors** Woodland walks and a native-apple orchard. **Dogs**: on woodland walk below shop only (on leads).

Access: ⬚⬚⬚⬚⬚⬚
Building ⬚⬚ **Grounds** ⬚⬚
Parking: 100 yards (narrow lanes). Electric vehicle charging point in top car park beside tea-room.

Find out more: 01758 780219 or plasynrhiw@nationaltrust.org.uk

Plas yn Rhiw		M	T	W	T	F	S	S
22 Mar–30 Sep	11–5*	M	T	W	T	F	S	S
1 Oct–4 Nov	11–4*	M		W	T	F	S	S

*House: opens 12.

Porth Meudwy

near Aberdaron, Gwynedd

 1990

Nowhere expresses the essence of the area better than this sheltered cove on the wild and rocky coastline west of Aberdaron. It was from here that the pilgrims set out to Ynys Enlli (Bardsey Island). Today fishermen still bring the daily catch into the cove. Don't miss the unique Aberdaron boats: small wooden beach boats

The fishing cove of Porth Meudwy, Gwynedd

designed to dance nimbly through the waves along the craggy coastline. **Note**: sorry no toilet.

Eat, shop, stay: shops, pubs and cafés in Aberdaron village (not National Trust). Four holiday apartments in Aberdaron.

Things to see and do: the Wales Coast Path – a birdwatchers' paradise – runs dramatically along the clifftop. **Dogs**: welcome, but please be mindful of other beach users.

Access: 🦽
Sat Nav: use LL53 8DA. **Parking**: ½ mile.

Find out more: 01758 760469 or porthmeudwy@nationaltrust.org.uk

Porth y Swnt

Henfaes, Aberdaron, Pwllheli, Gwynedd LL53 8BE

♿ 🏛 🏠 2010

This exciting interpretation centre, at the heart of the beautiful fishing village of Aberdaron, shines a light on Llŷn's unique culture, heritage and environment. You can experience the Bardsey Island lighthouse's retired optic up close, follow in the footsteps of pilgrims on a journey across the Sound in the video pod, catch up on what Llŷn's rangers are up to and form your reflective thoughts in the Sea of Words.

Eat, shop, stay: gift shop in visitor centre. Cafés, pubs and convenience stores in village (not National Trust). Henfaes holiday apartments (Meudwy, Enlli, Daron and Hywyn) are located at the centre of Aberdaron.

Things to see and do: **Indoors** Audio guide, children's scrapbooks, events during school holidays. **Outdoors** Walks and access to the Wales Coast Path. Adventure packs, beach fun days, seafood festival, guided walks and cycle rides. **Dogs**: beach access restricted during summer.

Access: 🅿 📷 🔊 ♿ Car park 🦽🦽
Parking: on site. Electric vehicle charging point behind visitor centre.

Find out more: 01758 703810 or porthyswnt@nationaltrust.org.uk

Porth y Swnt		M	T	W	T	F	S	S
2 Jan–31 Mar*	10–4	M	T	W	T	F	S	S
1 Apr–30 Jun	10–5	M	T	W	T	F	S	S
1 Jul–31 Aug	10–6	M	T	W	T	F	S	S
1 Sep–30 Sep	10–5	M	T	W	T	F	S	S
1 Oct–31 Dec**	10–4	M	T	W	T	F	S	S

*Closed 1 and 23 to 29 January. **Closed 24 to 26 December.

Exploring The Light at Porth y Swnt, Gwynedd: an exciting interpretation centre

Porthdinllaen

Morfa Nefyn, Gwynedd

🏛️ 🏖️ 1994

An old fishing village perched on the end of a thin ribbon of land stretching into the Irish Sea, with its clear sheltered waters lapping against stout stone houses, Porthdinllaen really is a jewel. You can watch fishermen bring in the daily catch, while relaxing with a drink at the Tŷ Coch Inn. In the summer you can view the ecologically rich seagrasses from a paddle board – and have fun trying to stand up. **Note**: nearest toilet in village, which can only be reached by foot. Steps down to beach.

Eat, shop, stay: two holiday cottages available in the heart of the village. Refreshments available at our tenanted pub, Tŷ Coch Inn.

Things to see and do: events during summer for all the family. Wonderful walking on the coastal path – maps and guides available at car park welcome cabin. **Dogs**: welcome, but please be mindful of other beach users.

Access: 🚻 ♿

Sat Nav: use LL53 6DA. **Parking**: on site for beach; 1 mile from village (no vehicular access to village). Electric vehicle charging point in Trust car park, beside visitor welcome hut.

Find out more: 01758 760469 or porthdinllaen@nationaltrust.org.uk

The old fishing village of Porthdinllaen, Gwynedd, above, boasts a perfect sandy beach, below

Wales

Porthor

Aberdaron, Gwynedd

[icons] 1981

Glistening clear waters and fine sands make Porthor, Gwynedd, a favourite of surfers and sandcastle builders

This wonderful beach is famous for its 'whistling sands' and glistening waters. The whistling happens because of the especially fine sand grains on the beach – perfect for building sandcastles. If the joys of sandcastles and sunbathing are not enough for you, then why not have a go at surfing? The sea here is perfect. In addition, the Wales Coast Path runs in both directions from the car park.
Note: nearest toilet in car park. Please remember to scan your membership card.

Eat, shop, stay: National Trust tenanted beachside café and shop offering everything from lunch to sun cream. Four holiday apartments in Aberdaron.

Things to see and do: famous beach and glorious clifftop coast path to explore. Children's adventure pack available from car park. **Dogs**: seasonal restrictions on beach apply from 1 April to 30 September.

Access: [icons]
Sat Nav: use LL53 8LG. **Parking**: on site. Electric vehicle charging point.

Find out more: 01758 760469 or porthor@nationaltrust.org.uk

Powis Castle and Garden

Welshpool, Powys SY21 8RF

[icons] 1952

The Herbert family spent more than 400 years transforming a medieval fortress into the comfortable family home you see today. Furnished with sumptuous fabrics and exquisite works of art from around the world, the interior reflects the Elizabethan to Edwardian periods. The UK's largest private collection of Indian treasures is housed in the Clive Museum. From weaponry to a gold bejewelled tiger's head, the collection is unique. The world-renowned gardens are an eclectic mix of Italianate terraces filled with herbaceous borders, a formal garden with clipped yews and a woodland area which boasts a number of champion trees.

Powis Castle and Garden, Powys: once a medieval fortress, the castle is now a comfortable family home

Eat, shop, stay: restaurant (licensed) and garden tea-room. Gift shop and plant sales. Holiday cottage, The Bothy, is located in the heart of the garden.

Things to see and do: Indoors Themed castle tours, daily introductory talks (May to September). Family trails. **Outdoors** Garden themed tours. Daily talks. Family trails. Additional children's activities during school holidays. Seasonal events all year.
Dogs: assistance dogs only.

Access: [icons]
Building [icon] **Grounds** [icons]
Sat Nav: postcode misdirects, enter Powis Castle. **Parking**: on site. Electric vehicle charging point in car park.

Find out more: 01938 551920 or powiscastle@nationaltrust.org.uk

Powis Castle and Garden		M	T	W	T	F	S	S
1 Jan–25 Mar*	11–4†	M	T	W	T	F	S	S
26 Mar–30 Sep*	11–5**	M	T	W	T	F	S	S
1 Oct–31 Dec*	11–4†	M	T	W	T	F	S	S

*Garden and restaurant: open daily from 10. **Garden: open until 6. Garden tea-room (opening times vary) and garden shop open. †Reduced catering offer in January and February. Closed 25 December.

Rhossili and South Gower Coast

Coastguard Cottages, Rhossili, Gower, Swansea SA3 1PR

[icons] 1933

A family discovers the many delights of Rhossili and South Gower Coast, Swansea

Perched on the clifftop overlooking the spectacular Rhossili Bay (Britain's best beach: Trip Advisor Travellers' Choice Awards 2013 and 2014), Rhossili Shop and Visitor Centre offers everything you need to enjoy beautiful Gower, from local information and advice, to tempting treats and gifts to remember your day. **Note**: Worm's Head island access restricted March to August. Very steep steps and slope to beach.

Eat, shop, stay: self-service refreshments and Swansea's famous Joe's ice-cream available all year. Three National Trust holiday cottages nearby.

Rhossili Bay: twice voted Britain's Best Beach

Things to see and do: visitor information and advice on tides, local beaches, access, facilities and walks available. Free family activities throughout the year. **Dogs**: welcome (on leads near livestock please). Beach is dog-friendly all year.

Access: 🅿️🚾♿️♿️📶♿️📷
Visitor Centre ♿️ Grounds ♿️ ➡️
Parking: large pay and display car park at end of village. Suitable for motorhomes (no overnight stays).

Find out more: 01792 390707 or rhossili@nationaltrust.org.uk

Rhossili and Gower		M	T	W	T	F	S	S
Shop								
2 Jan–16 Feb	10:30–4	M	T	W	T	F	S	S
17 Feb–29 Mar	10:30–4:30	M	T	W	T	F	S	S
30 Mar–2 Sep*	10–5	M	T	W	T	F	S	S
3 Sep–4 Nov	10:30–4:30	M	T	W	T	F	S	S
5 Nov–23 Dec	10:30–4	M	T	W	T	F	S	S
27 Dec–31 Dec	11–4	M	·	·	T	F	S	S

Car park: open 24 hours. *Shop: open to 6, August weekends.

St David's Visitor Centre and Shop

Captain's House, High Street, St David's, Pembrokeshire SA62 6SD

🏠 📷 1974

Overlooking the Celtic Old Cross in the centre of St David's, Wales's smallest historic city, the visitor centre and well-stocked shop is open all year. For a complete guide to the National Trust in Pembrokeshire, visitors can take a tour of our special places, beaches and walks using interactive technology. **Note**: sorry no toilet.

Eat, shop, stay: books, cards, maps, wide range of gifts and local produce. Walks leaflets available. Holiday cottages nearby.

Things to see and do: visitor information and advice about Pembrokeshire's special places; speak to the team about access, facilities and walks. St David's Head, Porth Clais, Solva and Abereiddi nearby.

Access: Building ♿️
Parking: none on site.

Find out more: 01437 720385 or stdavidsshop@nationaltrust.org.uk

St David's Visitor Centre		M	T	W	T	F	S	S
2 Jan–17 Mar	9–4	M	T	W	T	F	S	·
19 Mar–31 Dec	9–5*	M	T	W	T	F	S	S

*Open 10 to 4 on Sundays. Closed 25, 26 December and 1 January 2019.

From the high point on St David's Peninsula, Pembrokeshire

Why not share your pictures with us? #nationaltrust

Segontium

Caernarfon, Gwynedd

 1937

Fort built to defend the Roman Empire against rebellious tribes. **Note**: in the guardianship of Cadw – Welsh Government's historic environment service. Museum not National Trust. For Sat Nav use LL55 2LN. For opening arrangements, please contact Cadw on 01443 336000.

Find out more: 01443 336000 or segontium@nationaltrust.org.uk

Skenfrith Castle

Skenfrith, near Abergavenny, Monmouthshire NP7 8UH

1936

Remains of early 13th-century castle, built beside the River Monnow to command one of the main routes from England. **Note**: in the guardianship of Cadw – Welsh Government's historic environment service. Open every day all year.

Find out more: 01874 625515 or skenfrithcastle@nationaltrust.org.uk

Southwood Estate

Newgale, Roch, Pembrokeshire

2003

A timeless landscape of wooded valleys, floral fields and craggy cliffs, the Southwood Estate is full of scenic surprises. Follow the waymarked walking trails and explore the best of coast and countryside; spot flora and fauna and see how we're working hard to safeguard this special place.

Exploring the Southwood Estate, Pembrokeshire

Eat, shop, stay: shop, café and pub in nearby Newgale and Roch (not National Trust). St David's Visitor Centre and Shop nearby. Bed and breakfast at Southwood Farm (concession).

Things to see and do: walking trails and seasonal programme, including guided walks, talks, craft fair and children's holiday activities. Information points at Southwood Farm and Maidenhall car parks. Shearing shed exhibition telling Southwood's story. **Dogs**: welcome under close control.

Access:
Sat Nav: for Maidenhall car park use SA62 6BD; Southwood Farm car park use SA62 6AR. **Parking**: on site.

Find out more: 01348 837860 or southwoodestate@nationaltrust.org.uk

Stackpole

near Pembroke, Pembrokeshire

🏠🏛️✳️🐾🚡🎣🛏️🍽️ 1976

The coastline at Stackpole in Pembrokeshire

A former grand estate stretching down to some of the most beautiful coastline in the world, including Broad Haven South, Barafundle Bay and Stackpole Quay. Today, Stackpole is a National Nature Reserve, recognised for its abundant flora and fauna, while Bosherston Lakes are famous for their superb display of lilies and resident otters, and the dramatic cliffs of Stackpole Head are great for wildlife watching. You can uncover the history and heritage of this special place too; the former Stackpole Court site and nearby Lodge Park Woods reveal the story behind the magnificent designed landscape.

Eat, shop, stay: The Boathouse tea-room at Stackpole Quay offers hot and cold drinks, light lunches, sandwiches and a selection of cakes and cream teas. Stay longer at Stackpole's holiday cottages, the Outdoor Learning Centre or nearby Gupton Farm campsite and farmhouse.

Things to see and do: guided kayaking and coasteering. Wildlife walks and talks. Coarse fishing (close season 15 March to 15 June). Family events, from fun runs and beach activity days, to bushcraft with rangers. **Dogs**: under close control on the estate.

Access: 🅿️♿🚻📷 Building 🏘️ Grounds 🏘️➡️
Sat Nav: for Stackpole Quay use SA71 5LS;

Broad Haven South SA71 5DR; Bosherston Lakes SA71 5DR; Stackpole Court SA71 5DE. **Parking**: car parks at Stackpole Quay, Broad Haven South, Bosherston Lakes and Stackpole Court. Electric vehicle charging point at Stackpole Outdoor Learning Centre (SA71 5DQ).

Find out more: 01646 623110 or stackpole@nationaltrust.org.uk

Stackpole		M	T	W	T	F	S	S
Estate								
Open all year	Dawn–dusk	M	T	W	T	F	S	S
Boathouse tea-room								
17 Feb–25 Feb	10–5	M	T	W	T	F	S	S
26 Feb–29 Mar*	11–4	M	T	W	T	F	S	S
30 Mar–30 Sep	10–5	M	T	W	T	F	S	S
1 Oct–4 Nov*	11–4	M	T	W	T	F	S	S
10 Nov–25 Nov*	11–4						S	S
26 Dec–30 Dec*	11–4			W	T	F	S	S

*Reduced catering offer.

Stackpole Outdoor Learning Centre

Old Home Farm Yard, Stackpole, near Pembroke, Pembrokeshire SA71 5DQ

🏠🏛️🐾🚡🎣🛏️🔔🍽️ 1976

Located in the heart of the Stackpole Estate, our eco-award-winning centre provides residents with easy access to Bosherston Lakes, Stackpole Quay and award-winning beaches –

including Barafundle and Broad Haven South – as well as the historic site of Stackpole Court. The recently refurbished centre can house up to 140 guests and offers flexible accommodation with modern facilities, including a theatre, meeting and classroom space. It is ideal for groups, corporate clients, celebrations, family holidays and couples' getaways. **Note**: contact the centre for activity programmes, prices and availability.

Eat, shop, stay: self-catering or chef-catered options. Meals provided by experienced in-house National Trust catering team. Full entertainment licence for events with bar. Residents' barbecue area. Shop and information hub. Single and double rooms, farmhouse accommodation and new campsite at nearby Gupton Farm.

Things to see and do: events, including rock-pool rambles, bushcraft, guided walks, open-air theatre and concerts. Explore the area from an alternative angle with our kayaking and coasteering guided tours. **Dogs**: assistance dogs only.

Access: ⓟⓖⓚⓛⓙ
Parking: free for guests. Electric vehicle charging point.

Find out more: 01646 623110 or stackpoleoutdoorlearning@nationaltrust.org.uk

Stackpole Outdoor Centre
Open every day all year

Please contact the centre for more information on residential group bookings, courses and activities.

Stackpole Outdoor Learning Centre, Pembrokeshire

Tredegar House

Newport NP10 8YW

🏠❄️🚸🔔 2012

Tredegar House, Newport: tranquil retreat

Tredegar House is a striking example of Restoration-era design, cherished as a tranquil retreat away from the city of Newport. The bold architecture, sumptuous decoration, contrasting formal gardens and sprawling parkland are a grand statement of the Morgan family's flamboyance and theatricality. With tales of riotous parties, dark arts, war heroism and animal menageries, the Morgan household was certainly no ordinary one. In the grounds, the three formal gardens provide a place to reflect and relax, while the 36-hectare (90-acre) parkland offers woodland and wildlife just waiting to be explored.

Eat, shop, stay: tea-room serving light lunches, homemade cakes and hot drinks. Renovated shop selling souvenirs, books, gifts and plants.

Things to see and do: Indoors Yearly programme of events and activities. **Outdoors** Lakeside walks, formal gardens and natural play area. Dyffryn Gardens nearby. **Dogs**: welcome in the parkland, formal gardens and tea-room.

Access: 🅿♿🚾🚼📷📖🔄
House 🏠 Reception 🔄 Grounds 🏞🏞
Parking: on site.

Find out more: 01633 815880 or
tredegar@nationaltrust.org.uk

Tredegar House		M	T	W	T	F	S	S
House and gardens*								
10 Feb–29 Mar	11–4	M	T	W	T	F	S	S
30 Mar–30 Sep	11–5	M	T	W	T	F	S	S
1 Oct–4 Nov	11–4	M	T	W	T	F	S	S
Tea-room and shop								
6 Jan–4 Feb	10–3	.	.	.	.	.	S	S
10 Feb–29 Mar	10–4	M	T	W	T	F	S	S
30 Mar–30 Sep	10–5	M	T	W	T	F	S	S
1 Oct–4 Nov	10–4	M	T	W	T	F	S	S
7 Nov–16 Dec	10–3	.	.	W	T	F	S	S
Park								
Open all year	Dawn–dusk	M	T	W	T	F	S	S

*Gardens: open from 10:30. Last entry one hour before
closing. Christmas opening times available, check
before visiting.

Tudor Merchant's House

Quay Hill, Tenby, Pembrokeshire SA70 7BX

🏛 1937

Over 500 years ago when Tenby was a busy
trading port, a merchant built this three-storey
house to live in and trade from. Today, the
house and shop have been furnished with
exquisitely carved replicas and brightly
coloured wall-hangings which re-create
the atmosphere of life in Tudor Tenby.
Note: sorry no toilet.

Tudor Merchant's House in Tenby, Pembrokeshire

Eat, shop, stay: shop range includes specially
made Tudor-style pottery (design based
on finds at the house), pewterware, horn
cups, glass, beeswax candles and books
about the Tudors.

Things to see and do: you can lay the high
table, see the wall-paintings, try on traditional
costumes and play with replica toys, Tudor
Family Fortunes and superstitions scrolls.
Easter, Hallowe'en and Tudor-themed family
events. **Dogs:** assistance dogs only.

Access: 📷📖🔄 Building 🏠
Parking: very limited on-street parking. Several
pay-and-display car parks, not National Trust
(charge including members).

Find out more: 01834 842279 or
tudormerchantshouse@nationaltrust.org.uk

Tudor Merchant's House		M	T	W	T	F	S	S
12 Feb–25 Feb	11–3	M	T	W	T	F	S	S
3 Mar–25 Mar	11–3	.	.	.	.	.	S	S
26 Mar–21 Jul	11–5	M	.	W	T	F	S	S
22 Jul–3 Sep	11–5	M	T	W	T	F	S	S
5 Sep–4 Nov*	11–5	M	.	W	T	F	S	S
10 Nov–23 Dec	11–3	.	.	.	.	.	S	S

Open Tuesdays in Bank Holiday weeks, 11 to 5.
*Closed Tuesdays, except 30 October.

Tŷ Isaf

Beddgelert, Gwynedd LL55 4YA

🏛♿ 1985

Brimming with character, Tŷ Isaf lies in the very
heart of Beddgelert. Dating back to the late
17th century, this Grade II listed building is the
oldest property in the village and has fulfilled
many roles over the centuries – from tavern to
farmhouse and, now, shop.

Eat, shop, stay: fantastic range of local
produce and crafts, alongside National Trust
products, for sale. Second-hand books and
gallery upstairs.

Things to see and do: free family adventure
packs. Go for a ramble beside the river and see
how many activities you can complete.

Tŷ Isaf, Gwynedd: tavern, then farmhouse, now shop

Access:
Parking: car parks in village, not National Trust (charge including members).

Find out more: tyisaf@nationaltrust.org.uk

Tŷ Isaf		M	T	W	T	F	S	S
24 Mar–2 Nov	11–5	M	T	W	T	F	S	S
3 Nov–23 Dec	11–4	·	·	·	·	·	S	S

Tŷ Mawr Wybrnant

Penmachno, Betws-y-Coed, Conwy LL25 0HJ

🏠 ♿ 1951

Modest 16th-century farmhouse with huge cultural significance. Bishop William Morgan's birthplace celebrates 30 years as a museum. You can learn about William Morgan's ten-year endeavour to translate the Bible into Welsh, helping ensure the survival of the language, and view original copies of the Welsh Bible and exhibition. **Note:** access via narrow road from Penmachno. Once you reach forestry follow signs (ignore Sat Nav).

Eat, shop, stay: picnics welcome. Four holiday cottages available near Betws-y-Coed and Hendre Isaf bunkhouse at Pentrefoelas (9 miles).

Things to see and do: Indoors Enjoy an introductory talk, visit the exhibition room and browse the extensive Bible collection. Virtual tour also available. **Outdoors** Tudor kitchen garden, woodland walk and animal puzzle trail. **Dogs:** under close control.

Access: 🅿️♿🚻♿ Building ♿♿ Grounds ♿
Sat Nav: do not use. No access from A470.
Parking: 500 yards.

Find out more: 01690 760213 or tymawrwybrnant@nationaltrust.org.uk

Tŷ Mawr Wybrnant		M	T	W	T	F	S	S
15 Mar–30 Sep	12–5	·	·	·	T	F	S	S
4 Oct–4 Nov	12–4	·	·	·	T	F	S	S
Open Bank Holiday Mondays.								

Tŷ Mawr Wybrnant, Conwy: huge cultural significance

Carrick-a-Rede, County Antrim

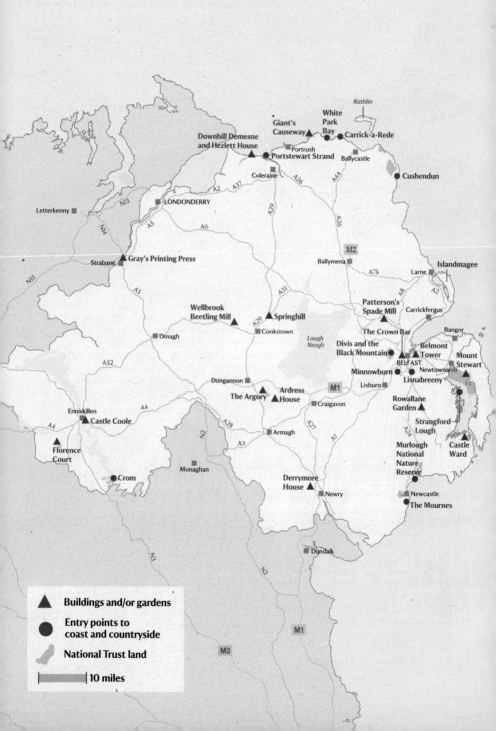

Rathlin

Giant's Causeway ▲

White Park Bay

Downhill Demesne and Hezlett House ▲ ● Portstewart Strand
Portrush ■
Ballycastle ■
Carrick-a-Rede ●

● Cushendun

Coleraine

A2   A37   A26

LONDONDERRY

Letterkenny ■

N13

A5   A6   A29   A26

N14

M2

Strabane ■ ▲ Gray's Printing Press   Ballymena ■   A75   Larne ■   Islandmagee

N15   A5   A31   A8

Wellbrook Beetling Mill ▲   A29   ▲ Springhill   Patterson's Spade Mill ▲   Carrickfergus ■

Omagh ■   Cookstown ■   Lough Neagh   The Crown Bar ▲   Bangor ■

Divis and the Black Mountain ●   Belmont Tower ▲   Mount Stewart ▲

A32   BELFAST

Dungannon ■   Minnowburn ●   Newtownards ■   Lisnabreeny ●

Enniskillen ■   ▲ The Argory   Ardress House ▲   Lisburn ■

A4   ▲ Castle Coole   A28   Craigavon ■   M1   Rowallane Garden ▲

A4   N2   Armagh ■   A27   Strangford Lough

Florence Court ▲   A3   A1   Castle Ward ▲

● Crom   Monaghan ■   Murlough National Nature Reserve

Derrymore House ▲   Newcastle ■
Newry ■   ● The Mournes
N3

N2   Dundalk ■

M1

M3

Legend:

▲ Buildings and/or gardens

● Entry points to coast and countryside

National Trust land

| 10 miles

Ardress House

64 Ardress Road, Annaghmore, Portadown, County Armagh BT62 1SQ

🏠🔥❄️♿ 1959

Family fun at Ardress House in County Armagh

Nestled in 40 hectares (100 acres) of rolling countryside, this 17th-century farmhouse, with detailed plasterwork and fine Georgian interiors, offers afternoons of fun and relaxation for everyone. The cobbled farmyard is the perfect spot for children to feed the resident chickens, and the nearby apple orchards are great for exploring.

Eat, shop, stay: takeaway hot and cold drinks and ice-cream available. Picnics welcome in the garden or woodlands.

Things to see and do: original cobbled farmyard, including dairy, smithy and threshing barn, miniature Shetland ponies, donkeys, Soay sheep, geese and chickens. Lady's Mile walking trail. Children's outdoor and indoor play. **Dogs**: on leads in garden only.

Access: 🅿️ Building 🦽🔽 Grounds 🦽➡️
Parking: 10 yards.

Find out more: 028 8778 4753 or ardress@nationaltrust.org.uk

Ardress House		M	T	W	T	F	S	S
House and farmyard								
10 Mar–25 Mar	11–5	·	·	·	·	·	S	S
30 Mar–8 Apr	11–5	M	T	W	T	F	S	S
14 Apr–30 Jun	11–5	·	·	·	·	·	S	S
1 Jul–31 Aug	11–5	M	·	·	T	F	S	S
1 Sep–30 Sep	11–5	·	·	·	·	·	S	S
7 Oct–28 Oct	11–5	·	·	·	·	·	·	S
Lady's Mile Walk								
Open all year	Dawn–dusk	M	T	W	T	F	S	S

House: admission by guided tour (last tour one hour before closing). Open Bank Holiday Mondays and all other public holidays in Northern Ireland. Closed 25, 26 December and 1 January 2019.

The Argory

144 Derrycaw Road, Moy, Dungannon, County Armagh BT71 6NA

🏠❄️♿🔥🍴 1979

This Irish gentry house can trace more than 190 years of history. Built in the 1820s for the MacGeough Bond family, the house and surrounding riverside estate came into existence due to a quirky stipulation in a will. The interior of this understated and intimate house still evokes the eclectic tastes and

The Argory, County Armagh: 190 years of history

Early autumn walk at The Argory

interests of the family. The rose garden, with its unusual sundial, pleasure gardens and wooded walks along the River Blackwater are ideal for exploring.

Eat, shop, stay: Courtyard Café serving home-baked scones, sandwiches, paninis and cakes. Gift shop offering a wide range of products. Second-hand bookshop (volunteer-run). Picnics welcome.

Things to see and do: **Indoors** Guided house tours and children's indoor Pest Quest. **Outdoors** Variety of walks and trails. Children's adventure play park with zip line. Events throughout the year, including Vintage Rally. **Dogs**: on leads in grounds and garden.

Access: 🅿️♿🛗👓 Grounds ♿➡️
Parking: 100 yards.

Find out more: 028 8778 4753 or argory@nationaltrust.org.uk

The Argory		M	T	W	T	F	S	S
House, café and shop								
3 Feb–25 Feb*	11–5	·	·	·	·	·	S	S
3 Mar–25 Mar	11–5	·	·	·	T	F	S	S
26 Mar–8 Apr	11–5	M	T	W	T	F	S	S
9 Apr–28 May	11–5	M	·	·	·	F	S	S
1 Jun–30 Jun	11–5	·	·	W	T	F	S	S
1 Jul–31 Aug	11–5	M	T	W	T	F	S	S
1 Sep–30 Sep	11–5	·	·	·	T	F	S	S
7 Oct–28 Oct	11–5	·	·	·	·	·	S	S
29 Oct–4 Nov	11–5	M	T	W	T	F	S	S
Grounds								
Open all year	10–5	M	T	W	T	F	S	S

*Also open 15 and 16 for local half-term; closed 22 and 23 February. House: admission by guided tour, last tour one hour before closing. Open Bank Holiday Mondays and all public holidays in Northern Ireland. Grounds closed 25, 26 December and 1 January 2019.

Belmont Tower

82 Belmont Church Road, Belfast, County Down BT4 3FG

🏠 ☂ 2013

For more than 100 years this prominent Gothic-style late-Victorian building buzzed to the sound of children playing and learning in its former life as Belmont Primary School. Today this inspirational space has been restored and adapted to offer classes, conference facilities and coffee shop.

Belmont Tower, County Down: inspirational space

Eat, shop, stay: freshly prepared food and delicious scones at Belmont Tower Café.

Things to see and do: community groups, such as Belfast Historical Society and baby sensory. **Dogs**: assistance dogs only.

Access: ♿🅿️🛗♿🛗
Parking: on site and on street at Belmont Road and Belmont Church Road.

Find out more: 028 9065 3338 or belmonttower@nationaltrust.org.uk

Belmont Tower		M	T	W	T	F	S	S
2 Jan–31 Dec	9–4	M	T	W	T	F	S	·

Saturdays and July: closes at 3. Open evenings and other times for booked classes and events. Closed 25 and 26 December.

Carrick-a-Rede

Ballintoy, County Antrim BT54 6LS

🚻🚶 1967

Connected to the cliffs by a rope bridge across the Atlantic Ocean, this rocky island is the ultimate clifftop experience. Jutting out from the Causeway Coastal Route, the 30-metre deep and 20-metre wide chasm separating Carrick-a-Rede from the mainland is traversed by an amazing rope bridge that was traditionally erected by salmon fishermen. Wildlife-rich and with views across the seas to Rathlin Island, this is also home to Larrybane old quarry, recently featured in TV series *Game of Thrones*. **Note**: timed ticketing system operates (details on website). Bridge accessible weather permitting. Entrance 119a Whitepark Road.

The rope bridge, above and below, at Carrick-a-Rede, County Antrim, connects the mainland with this rocky island and is the ultimate test of nerves

Carrick-a-Rede: the rope bridge spans a deep chasm

Eat, shop, stay: Weighbridge tea-room offering great coffee, delicious scones and sweet treats, hot snacks and light lunches. Gift shop area showcasing local crafts and unique range of Carrick-a-Rede souvenirs.

Things to see and do: coastal path – part of the Causeway Coast Way walking route from Portstewart to Ballycastle. Birdwatching and coastal scenery. Unique flora and fauna. Guided tours (by arrangement). **Dogs**: on leads (not permitted to cross bridge).

Access: [icons] Grounds [icons]
Parking: on site.

Find out more: 028 2076 9839 or carrickarede@nationaltrust.org.uk

Carrick-a-Rede		M	T	W	T	F	S	S
Bridge								
1 Jan–31 Jan	9:30–3:30	M	T	W	T	F	S	S
1 Feb–25 Feb	9:30–5	M	T	W	T	F	S	S
26 Feb–24 Jun	9:30–6	M	T	W	T	F	S	S
25 Jun–2 Sep	9:30–7	M	T	W	T	F	S	S
3 Sep–28 Oct	9:30–6	M	T	W	T	F	S	S
29 Oct–31 Dec	9:30–3:30	M	T	W	T	F	S	S

Bridge: open weather permitting; last entry 45 minutes before closing. Car park and North Antrim coastal path open all year. Closed 24 to 26 December.

Castle Coole

Enniskillen, County Fermanagh BT74 6HN

🏠🌳🔔⛲ 1951

Surrounded by a stunning landscape park, the majestic 18th-century home of the Earls of Belmore was created to impress. One of the finest examples of Neo-classical architecture in Ireland, the rooms at Castle Coole are brimming with opulence, luxury and colour. There are interesting pieces of history to explore, such as the servants' tunnel and ice house. The parkland, interspersed with mature oaks, woodlands and paths, is perfect for refreshing walks, while the outdoor play area is great for families.

Eat, shop, stay: Tallow House tea-room serving snacks, lunches and afternoon teas. Gift shop selling souvenirs and local crafts. Second-hand bookshop (volunteer-run).

Castle Coole, County Fermanagh: the majestic mansion, above, and elegant Saloon, left

Things to see and do: Indoors Events throughout the year. 'Upstairs downstairs' guided tours of the mansion. Enjoy the cosy Tallow House tea-room. **Outdoors** Events throughout the year, including summer music sessions. Trails and walks. **Dogs**: under control.

Access: 🅿️♿🚻👓📖📷
Building 🚶♿♿ Grounds ♿➡️
Parking: 150 yards.

Find out more: 028 6632 2690 or castlecoole@nationaltrust.org.uk

Castle Coole		M	T	W	T	F	S	S
Grounds								
1 Jan–28 Feb	10–4	M	T	W	T	F	S	S
1 Mar–31 Oct	10–7	M	T	W	T	F	S	S
1 Nov–31 Dec	10–4	M	T	W	T	F	S	S
House, tea-room and shop								
10 Mar–11 Mar	11–5						S	S
17 Mar–25 Mar	11–5	M					S	S
30 Mar–8 Apr	11–5	M	T	W	T	F	S	S
14 Apr–27 May	11–5						S	S
1 Jun–31 Aug	11–5	M	T	W	T	F	S	S
1 Sep–30 Sep	11–5	M		W	T	F	S	S

House: admission by guided tour (last tour one hour before closing). Open Bank Holiday Mondays and all other public holidays in Northern Ireland.

Castle Ward

Strangford, Downpatrick,
County Down BT30 7LS

🏠🏛️🏚️♿✿🛶🚣🍴🎣⛺🔔🍵 1953

High on a hillside, with views across the
tranquil waters of Strangford Lough, the
distinctly different styles of Gothic and
classical collide at Castle Ward. This eccentric
18th-century mansion, within a 332-hectare
(820-acre) walled demesne, is one of the most
peculiar architectural compromises between
two people. The former home of the Viscounts
Bangor, guided tours reveal the history of the
different façades. In the farmyard, you can visit
the water-powered corn mill, or stroll among
flowers and subtropical plants in the Sunken
Garden. The impressive laundry, tack room
and dairy give an insight into life 'below stairs'.
The extensive grounds are criss-crossed
by a 21-mile network of family-friendly
multi-use trails, while the woodland and
adventure playground are great for children.
Note: 1 March to 30 November visitor access
to livestock grazing areas may be restricted.

Eat, shop, stay: Stableyard tea-room. Gift shop
selling local produce and souvenirs. Second-hand
bookshop. Holiday cottage, bunkhouse,
caravan and campsite with glamping pods.

The classical side of Castle Ward, County Down

Setting off on a cycling adventure, above, at Castle Ward, and exploring the lough shore, left

Things to see and do: **Indoors** Guided house tours. Victorian laundry, dairy and corn mill. Visit the 16th-century Tower House. **Outdoors** Network of multi-use trails. Bicycles for hire (not National Trust). Farmyard with animals. Woodland and adventure playground. Tracker Packs and children's activities. Events throughout the year, including Easter Fair, Pumpkinfest, Jazz in the Garden and Christmas. Why not visit some of the iconic filming locations – Winterfell in HBO's *Game of Thrones*? **Dogs**: on leads at all times (livestock grazing areas out of bounds).

Access: ♿
Building 🏛 **Grounds** 🏛
Parking: on site.

Find out more: 028 4488 1204 or castleward@nationaltrust.org.uk

Castle Ward		M	T	W	T	F	S	S
Parkland, trails and garden								
1 Jan–16 Mar	10–4	M	T	W	T	F	S	S
17 Mar–28 Oct	10–6	M	T	W	T	F	S	S
29 Oct–31 Dec	10–4	M	T	W	T	F	S	S
House, stableyard and farmyard*								
17 Mar–28 Oct	12–5	M	T	W	T	F	S	S
Tea-room, gift shop and second-hand bookshop								
2 Jan–16 Mar	11–4	M	T	W	T	F	S	S
17 Mar–28 Oct	10–5	M	T	W	T	F	S	S
29 Oct–31 Dec	11–4	M	T	W	T	F	S	S

*Stableyard and farmyard: open at 10. House: last admission one hour before closing; timed tickets apply to guided tours. Corn mill demonstration: 1 April to 23 September, Sundays, 2 to 5. Gates and parkland close same time. Everything closed 25 and 26 December.

Crom

Upper Lough Erne, Newtownbutler,
County Fermanagh BT92 8AJ

 1987

Home to islands, ancient woodland and
historical ruins, this 810-hectare (2,000-acre)
demesne sits in a tranquil landscape on the
peaceful southern shores of Upper Lough Erne.
One of Ireland's most important conservation
areas, it has many rare species and is great
for relaxing walks, cycling and boat trips.
Note: 19th-century castle not open to public.

Upper Lough Erne at Crom, County Fermanagh

Eat, shop, stay: lunch, snacks and afternoon
tea, gifts and souvenirs available in visitor
centre. Convenience goods and outdoor
clothing also for sale. Holiday cottages,
campsite (tents only) and glamping pods.

Things to see and do: historic castle ruins.
Cot trips (Bank Holiday Mondays). Boat and
canoe hire. Children's Tracker Packs and
GPS devices available. Events, including
Outdoor Adventures, Easter hunts and
Music by the Lake. **Dogs**: under control.

Access: ▣ ▣ ▣ ▣ ▣
Building ▣ ▣ Grounds ▣ ▣ ▣
Parking: 100 yards.

Find out more: 028 6773 8118 or
crom@nationaltrust.org.uk

Crom		M	T	W	T	F	S	S
Grounds								
1 Jan–28 Feb	10–4	M	T	W	T	F	S	S
1 Mar–31 Oct	10–7	M	T	W	T	F	S	S
1 Nov–31 Dec	10–4	M	T	W	T	F	S	S
Visitor centre								
10 Mar–30 Sep	11–5	M	T	W	T	F	S	S
6 Oct–28 Oct	11–5						S	S

Open Bank Holiday Mondays and all other public holidays in
Northern Ireland. Last admission one hour before closing.
Tea-room open as visitor centre (closed October).

The Crown Bar

46 Great Victoria Street, Belfast,
County Antrim BT2 7BA

 1978

Belfast's most famous pub remains one of the
finest examples of a high-Victorian gin palace
complete with period features. **Note**: run by
Mitchells & Butlers. Open daily all year, 11:30 to
11, apart from some Bank and public holidays
(telephone 028 9024 3187 for details); Sundays
open 12:30 to 10.

Find out more: 028 9024 3187 or
info@crownbar.com

Cushendun

County Antrim

▣ ▣ 1954

Nestled at the mouth of the River Dun (Brown
River) at the foot of Glendun, Cushendun is a
very charming historic village steeped in
character and folklore. The surrounding hills are
a patchwork of farms, small fields, hedgerows
and traditional stone walls. Sheltered harbour
and beautiful beach. Views of Scotland.

The historic village of Cushendun in County Antrim

Eat, shop, stay: pub and restaurant facilities available in the village (none National Trust).

Things to see and do: attractive white Cornish-style houses designed by Clough Williams-Ellis. Explore the grounds of historic Glenmona House. Circular walking trail. River fishing, sea angling, boating, horse-riding and golf course nearby.

Access: 🚶 ♿
Sat Nav: use BT44 0PH. **Parking**: car park adjacent to Corner House tea-room and at Glenmona House.

Find out more: 028 2073 3419 (North Coast Office) or cushendun@nationaltrust.org.uk

Derrymore House

Bessbrook, Newry, County Armagh BT35 7EF

🏠 ♿ 1953

Resting peacefully in a landscape demesne, this 18th-century thatched cottage is rich in history and a great place for walks. **Note**: sorry no toilet. Grounds open all year, dawn to dusk. Treaty Room open 2 to 5:30, 7 and 28 May, 12 July, 27 August and 8 September. Last admission 45 minutes before closing.

Find out more: 028 8778 4753 or derrymore@nationaltrust.org.uk

Divis and the Black Mountain

Hannahstown, near Belfast, County Antrim

🏛 📷 ♿ 2004

Sitting in the heart of the Belfast Hills, this 809-hectare (2,000-acre) mosaic of upland heath and blanket bog is a great place for a wild countryside experience. There are four walking trails to explore, affording panoramic views across Belfast and a wealth of flora, fauna and archaeological remains to discover.
Note: cattle roam freely during summer months. Mountain environment and weather conditions can change rapidly.

Eat, shop, stay: tea, coffee and light refreshments available in The Barn.

Things to see and do: guided walks on biodiversity and archaeology.
Dogs: welcome, but please note cattle roam freely during summer.

Access: 🅿 ♿ 📷 🚶 Visitor centre ♿ Mountain ♿
Sat Nav: use BT17 0NG.
Parking: beside The Barn or on Divis Road, opposite entrance gates.

Find out more: 028 9082 5434 or divis@nationaltrust.org.uk

Divis and the Black Mountain
Coffee shop opening times vary throughout year.

Divis and the Black Mountain, County Antrim

Downhill Demesne and Hezlett House

Mussenden Road, Castlerock,
County Londonderry BT51 4RP

🏠 🏛 ⬟ ✿ ⬟ ⬟ 🔔 🍷 1949

The sheltered gardens, cliff-edge landmark and striking ruins of a grand headland mansion bear testament to the eccentricity of the Earl Bishop who once made this 18th-century demesne his home. Mussenden Temple, perched atop sheer cliffs, offers panoramic views of the famous north coast and is a great place for walking and kite-flying. Nearby at Hezlett House, life in a rural 17th-century cottage is told through the people who once lived there. One of the oldest thatched cottages left standing in Northern Ireland, it boasts a rare cruck frame and houses the Downhill Marble Collection.

Eat, shop, stay: tea and coffee facilities at Hezlett House and Bishop's Gate. Picnics welcome in gardens.

Things to see and do: **Indoors** Hezlett House guided tours on request (booking essential). **Outdoors** Numerous events throughout year, including Easter hunts and Kite Festival. Bishop's Play Trail. **Dogs**: on leads only.

Exploring the gardens and grounds of
Downhill Demesne and Hezlett House,
County Londonderry, above and left

Access: 🅿♿ 🚾 Building ♿ Grounds ♿
Parking: at Lion's Gate.

Find out more: 028 7084 8728 or
downhilldemesne@nationaltrust.org.uk
Hezlett House, 107 Sea Road, Castlerock,
County Londonderry BT51 4TW

Downhill and Hezlett		M	T	W	T	F	S	S
Downhill Demesne grounds								
Open all year	Dawn–dusk	M	T	W	T	F	S	S
Hezlett House								
10 Mar–25 Mar	11–5						S	S
26 Mar–8 Apr	11–5	M	T	W	T	F	S	S
14 Apr–17 Jun	11–5						S	S
18 Jun–9 Sep	11–5	M	T	W	T	F	S	S
Downhill Demesne facilities								
10 Mar–9 Sep	10–5	M	T	W	T	F	S	S
15 Sep–4 Nov	10–5						S	S

Open Bank Holiday Mondays and all other public holidays
in Northern Ireland.

Florence Court

Enniskillen, County Fermanagh BT92 1DB

🏠 🏛 ❀ ⚒ 🛏 🔔 🍴 | 1954 |

Florence Court enjoys a majestic countryside setting in West Fermanagh, surrounded by lush parkland with Benaughlin mountain rising in the background. There is something for everyone to enjoy at this extensive and welcoming place. On a guided tour of the Georgian mansion you can hear stories about the Earls of Enniskillen and their staff, who lived here for more than 250 years. Outdoors take a gentle walk or long cycle along 10 miles of trails in the adjoining forest park and see fascinating industrial heritage features, including the water-powered sawmill and blacksmith's forge. The gardens are home to the mother of all Irish yew trees, as well as the kitchen garden which is being restored to its 1930s character.

Welcoming Florence Court, County Fermanagh, above and below, is surrounded by lush parkland

Eat, shop, stay: Stables tea-room serving snacks, lunches and afternoon tea. Coach House gift shop. Second-hand bookshop (volunteer-run). Visitor Centre providing information, house tour tickets, retail and drinks to go. You can stay for longer and enjoy a holiday in the Butler's Apartment.

Things to see and do: **Indoors** Guided house tours. Laundry yard with washroom, dairy, ironing and drying room. Explore our forge, sawmill and carpenter shop.

Outdoors: Events and ranger walks throughout year. Children's Tracker Packs. Network of 10 miles of multi-use trails. Bike hire available from the Visitor Centre. Kitchen garden restoration project. **Dogs**: under control, on leads in Walled Garden.

Access:
Building **Grounds**
Parking: 100 yards to Visitor Centre.

Find out more: 028 6634 8249 or florencecourt@nationaltrust.org.uk

Florence Court		M	T	W	T	F	S	S
Gardens and park								
1 Jan–28 Feb	10–4	**M**	**T**	**W**	**T**	**F**	**S**	**S**
1 Mar–31 Oct	10–7	**M**	**T**	**W**	**T**	**F**	**S**	**S**
1 Nov–31 Dec	10–4	**M**	**T**	**W**	**T**	**F**	**S**	**S**
House, tea-room, visitor centre and shop								
10 Mar–11 Mar	11–5	·	·	·	·	·	**S**	**S**
17 Mar–25 Mar	11–5	**M**	·	·	·	·	**S**	**S**
30 Mar–8 Apr	11–5	**M**	**T**	**W**	**T**	**F**	**S**	**S**
14 Apr–29 Apr	11–5	·	·	·	·	·	**S**	**S**
1 May–31 May	11–5	**M**	**T**	**W**	**T**	·	**S**	**S**
2 Jun–31 Aug	11–5	**M**	**T**	**W**	**T**	**F**	**S**	**S**
1 Sep–30 Sep	11–5	**M**	**T**	**W**	**T**	·	**S**	**S**
6 Oct–28 Oct	11–5	·	·	·	·	·	**S**	**S**

House: admission by guided tour (last tour one hour before closing). Open Bank Holiday Mondays and all other public holidays in Northern Ireland. Open Republic of Ireland Bank Holiday, 30 October. Grounds closed 25 December. Visitor Centre: open weekends, November and December.

Admiring the roses at Florence Court, above, and the colonnade at the Entrance Front, left

Giant's Causeway

44 Causeway Road, Bushmills,
County Antrim BT57 8SU

 1962

Follow in the legendary footsteps of giants at
Northern Ireland's iconic UNESCO World
Heritage Site. The famous basalt columns of
the Causeway landscape, left by volcanic
eruptions 60 million years ago, are home to
more than Finn McCool. Its nooks and crannies
are dotted with dainty sea campion, and
defensive fulmars protect their cliff nests.
Windswept walking trails wind through this
Area of Outstanding Natural Beauty, with an
all-accessible walk at Runkerry Head and more
challenging terrain along the Causeway Coast
Way. The interactive exhibition and
innovative audio-guides unlock the secrets
of the landscape and regale visitors with
legends of giants.

Eat, shop, stay: light lunches and tasty snacks
available in Visitor Centre café. Causeway Hotel
bar and restaurant offer delicious lunch and
evening meal menus based around fresh local
produce. The award-winning gift shop
showcases locally handcrafted gifts and
exclusive Giant's Causeway souvenirs.

Things to see and do: **Indoors** Interactive
exhibition brings the stories of the Causeway
to life. **Outdoors** Audio-guides (11 languages)
reveal the landscape's secrets. Walking trails
for all abilities. Entertaining guided tours.
Family fun events. **Dogs**: on leads only.

**Formed by volcanic eruptions, the basalt stone columns
at Giant's Causeway, County Antrim, always fascinate**

Access: [icons]
Visitor Centre [icons] **Causeway Hotel** [icons]
Grounds [icons]
Parking: on site and park and ride in Bushmills village. Electric vehicle charging point in car park two.

Find out more: 028 2073 1855 or giantscauseway@nationaltrust.org.uk

Giant's Causeway		M	T	W	T	F	S	S
Stones and coastal path								
Open all year	Dawn–dusk	M	T	W	T	F	S	S
Visitor Centre								
1 Jan–28 Feb	9–5	M	T	W	T	F	S	S
1 Mar–31 May	9–6	M	T	W	T	F	S	S
1 Jun–30 Sep	9–7	M	T	W	T	F	S	S
1 Oct–31 Oct	9–6	M	T	W	T	F	S	S
1 Nov–31 Dec	9–5	M	T	W	T	F	S	S

Last admission to Visitor Centre one hour before closing.
Closed 24 to 26 December.

Bring out your inner Finn McCool at the Giant's Causeway

Gray's Printing Press

49 Main Street, Strabane,
County Tyrone BT82 8AU

[icon] 1966

The indelible story of printing is told behind this Georgian shop front in Strabane, once reputed as Ireland's printing capital. **Note**: open 12 to 4 (times subject to change), 31 March, 7 and 28 May, 30 June and 9 September. Last admission 45 minutes before closing.

Find out more: 028 8674 8210 or grays@nationaltrust.org.uk

Islandmagee

near Larne, County Antrim

[icons] 1996

An Area of Special Scientific Interest, the peninsula at Islandmagee has some of Northern Ireland's largest colonies of cliff-nesting seabirds. **Note**: paths uneven and steep in places.

Find out more: 028 9064 7787 or islandmagee@nationaltrust.org.uk

Lisnabreeny

near Belfast, County Down

[icons] 1938

On the edge of Belfast, paths through a wooded glen cross farmland to emerge at a rath on the Castlereagh Hills. **Note**: uneven paths and steep steps.

Find out more: 028 9064 7787 or lisnabreeny@nationaltrust.org.uk

Minnowburn

near Belfast, County Down

1952

Nestled in the heart of Lagan Valley Regional Park, where meadows and woodlands roll down to the River Lagan. Perfect for a short stroll or longer walk. Climb Terrace Hill to discover the garden built by linen merchant Ned Robinson, and stop for a picnic and to admire the views. **Note**: trails are uneven and steep in places.

Eat, shop, stay: Piccolo Mondo van (not National Trust) serves food, tea and coffee in car park six days a week. Lock Keeper's Inn (not National Trust) serving food, tea and coffee, ¾ mile along riverside path. Picnic tables in Terrace Hill garden.

The River Lagan at Minnowburn, County Down

Things to see and do: guided walks, including heritage, history and woodlands. Why not explore the walking trails, including the Giant's Ring and Terrace Hill trails?
Dogs: on leads only.

Access:
Sat Nav: use BT8 8LD. **Parking**: on site.

Find out more: 028 9064 7787 or minnowburn@nationaltrust.org.uk

Mount Stewart

Portaferry Road, Newtownards, County Down BT22 2AD

1976

The exquisite Central Hall, Mount Stewart, County Down

Voted one of the world's top ten gardens, Mount Stewart reflects a rich tapestry of design and planting artistry bearing the hallmark of its creator. Edith, Lady Londonderry's passion for bold planting schemes, coupled with the mild climate of Strangford Lough, means rare and tender plants from across the globe thrive in this celebrated garden, with the formal gardens exuding a distinct character and appeal. Explore the exquisite house, recently restored to glory. Hear fascinating stories about the Londonderry family, and enjoy a world-class collection of paintings and many other internationally significant items. For a different view of Mount Stewart, stroll around miles of new walking trails and discover a landscape lost in time.

Eat, shop, stay: locally sourced gifts in our shop. Garden shop selling a range of gardening items and plants specially propagated from our world-class garden. Tea-room with a range of homemade food and many products made from local produce.

Find out more: 028 4278 8387 or
mountstewart@nationaltrust.org.uk

Mount Stewart		M	T	W	T	F	S	S
Formal and lakeside gardens, trails, tea-room and shop								
1 Jan–2 Mar	10–4*	M	T	W	T	F	S	S
3 Mar–28 Oct	10–5	M	T	W	T	F	S	S
29 Oct–31 Dec	10–4*	M	T	W	T	F	S	S
House								
6 Jan–25 Feb	11–3						S	S
3 Mar–28 Oct	11–5	M	T	W	T	F	S	S
3 Nov–30 Dec	11–3						S	S
Temple of the Winds								
4 Mar–28 Oct	2–5							S

*Tea-room and shop: close at 5 weekends, Bank Holidays and public holidays. House: free-flow admission (guided tours on selected days); opening times may change. Open Bank Holiday Mondays and all other public holidays in Northern Ireland. Closed 25 and 26 December.

Things to see and do: **Indoors** You can explore the recently restored family home and discover a wealth of new treasures. Events throughout the year, including jazz in the gardens, Teddy Bear's Picnic and Red Squirrel day. **Outdoors** Various trails, walks and garden tours. The natural play area and walking trails will take you through a magical landscape of woodland and farmland, set within an iconic rolling drumlin landscape beside Strangford Lough. **Dogs**: welcome on short leads in all areas.

Access: 🅿️ 🄳 🚾 🔉 📷 📱
Building 🔌 🏛 🦽 **Grounds** 🔌 🏛 ➡️ 🦽 🦽
Parking: 200 yards. Two electric vehicle charging points in rear car park.

Three views of Mount Stewart's glorious gardens. Exuding a distinct character and appeal, there is something to delight, whatever the season

The Mournes

near Newcastle, County Down

🏛️🏊📷 1992

These famous wildlife-rich mountains (above) are criss-crossed by well-marked coastal and mountain paths. Great for exploring, the National Trust-maintained paths stretch from the shore into the heart of the Mournes, offering views over Dundrum Bay to the Isle of Man on a clear day.

Eat, shop, stay: picnics welcome. Nearest shops, restaurants and cafés in Newcastle (none National Trust).

Things to see and do: outstanding views from Bloody Bridge. Coastal path to St Mary's Chapel ruins. Birdwatching. **Dogs**: welcome under control and on leads.

Access: 🔬
Sat Nav: use BT33 0EU for Slieve Donard and BT33 0LA for Bloody Bridge.
Parking: for Slieve Donard, park in Newcastle; for Bloody Bridge, park on A2.

Find out more: 028 4375 1467 or mournes@nationaltrust.org.uk

Murlough National Nature Reserve

near Dundrum, County Down

🏛️🏊📷🐕 1967

Home to seals, Neolithic sites and Ireland's first nature reserve, Murlough is one of the most extensive examples of dune landscape in Ireland. A network of paths and boardwalks through these ancient dunes, woodland and heath make it ideal for relaxed walks and spotting a wonderland of wildlife. **Note**: limited toilet facilities.

Eat, shop, stay: beach café (seasonal opening, not National Trust). Picnics welcome on beach or in car park.

Things to see and do: explore the dune network and discover all about nature on one of the ranger-led guided walks, or enjoy one of the family activities which take place through the year. **Dogs**: on leads are welcome, restrictions apply when ground-nesting birds are breeding or cattle grazing.

Access: 🚾 Grounds 🔬
Sat Nav: use BT33 0NQ. **Parking**: on site.

Find out more: 028 4375 1467 or murlough@nationaltrust.org.uk

Murlough		M	T	W	T	F	S	S
Nature reserve								
Open all year	9:30–7	M	T	W	T	F	S	S
Facilities								
10 Mar–25 Mar	10–6	·	·	·	·	·	S	S
30 Mar–8 Apr	10–6	M	T	W	T	F	S	S
14 Apr–27 May	10–6	·	·	·	·	·	S	S
2 Jun–2 Sep	10–6	M	T	W	T	F	S	S
8 Sep–30 Sep	10–6	·	·	·	·	·	S	S

Open Bank Holiday Mondays and all other public holidays in Northern Ireland. Car park gates: open at 8 and close at 7.

Murlough National Nature Reserve, County Down

Patterson's Spade Mill

751 Antrim Road, Templepatrick,
County Antrim BT39 0AP

⌂ 🏛 ⛴ 🔔 🍴 1991

Travel back in time and witness history literally
forged in steel at the last working water-driven
spade mill in daily use in the British Isles.
Dig up the history and culture of the humble
spade and visit bygone life fashioning steel
into spades during the industrial era.

Eat, shop, stay: handcrafted spades on sale
and made to specification. Tea and coffee
available from drinks machine.

Things to see and do: guided tours
and demonstrations for all the family.
Dogs: on leads only.

Access: 🅿️🅳♿🄹 Building ♿🅴 Grounds ♿
Parking: 50 yards.

Find out more: 028 9443 3619 or
pattersons@nationaltrust.org.uk

Patterson's Spade Mill		M	T	W	T	F	S	S
30 Mar–8 Apr	12–4	M	T	W	T	F	S	S
14 Apr–27 May	12–4						S	S
28 May–26 Aug	12–4	M	T	W			S	S
1 Sep–30 Sep	12–4						S	S

Admission by guided tour, last admission one hour before
closing. Open Bank Holiday Mondays and all other public
holidays in Northern Ireland, 30 March to 30 September.

Patterson's Spade Mill in County Antrim

Portstewart Strand

Portstewart, County Londonderry

🏛 ⛴ 🌊 🐾 🍴 1981

Golden sands at Portstewart Strand, County Londonderry

Sweeping along the edge of the north coast,
this 2-mile stretch of golden sand is one of
Northern Ireland's finest beaches and affords
uninterrupted views of the coastline. It's an
ideal place for lazy picnics, surfing and long
walks into the wildlife-rich sand dunes.

Eat, shop, stay: award-winning Harry's Shack
with great new catering offer. Mobile beach
retail and information service.

Things to see and do: waymarked nature trail.
Barmouth Estuary bird hide. Events during
peak season. **Dogs**: on leads only.

Access: 🅿️🆆♿🅱️🅲 Café ♿ Beach ♿➡️
Sat Nav: use BT55 7PG. **Parking**: on beach.

Find out more: 028 7083 6396 or
portstewart@nationaltrust.org.uk

Portstewart Strand		M	T	W	T	F	S	S
Beach								
Open all year*	Dawn–dusk	M	T	W	T	F	S	S
Facilities								
10 Mar–25 Mar	10–5	M	T	W	T	F	S	S
26 Mar–29 Apr	10–6	M	T	W	T	F	S	S
30 Apr–2 Sep	10–7	M	T	W	T	F	S	S
3 Sep–30 Oct	10–5	M	T	W	T	F	S	S

*Open to pedestrians. Beach closed to vehicles one hour
after last admission. Opening times vary depending on
weather and tides.

Rowallane Garden

Saintfield, County Down BT24 7LH

❖ ▲ T 1956

Carved into the County Down drumlin landscape since the mid-1860s, this inspirational 21-hectare (52-acre) garden is 'a world apart'. The passion and shared vision of the Reverend John Moore, and later his nephew Hugh Armytage Moore, created a garden where you can leave the outside world behind and immerse yourself in nature's beauty. The formal and informal garden spaces are home to magical features mingled with native and exotic plants, such as drifts of rare rhododendrons. It is a great place for a leisurely walk or just to relax on a seat and soak up the atmosphere.

Eat, shop, stay: garden café with views across the gardens. Café gift shop. Second-hand bookshop. Pottery providing unique Rowallane Garden items and garden pots.

Things to see and do: full-year programme of exciting activities and events for all ages.
Dogs: on leads in garden.

Access: 🅿️ 🏛️ 🏬 ♿ Grounds 🏞️ ♿
Parking: on site.

Find out more: 028 9751 0131 or rowallane@nationaltrust.org.uk

Rowallane Garden		M	T	W	T	F	S	S
Garden								
1 Jan–28 Feb	10–4	M	T	W	T	F	S	S
1 Mar–30 Apr	10–6	M	T	W	T	F	S	S
1 May–31 Aug	10–8	M	T	W	T	F	S	S
1 Sep–31 Oct	10–6	M	T	W	T	F	S	S
1 Nov–31 Dec	10–4	M	T	W	T	F	S	S
Café								
5 Jan–25 Feb	11–3					F	S	S
26 Feb–30 Apr	11–4	M	T	W	T	F	S	S
1 May–31 Aug	11–5	M	T	W	T	F	S	S
1 Sep–4 Nov	11–4	M	T	W	T	F	S	S
8 Nov–30 Dec	11–3				T	F	S	S

Open Bank Holiday Mondays and all other public holidays in Northern Ireland. Closed 25 and 26 December.

Magical features mingle with native and exotic plants at Rowallane Garden in County Down

Springhill

20 Springhill Road, Moneymore, Magherafelt, County Londonderry BT45 7NQ

⌂ ❄ ♨ ⛺ ♦ ▼ 1957

Hundreds of years ago the Lenox-Conyngham family chose this idyllic spot to build their home and, after ten generations, this 17th-century plantation house is still regarded as 'one of the prettiest houses in Ulster'. The welcoming family home they created is brought to life on guided tours of its portraits, furniture and decorative arts. The old laundry houses Springhill's celebrated costume collection of 18th- to 20th-century pieces that capture its enthralling past. There is a visitor centre, a natural play area and short trails that are perfect for a leisurely stroll.

Eat, shop, stay: soup, scones, hot and cold drinks, snacks and ice-cream available from the Barn Café. Retail area with a range of items for the home and garden. Second-hand bookshop.

Things to see and do: **Indoors** Guided house tours and children's indoor Pest Quest.

Costume exhibition and children's dress-up area. **Outdoors** Woodland walks, children's natural play trail and Springhill nursery selling plants and shrubs. **Dogs**: on leads in grounds only.

Access: [icons] **Building** [icons]
Parking: 50 yards.

Find out more: 028 8674 8210 or springhill@nationaltrust.org.uk

Springhill		M	T	W	T	F	S	S
House, visitor centre, café and costume museum								
3 Feb–18 Mar*	11–5						S	S
26 Mar–8 Apr	11–5	M	T	W	T	F	S	S
13 Apr–27 May	11–5					F	S	S
1 Jun–30 Jun	11–5				T	F	S	S
1 Jul–31 Aug	11–5	M	T	W	T	F	S	S
1 Sep–30 Sep	11–5						S	S
7 Oct–28 Oct	11–5							S
29 Oct–4 Nov	11–5	M	T	W	T	F	S	S
Grounds								
Open all year	10–5	M	T	W	T	F	S	S

*Also open 15 and 16 February for local half-term; everything closed 22 and 23 February. House: admission by guided tour (last tour one hour before closing). Open Bank Holiday Mondays and all other public holidays in Northern Ireland. Closed 25, 26 December and 1 January 2019.

Strangford Lough

County Down

 1969

The tidal treasures of Britain's largest sea lough and one of Europe's key wildlife habitats await discovery.

Find out more: 028 4278 7769 or strangford@nationaltrust.org.uk

Wellbrook Beetling Mill

20 Wellbrook Road, Corkhill, Cookstown, County Tyrone BT80 9RY

 1968

Step back in time and discover how yarn was spun at Northern Ireland's last working water-powered linen beetling mill. **Note**: open weekends, 10 March to 30 September, 1 to 5 (admission by guided tour, last tour one hour before closing). Open Bank Holiday Mondays and all other public holidays in Northern Ireland. Closed 25, 26 December and 1 January 2019.

Find out more: 028 8674 8210 or wellbrook@nationaltrust.org.uk

White Park Bay

near Ballintoy, County Antrim

 1939

Embraced by ancient dunes, Neolithic settlements and passage tombs, this arc of white sand nestles between two headlands on the North Antrim coast. Home to a range of rich habitats for a myriad of wildlife, its secluded location makes it ideal for quiet relaxation and peaceful walks.

Eat, shop, stay: shops, restaurants and cafés in nearby towns (none National Trust). Picnics welcome.

Things to see and do: you can discover one of the first Neolithic settlements in Ireland with three passage tombs, including Druid's Altar. Part of the Causeway Coast Way, a section of the Ulster Way. **Dogs**: welcome on leads.

Access: P
Sat Nav: use BT54 6NH. **Parking**: on site.

Find out more: 028 2073 3320 or whiteparkbay@nationaltrust.org.uk

White Park Bay, County Antrim, above and below, nestles between two headlands

Ever dreamed of waking up in a National Trust house, which has a family history stretching back centuries?

Such historic houses make great places to stay, to hold family gatherings, a party or wedding – making it an experience to remember. You can stay at one of the three Historic House Hotels of the National Trust located in the Vale of Aylesbury, North Wales and the City of York.

Hartwell House Hotel, Restaurant and Spa

The most famous resident of this elegant stately home was Louis XVIII, the exiled King of France, who lived here with his Queen and members of his court for five years from 1809. Only one hour from central London, the magnificent grounds include a romantic ruined church, lake and bridge.

www.hartwell-house.com   01296 747444

Bodysgallen Hall Hotel, Restaurant and Spa

This Grade I listed 17th-century house has the most spectacular views towards Conwy Castle and Snowdonia. The romantic gardens, which have won awards for their restoration, include a rare parterre – filled with sweet-smelling herbs – as well as several follies, a cascade, walled garden and formal rose gardens. Beyond, the hotel's parkland offers miles of stunning walks.

www.bodysgallen.com   01492 584466

Middlethorpe Hall Hotel, Restaurant and Spa

Built in 1699, this quintessentially William and Mary house was once the home of the 18th-century diarist Lady Mary Wortley Montagu. Furnished with antiques and fine paintings and set in manicured gardens with parkland beyond, Middlethorpe Hall's country-house character remains unspoilt.

www.middlethorpe.com   01904 641241

Start planning your visit to a Historic House Hotel today

Themed index

General interest

Location	Activity	Page

Cornwall

Cotehele, Cornwall

Devon and Dorset

Finch Foundry, Devon

Somerset and Wiltshire

Glastonbury Tor, Somerset

The Cotswolds, Buckinghamshire and Oxfordshire

Dyrham Park, South Gloucestershire

Berkshire, Hampshire and the Isle of Wight

Hinton Ampner, Hampshire

The White Cliffs of Dover, Kent

London

Fenton House and Garden, Hampstead

East of England

Houghton Mill, Cambridgeshire

East Midlands

Longshaw, Burbage and the
Eastern Moors, Derbyshire

West Midlands

Croft Castle, Herefordshire

North West

Little Moreton Hall, Cheshire

The Lakes

Fell Foot, Cumbria

Yorkshire

East Riddlesden Hall, West Yorkshire

North East

Wales

Bodnant Garden, Conwy

Dolaucothi Mines, Carmarthenshire

Northern Ireland

Castle Ward, County Down

Additional coastal and countryside car parks

Quick stops

Studley Royal Water Garden, North Yorkshire

Collections

Location	Collection	Page

Cornwall

Cotehele, Cornwall

Devon and Dorset

Somerset and Wiltshire

The Cotswolds, Buckinghamshire and Oxfordshire

Dyrham Park, South Gloucestershire

Berkshire, Hampshire and the Isle of Wight

Kent, Surrey and Sussex

London

Charlecote Park, Warwickshire

The Lakes

Yorkshire

North East

Wales

Northern Ireland

Dunham Massey, Cheshire

Famous people

Viscountess Astor

William Wordsworth

Film and television

This is a small selection of the largest and most popular films and TV dramas filmed at National Trust places.

Chartwell, Kent

Golden Cap, Dorset

Alan Titchmarsh, *Secrets of the National Trust*

Sudbury Hall, Derbyshire

Alphabetical index

Photography credits

Make more of your membership

Your membership card gives you free, unlimited access to most of the places we look after during normal opening hours. Just bring it along with you every time you visit.

To make it easier to discover special places, your membership includes free parking at most of our places.

Some of our car parks (mainly those at coast and countryside locations) are now pay and display for non-members. At these, you'll be able to scan your membership card to get a free parking ticket to display in your car window to indicate that you are a member. Each time you scan at a car park you will help us to direct financial support to the places you visit, for the upkeep of facilities and for conservation projects.

You may also be asked to show your card at all staffed car parks. So remember: always bring your membership card.

And that's not all you get from being a member…

Visit special places abroad
We are part of the International National Trusts Organisation (INTO), a global network of charities and foundations which look after heritage sites of natural and historical importance. This means your current membership card may entitle you to free or discounted entry to other places looked after by INTO members.

For a full list of participating nations, visit **nationaltrust.org.uk/overseas-visitors/overseas-organisations**

Entry to places owned by us but maintained by English Heritage or Cadw may be free to our members. If this is the case, it will be stated in the entry's Important Note.

Carers go free
Carers and essential companions of disabled visitors also enjoy free entry to all places on request.

To make things easier, you can order an annual Essential Companion card by calling 0344 800 1895 or emailing **enquiries@nationaltrust.org.uk**

Four-legged friends
We love to welcome dogs wherever we can, but it isn't possible at all of our special places. To avoid disappointment, check the 'Dogs' message at the end of 'Things to see and do' before setting out. At our dog-friendly places you'll find water bowls, exercise areas and shady spaces.

Access
The symbols on page 2 indicate the access and facilities at each place.

Please ring before your visit in case a particular provision needs to be booked.

Photography
You are welcome to take pictures during your visits for personal use. However, to avoid disturbing fellow visitors, please don't use a flash or tripod when indoors. Also pictures taken indoors are at the discretion of the Property/General Manager, as they may need to get permission from the owner of loan items. Mobile phones can also be used – without flash please.

All requests for commercial filming and photography need to go through our Head of Filming and Locations (020 7824 7128).

Other ways to support the National Trust

As a charity, we rely on membership fees to look after special places for ever, for everyone. So from everyone who loves these places, and everyone who ever will, thank you. If you'd like to do more, here are some other ways you can support the places that matter to you.

Volunteering
We wouldn't exist without the passion and hard work of thousands of volunteers. If you'd like to learn some new skills, share your experience and find rewarding work, please visit **nationaltrust.org.uk/volunteer**

Donations
Every penny helps us look after places of natural beauty and historic importance. From supporting an appeal to leaving a gift in your Will, see how you can help at **nationaltrust.org.uk/donate**

Holidays
From grand manor houses and cosy cottages to rustic bunkhouses and camping in the great outdoors, we've got hundreds of different holidays for you to choose from. You can also join a Working Holiday and take part in conservation activities that help keep places special. For more information visit **nationaltrust.org.uk/holidays**

Supporter groups
Our supporter groups find enjoyable ways to raise funds. From group talks to group walks, enjoying days out to organising social events, find out more at **nationaltrust.org.uk/supporter-groups**

Events
From live music and open-air theatre to organised sports and conservation walks, we have a busy programme of events. Find out what's happening near you at **nationaltrust.org.uk/visit/whats-on**

Shops and cafés
Visit one of our cafés to discover a tempting selection of dishes and baked treats made using seasonal produce. Don't forget to pop into the shop to see our latest collections, inspired by the places in our care, and pick up a gift for yourself or a loved one. You can also shop online at **nationaltrust.org.uk/shop**

Heritage Lottery Fund
Using money raised through the National Lottery, the Heritage Lottery Fund (HLF) has awarded grants totalling well over £100 million to the National Trust in the past 20 years. Through these grants it has supported many of our most important projects, including Chartwell, Knole, Castle Drogo, Rainham Hall and Quarry Bank.

If you would like to know more please visit **hlf.org.uk** or **nationaltrust.org.uk/features/grants-and-funding** for information about our grant-funded projects.

The Royal Oak Foundation
Through the generous support of its members and donors across the USA, Royal Oak makes grants to the National Trust. Royal Oak members enjoy free access to National Trust places as well as lectures and tours in the USA.

For more information please visit **royal-oak.org**

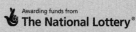

Have your say

Annual General Meeting
Our Annual General Meeting (AGM) each autumn is an opportunity for you to meet our Trustees and staff, ask questions and contribute to debates. Most importantly, you can exercise your right to vote on both resolutions and elections to our Council.

You can also vote online and watch the live AGM webcast. There will be more details in the autumn magazine and on our website **nationaltrust.org.uk/agm**

Please look out for your voting papers, information about how to vote on-line and resolutions in your autumn magazine. Please let us know if for any reason you don't receive your magazine.

Remember: the AGM is for members only; you're not able to bring a guest with you even if they normally visit regularly with you on a life membership.

Governance
A guide to the Trust's governance arrangements is available on our website **nationaltrust.org.uk/about-us** and on request from The Secretary.

Our Annual Report and Financial Statements are available online at **nationaltrust.org.uk/annualreport** and on request from **annualreport@nationaltrust.org.uk**

Privacy policy

Privacy Policy and use of personal information
The National Trust's Privacy Policy sets out the ways in which we process personal data. The full Privacy Policy and information about the National Trust's data handling processes are available on our website **nationaltrust.org.uk**

Our Privacy Policy and data handling processes will be updated in preparation for the implementation of the European Union's General Data Protection Regulation on 25 May 2018. To see these updates, please check the National Trust website on or after 25 May 2018.

Senior conservator, Heather Porter, working on the iconic Knole sofa in the Conservation Studio at Knole, Kent

Getting in touch

About a place and planning a visit

If you want to know something before you visit, have any queries about a specific place or would like to make a comment about your visit, then please contact the place directly. Telephone numbers and email addresses are included in the entry for each place in this *Handbook*.

You can also find regularly updated information about the places we look after on our website **nationaltrust.org.uk**

Or to find an event happening near you, visit **nationaltrust.org.uk/visit/what's-on**

Help during your visit

Your enjoyment is important to us, and staff are always happy to help with any questions you might have to ensure that you get the most out of your visits.

Many places also provide comment cards and boxes. Your comments help us to improve the experience we offer and make your visits memorable.

Online Help Centre

Whatever your questions, you're most likely to find the answer in our Help Centre **nationaltrust.org.uk/help-centre**

Help with your membership

Manage your membership online at **nationaltrust.org.uk/mynationaltrust** where you can:
· Register for an account;
· View your membership(s);
· Make updates to your details;
· Change your contact preferences;
· Manage your membership payments;
· Request items, including replacement cards and stickers.

You can also now use MyPlaces to record the places you have visited and the places you'd like to visit. For all other queries, please try the online Help Centre or contact the Supporter Services Centre.

Supporter Services Centre

enquiries@nationaltrust.org.uk
PO Box 574, Manvers, Rotherham, S63 3FH
0344 800 1895 (phone)
0344 800 4410 (minicom)
Lines open seven days a week (9 to 5:30 weekdays, 9 to 4 weekends and Bank Holidays)

National Trust Holidays

0344 800 2070 or **cottages@nationaltrust.org.uk**

Our online shop

If you have a question about an order or purchase made from our website, please contact our online shop order fulfilment team.
online.shop@nationaltrust.org.uk
0300 123 2025
Online shop call centre is open Monday to Sunday, 8 to 8.

If you'd like this information in an alternative format, please telephone 0344 800 1895 or email enquiries@nationaltrust.org.uk

Sponsor
Louise McRae

Publisher
Katie Bond

Production
Graham Prichard

Art direction
Craig Robson

Image selection
Chris Lacey

Maps © Maps in
Minutes™/Collins
Bartholomew 2015

Editor
Lucy Peel

Editorial assistance
**Anthony Lambert
Wendy Smith
Dee Maple**

Content management
**Roger Shapland
Dave Buchanan**

Design
Steers McGillan Eves

Origination
Zebra

Printed
Wyndeham Group

NT LDS stock no:
0010367

ISBN:
978-0-7078-0443-9